THE JOURNEY OF
eXPECTATION

…embrace it and
be empowered!

THE JOURNEY OF EXPECTATION... EMBRACE IT AND BE EMPOWERED!

©2025 Copyright by Elizabeth Bayliff
ISBN: 978-1-60920-119-7
Printed in the United States of America
Publisher: Ajoyin Publishing Jones, Michigan 49061 USA Contact: Pam Eichorn
Cover Design: James Nesbit / jnesbit.com

All rights reserved. No part of this book may be reproduced or transmitted in any form or by any means – electronic, mechanical, photocopying, recording, or otherwise – without prior written permission of the author, except in the case of brief quotations used in reviews, articles, or teaching, as permitted by U.S. copyright laws.

All emphasis in the use of Scripture is mine, along with personal paraphrasing built on various translations and versions being joined together for a broader perspective.

-Scripture Quotations and Citations / This book applies the "Fair Use" limit of 500 verses and 25% of book in any one version or translation.   -
Scripture quotations taken from the Amplified® Bible (AMP), Copyright © 2015 by The Lockman Foundation. Used by permission. lockman.org
Scripture quotations taken from the Amplified® Bible (AMPC), Copyright © 1954, 1958, 1962, 1964, 1965, 1987 by The Lockman Foundation. Used by permission. lockman.org".
-Scripture quotations taken from the Complete Jewish Bible by David H. Stern. Copyright © 1998. All rights reserved. Used by permission of Messianic Jewish Publishers, 6120 Day Long Lane, Clarksville, MD 21029.www.messianicjewish.net.
-Scripture quotations are from The ESV® Bible (The Holy Bible, English Standard Version®), © 2001 by Crossway, a publishing ministry of Good News Publishers. Used by permission. All rights reserved."
-Scripture KJV - The text of the King James Version of the Bible is in the public domain. Therefore, no permission is required.
-Scripture taken from the New King James Version®. Copyright © 1982 by Thomas Nelson. Used by permission. All rights reserved.
-Scripture quotations marked (NLT) are taken from the Holy Bible, New Living Translation, copyright ©1996, 2004, 2015 by Tyndale House Foundation. Used by permission of Tyndale House Publishers, Carol Stream, Illinois 60188. All rights reserved.
-Scripture quotations marked TPT are from The Passion Translation®. Copyright © 2017, 2018, 2020 by Passion & Fire Ministries, Inc. Used by permission. All rights reserved. ThePassionTranslation.com.

Dictionaries / Fair Use: Merriam Webster / https://www.merriam-webster.com/dictionary, Noah Webster - Websters 1828 Dictionary https://webstersdictionary1828.com, King James Version (KJV) Dictionary / derived from Noah Websters American Dictionary of the English Language https://www.AV1611.com

Disclaimer: All religious, spiritual, or other kind of shared revelation, knowledge, understanding, and application of what the author has written are from her personal encounters, experiences, interpretations, and applications. Each person reading this book is responsible for their own in the reading, interpreting, and applying of any content therein as each seeks God in their journey and process.

THE JOURNEY OF eXPECTATION

…embrace it and

be empowered!

ENCOUNTER, ENGAGE, AND EXPERIENCE
A 28 DAY JOURNEY WITH EARTHLY AND HEAVENLY
EXPECTANCY!

ELIZABETH BAYIFF

AJOYIN PUBLISHING
JONES, MI 49061

✧ FORWARDING WORDS OF WORTH ✧

Receive from the fruit of *expectations* expressed and arising by *His Spirit* through these ones who from *His* and their heart… what they're encountering, experiencing, and embracing in fresh ways by joining their *expectations* more with *His divine ones* and from a *heavenly* seated perspective as you *journey* forward.

"This book will help you find what an important role **expectations** play in our faith life journey with God. As you engage yourself in traveling through the book and the 28 days… may you discover as I have, your heart being awakened and come more alive as you see beyond with **expectancy**!" ~ **Karen**

"As I read about being a "carrier" I was challenged to turn up the power spiritually in my life by His Spirit and becoming a glory carrier of His **expectations** for my life and purpose based on His plans and promises. To know I carry a part in His kingdom coming on earth… that alone stirs my **expectancy**!" ~ **Connie**

"You have before you an opportunity and invitation to explore what a single word can have to do with God, you and others… especially when it is **expectation**… a word of worth and power. May you, as I have, encounter Him, the God of the universe, in a greater personal way like never before… as you embrace and enjoy the journey of **expectation** for the new… for the more!" ~ **Brenda**

"We've discovered and were reminded that every journey starts with the first step, which is done with **expectancy**. Come join the journey of **expectation** with Him… we're glad we have." ~ **Ted & Lynette**

When He speaks… we are wise to listen. This prophetic word of the *Lord* came forth in a timely way to propel the writing of this book… this *telling* forward. You'll encounter it later in the fullness of the experience it created and is linked to. The releasing of it now is to stir an **expectation** connection.

"I want My people to wake up now. I have new ideas, new compositions for them, and a new accumulation of data where they will put things together they have never put together before to advance." says the Lord. "I'm telling you, get ready!"
~ **Apostle Chuck Pierce** prophetic word of the 8/27/23 @ GZI.

✧ TABLE OF CONTENTS ✧

Forwarding Words of Worth	i
Table of Contents	iii
Dedication	v
Acknowledgements	1
SECTION ONE *Expectation's Formation… an ever evolving*	3
Section One Worthy Words	5
Introduction	7
Chapter 1 Encountering & Experiencing… an introducing	9
Chapter 2 Encountering & Experiencing… an acquainting	21
Chapter 3 Encountering & Experiencing… an aligning	33
Chapter 4 Establishing & Embracing… a journey of words	45
SECTION TWO *Expectation's Birthing… an establishing & embracing*	55
Section Two Worthy Words	57
Chapter 5 Worthy Words	59
Chapter 5 Establishing & Embracing… the Journey with "e"	61
Day 1 establish / E Names	65
Day 2 echad	73
Day 3 essence	81
Day 4 express	85
Day 5 encounter	91
Day 6 encourage	95
Day 7 eternal	99
Expectation's Reflection	103
Chapter 6 Worthy Words	105
Chapter 6 Establishing & Embracing… the Journey with "m"	107
Day 1 man	109
Day 2 M names	115
Day 3 mountains	121
Day 4 message	129
Day 5 ministry	135
Day 6 maturity	143
Day 7 manifest	151
Expectation's Reflection	161

Chapter 7	Worthy Words	163
Chapter 7	Establishing & Embracing… the Journey with "c"	165
	Day 1 create	167
	Day 2 communion	171
	Day 3 connect	179
	Day 4 covenant	187
	Day 5 C names	195
	Day 6 carry	205
	Day 7 celebrate	215
	Expectation's Reflection	225
Chapter 8	Worthy Words	229
Chapter 8	Establishing & Embracing… the journey with "3"	231
	Day 1 father / son / holy spirit	233
	Day 2 alpha & omega / beginning & end / author & finisher	241
	Day 3 body / soul / spirit	247
	Day 4 water / fire / spirit	259
	Day 5 righteousness / peace / joy	269
	Day 6 individual / collective / corporate	275
	Day 7 faith / hope / love	283
	Expectation's Reflection	289
SECTION THREE *Expectation's Manifestation… an emerging & empowering*		291
Section Three	Worthy Words	293
Chapter 9	Worthy Words	295
Chapter 9	Emerging & Empowered… from, for, and into now!	297
Chapter 10	Worthy Words	305
Chapter 10	Emerging & Empowered … for now and beyond!	307

APPENDICES — 319
"ION" Word List / referenced in Chapter 3 page — 321
10 M's List / Bishop Bill Hamon / referenced in Chapter 6 – Day — 322
The 7 Mountains Chart / referenced in Chapter – Day — 323
The Ship / referenced in Chapter 6 – Day — 324
The 7 Churches Chart / referenced in Chapter 7 – Day — 325
Albert Einstein's Letter to Daughter / referenced in Chapter 10 — 326

MINSITRY INFORMATION — 329
BOOK PODCAST OPPORTUNITY — 331

✧ A DEDICATION OF HONOR & LOVE ✧

To *You* first and foremost
oh **Eternal Expectant** *King of Kings* and *Lord of Lords*,
my *Beloved*, *Holy Lover of My Soul*, *Messiah*, *Savior*,
Redeemer, *Lord*, and *Truest Faithful Friend* that *You* are.

I love *You* and *You* are the only *One* worthy of any and
all *blessing* and *glory* and *honor* and *power* and *praise*.

For *You* are my *Alpha & Omega… Beginning & End*.

My ***expectation*** is *earnestly endearing*
and *exclusively* lies in *You*.

You are *Author & Finisher* of all things in my life.

You are *God my Father Yahweh Adonai*, *You* are *God the Son - Yeshua*,
and *You* are *God the Spirit, Holy Spirit*.
I love, worship, and serve *You* alone
in the *beauty of Your holiness, majesty,* and *sovereignty*
doing all as unto *You* in the fullness of who *You* are
and in *Spirit* and *Truth* as *You* desire.

May the words of my mouth, my meditation-thoughts, and every movement
of my heart be always pure and pleasing, acceptable before Your eyes,
YAHWEH, my only *Redeemer*, my *Protector.*

May *Your kingdom* come and will be done always, in all ways,
on earth as it is in heaven, and as it is written
for such a time as this especially in and through my life.

Expectantly and *eternally Yours*
with *all my love…*

e

✧ ACKNOWLEDGEMENTS ✧

In the spirit of love, gratitude, and giving honor where it is due... in this my first book through Him.

*To my loving godly husband, **Greg**... watchful vigilant one... my 'science guy' and an all-around gracious, more than patient participant in this process of shifting from a life built on self, soul, intellect, religion, and formulas to a life led by His Spirit grounded in His Word, will, and ways in a covenant relationship with Him, each other, and beyond. My on earth faithful and true whom I love and honor... couldn't have done this without you.*

*To our/my beautiful daughters **Victoria** and **Alexandria** who carry within them much of the presence, power, and purposes of God. Over the years you've heard me speaking of a "book" I'd one day write, sharing revelation and thoughts from time to time, and drawing from the well of Him in you both. Yet amazingly, the essence of it all never unfolded then as it was kept for such a time. Now in this place your love and support throughout life has meant everything to me as I so honor and treasure the blessing of you, Christ in you and His heart in you toward me. My heart is doubly blessed in the godly men He's given me (us) in your husbands – my 'sons in love' **Cody** and **Jackson**, in which I'm continually thankful to Father God for and their special place and part in our family.*

*My heart of love, honor, and gratefulness to my mother **Donna**, grandmother **Mildred**, great grandmother **Janie**, and grandmother **Blanche** for their unconditional love, roles in modeling, and living out life as godly women, women of prayer, and as the spiritual leaders you each uniquely were in my life. And yes... for the training up of me including the prayers you prayed in faith believing that I was trained up in the way I should go so ultimately I would not depart from it, becoming and being who He made me to be. Your devotion to our family, His family/church, and service unto the Lord truly deposited much.*

*To my/our "**book ministry prayer and support team**"... truly my family, that He led me to form early on. He is so very, very good to have deposited a yes in you each to become a part of this essential foundational piece vital for bringing me to this moment of the process and in this journey. He continually propelled us forward in this process of moving consistently from faith to faith, strength to strength in His grace upon grace for glory to glory – which is all His. My heart is full and I marvel still in how He has knitted our hearts together drawing out much from you each in our times of connecting and conversing as Holy Spirit directed. I honor and value Him in you, His voice in you, and the role of your heart, voice, input, and even editing in the writing of this book. By no means can "**thank you**" ever reflect the depth of my gratitude to you each **Brenda, Connie, Karen, Lynette** and **Ted**. What's fun is that you'll be blessed by their special "telling" portions too!*

To my precious sister and brother friends (family) whom over the years you've received from bits and pieces He would prompt me to share with you related to this "book" I was to write. The offering of your sincere listening ears, gracious spirits, and gracing me with an outlet have blessed me more than I could ever express. The blessing of your valued anointed input and depositing of a perspective uniquely yours, yet imparted by Him in what you'd receive to release as He'd reveal and direct in our divine appointments through times of conversations and connections ... and always for such a time.

It would be impossible to name all the ministries, the variety of ministering ones – 5 fold ministers, leaders, types of mentors, ministry team partners, prayer warriors, passion filled worshippers, lovers of the Lord and His Word... those that He has moved through to touch, teach, and impart much into my life in part bringing me to the place He has. They are made up of men and women, of a variety of ages, various 'religious/spiritual' backgrounds, and have all imparted into my life from Christ in them and their hunger for more of Him in their life out of their great love for and lifestyle of worship where all is unto and through Him and their hearts to model His servant leadership in all areas of life.

My profound love and honor, with deeply heartfelt appreciation and recognition to all, particularly the ministries He's made a way for my family and ones together with me to partner with so His Bride - His true church can arise, as His ekklesia so His kingdom can come and will be done on earth as it is in heaven ~ New Life Christian Ministries, Glory of Zion International – House of Zion/Kingdom Harvest Alliance, Aglow International – Great Lakes Ohio Valley Region, Ohio/NW Ohio Area, NW Ohio Apostolic Group – Firstfruits, Curt Landry Ministries, Come To The Table /Midrash and more, and the rich deposits made from the seasons of life connected to all with Daughters of Zion, Findlay Prayer, Son Center House of Prayer, Emerging Streams, International Fellowship of Chaplains, Wagner Leadership Institute/Wagner University, Marion Christian Center - Christian International, and Shekinah Christian Center.

Along with those above, the special place in my heart for the ministries He's connected me to over time regarding the apple of His eye – Israel, our grafted in identity as One New Man humanity, and understanding the fullness of my identity - inwardly and outwardly and inheritance in my/our covenant with the God of Abraham, Isaac, Jacob, and Yeshua.

*A special closing note of honor and appreciation to all those who 'sowed' into the publishing of this book. May God reward you richly for your generosity and bless your seed a hundred-fold. To **Leah** who offered her expertise and wise counsel, **Robin, Alexandria, Victoria**, and **Pam** who offered their insight, editing skills and support, **Kelli** (WTLW TV44) and **Alexandria** who graciously offered their tech support. Additionally, **Pam** and all those at **Ajoyin Publishing,** and **James** and **Colleen Nesbit** of **James Nesbit Prophetic Art** for the anointed cover. Truly you each have brought essential elements and finishing touches together in ways that fulfilled my expectations and beyond!*

I am truly a more loving, honoring, gracious, and Christ-like woman of God and person because of Him in all mentioned and those ones I've not mentioned, but have been or are significant in my life's journey and the process I'm in together with you in Him.
With much love, honor, and appreciation… ~ Elizabeth "Beth"

e

SECTION ONE

✧ EXPECTATION'S FORMATION
...AN EVER EVOLVING

✧ SECTION ONE: WORTHY WORDS ✧

*In the beginning... God sent His Spirit to hover... to brood... over the face of the waters... over the deep, the dark... what was formless, void and empty... over what He created and was then known as the heavens and the earth. But for the earth – He knew He **must** send His Spirit to resonate and release over... through an infiltrating... saturating... **m**arinating... of His Divine essence in His **m**ost Holy Breath for a **m**anifesting of what it was to and would (**expectantly**) become. And then Yahweh, Himself Almighty... Elohim... Master Creator... brought up out of Himself... the very Source of Him... filled with the fullness of the sustenance of the life giving Force in Him... words... words that as spoken (in **expectancy**) carried within them the creative power of His Divine essence... something the earth had yet to encounter and experience. This "telling" as it released for the earth to receive... "Let there be". "Let there be light"... and light was birthed in the earth... in its beginning... as it began to break in... break through... break out... and burst forth... for that's what it was purposed (**expected**) divinely according to Elohim's original Master design to do. And He... with all of heaven **expectantly** looking down... saw what He said come to life and **m**anifest as light. Yes, His Light... and it was pleasing... beautiful. For the essence of the Divine eternal energy within it even... as He directed... dispersed and dispelled the darkness... it was good... very good.**

*Now... the entire universe is standing on tiptoe (anxiously awaiting **expecting**), yearning to see the unveiling of God's glorious sons and daughters - **expectations m**anifestation of the sons of God! For against its will the universe itself has had to endure the empty futility ("the purposelessness, frustration, chaos) resulting from the consequences of human sin. But now, with an eager (earnest) **expectation** (anxious even persistent **expectation**) all creation longs for freedom from its slavery to decay and to experience with us the wonderful freedom coming to God's children. To this day we are aware of the universal agony and groaning of creation, as if it were in the contractions of labor for childbirth. And it's not just creation. We who have already experienced the firstfruits of the Spirit... the **expectant** awakening of the Spirit now in us... also inwardly groans as we passionately long to experience our full status as belonging to God - His created ones —including our physical bodies being transformed. For this is the hope (the **expectation**) of our salvation.**

*God conceals the revelation of His word in the hiding place of His glory. But the honor of kings; we are His kings and priests, is revealed by how they thoroughly (with expectancy) search out the deeper **m**eaning (**expectantly**) of all that God says.**

*My soul... **wait** silently for God alone, for my **expectation** is from Him.* For **in Him** you... me... we, **live** and **move** and **exist** - that is, in Him we actually have **our being**. For we are actually His children – sons and daughters who choose Him.**

---

* Footnotes: See Genesis 1:1-3, Romans 8:19-24,. Proverbs 25:2, Psalm 62:5, Acts 17:28, 1 John 3:2, Galatians 3:26, 2 Corinthians 6:18 – all emphasis is mine and personal paraphrasing built on various translations and versions.

✧ INTRODUCTION ✧

Oh the waiting... enduring even to experience as earthen vessels the exhilaration from the excitement that stirs, with its underlying ever present form of anticipation... and its own kind of delight filled energy that arises in the **encountering** and **experiencing** of such **expectancy** as penned in *His Word*. Just as the **earth**... *yes, all of creation*... in its groaning and laboring... along with extreme eagerness joins in the awaiting of the *glorious revealing* that will unfold in those that are the vessels called **"sons"**... to the point of *"standing on tiptoe"*!

- ❖ *Perhaps...* there's a kind of general recollection happening right now in the unfolding of your memories, as there is in mine through the use of the phrase: *"**standing on tiptoe**"*? And, could it be it's bringing a sensation that's awakening... even arousing a sense of child- like reflection and wonder... possibly connected to what you were *expecting*? In that moment... in life... for yourself... of yourself... for others... of others... connected to words spoken... promises made... even regarding *God's*?

And *then*, you know how what we *expect* begins to align and assign itself in *what could be – should be – would be – ought to be*... and in what we've come to call or we could describe as the *forming* of an *expectation*... for what is *expected* and even more when we expand it to include the *expectations* of many... multitudes in some situations... and whether it is in life naturally or spiritually... or whether it is in facts, deception, lies... or truth.

The *what's to be expected*... a starting of a formation in the stirring and whirling... in the imaginations and thoughts twirling in the here and now. Yet, for a time it's about what's just beyond. Yes, that's exactly what we call *expectancy* – you know... where you *expect* and *see*... whether it's how you think or imagine it might be. How it forms and is birthed... manifesting right in the very midst of the continual *ebb and flow* of life – your life, our lives. The world around us even... including how it has or hasn't manifested in full or part.

- ❖ *Perhaps... there might be a different kind of recollection unfolding in your memories right now, as happened to me in writing this beginning. For emerging in life, there can happen in the world of the <u>un</u>expected... a not always "on your tiptoes" kind of moment... with a result, where either way – positive or negative – something happens... manifests... and it wasn't on your radar... it catches you even off guard. Therefore, you may not of had a grid for what it now leaves you expecting... let alone the expectancy it starts to "breed" and can "carry" into where you are... are going... or thought you were.*

Let's journey now into such a moment... into such a time... quite some years ago where an *experience* that I *encountered* has now become a catalyst for carrying the seed to shape the becoming of the *introduction* of *expectation* in this book. May you enter in *expectantly* knowing He goes before and *with you, me... us*. In sincere and fervent *expectancy* know I'm joining you in the *journey* that's before you ~

✦ CHAPTER 1 ✦

✦ ENCOUNTERING & EXPERIENCING… AN INTRODUCING

Like a sign in the road telling me to *"turn around"* coupled with a knowing that it was ok and that I'm "allowed", so to speak, to share here something that happened in my life's journey… where my **e**yes were opened in an **unexpected moment** and where some things that had been happening started **m**erging and **c**onverging **together** to form a type of focal point. Becoming like a **c**atalytic agent… it prompted me to now go *"this way"*… and to let what was being brought before me *create a way* to release in written words and with you, a greater awareness requiring my attention and aligning in a *more conscientious* kind of way with **expectancy** in general and personally, and in this introducing.

With the ongoing *existence of expectations* and their **relevancy** and **connection**, **naturally** and **spiritually**, to everyday life and all while **m**oving forward in life's journey, there's been for some time a continual *process* where I'm discovering a need to *look* and *look again*, but not for the turning around to *look back*… only to *look again* for the *looking* beyond. So that in **my expectancy**… I become well able to **"expect and see"** **m**ore often another realm of possibilities. At *His* bidding I was strongly sensing in this *"look"* it was ok to turn… so I turned. Where it took me is beyond what I'm **c**apable of sharing, let alone writing about without *Him*… and by *His Spirit, Holy Spirit*. Oh… what *expectant* help **c**omes from *Him*.

My heart is and has been for **m**uch of my life to *fully love, worship and serve Him* to some degree or another. Accepting that *He's* wrapped me in *His love, plans, and purposes for* **my** *life*… well, I discovered over time and still am… that I **m**ust rest *my expectancy* in this **c**oupled with how *He* brings it all together… as *He* always has, does… and it's always good. Perhaps you've discovered and know this somewhat like me… where the bottom line is *obedience* is key – it's as *He requires, desires, and delights* in from *you*… *me*… *us*.

✦ IN THE BEGINNING…

There is a beginning… and within it a beginning in *Him*, who we know is the *Beginning*. A beginning that becomes an amazing ongoing **encountering, engaging,** and **experiencing** with unlimited **expectations** that build together to establish things in our lives.

"Abba," I found myself asking *Him*… *"When was my 'In the beginning' into this journey… into what You've revealed, have refined over time, and now I define as* **"expectation"** *at work?"* Everything within me knew it would be beneficial… even needful, to know as I've thought I knew what **m**ight be **m**arked as a *"starting point"*. There was however, something brooding within that was saying, *"There's more"*. And, I sensed a drawing to ask then… *"Where do I begin?. You know and I know it's already written in You… in Your book about me… this writing."* So with a **c**ertainty arising in a form of knowing… all the while a kind of *expectation* was ascending in the fact that yes, it's been written… but the writing is now before me… a beginning with future fruit attached… of a long awaited adventure and *expected journey* and with it… an end – *His* **expected** end. As it really is all about *Him*.

And there it was, a *'for such a time'*... from those appointed divinely aligned times in *His* timeline for you and for me... as it started unfolding and began with two words... *"Tell them."*... again, later *"Tell them."*... two times at a worship and arts conference I had attended I encountered a kind of *spiritual hearing* that was new to me, yet as real to me as a person like you, were standing next to me speaking in a normal tone of voice.

Upon returning home, as I entered the township I live in, again I hear, *"Tell them."* – that's the third time I thought – hmmm, three (3) is an important number biblically I recalled. For *He* had begun to draw my attention often to numbers in *His Word* and in life, while communing and conversing in my times with *Him*... which was interestingly inspiring a budding ***expectancy***.

Much stirred within to know whose voice this was, why is this voice telling me to *"Tell them"*, and what am I to *tell them*, not to mention – who is them?

Again... the next day after church during lunch at a restaurant owned by family, very loudly and distinctly I heard, *"Tell them."*, and this time it was in a more unlikely atmosphere like the times before. And before you know it, I ended up asking my husband, *"Did you hear that voice? That voice speaking to me?"* *"No"*. Well I knew I heard it and it was now the fourth time within three days. Each time it was a clear audible voice, which I believed to be *His* or at the very least by *His Spirit* or possibly a godly ministering angel *He* sent to speak to me these words, *"Tell them."* But why, why now... and why me?

Here I was contemplating it all... giving serious consideration that it was *God* definitely trying to get my attention. But in order to respond... and, to this *"Tell them"*, I first had to have an ear to hear and receive these words from whomever it was, and what they were *telling* me. I don't recall asking, *"Lord, is that You?"* But, I distinctly remember a type of assured sensing it was *Him* since *He* had been growing and training me to know *His* voice.

There I was, not only hearing these words... but actually listening to them, believing they were from *Him*, and giving them a place in my mind, my thoughts...mixing together with my overall thinking which was beginning to consume me. For this was an exceptionally unusual encounter – at least for me.

There was a hearing of words, a receiving of the words, with a way being made that caused me to start to believe these words – that yes, there is something I must *"Tell them"*. So, you could say there was a convincing that created a kind of *"conceiving"* from the words released and being ***embraced*** and as a form of ***engaging*** began.

Oh... the power of "words" to create a place within of *anticipation, wonder,* and yes, ***expectation***. I longed to discover the purpose in this encounter and knew I needed to know – *Is this You Lord?* I was in a very transitional place in my walk with the *Lord* as the very core of me was crying out for more of *Him. Perhaps*... you can relate because you've encountered something similar and hungered or are hungering now for more?

It wasn't just the power of the words "*Tell them*", or even the extreme sense of a yearning and desire to truly know what this all meant, but additionally what would follow… and it intensified everything.

What added to this powerful time of *His* moving and speaking was *what then* immediately happened in that timeframe. I experienced another encounter… which was not something I *expected*. Later that Sunday into Monday, I entered into what I call a *"live"* type of interactive vision in the middle of the night.

Let me recap and share here… I had just come from an incredible, appointed time of *corporate worship,* much needed *teaching,* and genuine meaningful *fellowship* at an anointed worship/arts conference where many among those gathered were of a more Charismatic Pentecostal way of believing; I was not. Yet, not opposed to such obviously as I choose to attend… due to my grandmother aligning herself in that way, so I had some familiarity but primarily as a child, and had come to know quite a few friends who did.

Little did I know however, that all of this was just part of *Him* drawing me up higher into an *insatiable desire, deep hunger,* and *personal cry* out to *Him* for more… and a more, that was becoming clear could only be satisfied by *Him.*

There I was awakened in the middle of the night by a bright light that immediately made me sit up in bed. I sat there with an intense sense of wonder asking myself what is happening… am I in bed or am I somewhere else? For what appeared before me and around me put me in a place I was not from.

A desert was where I appeared to be and beyond it in the distance I could see an oasis with many palm trees. It was like I was *"transported"* there to a kind of scene in the Bible you could say… to the place I was now "in".

There appeared 12 men of Bible times before me. I didn't count them. I just knew there were 12 and immediately wondered who they were… not knowing fully whether they were representing the 12 Tribes or the 12 Apostles/Disciples, but felt confident they represented godly important men on a mission. They were walking slowly, steadily across the desert with staffs in hand, behind what appeared to be a white dove flying in the sky with an olive branch in its mouth leading the way, and what looked to be like a scroll or book/bible opened with wings supporting it as it was flying closely behind the dove, but before these men.

As they walked forward, passing in front of me at about what seemed a distance of 20-30 yards away, they all turned their heads looking intently at me… when from them I suddenly heard a unified speaking of words clearly saying, *"Tell them."* WOW!

Where am I, what is happening, and is this real? As my heart was racing and my thoughts stirring in the midst of this amazing encounter happening in my bedroom. They then began to draw nearer to the oasis area… and suddenly it was all gone as abruptly as it all came.

Immediately I awakened in our bedroom where it began and started asking my husband, *"Did you see that? Did you hear that? I can't believe what was just happening."* He didn't hear or see anything and went back to sleep. It became very clear this encounter was for me, as he didn't seem concerned or alarmed. There now lingered the unexplainable weightiness of my amazement at the astonishing encounter I just experienced, along with the complexity of my "why"… which was creating a greater depth of *fascination, anticipation,* and again – **expectation.**

Sharing this experience wasn't really something I could do as I didn't really understand it myself…. and, who did I know who would? He did lead me to call and ask a newer friend of mine… a mighty woman of *God* and kind of spiritual example /teacher in my life, and just happened to be at the worship and arts conference I had attended… and was spirit-filled. *"Can we talk… something significant is happening to me spiritually and I'm not sure what."*

She greed to have me come over to her home so I could share, we could pray, and I did on that Monday Memorial Day of 2001 while things were still *"fresh"*. The *Lord* met with me there in some very powerful and interesting ways that day… as I ended up inviting and asking for the fullness of *Him* I had longed for to come and by *His Spirit - Holy Spirit* to baptize and fill me afresh. This life changing encounter ended with me saying to *Him*, *"Ok, I will tell them – whatever it is I will."* My sure response surprised me a bit, as I entered fully back into the natural setting of where I said that. Yet, across my face there came a long awaited anticipated smile that expressed not only the intensity of **expectancy** in my heart, along with a knowing that *He* was doing something very NEW in me… and more of *Him* was here!

I knew I would never be the same and this *experience* would *change, challenge, influence,* and *direct* much; little did I know actually everything. Especially in how I would now come to **expect**, what I would **expect**, from who and how would I **expect** it… you get the idea. *He* would require and desire I enter a new level of inquiring and acquiring of *Him*… and, certainly in regards to what *He* would **expect** of me… for me… and even I of myself… in this calling up into the more I had cried out for.

Personally, up to this point what I had encountered of experiencing *Him* in my life and walk with *Him* was at best, in what I identified and knew *Him* then to be as *God the Father and God the Son – Jesus*; knowing very minimal of *Him* as *God the Holy Spirit*. The continual change I would come to begin knowing and growing in began as the fullness of *Him* by *His Spirit – Holy Spirit*, who now had an intended place in *leading, guiding,* and *directing* me… as well as, *helping, comforting, revealing truth, advocating, and teaching* me as only *He* could. This is who the *Word* says *He* is and what *He* does became reality… yes, mine.

It is *God's* heart and the essence of *His* great love for us in *His* divine design… for and to our connection and interaction with *Him* … and *Him* with us in what many, including myself – perhaps you too, have come to call *His "original intent"* (OI). This is as *He* designed it *in the beginning* to be… as *relational* before it was ever about being *functional or structural*… grounded in authentic personal continual communion as one with *Him the One*.

He is the *Beginning (Alpha)* and we see this there… in the *Garden* of *Eden*. *He* is the *End (Omega)* and we see this there where the end is only to begin again in *Him* and eternally. *He* is as well, the *Author* and *Finisher He* is in the *constancy, consistency, and continualness* of *His* moving in the *times, seasons, and cycles* of life… yours… mine…ours.

This is good to *know, remember, and rely* upon as one pursues writing what *He* has revealed and released for such a time ... especially when the **e**ncompassing timeframe has been over a twenty four year span... and actually I'm **c**ertain of the realm of its **e**xistence beyond.

Grounding my life and what is written here in these pages in what *He* says... agreeing with it and aligning it in what *He has, is,* and *will* reveal **c**oncerning *His Word, will and ways*... is **m**andatory. There has been a **m**aturing and growth within me that has been and is a vital essential **c**omponent within the *forming, birthing,* and *creating* within this ever existing realm of *expectation* and all ahead.

This **e**stablishing has been in *Him* both through the written *Word* and in *Him* as the *Word*. Both **c**onnecting what *we... you and me...* **c**ome to *expect* to actually happen since *He* tells us that *His Word* goes forth accomplishing what is sent to do... not returning void or unfulfilled... but is fruitful even prospering us... in its **m**anifesting.

- ❖ *Perhaps...* you have or are discovering what I'm sharing happening in the *process* and purpose of *"expectation"* in your life? Maybe you're even beginning to encounter more and more how much it really is not by our might, nor by our power, but by *His Spirit*, and it within us. That *He* enables us to develop this awareness and root our *expectancy* in what *He's* established in and for us to do... to be... with and in *Him*? Trust in this either way... for *He* plans on meeting you as you *journey* through reading about **expectation to engaging, embracing, and being empowered.**

It's time now to identify that not only as *His* creation...but as *His* children... **He** has established and is establishing, based upon the fact that *He* placed *Himself* in *His* fullness – *Father, Son,* and *Holy Spirit* in us – *fashioning, forming, molding and making* us in the expressed image and likeness of *Him - Them*...even setting eternity in our hearts – the hearts of **m**en.

Yet, in this divinity and definitiveness of *His* design... *He* desires a partnering with us, but it has to **c**ome in our own will **c**hoosing to partner with *His* plans and purposes. For its the same free will *He* gave from the beginning... and now it **c**omes in the opportunity of the invitation to enter into the being *saved from sin...* being **born again**... to being *His* **c**hildren as *He* originally intended. Filled with *His Spirit - Holy Spirit*, living now from our new **m**an – as a new creation. Not just as *Jesus*, our *Savior* with salvation working in and through us to become new... but by *His Spirit* living in and through our spirit... in which it all begins to work together to enable us to experience everything *He* has promised and purposed for us to be... including spiritual gifts and the fruit of *Holy Spirit* **m**anifesting.

For it is our identity and inheritance in *Him* – in *Them*, the fullness. So how **c**ould my hope... my perspective... my outlook... yes, my *expectation* truly rest in anything... anyone... but *Him-Them* alone? How about yours?

Is this not the hope that does not disappoint? The *expectant* hope that's not a form of fantasy filled with ungrounded, unfounded possibility or potential... because we now open ourselves to **experiencing, encountering** the endless *expectations* of what the essence of *Him* as God... our *Father* and *Creator Elohim* can do through who *He* is in and through us. Coupled with how *He* **m**oves **c**ascading into and through our soul... *mind, will, emotions,* and our hearts with *His* heart…in such a way leads to what I call a *togethering*. Where by *His Spirit* who lives in us fully now truly moves to evokes our *expectancy* and so much more.

Oh the unfolding in theses writings… in the uniqueness of style and in the freedom of form… and in formations forming… creating a framework for what becomes the *paragraphs, pages, chapters*… of a book. In the way that *He* authentically *put in me, ordered me,* and *called* me to "Tell them"- *you*. Within this *telling* you will most likely begin to see and encounter some unique ways and methods authentic to me… especially in this becoming and being a writer… an author… and together with *His pen* by *His Spirit* moving in me to manifest in a *birthing*.

As shared, I am not sure exactly when this all truly began, but for me… where I am now… I most see it as a truly amazing… godly divinely aligned and assigned adventure…within an appointing of times within my life's "timeline" that's been a continual *journey* together with *Him*. Learning to write through *Him* in me… where writings in journaling, songs, teachings, and more have manifested playing a role in the fashioning and forming… molding and making of a writer. But, as for the end product of a book by me as an author… it was as if I was always placed in a type of *"holding pattern"* so it seemed. *His*, not quite yet.

The waiting… because *He* didn't want me to be like *Sarai (Sarah)* in the *Bible* – the wife of *Abram (Abraham)* and preempt *His* plan and timing by bringing forth… and conceiving something through another means not of *God's intent*. A womb… or wineskin of sorts… that contained a mind skin… not fully mature or ready to hold *new wine*, let alone *new paradigms* in the needful necessary *process*. And yes, there was a time when I laughed out of fear and unbelief too… at the thought of a book being birthed through me… especially with any *spiritual* kind of relevance, let alone any form of relativity.

Originally… I didn't see it this way, but over time *He* opened my eyes to see… and to see that in the waiting… the weight of *His* presence and purposes processing and preparing me… consuming more and more of me… releasing more and more of *Him* in me… for what this endeavor essentially required. And, in the refining progression of it all… all *He* desired was for me to *learn, mature,* and *develop* with *Him* in the *process* and *journey* and through all that truly mattered.

The laying it down like *Abraham*… for I loved what *He* had given me to receive conceiving and giving birth to a type of *prebook* - my type of "Isaac". In all *His* knowingness *He* knew it now required the building of an altar and a laying down of it all there like Abraham… and more than once. For you see, the essence of *expecting… expectancy*… for me – well, it had to be in *His* time… which wasn't always easy to *embrace*… but over time it truly *empowered* me. Be encouraged if you are there… or see this kind of requiring coming.

Oh… the movement in the moments… *"for such a time"* moments in life… that enter into the *journey* questioning relevancy and relativity. Perhaps… like *Esther*, there is a time of preparation that must go before. For her it was a year… for me it went beyond a year… into years…many years… until there came my *"this is that – for such a time"* moment… and accordingly I am… we are here. He is good ~

Looking through the lens of now and embedded in my asking "How now?"… a more broad and beyond way has surfaced with an underlying dimension displayed and exhibited in *encounters* and *experiences* that run throughout *my* childhood, teenage… and my entire adult life… that are still unfolding... where a need to *look and look again*... not to *look back* let alone go back... but to *look again* to remember *Him* and what that **means** for the here, now, and to *look beyond*. It is an unfolding... and yours **may** be unfolding in a greater way too.

✧ IN THE BEGINNING… KNOWN & UNKNOWN…

In this *journey* of life, when do we really become aware of the innate inborn role of our *expectancy* and *expectations* – what they create and roles they've played... play, in it all other than to say... <u>how could they but not</u>? Remember, even the earth *expects* as it groans travailing with *expectation*. Did not the darkness of an earth formless, void even *expect*... as it encountered the *Spirit* of *God* brooding and releasing *words* filled with the *Spirit* of *Life* – from *Him* who is *Life*... spoken... giving place to light and life emerging?

Afterall, the plain and simple of it is that *expecting* is an absolute part in and of everything that we do... and are... have been... and will be... without us fully recognizing its ongoing never ceasing place most of the time. It's like its implanted and embedded in the very fiber of us. Hence you could say... is it not just a faction and function within that of our DNA...naturally, spiritually... but as well, within it there exists this eternal ebb and flow of our creation *Creator* connection where lies the heart of a purer *expectation - His!*

In what we *expect* there is an evolving constantly through the *forming, reforming, adjusting,* and *readjusting*. The changing, shifting, realigning, reassigning, or relinquishing of what we *expect*, why we *expect* it, when we expect it, how, and yes, even where. It's as constant as day turns into night and night back into day... the distinctive yet differentiating work of *expectancy*.

With it all tending to happen in a seemingly kind of knowingly and unknowingly, willingly and unwillingly, or intentional and unintentional kind of way within the broad scope and spectrum of *expectations* full of *expectancy*.

To share with others through writing in a way that recognizes and respects giving a place to my *unique* way of embracing the role and *process* I've grown to learn and respect that this thing called *expectation* plays and *expectancy* has created... it is important to me. I believe it is now becoming more so to you. With that in mind, there are a few things I'll share to establish and enlighten some foundational aspects that I believe will help you as the reader to *enjoy, benefit,* and *be blessed* in this *journey* by the more *He'll* deposit then through it.

Things which will clarify my personal style... as you're probably already noticing... revealed and reflected in my writing, how it goes with my way of thinking, and momentary meditating, how it's becoming and evolving more and more around my communion and conversation with *Him*... *His* ways, and how this influences my way of expressing topics, themes, and terminology; wording that this book presents to you... not just as a reader... or a participant... but it is hoped in a way that it "*touches and speaks*" to you as a child of *God*... my brothers and sisters in *Christ*...our *Father's* family whom *He* loves.

Here are a few key areas that reflect my personal *character, nature,* and *integrity,* as well as my heart to *encourage, edify, equip,* and *empower*... as it all becomes a part of the making of my "*unique way*" of expressing in and through thoughts, words, and my writing style. There's an intentional attempting to honor the integrity of sources and subject matter over time gained... staying true to what I believe *He* requires and desires of me. *Thank you* in advance... for freedom and grace to flow as the *Spirit* has led me to go… in the doing and being as an "author" and of *Him* in me. *Perhaps*… a witness of ***expectancy*** will arise?

❖ POSTURE & POSITIONING… the taking of a stance and standing in it be-cause you have, are, or know you will discover what is good and right in *His* sight. To position oneself furthermore, in that which *He* requires and desires… for pleasing *Him* must be the foundation that the *revealing, reflecting, and releasing* from *His* heart to mine and mine to you – yours… flows through in writing and regarding all things and in all ways… because, it always matters. *He* sees… *He* knows… and *His* good and righteous *opinion, acceptance, and esteem* of me is a significant part of my ultimate ***expectation.*** So, as I go low… and lower still as a laid down lover and servant of the *Lord*…this posturing in its positioning cannot remain steady without knowing and receiving *His* love as the exclusively all- encompassing element it is in what makes up and holds the foundation solid… especially as this new portion of my identity and purpose as an "author" awakens and arises. May you discover a new posture and positioning as you align in *His* purposeful ***expectancy*** for you.

❖ PURPOSEFUL PARTNERING… the continual intentionality and investment made in knowing and showing that alone I am nothing… but in, with, from, and through *Him* something… in which all things then are possible. For *His* grace is sufficient and surely that grace upon grace by *His Spirit* is what has kept and keeps me… us… moving from faith to faith… strength to strength… glory to glory… and for *His* glory so *His* kingdom can come and will be done on earth… in our earthen vessels… as it in heaven. Not to mention the extreme honor and blessing it is to partner with *Him*… and in its design be reflective of *His* heart… and *His* plans and purposes for *His* kingdom for us, you… me. May Your purposes prevail as we embrace such with exceedingly great ***expectation***!

❖ PONDERINGS & PARAPHRASING… the giving of one's soul: mind, will, and emotions to *Him* for *His* reasonable service… *His* good and perfect will which is holy and acceptable unto *Him*. For indeed being not conformed, but transformed in the renewing of my mind… your mind… our minds… daily… helps keep our thoughts… our ponderings in greater alignment with truth… with *His Word – will – ways*. Therefore, when I take freedom to create my own form of *"paraphrasing"*… from the variety of versions and translations coming together to reword, translate, summarize or reasonably infer… it is through the filter of the fullness of *His Word,* by *His Spirit,* representing *His* heart. The end product of such a filtered perspective or perception expressed… brings depth of agreement into it all… in dimensions of what *He* has said and ***expects***. This kind of grouping of words works in and through us…creating an ***expectancy*** that sees and ***expects*** beyond normal borders… and helps enlarge us, especially in a more <u>*conversational, relational, and relative*</u> way. May the ponderings and paraphrasing come together in *You* first Lord, and be what *You* ***expect.***

❖ PARTS, PIECES, & PAUSES… the understanding that we see in part, hear in part, know in part, and therefore, speak in part… and, what's spoken in written words in part is foundational in this book. The parts and pieces that unfold reveal to you the reader… just as they do and have done to me the writer… in a uniquely amazing, powerful exclusively enlightening and ***expectant*** way. And yes… the *three dot pattern* used called an *"ellipsis"*… like seeds sown and scattered… they matter. In their cultivation and connection of what they can construct and confirm. You see if truly it is that as *He* is so are we, am I… and that in *Him* every part of me and you is to live, move, breathe, and have it's very being.. the gaps and breaths… the *parts, pieces, and pauses*… the *selah* moments within them have substance… carrying even a sustenance from *Him* within them when submitted to *Him*. So, expansion of *Him* in us connects us to and casts upon the horizon a fervent and effectual hope. May the parts and pieces in all their pauses… make a way as *You* reveal and release **expectancy**.

✧ PEARLS OF PURPOSE… the overwhelming… never ending… perfect plans of *God* in our eternal purpose in *Him* in the fullness of *Them*. Such fullness and fruitfulness of what they have released into my life… and I believe yours too. Those *pearls, gems, treasures, nuggets… precious prizes* of sorts containing within them some sort of certain value… a price because of a sacrifice… a purifying in a process required… from a trial or test in a time of temptation or tribulation… in your life… my life… our lives. But, we are better and not bitter because of them… and they reveal more of *Him* being who *He* is … doing what *He* does as the *Redeemer, Restorer, and Reconciler He* is. And, we now have this strand of such *pearls* in our lives. What do we do with them… how do we wear them… with whom do we share them… allowing them to point to *Him*? Our *Refiner* who produces them in us… and in them what we **expect**… and even reject in an **expectation** <u>not of Him</u>. Those things, yet hidden in a kingdom, but from a personal *process* and perspective we are to produce… purchased at a great cost indeed. The essence of what's collecting and connecting… merging and converging…in and through them… these *pearls*… a deeper depth of who *He* is and how *He's* at work in us. May life's pearls made by *His* kingdom aligned in providence within you carry valued **expectations**.

✧ POINTS, PATTERNS, & PRINCIPLES… the seat of our contemplations together with considerations… each in their *elaboration, exaggeration, enhancement, enlargement, embroidery* even… with an enticing that attempts to come within thoughts, *reflecting, reviewing,* and even a *rehearsing*. Do not reject the requiring of an examination with further exploration to know that we know they are formed and are joined together or not within the principles *He* has presented to us in *His Word* and by *His* modeling and manifesting them according to *His will* and *ways*. *He* has required that in *points, patterns, and principles* of me and when I share such it is from a *process* I've entered into **expecting** *Him* to reveal the "how now" of **expecting** and such revealing continually.

If… since we are *"seated"* with *Him* in heavenly places postured and positioned through the righteousness of *God* in *Christ Jesus* then what we *see, say,* and *share*… like in these writings must manifest a form of evidence. A fruit that contains and carries an indication of godly biblical ethics, values, morals, and beliefs that are *rooted, grounded, and established* in TRUTH – *His* and *His* alone which is always established in love. Facts are that – facts. But truth is truth. And for me… and how I bring forth such, is to make every attempt to align what is written in *Him* /*His Word* alone as the *way*, the *truth*, and the *life* it is – He is. So that how it influences and produces what I come to **expect** and release to you the reader to receive… well, as it has been in my own life… and more importantly as *He* says - it will be. Let us **expect** that we and even others, will know the truth and the truth will set us free. May such **expectancy** arise filled with truth… and what *He* who is the *Truth* holds for us!

✧ PRUDENCE… the voice of **expectation** and what carries within it… *"she"* calls and draws me to a place of knowing… just as *He* says of *"lady wisdom"*. Reminding, I must be wise, discerning, cautiously considering, always coupling my thoughts in what *I*… *you*… we **expect** as likened to these few points mentioned. These key actions you're considering, have the weight of their affects and consequences, and the counting of the cost in sharing… releasing revelation given by *Him* through *His Word*, through other trusted sources, and through life experiences with encounters. Words in all their meanings and implications… now as written words… my words in a book… **m**ade public… no longer private… with all the testing and trying of them… in being accountable to *Him* … to others and to you the reader for them. *He* did say *"Tell them"*. Yet, **m**ost importantly and significantly, obedience to what *He* has said and led is what's **e**ssential. And, the affect /effects of such in the **e**ntirety of *the process* over the years and ongoing in my life… in yours… in the life of a believer… a **c**hild- son or daughter of God… me… you… us… well, *prudence* is indeed key. **M**ay the pure voice of what is *prudent*: *wise, sensible, practical…* be the **c**onduit of what *He* **expects**.

✧   PROVIDENCE… the **e**lement and role of the providence of *God* that holds within what *God* foreknows, has planned, purposed and provides for by **m**eans of *Him* being the triune *God* of the *Universe* that *He* is, is vital. Settling it quickly is key… whether you believe in such… as I had to **c**ome to a position of belief for me so my ***expectation*** would and will align accordingly… is **e**ssential for you too. That you determine in some form or fashion as it is written in *His* book about you/your life… me/my life… what we ***expect***… at its **c**ore **m**ust encompass *His* **m**eans and purposes for which *He* **c**reated in a general way… an individual way… **c**ollective and **c**orporate way.   So, required in the foundations of my ***expectancy*** to write and publish this book… an intentional inclusion of knowing and trusting, as **e**very biblical based writer has had to do… not that I am fully in that **c**ategory… but in the simplicity the example offers… and in remembering one of the life principles I **c**ling to in the divinely inspired *as it is written*, *"Whatever He says… do it."* Oh how providence smiles with ***eternal expectancy*** at ***His expected end.***

For we **m**ust realize that in *His* all supremacy, sovereignty… omnipotence, omniscience, and omnipresence, I align myself providentially allowing *Him* to guide me, attempting to always release my ***expectation*** to *Him*.   And through it all, I ***expect*** I will see *Him* **m**ove in ways only *He* **c**an just as *He* has for me **e**ven to write… let alone publish this.

Oh… the **c**oming together in the *togethering* of *Him* and by *His Spirit* of it all and in it all… my heart is desiring to delight in and disclose … inditing… **c**omposing… yes "penning"… things that are good… that **m**atter:… that point to and speak of things that are lovely and of worth. Yes, **"*worthy words"***…written by the *"tongue"* of a ready writer now… words that touch the *King*… and to those *He* has drawn… **c**onnected to this writing… not only to **e**mbrace expectation and be **e**mpowered by it… but to invite and allow *Him* to be the *Source* and *Force* of all our ***expectations*** … within the words written, that will serve to partner with *Him* and *His Word*… *His* heart of ***expectancy*** toward and for us.

Come away… come up here… come in… **e**ach word and the ***expectation*** it **c**arries **c**alls… as *He* is **c**alling… for *He* is the *Word*. Like the sound of a trumpet… yet with a beckoning intimate invitation that **e**ntices you bidding you **c**ome… almost as a *Lover* **c**alling the one *He* loves…saying **c**ome away with *Me*. Come into **M**y **c**hambers… **c**ome receive so you **c**an believe and **c**onceive and be what you **e**arnestly ***expect*** through life in and with **M**e…

And, as this voice **c**ontinues to speaks… **c**ommanding the forward to **m**ove ahead and into the beyond… in the **m**omentum released within this invitation to an introduction… *"opened and accepted"* with ***expectancy*** and ***expectantly*** much like to an "RSVP"… we respond now in undeterred faith knowing we will ***expect*** and *see* as we've responded to entering in.

Oh… the reliance one **m**ust place upon the relevancy and relativity of the **m**anifesting of the **m**ultitude and **m**ultifacetedness of such expressions of ***expectation.***   <u>Not</u> **e**ager to **c**reate a formula… as **m**ight be suspected through lingering thoughts layering within this introducing and *stirring, stirring, stirring*… but a ***relative, raw, and real relationship*** with and in *Him* who is our ***Everlasting Expectation****…* and established in and through *His Love*.

❖ *Perhaps*... as ones who are joining this journey of what *He*, **my Everlasting Expectation**, has told me to "*Tell them*"... you, and it's in obedience I release... it seems it might be the time to present a question that's been stirring... **"Is He that to you – your Everlasting Expectation as Lord in your life?"**... I know not. But whether you are *new to the faith* and your born again life in *Him*, a *mature seasoned believer*, or *anywhere in between*... and yes, I believe there are ones who may consider themselves "*none of the above*" Each and all are invited now to continue on beyond this introduction into this *journey* of *expectation* with me... with us. Yes, together... in the *togethering He does of* you... me... us, in *Him as Father, Son, Holy Spirit* and as one. *One, in the One.* Oh such *expectations* in us...as these ones who are *expectantly* arising as one!

Let the adventure of *expectancy* begin...
Let us emerge *expecting* together with *Him* to enter in...
Let us cross the threshold *expectant* of more in *the journey*.
Let every *expectation* as we *embrace His Worthy Word* and its *empowering*...

Now faith brings our hopes (expectation) into reality
and becomes the foundation needed to acquire the things we long (expect) for.
It is all the evidence required to prove what is still unseen. This testimony of (expecting) faith is
what previous generations were commended for.

Faith (expects to) empowers us to (expect and) see that the universe was created and beautifully
coordinated by the power of God's words! He spoke and the invisible realm gave birth
(expectantly to all that is seen. And without such faith (expectancy)
living within us it would be impossible to please God.

For we come to God in faith (expecting and) knowing that He is real and that the rewards the
faith (the expectedness) of those who passionately seek Him... they lived in hope (expectantly,
yet) without receiving the fullness of what was promised them.
But now God has invited us to live in something better than what they had
faith's (expectation's empowering) fullness!

(Portions of Hebrews 11 from various versions and translations with
all emphasis and words in parenthesis mine.)

CHAPTER 2
✦ ENCOUNTERING & EXPERIENCING… AN ACQUAINTING.

*You are so intimately aware of **me**, Lord.*
*You read **my** heart like an open book and you know all the words*
I'm about to speak before I even start a sentence!
*You know every step I will take before **my** journey even begins.**

Oh… to encounter and experience being introduced to the *journey of words, sentences*… let alone their telling of a type of **m**eeting, **m**oving, and **m**anifesting of *God* in one's life… perhaps aligned in some form as a *"testimony"*… a remembering and retelling of something that has happened is always an adventure stirring up a place for **m**any expectations… good… bad… and indifferent.

And typically, by our very nature… in their telling or testimony… a form of **m**easuring, gaging, evaluating, or discerning perhaps, that begins playing a role in determining whether there is a desire for **c**ontinuing past the *introduction* into what they'll share next. You could **c**all it… an *acquainting*. This holds true not only with people and within the happenings of life… but in our relationship with *God* and through *His Word*.

*To **acquaint m**eans to inform or familiarize by becoming familiar with, to explain, to notify about something, somewhere or someone and in varying degrees.* And yes, it **c**onnects and extends into *considering, appraising, evaluating, or reviewing* for one's self… *forming an opinion based on a small portion of information and weighing it for the value it contains*. Only you **c**an determine its relevancy and worth to you… in your life… and for now. Only you know what you *expected* and now *expect.*

There's a wide-range in the types of ways one **c**an approach traveling on the path of *expectation*. One is simply **e**valuating things along the way. So how's your *expectation* as a reader forming now as we've started off? It **m**atters.

For there… before us in the road are always signs requiring we **m**ake decisions… determining some things… with all of it affecting what we *expect*… and within each option *expectation*s that reveal what they entail. And, over time you become familiar with **c**ertain aspects of the daily **c**ontinuation of *expecting*. Yes, so **m**uch becomes routine… assumed.. and out of habit. A reliance forms… **c**ausing us to expect **c**ertain things to be **c**ertain ways… and to be about **c**ertain connections. Here's a present type of example: from a title of a book we think we know what it's about, **m**ake a decision to read it… and thus, based on that, the *expecting* begins.

Only you know the *what, why,* and *how* of it for you… and if you're willing to press forward with **m**e in this "*telling*"…**m**ay I suggest, if you haven't already… ask *Him*. He knows where you are in life and what you're *expecting* in every aspect of life – including the time you'll spend reading, particularly since its a *process* within a greater *journey* too.

It is with great certainty, I *expect Him* to bring **c**larity so you **c**an determine whether you're one of the ones to enter into the fullness of the *"telling"* through these writings *He's* ordered.

As you've probably ascertained… it's a different kind of trip… and requires you hold loosely to what you *expect* from it as it's not a literary masterpiece… but a real, raw, imperfect piece that's more about *the process* you will *encounter* and *experience* through it, if willing, as we journey along ***expectancy's*** way... not concerned about arriving at some *destination,* but what *He'll* reveal and it's connectedness to mine, yours, our... ***expected end*** in *Him.*

So, here we go... with our anticipation arising as we're letting go of our surmising and calculating... allowing the *unknown... unforeseen...* and *unexpected* of our own ***expectancy*** propel us into a new kind of adventure... where together we'll be *enlightened, enhanced, expanded,* and *enlarged.* Could it be there's an ***expectancy*** innately as well... for a greater knowing of the extreme vastness ***expectations*** actually hold*?* Let's find out ~

✧ THE AGAIN...

As I've shared... for me... *my life's journey* was being presented with a whole new kind of path... and I believe it to be best described as new direction and intense determination coming from *Him* by *His Spirit* to me... so you could say it was creating a new phase *in the process* where ***expectation*** was starting to form and be *spirit born... spirit filled... spirit fueled... and spirit led...* and in the how and why it was because I was now spirit born, filled, fueled, led.. and by *His Spirit – Holy Spirit.*

It was certainly becoming clear... my life was changing...it was not the same – I was not the same. I recognized it in part and others sensed something was different too... as little by little it was again as shared, becoming (and still is) less and less by my might or power... *but by His Spirit.* For by *His Spirit He* began to *realign* and *rearrange* as quickly as I yielded to giving *Him* a place and placing more and more before *Him* in *the process* that was at work... and ***expectations*** that were being made new!

Venturing forward I willing went onward into this new... from just *having* and *living* what one could say was a *basic Chrisitan foundation* and a predominantly, although somewhat beyond introductory *"religiously"* formulated type of relationship with *Him. Looking back* from here... as I *look again,* I can see how there was always some form of underlying *drawing, wooing, calling...* into more... and it being more of *Him.* Possibly, you share such an unfolding of *His* invitation in *the process* of your life's quest?

Quickly as things shifted... my intentionality in responding to this stirring... this leading by *His Spirit – Holy Spirit...* where I discovered my ***expectations*** were forming somewhat differently... because now not only was *Jesus* with me and living in me... the *Spirit* of the *Living God* was brooding over, through and in me... and over every day and every aspect of my life. This taking root with its greater possibilities... and such interesting potential, it seemed to always be perpetually presenting an availability now... yes, opportunities for more. Isn't that what I had cried out and longed for – wasn't that what I was ***expecting?***

Truly a greater *acquainting* had begun as this *journey* continued on... with new ***encounters*** and ***experiences*** presenting their *signs* that invited me with a type of *"turn here"... "stop ahead"... "keep straight"... "yield"....* But, would I choose to ***embrace*** what they were suggesting... offering... in their invitation...to enter into the way spiritually and relationally by the *Spirit* and with my born again spirit rising in a new founded spontaneous variance of what some might say is a type of religiosity and ritual, but I knew it was not created by man or my soul like the past... and so where would this all lead and take me to?

Let's now enter into making a turn into a part of this trip where an acquainting with an *encounter* brings a degree of *expecting* meeting the un*expected*. An experience that would be etched in my memories... as it began to make out of a moment... an embedding of itself into a type of *style* and *form* influenced by what was *experienced*... and in ways I would not have imagined. Let alone, I never thought that it would all end up creating and providing an underlying framework for a diverse variety of future *expectations* and explorations that will open up to you... as they're included for you to *journey* through and explore.

But first, let's return for a minute... to the introductory picture painted in *His Word*... where all the earth ... even the whole of creation... is eagerly awaiting and longing with earnest *expectation* for something that could be, yet with a confidence is... defined as an *expectation of God's* and it manifesting through *His* creation. And... if we'll claim such... we might even see a type of connectedness to *providence*... in this *expectation* for and of the manifestation of the *sons of God* to be revealed and arise in the earth.

You might say that in essence... it's in *His* design. That *He* created a canopy of hope which is hovering on the horizon... and entwined within the fiber of it... something that makes it so much more than *expectation*... or else why would all of creation and all the earth... be waiting... *expecting*... with that extremely intense level of *expectancy*?*

*For surely there is a future... a purpose... even an eternal (expectancy filled) purpose... in and for such... where there is certainly hope hovering... indeed. Does not this hope become as well an (expected) anchor? Undoubtedly it will not be cut off – for He is not a man that He would lie?**

Therein lies *expectation*...

As *His* created ones... along with being part of the whole of creation in the earth... it would reason that we are waiting *expectantly*... as it happens, to the point of persevering and pressing in, for the *expected* outcome *His Word* speaks of... together as we long, hope, and believe with *expectancy*.

However, there is an element of *what will be will be*... right? For in being it will become... especially since it must be through and in *Him*; this manifestation of sons forming since the cycle of creating and producing began. And, an *expectation* for the *reproduction* of those who now are reproducing... *His* created ones creating... and, not just in the *expressed image and likeness of Him*... the *Creator*... but *Them – Father, Son, Holy Spirit* – the *Three* and as one in the *One*.

The outcome will come... and what comes within the result of what is produced will play its part to *form* what we become... *sowing – reaping – being – becoming*. Because that is the *fruit* of the very *spirit*... of *God's* essence and energy... the truest *life force* of *expectation.*

Until then, we see its *forming*. We behold it... we believe for it... and, besieging it as much as humanly possible... it can become in its outcome... all that we imagined it to be... as it is wrapped up in this thing called our *expectation.*

Now, based on our intentionality and the intensity within the reality around us, indeed even as we have perceived, so shall it be. For we drop the anchor of our hope confidently in it... the prospect... and as much in the promise – the *expectant* promises connected to being grounded *expectantly* in *Him*.

Ultimately, our intent with intentions are connected to and can be driven forcefully by our motivation which together creates and cultivates the basis of and for the forming of one's **expectation**.

We expect to **encounter** and **experience** what we've been *perceiving, believing,* **expecting**. Remember… *surely our* **expectation** *will not disappoint… anchored in the hope He brings into life with His Word being a lamp to our feet… and a light to our path… as on it we move forward trusting and leaning not on our own understanding… inviting and allowing Him to direct us in the way.**

Oh… how I still marvel at times at life's *happenings* and how they often tie into some of life's *"agains"* in *the journey* ~

For years now there has been such a *personalized process* with an *ongoing unfoldings* of expecting within me… and between *He and I*. Just as assuredly there has been *with you – and between He and you*… because *you… me… we*, can't avoid it when we're *His* and responding in *love, service,* and *worship* continually to *Him*.

Now, regarding an *again* place in *the process* where I have determined that in part what has transpired has carried a transforming view of the importance and priority I…we, must place on *honoring, valuing, and treasuring*… this multilayered, multi-faceted, meaningful purpose filled life happening simply called *"the process"*.

Ultimately because it is how *He* enables us to **encounter** *and* **experience** more of *Him*. But undoubtedly, it is how I've discovered, and still am… being the *me He m*ade *me* to be. In everyday life and its greater *God* directed *go, do, and be.* Which I liken unto where I am at with you now as we're *connecting* in this *amazing journey.*

I knew in part then, but not like I do now… all the change I was experiencing as my hunger and desire for more of *Him* essentially became primarily about that *process – His process* in and through the **encounters**… the **experiences**… and the greater relevancy and priority of *the journey* being with **Him** in it all. Which requires an intentionality and growing intimately in a way that doesn't come through manmade *formulas… rituals… or routines*.

You see I heard *Him* once whisper to me and its true… **"The end product matters, but not at the expense of the relationship with Me that's fired, formed, and forged in the process."**

Oh the *pearls* that have been *formed*… and the necklace they are *forming*. Yes, all in *the process* and *processing*… or one could say the **becoming**… **becoming the being** and *being it* like *He* designed *me, you… us,* to be. Image that… *He* actually desires being in it all with us.

And, there's nothing like the "re"… *the again,* of *God*! It begins with *Him* presenting a type of invitation again, which for me was in the middle of the night through another mysterious type of encounter… sound familiar? *Again*… I experienced my sleep being interrupted… except this time with a gentle nudge awakening me encouragingly to get up and *come out here*. Choose quickly *His invitations to come,* for sleep remains there calling *"come back"*.

"Here" found its rendezvous point in my family room, where at that time I often ended up being drawn to spend special time learning to genuinely *engage* in communing with *Him*. It was indeed unbelievable in many ways… this time of *"acquainting"*… through talking honestly with *Him*,

listening to *Him* as well, learning to be still, sometimes journaling… but always learning **m**ore about who *He* was (is), what *He* desired, and required of me in my life. Yet, in a grander picture with a true sense of purpose for life in *Him*, with *Him*, and with others who love and serve *Him*. But not settling anymore for the *"I'm a good Christian, I go to church, and I live a good life"* kind of person… or way.

> ❖ *Perhaps*… you are recalling… remembering a time in your life when you began to enter into **m**ore of *Him* in your life… in the *daily workings* of life… in the *times and seasons* that **c**ome and go… some good and some not so good… where things shifted into a **m**ore intentional… even intimate kind of **c**onnecting with *Him*. **M**aybe during that time you **c**onnected further with *His* purposes and plans for you? So where are you now with the inclusivity of *Him* as *God* in your *journey of life*… and with what you're **expecting**?

For a season, these times **e**volved around me learning about *Him* through learning **m**ore of *His Word* - the *Word of God*. A program **c**alled *"The Worship Network"*™ would typically be airing on television during these special times of **m**eeting. They provided a *"connecting point"* for me with *Him*. If you're not aware of it **m**aybe it's something to explore?*

At first, I would put this show on simply because I **e**njoyed the quiet reflective worship **m**usic playing with beautiful scenes of nature scrolling in the background. It didn't take long however, that the scriptures based around a life topic with a theme, began to be highlighted… as if they were drawing and **c**alling me. I sensed an adamant desire stir to pay attention and begin to focus on them… writing as **m**any of them down as I **c**ould as they were being released in their revealed timing within. Plus, it was getting **m**ore of the *Word* in me.

Then these revelations through *His Word* brought **c**onnections… which led to some interesting **c**onfirmations which **c**arried and **m**ade way for the *forming* and *creating* of *expectations*… that I had… *He* had for me and it was good… very good. The things being birthed and yes, **m**anifesting. You know… *He* has an *expected* journey for us too.

These *peaceful, uplifting,* and *encouraging* programs… with their timely themes presented to me an opportunity to spend time alone with *Him*, that didn't take me away from my husband or family and at the same time seemed to be an almost *orchestrated* way of *Him* getting *His Word* in me and getting me to spend time with *Him* – who is *the Word*.

Most of these night time *"excursions"* would **e**xtend to about an hour or so a **c**ouple times a week and eventually became less until that season ended. However, during that time, it was like time stood still and in returning to sleep I'd most often awaken to find **m**yself *refreshed, renewed,* and *refilled* in a way that I'd now define as becoming **m**ore *empowered*.

Hence, that became my *expectation* as I began to sense *His* delight and dare I say, *His expectation* that I would *come away* when awakened and invited to. It became intentional as I've shared. Necessary **e**ven, and the *reward* of a deepening depth in my relationship and **c**ommunion with *Him*… which was all the **m**otivation I *needed, welcomed,* and *embraced.*

It was an **e**stablishing of me in *His Word, His Word – Him*, being **e**stablished in me, and a foundation being laid for *expectation* to align with the biblical principles of truth. Particularly in that *His Word,* we know it goes forth working… accomplishing… and does not return void doing what *He* intended for it to do.*

Truly, there were even times where *the washing of the water of the Word* and *Him* as *Living Water…* engulfed me with *inner healing… forgiveness… restoration,* and more… and all along *expectancy* was working… moving in the midst of it all – *His* and mine.

Speaking of moving in the midst… *He* really does want you to understand the value and importance of *the process…* all that's going into *becoming the being* – *He* highly values and genuinely desires being involved in it and the progressing developing with us. So if sometimes it seems I'm repeating or lingering in a sense… just know we'll get to where we're going … but in the meantime enjoy the *ride…* yep, it's a *process* with reminders.

The *again* as I began to say… it did really happen. One night, I found myself being drawn into another middle of the night moment. I went willingly and *expecting…* but I wasn't even close to *expecting* what I'd encounter – a true un*expected* experience as you'll soon discover.

Our *Fathering God* in *His* all-knowing knew. Because don't forget… *He* knew my heart's desire (*He* knows yours too) to continue to grow more in the knowing of *Him, His Word* and even knowing *Him as the Word* – which at that time I'm not sure I really realized what that meant. But it became apparent… *His* intent this night was to present something to me in the form of an *up front and center come alive* kind of approach. And yes, I went *expecting* to become *acquainted* more with *Him.*

Starting to drift off into a bit of sleep, although I had come *expectantly…* suddenly I was awakened to the television screen appearing bigger and brighter than usual displaying a commercial with a scene that included a man I presumed to be a scientist… and I wondered, *do I know him*? There in a classroom setting wearing a suit with a white unbuttoned lab coat over it, along with his white and gray haphazardly style of hair all in place, stood this man… whom I presumed to be a renowned *science guy.* But not my husband, if you read my lovingly fun description of him in the *Acknowledgements.*

Now I suspect, that some of you know exactly who he is just by how I'm describing him. You may know him to be a brilliant physicist and *Nobel Prize Laurette.* But I think we'll agree, he wouldn't most likely make a top ten men's list for best hair! The man in the scene on the screen was indeed, *Albert Einstein…* with his back to me as he was intently writing on a chalkboard in this surreal classroom scene. The board was full of chalk writings that appeared to be scientific mathematical formulas consisting of numbers, letters, and symbols.

Then, in this encounter… which was in our defined reality a commercial on the television in my family room, but not at this time for me, where a good sense of suspense was certainly hovering there. Suddenly… it became another form of a lifelike vision experience as the room brightened, the screen expanded more…appearing to *come alive* into creating an actual *lifelike scene* in the room where my seat was right up front and center. Wow!!! *What is happening and why?* These thoughts seem to come with such godly encounters and are good.

Enthralled, fascinated, and *captivatingly* taken in by it all – it continued.

Mr. Einstein then turned to face toward me, with his bright eyes in a piercing stare… full of life, light, and an animated type of expression of excitement as displayed by the evidence in the twinge in his shabby full eyebrows that said *"Look"*. With all this stirring like electricity in the excitement and wonder in the room and within **me**... his expression appeared to be beckoning me to *look...a look more closely*. It carried in it and transmitted a curious kind of ***expectation*** that I would... and so I did. I looked directly at him, into his eyes... intentionally and intently... and into a kind of wonder-filled inviting beyond what appeared there.

As the chalkboard behind him called out to *look again* too, full of its scientific mathematical writings displayed where he had written, **"E = mc2"**. I know that formula I thought, recalling in my reflecting later that it was connected to something called the *"Theory of Relativity"*.

The scene displayed on the screen became brighter... coming more alive as it all honed in on him and the formula he had written. He had turned and using the chalk to cross out the **"2"** in **E=mc2**. For a moment... time suspended it seemed. He then wrote the number **"3"** above the 2 which had been crossed out so it now read, **E = mc3**. The three was larger than the two had been and was starting to pulsate like a flashing neon marquee as he turned back around toward me with that piercing stare – which *again* was a *look* that said *"Look..."*.

So *again*... I knew within this scenario that was playing out *God* was connected somehow and wanting me to *look and to **expect to see*** something through what was written and then changed. That there was some kind of revelation being displayed for me to *see* and *seek Him* regarding it. For there was a *'God kind of sense'* that this was a type of connection with an ***expectation*** of me. *What was I supposed to see in it or do with it all?* And then it all ended.

Remarkably as the ending came... in a brief, but intense moment right before it did... it was like I saw the eyes of *Jesus* through his eyes – *Albert's* eyes, and I sensed very adamantly that *He – Jesus*, not only desired me to pay attention to what was just shown to me, but it was now clear to me that *He* was truly a part of this encounter... as the stirring of ***expectancy*** coupled with ***expectation*** was being imparted from *Him* and activated in me... and within a place in me that felt new.

Right then and there, in that moment I was certain that *He, God,* was of course the **Source** and **Force** behind *Einstein* too as *He* loved and fearfully made him. But I questionably wondered did he, *Albert,* a man of intelligent brilliance know? Surely, he believes in *God*?

Taking a deep breath was required so the taking in of it all by *His Spirit* could begin to have its way. Quickly the 2 becoming a 3 – obviously it was a type of *key* to something more... yet what? And, accordingly the seed of ***expectation*** fell establishing a place for the more to be revealed as it took root within me.

Although I did not at that time fully make the connection in a clear and apparent way... I know that I know that I know now... from developing along the way and the perceiving within the *look* of the *"Look"*... and the *"Look"* again... that yes, I heard within and from something embedded in *his look*... *He* was there in the midst and the *beyond* of this godly spiritual encounter like mine in my family room on a TV screen. For confronting and calling me was and became another form of... **"Tell them"**. I *'heard'* it in their eyes... yes, I did.

Within *"expectation's"* attempt... in its *personified* kind of way... it began to establish itself as I found myself in serious wonderment with an excited ***expectant*** kind of *"I've not been this way before"*. What possibly would *He* reveal to me... how to me... why to me...when to me... and what exactly was this **m**ystery of the "**3**"… on what appeared to be a flashing **m**arquee in how it stood out, not to **m**ention… the formula change of **E = mc3?**

For over twenty years I've been on a *journey of search and discover* on and off, of what has become layers and layers of **m**ultifaceted revelation of what *He* would lead me to or open the door for within the **m**ystery of **E = mc2** (sometimes written as **e=mc2**)now as **e = mc3**… and it never really went that far from my thoughts without coming up *again* in some way or another… or for too long.

It's interesting that I am *Elizabeth (His e)*… a *daughter, sister, wife, mother, friend*…. I am a college educated education **m**ajor, but not by any **m**eans was it to teach the subjects of science or math. However, my last few years of teaching I did assist directly in both subjects with **m**iddle school learning challenged students where often I was feeling just as challenged as they were! We can add a bit of my sense of humor here… since now I'm a blonde who's platinum white and gray! But, *He's* made and wired me this way… and I'm good with that!

Come on… *God* really does have a sense of humor and there's even a scripture that says, "*He laughs.*". So I **expect** *He* did then, is now, and has done so many times and will in *this journey* where I've grown, am growing, and have *learned to laugh* with *Him*… especially in *this journey* with "**e**"… "**m**"… "**c**"… and "**3**"!* You'll see and possibly hear *Him* laugh too.

Yes, I am blessed to have had some higher education and training both secular and spiritual in **m**y life path… but *His* training me is first and foremost. Here in the *again* comes the ask: *why was He choosing to speak to me in this way?* What was *He* trying to reveal, say… and how did this in any way connect to my purpose? You know…*the plans and thoughts He has for us* in general and are aligned with what *He has written in His book, about you, us… me.**

In the world a phrase you **m**ight hear some say is, *"It doesn't take a rocket scientist to figure that out."* **m**eaning it's not that hard to figure out or understand. You gotta love the simple truth in that. But for me in this **m**atter, that was not exactly the case at first. It wasn't like I just couldn't wait to start searching out a scientific formula like **E=mc2** as shared in the *Theory of Relativity: General or Special.*

The seed of *expectation* did get planted… none-the-less… as I found it coming into **m**y thoughts with curiosity and driving within me a deeper kind of general seeking of *Him, His Word*… in a simple kind of searching that developed as the valuing of being willing to enter into the *exploration* and *examination, e*specially with any *expectation* for *Him* in my life *journey* to always lead the way. *He* really is best being in the driver's seat with us!

Him leading me, yet sometimes from a familiar intellectual needing to know… and not always a *"Father, what is the needful thing I need to know?"*… kind of pursuit. Enveloped within it all was the discovery to learn the importance of the need to be growing and gleaning of **m**uch in the various ways *He* meets *you, me, us*… in the *unfolding of the process* in knowing *Him* spiritually or cognitively. Truly we find our *expectations* change as they evolve through it all in life. Oh… the *ebb* and *flow* as we learn to believe through what we receive.

Eventually a door opened in *His Word* where a truer and solid foundation was laid for one of **m**y life verses to emerge, *"It is the glory of God to conceal a matter, the glory of kings to search it out."* Proverbs 25:2. Searching it out sounded like and carried within it a kind of *fun*… after all being a teacher for me included the idea of being a *lifelong learner.* Add to that the likely possibilities of *"gems and treasures" He* would send me to discover in *the process...* glory indeed! For *He* too promises... *you will seek Him, and you will find Him, when you search for Him with all your heart.** It's a keeper and lifer for me as they all are.

Oh... the power of a seed planted and all its potential... especially the seed of *expectation.* However, some may argue that there's not always a "beauty" in it for *expectation* is a peculiar thing in that intention along with our motivation play a role as the source for *expectation* determining whether positive or negative will come forth from something desired or undesired... something good or evil – right?

> ❖ *Perhaps...* you can remember a time when a seed of *expectation* awoke in you because a thought you had regarding something *He* said to you, about you in *His Word,* about your identity in *Him,* your inheritance from *Him, His* promises... plans or purposes for you... even us being *His.* Did that seed grow...*forming, birthing, manifesting* what it carried *expectantly*? How did it **manifest**? Was it good? Did you grow in *the process* discovering more of *Him* and *Him* in you? Oh that you have, are, and will ~

With that said, my thoughts interestingly are finding their way to a story of a young man who was sold into slavery by his own family – his brothers in this case, due to their jealousy of him because of his relationship and favor with their father, along with a dream *God* gave him about his future... and yes, in included things about their future too, just not how *expected.*

This stirred up much jealousy among them which became a catalyst that led to what began his *adventurous journey* of going from a pit that they threw him in believing for him to die, to being purchased as a slave, and more! As things moved forward in his life he then spent time in a prison, ending up in a palace, and eventually rising to a position of great authority.

Amazingly it all led to a *supernatural set up* and opportunity to save not only his true family – the same brothers that through him in a pit... along with his people in general, during a time where famine was striking the land.

Not what one would *expect...* nor the results to be experienced after being left in a pit to die.

Yet, in the moment where he is amazingly reunited with his brothers, he speaks to them from a place deep within himself where his *expectation* has been influenced by a greater source within than his own intention and motivation, as it became grounded in restoration and redemption due to a greater purpose at work... and *working it all together for good.*

Therefore, he could only speak from the place in him which in his own life had **encountered** a type of providential rescuing connected to the greater eternal force of *God* at work that was constantly moving and influencing him in his extreme life experiences with varying *expectancy.*

Actually even to the point of now enabling him to compassionately and sincerely declare to them, *"You intended to harm me, but God intended it all for good. He* **(expectantly)** *brought me to this position so I could save the lives of many people. No, don't be afraid. I will continue to take care of you and your children."**

One cannot help but believe this probably wasn't on their radar of things *expected* …for it had not yet been revealed to them that he was the brother they had left to die and then sold into slavery. Now, in the unveiling one can only imagine how the waters of *expectation* began to stir in him, in them, and as the good news was shared with all including his father. Oh… *the process* in the life of *Joseph* uncovered in this case.

Proceeding… let us keep this in mind because we can all become "enslaved" by our own *expectations* that influence and drive us… coupled with questionable intentions and impure motivation that only benefits and blesses self… denying access to the door of a bigger plan and purpose lingering in *His*… for you. Even that of *you… me… us,* together with others.

The seed of *expectation* undeniably holds much potential… and eventually power, as it takes root in us through the gates of our eyes, our ears, our mind, will, and emotions… not to mention the soil of the garden of our heart. Expressly with the one(s) *expecting* as well as those being affected or influenced in *the process* unfolding as choices, consequences, and everything in between falls into a place playing a part in the eventual outcome and result.

On this path… a pattern of response was developing and emerging, assisting in *leading, guiding,* and *directing* in becoming more aware of the role of *expectation* in my life… not even realizing it at times… let alone acknowledging the significance of the role of what I *expected*.. even the part played by the *expectations* of others fully. It became evident in all this that the *Holy Spirit* was doing a work in and through me and it all… as only *He* can.

Over time, I found myself entering into life *encounters* and *experiences* where I would be led to *"look, look again (not back), and look beyond"* when presented with situations about what was my part/piece. The role of *expectancy* was so very vital in how I'd perceive and receive in my thinking or how it would… or could play out depending on the role I'd allow *Him* to have. You could say there was an earnestness beginning to be identified as an essential part to forming any *expectation*. After all… there is and *He* has an *expected* end.

The role of *intention, motivation, imagination, cultivation, perception, perspective, and projection* were a few elements that became evident, especially over time, with some aspects and their predominant influence in the result of the fruit of what came in *expecting* because of the impact of *expectations*. Just as we saw above.

Within this type of intentional pursuit through the *process* of the layers of life and revelation being released and received from *Him,* I found myself moving into a place of greater surrender and sincere submission to *Him* for *His* good and perfect will…and, predominately due to *Holy Spirit's* lead. I was coming more alive as a *born again new creature*… as my spirit was now fully spirit filled and *Holy Spirit,* the *Teacher* that *He* is, was teaching me much. Oh… how *I… you, me, we* need *Him. Jesus* said we would when *He* had to go

In the depth of this unfolding was a stirring producing much; even drawing up a deep, genuine longing within me attached to *expecting* that seemed to have a pre-determined assignment to this void within to be filled… and that I can only define as… a *longing for belonging* to *Him* – as fully *His*. Now I know only in part… but over time, I have come to ascertain that both in its origins in me and *His* divine nature in me… longing *expectancy for belonging fulfilled* lies alone in *Him*.

Conceivably, you've encountered such... deeply seated in the well of *expectation* in you?

Initially part of me was surprised at a revealing... yet recalling it now, it was pretty early on *He* had unveiled to me something kind of profound connecting it with *expectation* in the formula of $E=mc^3$. So clearly, as if *He* was standing right there with me I heard *Him* passionately, personally, and powerfully say, **"It's about a relationship; it's not about a formula my daughter."** Oh my ~

Do you not (**expect** to) see it, do you not know... behold (in **expectancy**) *a new thing I am doing, before it springs forth do you not* (**expectantly**) *perceive it? Is there not an* **expectation** *to believe and receive it* ... * Purely in *Spirit* and in *Truth*... godly **expectation** beckons such questioning.

✧ A GREATER ACQUAINTING...

Oh... to *look, look again, and look beyond* from where you are now, from who *He* has made *Himself* known to you to be, what *He* has done, how *He* has done what *He's* done, and why *He* has done it when *He* did... much stirs in the cultivation of the motivation and intention of remembering *Him*...putting *Him* in remembrance (*He* **expects** us to)... and *Him* bringing us to remembrance.*

There's just something about the *"re"* of God ... remember, it means *"again"* - *to do over, to happen, or make happen again*... indeed, I'm in awe of *Him* as *He* moves in the *ebb and flow again*, and *again*, and *again*... for there is now and forever will be an **eternal expectation**.

Don't forget... when you sense a kind of *repetition*... an *"again"*... in the sayings of what's being said... positioning one's self to encounter the *"again"* as an opportunity to apprehend an enhanced reflection is good and recommended. For these varied ways of repeating, almost like the ripples forming from a stone cast upon the waters... many rings form... and all are connected to the stone that produced them.

Producing a fuller picture of what I've discovered... and am discovering... and will continue to in that the rings... the layers... they do all matter. The varying ways they enlighten and influence you... me... us so innately and inherently bringing us back to the place of a single moment or thought... where something that we **expected** connects... and is now causing us to ponder looking again in **expectancy**. And, more often now through *His* lens.

Such turning... and even a *returning* back to where it all began... especially if you are sharing this exploring in *this journey* with *Him*. *He* may just take it back to *"in the garden"*... in that beginning... where they – *Adam and Eve* (humankind) and creation were in communion being one with the *One, Creator God Eliohim*, in what many and I call... the place of *His* "*original intent*".

If *you*... we, don't understand *His* heart from the start... then can we truly know what to **expect** as *His* created ones... or what *He* **expects** in, from or through us *His* created ones... and overall... in it all?

He is intentional in *His* pursuit of *His* **expectations**... predominately and principally... as the *"re"* God that *He* is – *Redeemer, Restorer, and Reconciler*. Titles yes, but oh what they represent and how they are presented in *Him*... in the core of the foundation of who *He* is in *the process of the journey*... and, expressly as *Love*.

This opens a way for us to agree... that within there is, as said before... a longing in it all for some kind of belonging... a connection of *Creator* with *His Creation*... so deliberately and divinely placed and positioned... embedded and encompassing all we **expect**... in that unseen dimension... where that thought hovering out there... and in there... is in the core of our being and us being. Where somehow we see that belonging comes before we step into the greater becoming... and being.

Remember... *He* did set *eternity into the hearts of men*... your heart... my heart... our hearts... the hearts of *His* Church, *His* Body... *His* Bride ... because its foundation connection of *His* beginning and *Him* as the *"Beginning"*... draws us into this ***acquainting*** with *Him*... and with an ***acquaintance*** already eternally established in ***expectation*** that *He* is a covenant God...and *His* ***expectancy*** rises in *His* eternal love.

Oh... that *expecting*... especially as it gives birth and **m**akes way in the earth for the **manifestation** of the ***earnest expectation*** that was, and is and is to come in the *Son* who came and will come *again*... and in the *sons of God* as we arise in *Him*, like *Him*, for *Him*, and *expectantly* for *His* glory. Oh what *hop*e in the ***expectation* of *His* expected end!**

Selah ~

---

* Footnotes: Chapter 2 / See Romans 8 , Proverbs 23:8, 3:5-6, Numbers 23:19, Proverbs 25:2, Jeremiah 29:11-13, Gen. 50:20-21, Isaiah 55:11, Ephesians 5:26, Psalm 2:1-4, Isaiah 43:18-19, 42:8-9, 43:26, John 14:26, Luke 22:19, Romans 8, Psalm 45:1 - all emphasis is mine and personal paraphrasing built on various translations and versions.

CHAPTER 3

✧ ENCOUNTERING & EXPERIENCING… AN ALIGNING.

We're now entering into a place in the greater *journey* where *aligning's* role is key. There's been an enlightening in the sharing of *encountering and experiencing* through "*an introducing*"… which was revealed in my *In the beginning* and *His* assigning a *tell them*. *An acquainting* which presented the idea of the overall and inner workings of *expectancy* and *expectations* as shared in their *forming, birthed or birthing*, and even some examples of what's *expected manifested* and the more connected to their *manifesting*.

A prospect unfolded in one significant form of an *encounter experienced* through the possibility and potential of "$E=mc2$" – *Eistein's Theory of Relativity*. How it has presented to us in a way, as an *unusual road* to consider in our travels into *expectancy*. Where through a different kind of lens or perspective, it was impressed upon *me*… *us* that it could be… maybe even should be in some dimension $E(e)=mc3$. With that strong sense of suggestion that came in the number change from 2 to 3… the 2nd power to 3rd **power**, well… it matters. Especially in ways potentially connected to what's *relative* and *relevant* in "*the process*".

Within it all, there's been a kind of *introducing and acquainting* in a simple cyclical kind of way… presenting an underlying necessity of recognizing and giving place to "*the process*" therein. Therefore, *aligning* what's forthcoming in our apprehending must come through some expanded defining and essential grounding yielding itself to *an aligning* designed to set us up for the adventure we're on with $e=mc3$ and likely some godly connections ahead.

It is my hope and without being presumptuous… that some level of *expectancy* is indeed calling *you… me… us* to "*expect and see*" more. And not just the more of it, but in the suspense or uncertainty of where is this headed, what does a scientific formula have to do with it anyway, and does it truly matter? Yet we know… *expectations* are a part of the door opening to the *unexpected* too… particularly when *He* gets invited and involved!

Oh… the beginnings. Don't forget the *starting point or place* is key to the initial forming that comes in and through our *thoughts… imaginations… opinions… perceptions… perspective… assumptions* as they align and more so as they're being laid out before us… which we will discover, over time. Indeed, much goes into them, along with their part or piece they play in their role within the *formation* of *expectation*.. which is vast.

The idea that it – *expectancy,* with its *expectations*… has a kind of "*voice*" has an place too… in its taking on a form of *personification* as has been somewhat implied. So one might *define, describe or express* this type of "*expression*" as the "*voice of expectation*".

If that's true… which let's for the sake of our *journey* ahead embrace that it is in a godly creative and open to discovery sort of way as led by *His Word* and *His Spirit* moving in our midst in this "*telling*". Because in actuality… there is, what can be designated as a *form of a voice* that speaks in something *inanimate* or today one could also say in an *inorganic* way … such as is experienced in our *thoughts, imaginations, insight…* our *perception* of all going on in the world – our world around us.

It's not an *actual outward voice*… but it is heard inwardly and affects us just as a *human voice* does entering in and into the grander *process* of the ebb and flow of who we are… how we function… and predominately the foundation for how the continual and constant cycle of the cogs on the wheel of what makes up **communication … conversation**… with others and the inner *speakings*… even *tellings* within ourselves that arise and desire a place.

Presented here is simply the idea that together these may be better known as multiple *ponderings*… *considerings*… *musings*… *reflectings*… from the *process* of meditating on and contemplating of them. And in that exact moment… a determining in the giving of a place to them within us – our *conscious, mind, and inner state of awareness* happens where they can start to dwell and occupy coming together… creating a type of ***aligning*** as they connect and converge with layers of ***expectancy***. The "s" added is mine for what I've come to call them… the many layerings upon another because *together* they influence what we ***expect.***

❖ *Perhaps*… you've even noticed how the "**dot dot dots** …" can present and create a type of space carrying a suggestion for you to consider… as the potential of a different forming of an *aligning* or connection related to context of what's been said… with emphasis… or like a "*selah*", a place for a pause… or the taking of a moment, spiritually even… presenting an opportunity for *Him* to reveal or release. To not just take in what is being said in a word or words… but for but a brief bit of time to think upon these words and their meaning when you're led. This applies only if you invite and allow them to in *your process*. In and of themselves, they – the *dot dot dots*… are just that and my style. They can give more of a *voice* to a word or set of words. To you they may generate a form of annoyance or meaninglessness… because you've not been this way before… and you're not real sure about the time you want to spend. That's understandable and as always it's your choice. It's your *journey*. I hope you'll at least consider them as led and reread to enhance and enlarge perspective and more! This grammatical marking structure is called an *ellipsis*.

When taking it all in remember, what is being shared gives a potential place for any *internal monologue* forming. You know, that conversation one has within oneself that is created by thoughts heard and received taking on *one's own voice* and may include a type of *talking back* interchange as a response.

This is not unusual … as we know thoughts are made up from the *power of suggestion* and the identification with the meaning of the *words, images, symbols,* and all the *inner workings* that search for somewhere to land, to move on to, and out from… or they leave moving out.

The variety of ways and degrees this all tries to take a place is amazing… and part of the fearfully and wonderfully made humans *He* created us to be. The ground that receives and conceives of these *'seeds'* sown… that form the *what, how, when, where, and why* you *expect* what you have *expected*… are *expecting*…and will produce what they contain, carrying a power to *make, mold, and fashion* each and every **expectation** we have and will have.

From such a place of consideration and conjuncture… let's be open enough to acknowledge and accept in a basic way as suggested before… that ***expectation does have a type of voice.*** That *voice* takes its posture and place positioned within **expectancy**… and the place it takes matters making a difference to one extreme or another.

Going about in this *journey* of life the **voice of expectation** as I've discovered, rings out clear for the most part... usually **expecting** to meander or maneuver its way *good, bad or indifferent*. From connecting to and with the *voice of one's soul* that's made up of our *mind, will, and emotions* in general *Greek* thought... and extends its connection with the *voice* of *our body*. which in its own way per say, speaks.

This affects much... especially a continual choosing of how *you, me, we*... **align** with what we **expect**... why we are **expecting** it... how that affects and influences our **expectations**... not to mention the role of what *you, I, or we believe*. What's **embraced** enters into what's *believed* forming a joining together and can with an extended spiritual significance. For every aspect carries a *voice* vying for its place and position within *you... me... us*, aligning our **expectancy** and for what we'll encounter or experience... which affects not just *you... me, or us*... but others too. *God* as well, wants to be **embraced** and believed in this *process*.

*"Never doubt God's **mighty (expectant)** power to work in you and accomplish all of this. He will achieve infinitely more than your greatest request(or **expectation**), and your most unbelievable dream exceeding your wildest imagination! He will outdo them all, for His **(expectant)**miraculous power constantly energizes you."**

Could it be a there's a type of "e=mc3" effect in all that's being connected and *aligning*?

As one whose life is dedicated and surrendered to living for *God* as a *born again child* of *God* through **Jesus Christ, Yeshua** alone... the **voice of my spirit** is aligned in *Him*– which is alive now in the **new creature in Christ Jesus** that I am. That new man – mine, yours... well, he's in the front seat now as the driver saying, ♪ *"Jesus takes the wheel"*!* And telling *Holy Spirit* as the *Helper*... the *Teacher*... the *Revealer*... have Your way!

It's a time and place where the *voice* of the fleshy old nature of our soul... and the voice... in its fleshy old nature in our body... they take the back seat where the input is considered secondary to *His* through *Holy Spirit* to our spirit new man. Therefore, the old man's voice doesn't make the choice or determine the course that our **expectations** have taken like before.

Does this ring true for you? It should if we're living out of the NEW and Christ in us. Or more realistically and honestly... does it most always or sometimes here and there ring true? It would be nice to be able to respond with a resounding yes. But as am I or you, so is the *voice of expectation*... our **expectations** within us. There's certainly a *process* going on and ongoing. But then... it's a *journey* – an adventure... right?!

Last time I checked... I'm still **becoming the being**... the being of one who desires to live out *His Word* that says, **as He is, so am I**.* The *I AM* and *His voice* is surely in me and having more of the majority of say. So let's just say I'm doing ok... and I'm believing you are too. Actually more than ok... because my **expectancy** is not only **aligning** with what's good and right in *His* sight... but its **aligned** more in agreement with *Him, His Word* - which is *His voice* at work in my life, and boy is that overflow carrying a continual **expectancy**.

If the *voice* of my spirit ... your spirit, in specific our *born again spirit*... is to maintain this position, it's good to be postured in being able to identify with and always seeking to give priority to the greater **voice of Truth** that beckons us... drawing us... desiring to lead... guide... direct... correct... posture, and *position* us for success... in our true eternal *identity* and *purpose* according to the plans written. *His incredible eternal purpose plans written (**expectantly**) full of amazing things including the thoughts He thinks of and has for us. That point to a bright future radiating with (**expectant**) hope… which aligns and manifests from the One who loves and created us.* *

The voice of *Yahweh our God… Elohim our Creator. His voice* comes to us as *Father*… as the *Son Jesus – Yeshua*, His Hebrew name, and as *Holy Spirit*. All these *Godhead* expressions of *His voice* are also the **voice of Truth** that's reliable… faithful… trustworthy… full of revelation… and carry in them a sure and pure *Source… the Spirit* of the *Lord God… the spirit* of *wisdom* and *understanding*… the *spirit of counsel* and *might*… the *spirit of knowledge*… and the *spirit* of *honor, awe, reverence*… that is, the *fear of the Lord*.*

A *voice* established in the godly divine essence of *love*.. that eternal everlasting force of *He* is as *God*. For *God* is *love*.

Interestingly, in the *Hebrew* there is a word that means *voice*, "*qol*". It can mean *sound, voice, or noise*. We see it first mentioned in *God's Word* in Genesis 3:8: "*And they heard the voice (**qol**) of the LORD God walking in the garden in the cool of the day: and Adam and his wife hid themselves from the presence of the LORD God amongst the trees of the garden.*" They chose to move into hiding as *His voice* brought a greater realization in manifestation, that they did not heed what *He* had required in *His telling* them… so an awareness began for them to know the **voice of sin** because of the voice of another – an enemy. Now an **aligning** in their relational communion and how their conversation would unfold… it changed. *His voice* became for them… and can be for us a catalyst that creates an **expectation** of its own and it's always godly good. However, the *enemy's voice* will try to convince you of the same.

May we invite *Him* and it, *His voice* in… *allowing, submitting,* and *surrendering* to *Him* – to the real pure love within it… letting it take its place as the predominate *Source* … behind the force attempting to constantly influence our *journey* of **expectation**. From its forming in conception… to its awakening in birthing… and its arising according to all *He* has said… what I…yes may we, come in faith to **expect** when we let *Him* be in the driver's seat… with *His* voice as our "*GPS: God's Positioning System*". Now that's **alignment**! And through *His* love for us moving in our assignments as we partner with *His kingdom system* by *His Spirit*.

So, ♪ *"Jesus take the wheel!"* now… and for where we are **expectantly** heading ~

Oh the joy in the *journey* when *His pure, unadulterated, unchangeable, unfathomable love* is along for the ride… moving in the midst and *driving* what we can expect and even being there for us and with us in the un*expected*.

What a colliding > merging and converging within life and within us … as we're on life's course. With **expectation** continually entering and exiting as it does… and interestingly enough one could say in the embodiment of… or dare we say a form of… *personification*.

*Can't you hear the **voice of Wisdom** (some call her a Lady)? From the top of the mountains of influence she speaks into the gateways of the glorious city. All the place where pathways merge, at the entrance of every portal, there she stands, ready to impart understanding, shouting aloud to all who enter, preaching her sermon to those who will listen. I'm calling to you, sons of Adam, yes and to you daughters as well."* * **Expectation** personification…His.

Indeed... can't you hear it's *voice*... it's there continually taking its place. But ah,... do you hear the extraordinary sound within *His voice* projecting from its place and *process* of permeation within such wisdom? For it carries the light of *His Truth* which brings life as it contains the *frequency of love*... truth in love. Which enables *His expectation* to purely be conceived and then contained within ours... and for breakthrough. We must hear. We must listen. We must choose to enter thru such a gate on our path... ready to receive *expectantly*.

Some subtle, yet in many ways significant... are the *other voices* that beckon us to *"come over here onto my path"*... and give ear to what they are saying. With that in mind... I'd like to propose in the *aligning* that is taking place, we take a kind of pit stop, pulling aside to prepare for what lies ahead in this most preparatory part of the *journey* of *expecting...*

Little by little... the route we're taking puts a demand on us to determine what is the good of *God* and goes with us... especially if we're intentional in following the way *He* has, is and will make for us.* Or... what must go because its influence and role is possessing a place and playing a part seems good, but is not productive or profitable for *prospering, prevailing,* and *possessing* the ground *He* wants us to take and possess along the way.

There is a place... a moment when and where we choose... do we *trust* that *He* will always make known the path... the one that *He* says leads to life... filled even with joy and pleasure for us to taste and see.. For as our hearts and *His* heart *align* because we hear, know, and we are *acquainted* with *His voice*... *His voice* above all others... no other will we follow.*

Be aware... such a *voice*, you know, an*other voice – voices* even... is what can be defined as ones arising from the **seat of contemplation**. Again, for the sake of simplicity and to not get mixed up in what the world would say... it could be said this *"seat"* is that place where what we're considering whether or not they are coming from the *voice* of our considerations... contemplations... things containing ideas or strong suggestions... they place before us in our mind through things coming at us, happening around us, presenting something that you hold and consider because it is or seems like such a part of the something needed, necessary, desired. In a *setting, circumstances,* or with *issues* you're *considering, confronting, or combating.* They come to take a seat, a place in their getting comfortable and sometimes too comfortable... It's important to discern what I'm referring to here in this *processing*.

Many times they like to connect merging together with things from our past reminding us or awakening us to a way to consider now that's actually grounded in something *familiar.* And now, speaking cunningly as they do to make what is presented look like a reality or a better way, when in reality it's all just attempting to appear as real.

Stop... look... listen... yes it's a primary kind of principle to apprehend. As it carries great strategy when it comes to the *considering* of such. Don't forget, it was *another's voice* other than *God's* that came in a cunning way asking of *Adam and Eve* in the garden through a clever crafty presenting of an opportunity by beginning with a simple question, *"Did God really say... surely you won't die?"* opening a door for the turning away from an *expectation* of life *He* had of and for them... along with the blessings they were experiencing and encountering already by remaining within communion in Him with its confines and conditions... to death contained a contaminated *expectancy* connected to a thing called **SIN**.

*"Blessed is the one who finds wisdom... She is **m**ore precious than rubies; nothing you desire(**expect**) can compare with her. She is a tree of life to those who embrace her(**expectancy**); those who hold her firm (in **expectation**) will be happy."**

They had **e**xemplified the image of *God* as humanity... and as they were intended too. Well... everything quickly **c**hanged, along with the pattern and prototype they were to be living out of and from – His, the *Creator's* ***expectation*** in them... that **c**ame in and as *His original intent* as He blessed them lovingly saying, *"Reproduce... be fruitful... replenish by populating... and go ahead and subdue it... reigning over it... the earth... and all creatures living in it."** This was *His* ***expectancy***... and when from a posture of their **c**hoosing to ***expect*** the same in their ***aligning*** as one with *Him*... it was a **m**utual ***expectation***.

Oh... how the **e**xpansion and **e**nlargement of *other voices* filled with *enticing, alluring,* and *deceiving words* and the future of and *ongoing invitation* to **e**ver be presented with its ***expectation*** as temptation **c**rouching **c**ontinually at their door... that would now **c**ome... after what they had done in their **e**ating of *The Tree of the Knowledge of Good and Evil*.

Instantly it removed their divine godly ***alignment*** of **e**xclusivity in their **m**utual ***expecting*** of being *together* in **c**ontinual **c**ommunion... it altered the way of *agreement* they knew and how they'd now have **c**onversation. For, there'd be no **m**ore walking and talking in the *cool of the day* as it was. Their **c**hoice of sin brought radical **c**hange to the place they were to live in, occupy, and **e**nlarge. They were **m**oved out away from the garden and being one..

It's interesting how ***evil*** backwards is ***live***... and ***love*** backwards is ***evol***.
Things through the **e**vil that **c**ame in sin **e**volved rapidly moving them away from *Father's heart*; what was good, full of life... very godly good. Yet *Love*... was at work in the **m**idst.

But words, they have purpose and they're filled with power... the power of life or death, blessing or **c**ursing. And when released... spoken, they **m**ust and will *align* with some form of ***expectation*** either in what the word **m**eans with its **m**ission and **m**otivating **m**essage applied. Or, what the word will do just on its own... when set into an action **c**onnecting with other words, other things we ***expect,*** and are ***expecting*** in all their ***expectancy*** to do. Lying in the heart of it all ultimately... is to *make* or greatly influence something that is happening that you or others want to happen. If by others... it may be what you <u>don't</u> want to happen.

Let's **e**nter into a further **e**xploration of what **c**ould be a kind of **c**atalyst... propelling this kind of **m**ovement... **c**arrying in it a type of **m**eaning and with a **m**ission... which in its beginning, one **c**ould say, is instantaneous in **m**ovement... straight out the gate... off and running. But, not always so **c**lear in **m**eaning or obvious in **m**ission.

This requires we explore **m**ore about the role *certain words* **c**an play... another words, words with their part. Definitely, we're determining, the piece they are and part they play in the *forming... birthing...* and *manifesting* are key to what we ***expect*** in our *journey*. As we take some time to deliberate and define **m**ore **c**learly... recognizing and giving attention to such, we arrive at a place that **e**ntails... and **m**any times requires us... to know just how **m**uch of a *role* certain words have... play, in what they **m**ean along with their **m**ission in the overall structuring and scheme of things unfolding.

What is revealed to *you...me... us*, in these searchable, teachable, approachable, viable... yes, *worthwhile* **m**oments of discovery within what we are *expecting* – in the natural and in the spiritual give regard to our want and needs... our desires. Even what's required by us, others, and *Him*. So when you take time to **c**onsider *His perfect will with His divine desires and requires...* along with *His purposeful, passionate plans* for your life... such **c**onsideration **c**an expand, enlarging, and setting up an end beyond what we **c**an think or imagine. Exactly how that happens is all up to *you... me... us*, and our *faith*... which is part is our *expectancy.*

Remember, the *voice* of *expectation – a faith filled voice,* is just that – a *voice*. *"Whose"* or *"what" voice* is that which is *"speaking"* and how we **c**ome to understand things attached to what it is saying... is **c**ritical. **M**ost often we pursue **c**larity to that of the *voice* itself...not wanting it to be an *echo...* an *expectation* of the past trying to attach and **e**mbed itself in the present. For we desire typically, the voice of what we *expect* to be assigned to the gift of the present *He* offers. Remember, we often have not because we ask not.

This type and way of purpose filled reflection... originating from healthy, hearty, and sincere **c**ontemplation with **c**onversation... **m**akes a way that **c**onceivably you are able to see or are beginning to. A way that invites and preferably allows the **m**aking of a way for the beyond in your thoughts **m**oving into *perceiving, believing, conceiving...* for revelation *He'll* release for you to receive. It is designed to help you press through for breakthrough... and the breaking off of anything attempting to *deter... distract... discourage...* especially through *the little foxes that come to spoil the vine.** And, *the thief that comes to kill... steal... destroy.** What is **m**eant to bring you into a place of *growth... exploration... innovation... and creation* of and through *expectations* that *He* desires bring us joy in *the journey.*

Let's **e**nter into a time of observation of what the little foxes use to get *access*. Access that will affect the information you're taking into **c**onsideration leading to activation with application. You'll notice the foxed *do, have,* and *will* take access. We **c**an see the probable place for such in each word presented as we look at the word in its defining and establishing of its own **m**eaning... and as it is extended with the adding of a suffix: *ion,* on its end.

When *ion* is added to the end of a word, it implies there is an <u>**_action required_**</u>. An action that affects the **c**ondition or state of the base word from being just that into becoming a word that *pertains, relates,* and *refers* to **m**ore. Plus, what its "effects" have on what we *expect.*

As you go through this **list of key "ion" words**, it is suggested you <u>read each word aloud</u> and <u>ask yourself</u> what do you know this word to mean? Let their **m**eaning known to you, along with the *synonyms*: words that **m**ean the same listed beside it, **c**ome together with what has already been given a place in *your thoughts... your prior knowledge, understanding, and wisdom,* as well as life *experiences* or *encounters* the word **c**onjures and stirs up particularly in regards to its influencing role toward *expectancy*... and our *expectations.*

Read, recognize it for what it is, and **m**ove on ~

PERCEPTION... interpretation, your understanding, **m**eaning of or assigned to, a view of
PERSPECTION... perspective, viewpoint, outlook, standpoint: true or relative to a subject
VISION... see, sight, perceive visualization, observation, image, imagination, future plans
INITIATION... to start, begin, **c**ommence, inception, to **m**ove forward into without asking
MOTIVATION... incentive, inspiration, stimulation, impetus, possess enthusiasm...

SATISFACTION… pleasure, approval, gratification, fulfillment, experience contentedness
VALIDATION… proof, to endorse, authenticity, genuine, justification, connection…
INHABITIION… occupancy, dwelling, residence, lodging, possessing, settle, inhabit…
LIMITATION… restraint, restrict, control, constraint, hinder, obstacles, being limited…
CONFUSION… confuse, mixup, misunderstand/perceive, uncertainty, doubt, a spirit of
INTIMIDATION… fear, coercion, bully, frighten, alarm, threaten, scare, a spirit of this
DECEPTION… lie, trick, sham, delusion, witchcraft/cultic, suspicion, deceive, a spirit of
PERVERSION… distortion, falsification, twist, pervert, manipulate, skew, a spirit of
ESCALATION… escalate, heighten, increase, surge, intensify, spiral, amplify, enlarge…
EXAGGERATION… embellish, overemphasis, overstate, mock, fake, imitation, a spirit of
SUGGESTION… idea, recommendation, counsel, assumption, theory, speculation, thought
PROVISION… supply, provide needs, give, equip, assistance, benefits, blessings…
REVELATION… reveal, expose, disclose, present, bring forth, acknowledge, a spirit of
IMAGINATION… mind's eye, curiosity, perception, embellish, exaggerate, fantasize…
JUSTIFICATION… defense, explain, reason, justify, rationalize, validation, corroborate …
IMPARTATION… convey, transmission of information, carry into, deposit, enlighten…
DIRECTION… lead, guide, show, route, path, to make or put right, rectify, amend, correct
SUBMISSION… plan, suggest, surrender, submit, yield, compliance, honor, respect…
ACTIVATION… start, begin, initiate, apply, adhere, display, appear, show
APPLICATION… use, function, operation, utilization, practice, purpose, claim, apply…
MANIFESTATION… appear, display, show, exhibit, presence, indication, proof, express
STAGNATION… stagnate, decay, deteriorate, sluggish, inactive, mediocrity, complacency
RECOGNITION… cognition, awareness, identify, reason, understand, insight, credit…
RESTORATION… repair, renew, recover, reclaim, improve, return, redemption, restitution
RECONCILIATION… resolve, reunion, return back to, rectify, settle, make right…
CELEBRATION… celebrate, rejoice, honor, festivity, praise, acknowledge, worship
PRESUMPTION… belief, conjuncture, supposition, presupposition, high likelihood
ASSUMPTION… guess, speculate, assume, take up, infer, hypothesis, suspect to
* Note: *Presumption* is accepting something as true even if not for certain. *Assumption* is accepting as true, certain to happen, without proof, believing without evidence
SITUATION… state, condition, circumstance, state of things at hand, in varying degrees
DIRECTION… path, way, course, track, route, how to, guidance, lead, order, manage…
CONVERSTATION… communicate, talk, chat, listen, share, exchange, dialog, discuss…
COMMUNION… union, intimacy, closeness, coming together … relationship

What has been released and imparted to you in these words – their meaning and what the potential and possibilities they carry to influence and play a role in *expectancy*… and revelation yet to come… will be such an asset in this *journey* of *expectation.* Recognition this type of revelation presents, even in some ways requires, that you *embrace* it to the point of knowing the role it plays… especially if you want to be *empowered* all along the way you are traveling on this path and in the *journey* of your life… and with the potential of creating an awareness to help *empower* others too. So *embrace* and *engage* with what is revealed.

❖ *Perhaps*…. these each in their own way either <u>hinder or help</u> *expectancy's* success? Only you know when you view them as potential *sources, forces - a spirit of,* and *voices* that affect the effect that you *expect* with your *expectations.* And, we really must address the *expectations* that others have of us... that we have of them, or we carry a piece/part in theirs of they in ours. *He* knows – seek *Him* for clarity.

Indeed... consider carefully the conversations you're having within yourself and especially when it's just you... and there's no other good or godly voice of counsel or covering. The information the conversation carries can begin to suggest, present, or quickly attempt to shift you into an *aligning* with what means to influence *immediately, intentionally,* or sometimes *inconspicuously...* what you *expect.*

When *expectation* is becoming and being potentially more than just your own *thoughts, perceptions, revelation, or power of suggestion* stirring things in an agitating way vs an *expectant* hopeful one... be aware and alert to an attempt of *sabotaging* spirit trying to enter the *process* through an *other voice* or means. It's motive is to take action, to influence, convince, and lead you in a direction most often... that is not good. Nor will it go the way you thought or the way it should leading to producing something undesired, un*expected*.

Equally it can move to confuse and bring chaos or crisis into any connection *God* wants to bring to you by *His Spirit, Holy Spirit* so that *His plans, promises,* and *purposes...* what *He* has available for you to partner with *Him* for... it can be revealed, released for you to receive, and potentially so you conceive from the good seed of *His* **expectation** and **expected end.**

This form and source of action... it will guide and direct you into an increase in faith... which enables you to "*take the chance*", so to speak, that the manifestation for what you and *He* are *expecting* is truly there. Good fruit will come forth... and more importantly... it tends to be lasting fruit - the *fruit of His Spirit* produced in you, in your spirit, and by *His Spirit* strength.

The more we *align* our path with seeking first the *kingdom of God* and *His* righteousness – through our right standing in *Him, the Word* says that the things we have need of will be *added* unto us.* Another words, we will see *Him* bring forth and provide in a way perhaps we didn't think *He* would, didn't think *He* was aware of, and therefore didn't *expect* Him to. But because of *His goodness, faithfulness,* and *all-knowing He* does.* My how *He* loves us and meets us so wonderfully.

In this *process* I exhort you to be encouraged, encourage yourself, and encourage others. For in our openness to the "*addings*" of *God* that will come... either to extend what *He's* revealing to *you... me... us,* by providing another way to look at it, or to replace altogether the way we've ordered the *forming*, are preparing for the *birthing*, and will see the timely *delivery* of the **expectation** at hand... the one *He's* highlighting before us.

This connection with *Him* promises to provide. *He's* secured this faithful provision for us in our identity and inheritance in *Him*. All of this matters and is ours to *pursue, press in* toward with all *perseverance* to *prevail* in receiving the benefits and blessings in being <u>*His*</u> and trustingly **expectingly** of *Him...* in both the *process* and *journey* with *Him*.

It truly is the idea that we know now - we *look*... now let's *look again...* and let's *look from here...* where we are now... so we can *look beyond* into the potential and possibilities that *He* reveals and *align* our **expectancy** in that which reflects *His heart, plans,* and *purposes* for *your life... my life... our lives.* Oh the power of *looking* ~ **expect and see.**

Connected to these key *ion* words are often words that *align* to and within the answering or determining dynamics like that of: *who... what... where... when... why...* and *how...* that couples with and within the *process* of the path of *expectancy* we're on. It makes way for a good and necessary healthy kind of *accountability* with ourselves... with *Him*... and others involved. This part of the *process* also matures and develops us into being more of who *He* created us to be, and what *He* purposed us to do. We decrease as *He* increases... more of *Him*... less of *you... me... us.** Let's *expect* it in ourselves and lovingly in each other.

Personally, I've encountered all the words mentioned, but have discovered that these seven are key *"ion"* words that are *"flagged"* for me as I in my way *process* things: **perception, presumption, assumption, validation, communication, intimidation,** and **projection**. They can affect significantly the dynamics mentioned above in determining what we're *expecting* and why we're *expecting* such, and even why we're not anymore. As you'd *expect,* it's different ones (and this list is not all) in varying situations, with different people, through a variety of issues, and circumstances that play a role in **expectation's** formation and beyond.

But again, the awareness and discovery of which is influencing us is a valuable key and dramatically impacts what then comes into *alignment* and the shaping taking place.

There's a *rule* so to speak, that I'll introduce to you that can help you as well. It was shared with me during an important season of life where I needed to really know if I was on the *right track* with my life... decisions I was making... the path I was taking... and clarity needed to come so what I was *expecting* would be better aligned. I'd also be more confident... because that alignment would be for the *track* that was best for me to be on.

When we're traveling somewhere it's vital to know not just the destination... but where will be the *"point of departure"*, the place you'll leave or take off from. It's no different on this *journey* – what is our destination? Let's go with what the title suggests: ***"embrace it and be empowered" by or through expectation.*** Where do or did we start off knowing we were entering into what we're *expecting?* Because once you've departed you're now on your way to a destination, a place, a location which has an *arrival point* that eventually allows what we're *expecting* to manifest, fulfilled in part or whole...so as we know it we've arrived!

Once you've departed and are on your way, remember, there are things that may attempt to or can gain *access* to you *"in route"*... some *good*, some *not so good*, and some actually can be very *disruptive*, even dangerous. These would form what we will call a *"point of access"*... something or someone enters into the *journey* affecting the trip. So, immediately what we were *expecting* has to shift, change, modify, or be completely abandoned. Interestingly some of *this process* as we know can happens so spontaneously... in seconds, minutes... and some of it is *a process* over a greater length of time.

That's why it's important to determine: is this the *point of departure* and how you will actually depart. In general let's say it's either *you yourself, someone else, or God* (what/who you believe in) leading you... because either you yourself or they are whom you've entrusted to influence this important *starting point* since they most likely know where and or at least important information about where you're headed.

Because the *potential of access* is always there, and even on going in some situations, every *point of departure* has with it *points of access* the need for us to be wise to consider, seek more information about, or spiritually, we can always seek *Him* about. Remember, things / people… they either *hinder or help* when given access to our going forward from where we are to where we want… desire… *expect* to go… be… do… things that are important, special to us and to *Him* too. Yes, some of this as we mature becomes routine, habit; but be aware.

It's no different than an actual *street, road, or highway* being marked letting you know how to *drive, steer, navigate,* and *determine* how best to keep focused and headed in the right direction… safe. For example there are all kinds of *"signs"* to *inform us, create awareness,* and *direct us* in the safest way… and not just for us, but those around us… as our *expectations* certainly affect more than us… ♪ *"Sign, sign, everywhere a sign… blocking out the scenery breakin' my mind… do this, don't do that can't you read the sign."** I know, I just dated myself… but it was a popular song with a catchy tune and lyrics that did make you STOP and THINK… *selah*. And, wonder just who's *expectation* is it and in what or who are we really *expecting*?

Stop… go… turn ahead… detour… dead end… one way… turn only… do not pass… crosswalk… curve… yield… and yes the… dot dot dots on the road… which then *determine… inform… limit… control* much… and so it is in this continual *journey* with our *expectations.*

So these signs… in the world, in our lives… all around us… even from *Him* and in *His Word…* are all trying to tell us something… and that something *projects* something into our *perception,* our *imagination,* where *presumption or assumption* tries to often bring a form of *exaggeration* with it… and next thing you know an *expectation* is birthed. Then we're walking and living it out wondering why or how did this happen, this isn't what I *expected…* and am I even going in the right direction?

That's the power and even a beauty of it all… the ***ion*** words are constantly there taking access as they represent action either in making how we departed *good, not so good, or questionable…* and that's when we must always remember and rely upon the fact that in life's *journey… "course corrections"* are factored in – especially in and with *Him*. And, you can *reset, recalibrate, or recalculate* your system at any time. You can have a new thought… a new perspective… or new directive that comes to you… which is what propels in part the formation of the continuality of *expectation.*

As we continue… the next section will present you with *special words* that open up the world of opportunity to *see* and *selah…* to *formulate* how you typically engage in and navigate *forming… birthing…* and walking out your *expectations…* as well as those others have of you… or are connected to you. To *expect and see expectantly!*

- ❖ *Perhaps…* you'll find for you… as I have for *me… it became, has,* and *is becoming* so much more simplified… as it's NOT a formula or a ritual required by *someone, some thing, some belief,* or *supporting some "theory"*. Instead… what makes it all relative … what keeps it all real… is realizing that through an intentional desire to enjoy *life's adventure* and the *expectancy* it holds… well, it is more about not going it alone… but genuinely inviting and allowing *Him* to join *you… me… us* … and those *He* connects us to. It's relational and found in relationships! What a venture it has been and we *expect* it will be as we come together and into more *expectancy*!

As you might have noticed… I enjoy ♪ music and often lyrics are what *He* uses to speak to me connecting and confirming things in types of experiences. So I can't help but think in this moment of **m**y beloved sister friend *Sandy* whose gone to be with the Lord. There it is, her phone is going off with her, me, or someone singing along to her ring tone … ♪ ***"Jesus, take the wheel. Take it from my hands. 'Cause I can't do this on my own so I'm letting go. So give me one more chance and save me from this road I'm on… Jesus, take the wheel."*** *

Oh… the ***aligning*** for the assigning as we're arriving now at our destination… only to depart with a new sense of **e**xcitement for the **e**xploration ahead and through our ***expectations!***

---

* Footnotes: Chapter 3 / *See Genesis 3:8, Lexicon H6963 voice/qol or Strongs Concordance. *See Proverbs 3:13-18, Ephesians 3:20, Proverbs 8:1-4, 1 John 4:17, Exodus 23:20, Psalm 16:11, Jeremiah 29:11, Song of Solomon 2:15, John 10:10, Isaish 11:2, Matthew 6:33, John 3:30 - all emphasis is mine and personal paraphrasing built on various translations and versions.
*See Song lyrics: "Signs" / Five Man Electrical Band - https://www.songfacts.com/lyrics/five-man-electrical-band/signs *See Song lyrics: Jesus, Take the Wheel / Source: Musixmatch Songwriters Hillary Lindsey / Brett James / Gordie Sampson …. Jesus, Take the Wheel lyrics © Reservoir Media Music.

✧ CHAPTER 4 ✧

✧ ESTABLISHING & EMBRACING ... A JOURNEY WITH WORDS.
MEANING & MISSION / MEDITATION & MOTIVATION
MOVEMENT & MANIFESTATION

It's time for us to enter into these days ahead in a greater **m**easure together... as reader and writer... ready to **e**ncounter with great **expectation** as well as a hunger for greater **e**xploration with what *He*... who is the *Beginning* and *End, Author* and *Finisher*... is revealing about a work that has begun in a form of this books telling... yet, is unfinished till we come together to its end. He **c**ontinues with me in the writing of it from how *He* helps me to write what I believe is a form of what *He* has already written...and is being revealed to me as I've received to release to you to receive in part. The other part will **c**ome directly from *Him* to you in the *process*. *He* truly wants you to ***engage*** and ***embrace*** in ***expecting*** such and **m**ore!

As you receive from what has been revealed to be released... and it begins to unfold on **e**ach page as we **m**ove on into the *journey*... and in and through **words** specific words. Words that have been highlighted... **m**arked, branded as by *Him*, if you will. A ***word worthy*** of paying attention to... of honing in on... as they will become a significant focus and part of forming sentences, paragraphs, and portions in the days ahead... that **c**arry **m**uch in them. A type of **e**nergy **c**reating a type of synergy – *interaction, collaboration,* and *interfacing* within the ebb and flow because *He by His Spirit* will **m**eet you in them and by *His Word* **c**onnections too.

For a discovery awaits us... in these words... as these words are presented in **m**any forms and formats. For that has been my life...**m**aybe in some way yours too? I'm reminded of the figure 8 and when sideways it becomes the symbol of infinity... one loop **c**onnecting to the other only to return to begin again. A bit like the style of my writing of words that's unfolded and unfolding... just as *He's* wanted it to be. Yes, likened unto a *wheel within a wheel*. But then, *Jesus... take the wheel!*

In the beginning... let us remember He is the Beginning – Alpha... and that's before all time... was the Word... the Living **Expectant** *Expression of Elohim Himself – as Christ – Yeshua, Jesus. Yet, as God Himself. He was already there... continually existing in the beginning co-eternally with God. And, through His creative inspiration... He, as this Expression that was alive – living... all things were made... they came into existence... into being.. through Him the Living One - Life. And, without Him... not even one – no not one thing – existed apart from Him... for a fountain of life was in Him... along with the power to bestow... yes give – grant, life. Oh, this life... this Life... was the Light of men and was for all humanity. A light... the Light that would never fail to shine on – in – through the darkness... and, the darkness could not overcome or overpower it... because it didn't comprehend, appropriate, or absorb it... and still is unreceptive to it.** Where was its **expectancy**?

Life... light... **c**oming through and created by words... and the *He* as the *Word* in the **mi**dst **m**oving. And, I... well, I'm **c**ontinually fascinated in the way and what I'm learning from *Him* regarding such... as I believe you in your own way have been, are... and possibly will be in *this process.* The *process* where through them – the words, arises an extreme **c**uriosity containing such a profound value embedded in a deep respect and appreciation *He's* developing in **m**e for words and *Him* as the *Word*. For **e**ach of their parts, pieces, and portions have a place in the rhythm of life... and how *He* seems, no appears to be indeed a type of or the actual *Originator* of. The *One* who perhaps is drawing and **c**alling *you*... ***me***... *us* to them... yet, *He* is them. Father, You know... help them to know the heart of what's said.

It **c**an almost be surreal at times... the words that seem to **c**ome to the forefront... like on a **m**arquee... flashing, standing out... as if they're saying *stop, look at me*... take a closer look. Go ahead... **c**ome into what I have for you.. and let me show you. Almost like there's an invitation into a type of **e**ncounter. Yes, an **e**xperience intertwined with a *word*... the *words*.

So, in a **m**ore "technical" way of seeing this **working of words**... this wonderful **weaving of words** in and through the forms they take on – *past, present, future*... and the format – *noun, adjective, verb*. An arrangement they fall into as a type of framework **e**merges... that will attempt to present to you with the opportunity to step into a place of **expectation**.

Positioning yourself within the *process* is key as what you start to **expect**... it lingers... just hanging around out there, so to speak. Almost ike its suspended by what is yet to revealed... opening up a realm of greater understanding... another *view*... *outlook*... *notion*. So... you posture yourself as you start to receive from what you **expect** and are suddenly **expecting**. And, in the **expectation** it is all birthing... as what its *forming, in the creating*... it begins to take on its own kind of life! In a sense, like when *He* spoke with words **c**reating life.

In and through the unfolding of the laying of foundations through words you've read to this point... and now what you're being prepared for as we venture ahead... **c**an you sense a type of invitation awaiting? A bidding **e**ven to **c**ome... to **e**nter **m**ore intentionally into where you are... into what the **m**oment, the day, and this time holds. Through what is shared and in the way it's being shared... in the way *He's* unfolded to me for *telling* what I've **e**ncountered ... and **e**xperienced. And it, suggesting that there's things *He* has for you in it all.

Even as will be shared throughout... it is and will be an ongoing thing ... this type of *wooing, drawing*, and **c**alling from *Him* to us to **c**ome and **e**ncounter... is not just to **c**ommunicate with me... with *you*... *with us*. It seems... yes, I believe there's a need to acknowledge that indeed the underlying desire and divine idea of it all... well ideally, it is that **expectation is better grounded and established in relationship VS** (versus) **rituals and formulas**... whether in thought or deed. Could it also be for us personally to come into a **m**ore *intentional continual, intimate* form of union **c**ommunion in the *dance* of the *process* and the *journey*?

It's a relationship... not a formula. Where the essence eternally in the energy of what I **expect**... you **expect**... we **expect**... what *He* **expect** in this **embracing** and **empowering** of words is designed to **m**anifest in the **m**oving, in the **m**aking, the **m**olding, and **m**erging together. In the **c**onnecting through **m**ore than the simplest **m**eans and **m**ethods of **c**ommunicating...but in **c**ommunion, the desired joining. For in union... **c**ommon union... shared and **m**utual... a delightfully almost **c**reated way **e**volves. Like in a sort of set of **c**ircumstances that **c**ollide, **c**onverge... creating something beautiful and it being in us *togethered* in *Him*... one in *Him the Word*.

Expressly... *"The purpose of the written word is always to lead us to the Living Word"*... (anonymous) *Selah* ~

Recognizing the *relative* role and *relativity* of both realms... divulged in their dimension and diversity... and the difference therein which is vital, essential and even connected to an eternal outcome. If we look at the word *"relative"*... in and of itself suggests a **relationship.**

? Will *you...me... we...* allow the ritual in the rhythm of life to *deter, discourage, or distract* us from *relationship*? That which is rooted in the *formalities* and *formulas*... the *religion* and *rationale* or the *routine and repetitiveness* not to mention the often lack of *receptiveness* that continues to direct not only the course I'm on, you're on, we're on... or what we *expect*?

? Or will I respond to the *divine drawing... wooing... calling...* of a *Creator* ... to *His* created ones to return...turning back, to turn toward...and to enter into the *expectation* of the NEW... that which all the created earth and creation groans and travails for? Is this not in *His* heartbeat of love and *expectancy... original intent* – what *He* in *His* heart and divine design meant?

To be the source - *Source*... the very life force – *Force*, of what *I*... *you*.. *we* **expect** in the continual consistent caring, communing, and fellowshipping... of the oneness of communion and conversation with the *One*. To know that in *the process*...when we convene all this... our communion and communication breeds a kind of creative constant calculation... where *words* are involved especially in *expectation* and in our relationship in and with *Him*?

What these carry within them – the words ritual/routine/religion OR relationship. The first few offering either a type of predetermined, predestined result...often void of inviting and allowing our relationship with others... let alone *Him*... to grow as they can close or open doors. Doors that when opened to *Him*... offer a way that is more authentic... genuine, sincere, intentional, purposeful, rewarding, edifying, encouraging, and empowering.

With everything working toward what we hope for... long for... believe for... *expect*... becoming available in and through life with *Him*... such a presenting of an optimistically and overwhelming better outcome starts to be established in such *expectancy*... even eternally. And *words* are at work in and through it all... **words of worth.**

Prioritizing relationships... especially with *Him*... begins to influence and inspire ...even mold and shape. For *He* knows every detail... and each plays a significant role in *expectation*... over such dogmatic... even engrained and entrenched reactions... responses... reflections. You know that this is just what I've...we've... come to *expect* to be the likelihood...the probability and prospect of what will result. Well... such priority extended is significant. Let our *words* align.

Take courage... lean into *Him*... learn to look at, consider, pay attention to... the things we've been or allowed to condition us in what we *expect*. Whether something is of value... importance, necessity, or something that appears to have a purpose... or a place in our *expectation(s)*. Not to mention the fact that it plays a role; negative or positive in producing a sense of pleasure or satisfaction or not, as we see the fruit and the role of *words* within.

And if we're honest, we'll quickly begin to see and acknowledge that it's really impossible to deny we were created for such... and for *Him*. For **He, the Eternal**... had and has an *expectation* in and for *you... me... us...* and its *everlasting*.

✧ EXPECTANCY'S ETERNAL ECHO…

As a **word of worth… *significant from its beginning of being presented*…** be encouraged allowing yourself to enter in to a type of encounter with the "*word*". Let your thoughts be open to what this **word of worth (wow)** is designed to bring to the *process* of **expectation** *forming… birthing… and* **manifesting** in the **m**idst of this time and season of your life.

A simple way to give place to the highlighted **word of worth** is to consider the following when encountering and experiencing it: what is meant in the part it plays in establishing something or someone… how that that leads to an *embracing*… how the *multifacetedness* of the **layers** in *unfoldings, addings,* and *removings* of words affects everything we *expect.*

Words where their "role" is being emphasized is very probable way to contribute… even conceivably bring about a new way of *expecting*… which is a needful, possibly necessary, neglected, or avoided component of what has gone before into our ways of *expecting* in the past. A part and piece that's now being presented holds within it *possibility … promise… prospect…* a potential of a connection to purpose… yours. And, His for *you… me… us.*

Just as it was *in the beginning*… the earth, in its initial state of being *dark, void, formless*… longed for something… someone… to give it form, life, and yes, purpose, and that's why we must always enter in with *expectancy*… ours and inviting *His* to join together with ours.

✧ EXPECTANCY HOVERS… BROODS…

Hover and brood Holy Spirit… over **me**… *us*… *over this process and establishing with the essence of eternal expectancy… over what is yet formless but forming… waiting to be birthed … waiting to break open your Word… and it within* **me** *… so that Your revelation-light… begins to shines out… and shine upon the forming. Let insight into Your plans… enter my… our open hearts… and mouth… and fill us with Your Word as we learn to desire… even crave… what You require… turning our hearts to You… and You turn Yours to us showing us Your grace… like You so consistently do … to each of Your godly followers… and especially Your laid down lovers. Those who hunger and thirst for You… whose* **expectation** *lies in the prepared place… arranged path… that is filled with only Your promises… and not my futile perspectives… opinions… and plans… that often open a door to sin … and its desire to have dominion over* **me**… *over us.**

Let the entrance of **You as the Word**… and **Your words**… let them break forth … and **m**ake way for *light… life… and truth* to come *hovering, brooding,* and *continually.* For *Your* words… they do that. For *You as the Word* are that by *Your Spirit…Holy Spirit…the Spirit of Holiness.* And oh… the beauty and power discovered in such gives way to understanding the simplicity of this kind of creative power…in *the journey* and *process* of *my… yours… our* lives and **e**very formed **expectation** therein and to come.

✧ HOVERING & BROODING… MEANING & MISSION

Words of worth take on their identity through their **meaning** and how they are defined by and in the world. In *academically, grammatical,* and *intellectual* definitions…formal and informal definings… come legitimate and valid **m**eans. Yes, by ways and **m**eans that could be determined invalid, in error even, or that really have no worth to what is at hand. They are rendered *worthless* and of no value to where our *focus, attention,* and *consideration* should be given as we contemplate and consider them.

In and through the defining of words we learn their meaning… as well their purpose. Or another way to view it would be to see it as the *mission* and the *mandate* of a word in whatever form it takes on (i.e. noun, verb, adjective…).

As we use words… especially these **words of worth** we'll focus on… placing them in a type of statement in sentences… and an expression of their nature forms. They appear to take on a form of life… which creates movement, which means *expectations* are *forming, creating, birthing, and manifesting*. It's what they do… it's in what we *expect* of them.

For it's a natural response in the *ebb and flow of life*… as they are attached to everything… everywhere. They're at work affecting everyone and in every situation – especially in the ordered routine and the mundane things of life all of the time. You can't escape them… as you'll always be *expecting* something!

Initially… whether a **word of worth** is directly relevant to what we are pursuing within our personal realm of a *specific expectation*… there are things to consider and not push aside. Just because we don't always see it or sense it… that is, an immediate confirmation or connection to the present word… we'd be wise to not rule it out its part to quickly. Yes… un*expectedness* is always lingering… in good ways as well as not so good.

So, let's not neglect to consider… the *"character"* that *words* and their unique meanings can take on becoming **"alive"** or **"rhema"** *… a divinely inspired impression brought forth through your… our, natural understanding… which by design is meant to provide us with a type of explanation that gives way to clarification. Thus, it influences the degree of our *expectation* either through assurance or even bearing a type of witness, one way or the other.*

One thing is for certain… there is **POWER in WORDS**. Yes, *life or death lie within them… blessing or cursing… a creative force that releases as they do.*

Remember, *in the beginning was the Word … and that Word as a living expression was with God…* and **it was God**. *It dwelt in our midst… full of (**expectant**) glory… full of grace and truth… and still is with us… alive.* It is the means by which *God* created all things. And, there is always and in all ways, the *expected* beginning as well as the *expected* end of *God*.

It, *the Word… defines, describes,* and *discloses* valuable information to us about *Him… His* nature… *His* attributes, and *His* characteristics. The *Word* (full of *expectancy*) it is written… it is spoken… *it is alive,* and *active**. One could say that it is *all inclusive*…for everyone.

In this connection between *God* and *His Word*… because **He is the Word**…and *the Word is the* **Most Worthy One**… and the *only true Word of Worth*. We can continue that line of thought into the *words of worth* He has highlighted and assigned to each part bringing forth pieces… a portion of what *He* desires us to see, hear, perceive, learn, know… as *He* has, is and will continually be available to us in this *processing* making known to us what we need.

So, embrace the establishing of the worth *He* is assigning to it… and aligning it with. What *His plans, promises, provision,* and eternal *purpose* for *you, me,* and *us* are connected to **word of worth** on earth and eternally. Remember, what *His Word* says, which always gives a place to see potential for how in its *beginning* it was created for something and by **the *Word*** who created all things.

This connection then spans beyond time for *He is time*... and beyond just *Him* and *Him* being the *Word*... **to *Him* being the *Word* in us** and **in all things.** When we as *His* creation by our own choosing in the free will *He* gave us as *He* created us with choice... respond to an **expectation** *He* has and has made known ***in His Word as the Word He is...*** let's do it well.

As *His* creation... to come to *Him* and become like *Him* is a choice; to be *His born again children*. And **He as the Word,** choosing to *live in us,* inhabiting and taking up residency in us, those who connect, communicating, and communing with *Him*... in *Him*...through *Him*... as *His*... may it be this way for us each and in all facets of our relationship then. May we ascend to apprehend, and then descend... to become more like *Him*... **the Word.**

For... the words He speaks to us... in His Word... in our lives... through these **(expectant) words of worth** *He speaks... that possess His Spirit... and His Spirit (with all* **expectancy***) is and brings life... therefore, they are full of truth and life.* *

He is waiting... *He* desires for you to invite *Him*... allow *Him*... to come into each day and through each *word*... as the **Word that He is**. **Encounter** and **experience** how *He* will meet you there. How *He'll* move drawing you into *His* moving and meanings... and into deeper meaningful purpose-filled ways. In what *He'll* begin to reveal, *He'll* also release for you to receive... to help ground and establish you in truth... providing a sure foundation.

For the *earnest* of our **expectation** in *Him* to manifest as the constant light *He* is... with *Him* providing as *He* leads the way and by *His Spirit*. In *this process*... there is a *deciding*... a *determining*... a *delineation* continually required... of whether what we **expect**... in our **expectations** is realistic or unrealistic... doable or undoable... aligned in Truth or not.

Whether it is in *His* timing or not... in what is good and right in *His* sight or not. Plain and simple...we must ask, *"Is it fashioned, formed, created, and birthed in Him by Him in you?"*

As *His Word* has its perfect work in us in this place and *the process* of it all... it provides a way for *Him* who is the *Way – the Truth – the Life** ... to move in what *you, me, we*... are hoping for... believing for... and not in presumption or assumption... or even apprehension or a form of calculation... but truly trusting and knowing that ultimately with *God* all things are possible. For *His Word* goes forth to do what it was assigned to do...in its mission of going, moving, and working - it does not return void.* Yes, there is *God's* **expected** end.

*... to everything this is a time... purpose... season, and reason under heaven (***expect*** it). Just as the grass withers... just as flowers fade... it is true for the word of our God... for it stands (as* **expected***) and it endures forever... for He makes everything (as is His* **expectation***) beautiful in its time... setting even eternity in the hearts of* **men.** *

✧ EXPECTANCY AWAKENS... STIRS WITHIN...

*Be strong and let your hearts (***expectantly***) take courage...all you who wait for and* **expect** *confidently the LORD! For this is the (***expectant***) confidence that we have toward Him, that if we ask... praying to Him for anything (***expectantly***) according to His will He hears us. And if we* know that He hears us (as **expected**) in whatever we ask, we know that we have the requests that we have asked of him.* Stir **heavenly expectancy** on earth as it is in heaven.

✧ HOVERING & BROODING... MEDITATION & MOTIVATION

Words of worth are presented ... creating an awareness that they are there. They come with an invitation... even an idea in mind of there being a need... a need to spend some time with and in that word... meditating... lingering in the presence of its meaning and mission filling the atmosphere. Having *Him* with you there from a personal invitation... delights *Him*.

Through a variety of ways revelation and insight they come to us. This gives place for them to play a role... as they can motivate us to want to know the **word of worth's** part and how we might expect it to form. In as much as whether we're to pursue and continue through with such an *expectation* we might have... and to be in faith believing for it to come to pass.

Since *expectations* are formed mostly by how we interpret and *process* information... that information is key to what we believe about a matter. **Words of worth** presented will have information shared about them... which by taking it all in... the *processing* begins in the matter it is attached to. Thus, its forming is considered to be innate, distinctive, characteristic of, essential even... or it takes on a more instinctive, intuitive, natural. or automatic kind of response in *the process*.

This opens up to us why it is important to understand the *source/Source* behind or connected to the revelation or insight you receive... it undoubtedly matters. As its influencing role sways, persuades, and can impact much. Determining the direction one way or the other... in what, where, why, when... and how *you... me... we...* come to *expect* is impacted also.

Whether directly or indirectly... motivation comes into play in it all as what influences or motivates you... that driving force... it will affect you. The effects ultimately impacting then where we go and how we get to what is formed in what you... me... we are *hoping* for... *desire... look forward to...* and *believe* will or will not **expectantly** happen. *God* help us.

When we meditate on *Him... His Word, will,* and *ways...* together with *His plans, purposes, promises,* and *provision...* and it all being connected. To that of our identity and inheritance as *His* children... *His* sons and daughters. Well... that can lead us to an encounter with *His* grace which enables... even anoints us to *press*, to *persevere*, and to *pursue* fully what we are *expecting*. Especially when the motivation stems from obeying and pleasing *Him*. And... what pleases *Father* always bears good fruit that has blessings and provision attached.

✧ EXPECTANCY ARISES ... APPREHENDS

I will declare the decree: what He... the LORD... hath said unto me*... and out of these words filled with **expectancy** will *flow* and *grow... apprehending* and capturing the moments that collide propelling forward what *I'm... we're,* **expecting**. Either to a place with weak, faint filled affirmation... or strong faith filled confident calculation... for what *He* has said... and has us speak then through *words* into the atmosphere of *expectancy* in our *speakings*.

"*You will also decide and decree a thing, and it will be (as you* **expect***) established for you; And the light of God's favor will (***expectantly***) shine upon your ways.*"*

There in the establishing arises a time where one *decides*... yes, one **m**ust *determine* is it by *God* – that *did God really say* **m**oment... or what's becoming to be in our *expecting*... is it being established of flesh...**m**an? *Holy Spirit* lead us by our spirits to apprehend rightly.

And, I'm reminded in this pivotal place of reading about a type of scale which was **c**alled the "*Scale of Expectation*". It **c**laimed that one **c**ould **c**lassify and assign a value of 1-5 to one's *expectations* into five **c**ategories: 1) **M**uch more than *expected*, 2) **M**ore than *expected*, 3) As *expected,* 4) Less than *expected,* and finally, 5) **M**uch less than *expected*. **

Surely, we **c**an see a type of purpose in such... in its somewhat to be *expected* simple *formula*. *Lord*, we submit this to *You* and know *You* know if this type of *tool* would be a help or a hindrance. Especially as we lean **m**ore into *You* for discerning and determining where we are in our *expectancy*, what we're *expecting*, and how our **m**editation and **m**otivation would be influenced by it. You led to include it *Lord,* since in some ways tools like this **c**an be good. But ultimately... we want to apprehend the good of *God* as a fruit from the *Tree of Life*.

*For those who wait for the LORD... who **expect**, look for, and hope in Him. They will gain new strength and renew their power; they will lift up their wings... and rise up close to God... (**expectantly**) like eagles rising toward the sun; they will run and not become weary, they will walk and not grow tired (as **expected**).* * *Oh* the willingness to **wait**... now that's a word!

✦ HOVERING & BROODING... MOVEMENT & MANIFESTATION

Words of worth carry within them the power to initiate a form of **m**ovement... a taking on of action first starting in a thought... that **c**reates additional pondering and **m**editating which become the **m**ethod of what we think forming... and **m**akes way for the birthing of *expectation* and **m**ore! As a **m**an thinketh... so is he... so be pure in your thoughts.

When these **m**oments of **m**ovement **c**onverge **m**erging together... there indeed **c**omes a time for the prospect, possibility, **e**ven what is probable or predictable to **m**anifest. Just a word of **c**aution here: be aware of how a sense of urgency... or a need to **m**ove on **m**ore quickly... **c**an *derail, deter or discourage* us in our *expectation* of self, others, or *God* – especially in *His* time. Interestingly that's tried to happen in writing this *telling*.

Encounters and ***experiences*** in this *ongoing process*... related to all *expectance* is forming ... we quickly learn of the **c**ertainty of **c**ertain effects that occur. Simultaneously, the ability to **c**ontinually be *processing* it all as we give way to a variety of stimuli... well, the exposure of a deluge of information... along with recall and reflection of past experiences **c**an **c**ome.

What is **m**anifesting in these **m**oments and **m**ovement **c**an become not only overwhelming... but **c**onfusing, **c**reating a place for doubt... unbelief... and **e**ven fear to affect what we do or don't do... ultimately generating effects that emerge and possibly **c**hange our *expectations.*

Quite often we **c**an **e**ven determine a point of reference.. or a *reference point* ...where our *expectation* began developing. We discover in our *life's journey*... that it's good to know at what point did what I *expect* start to form? Why? Knowing such **c**an bring a sense of orientation for how we got where are, where we're going, and **m**ore. It helps keep the door **c**losed to regret and the **unexpected** as well as the enemy and those little foxes.

In our attempt to judge or discern what's revealed about something... or something about ourselves or someone... don't forget, much influences what we begin to think we *know, understand, perceive,* and *receive* in information – be it facts or truth. In *this process*, we begin to assess and evaluate... and determine what we're taking in – does it matter? Does it have a place? Should I give it a place... let it have power even... in what I *expect*... in my *expectancy*? Truly taking more time than we typically might... especially in important and significant moments in life's *journey* and this *process* is often needed and wise.

Don't forget the importance to know who is the source/Source in all of it. For, whatever we grasp as having value or importance... it then has the potential to lay a foundation for what we will *encounter* and *experience* in all *formings, birthings,* and future *manifestations* of *expectations.*

- ❖ *Perhaps*... this is the place... and the time to inquire of you regarding **"e=mc3"** and it's relevancy and yes, its relativity to *words*. After all "*energy is = equal to, the mass and constancy of light squared 2*" is the formula Eistein established right? Yet, *He* suggested to me in that middle of the night moment, that it might be good to also look at and understand it as a **"3"**. Now I believe there's a chance you've been noticing the **highlighting** of *words* that start with **"e, m, and c"** (yes, 3 letters) in this *journey*. Ah ha... you have and if not, you know to notice now! It's my way of revealing that there many important *e, m,* and *c words* and in my *journey* up to this point they were and are always being noticed by me! Have fun catching the ones I missed! So what about the **3** you ask? *He* has over time shown the importance of 3 biblically and referenced as well that to the **3**rd **power** is the <u>**fullness of the power of Him in Them – Father, Son, Holy Spirit**</u>. In general then... the **3rd person** <u>**Holy Spirit's**</u> **power**, brings an enabling and empowering in truth and in love, for the *fashioning, filling,* and *fueling* our *expectation*. Plus, at times you see the ***power of 3 words*** coupled together in *italics* to make an enhanced point in patterns of connection they carry. So, fasten your seatbelts *journeying* ones, because there's more coming as we move into an *expectancy* for how we'll explore **words of worth** manifest and more.

Manifestation means movement has happened to and through our *expectation* because of our *expectancy*... and movement matters because it is greatly exhibited in and through and becomes the result of *words* at work. As shared, *words* and their *meaning and mission*... influence our *meditation and motivation*... which then influences and helps determine where movement is and it helping *manifest* the end *product* in the *process* and what we *expect*.

It's like the fruit that falls from the branch of tree. The type of tree is the deciding factor that lets us know the kind of fruit we should *expect* it to yield; to fall from it. We don't *expect* an apple to fall from an orange tree. Even more so... it really starts in the kind of seed... the power and potential it carries and has to become what it is meant to become.

Much goes into the keeping and caring of the tree so it flourish and yields a good crop. Just like much should go into the *words* (seeds) we entertain... because they take root quickly and begin to ground themselves... establishing eventually what becomes their fruit. Like sin being the fruit of the *Tree of the Knowledge of Good and Evil.** May we stop eating of and giving place to those words and embrace the *Tree of Life* with its **words of worth.**

What we embrace as we adventure into becoming **m**ore aware and intentional of the ***words*** we take in, chew on, and **e**at as we *journey*... **m**ay they be *rooted, grounded,* and *established* in and from *Truth* – which is always wrapped in love. Which is revealed to us in the **Word** and through **Him** as ***the Word***... who is <u>**the Most Worthy Word**</u>... and our ***Tree of Life***. *

*... And now Father God, I... we... wait...for **m**y soul it is eager as it confidently looks into the future...* **expecting** *a response from You. Yet, as I wait, rooted and grounded in You... all the while I'm moving forward in boldness and faith...* **my**... *our hope, it is in You as* **my** *expectation now comes from and is finding its establishment* **m**ore and **m**ore in *You, Your Word, will and ways. My hope... surely it will not be cut off... for Your efforts are never in vain... and in You neither will* **m**ine *be. So I rest... I trust... remaining steadfast with* **expectancy** ... *partaking and eating of Your Word.*

Redeem time, restoring and renewing as only You can my... our **expectancy** reconciling our **expectations** *in our life's journey* to align with *Yours*... so any proceeding ahead springs forth from being grounded in Yours.

You have reversed the curse... so **m**ay we look now... and see that before us is a Tree... pleasant to one's sight... good for food. **M**ay our **expectant** desire be to taste and see that the Lord is good no longer imprisoned by hope deferred... for it is **The Tree of Life** in which we can **expectantly** partake.*

* Footnotes: Chapter 4 / *See Psalm 31:24, Psalm 119:130-133, Proverbs 18:21, Deuteronomy 11:26-29, James 3:10, John 1: 1-3, John 6:63, Psalm 27:14,31:24, 39:7, 62:15, Prov. 24:14, John 14:6, Isaiah 55:11, Ecclesiastes 4, Isaiah 40:8, 1 John 5:14–15, I Corinthians 15:58, 2 Corinthians 3:12, Hebrews 11:1, Proverbs 13:12, Job 22;28, Isaiah 40:31 and Genesis 2, 3 - all emphasis is mine and personal paraphrasing built on various translations and versions.
*See G4487 rhema /Strongs Concordance.
*See G3056 logos /Strongs Concordance.
*See SnapSurveys.com / Scale of Expectation

SECTION TWO

✧ EXPECTATION'S BIRTHING
…AN ESTABLISHING & EMBRACING

✧ SECTION TWO WORTHY WORDS ✧
✧ EXPECTATION'S BIRTHING… ESTABLISHING & EMBRACING FOR THE JOURNEY BEFORE US

*In the beginning, God (with **exuberant energetic expectation**) created the heavens and the earth. The **earth** was completely formless and void (yet **expectant**), and darkness was draped over the face of the deep. And the Spirit of God was (**expectantly**) hovering over the face of the waters. **

*For by Him all things were created, in heaven and on earth, visible and invisible, whether thrones or dominions or rulers or authorities—all things were created (in **expectation**) through Him and for Him. **

*My grace is enough; it is all you need (rest, trust **expectantly**). My strength comes in your weakness (full of **expectancy**). I just let Christ (**expectantly**) take over! The weaker I get, the stronger I (**expect** to) become! **

*Don't worry about anything; instead, (**expectantly**) pray about everything. Tell God what you need (your **expectations**), and thank Him for all He has done (fulfilling **expectations**). Then you will experience God's peace, which (we **expect** to) exceed anything we can understand. His peace will guard your hearts and **minds** as you live (**expecting** always) in Christ Jesus. **

*You **m**ade all the delicate, inner parts of **m**y body and knit **m**e together in **m**y **m**other's womb (full of **expectancy**). Thank You for **m**aking **m**e so wonderfully complex! Your workmanship is (**expectantly**) **m**arvelous… how well I know (and **expect** of) it. **

*So do not throw away this **confident** (**expectant**) trust in the Lord. Remember the great reward it brings you – things He is (**expectantly**) birthing in and through you. Patient endurance is what you (**must expect** to) need now, so that you (in **expectation**) will continue to do God's will. Then you will receive (in **expectancy**) all that He has promised. **

*For you know (can **expect**) that when your faith is tested, tried in the fire even, your endurance has a chance to (**expect** to) grow. So let it grow, for when your (**expectant**) endurance is fully developed, you will be perfect and complete, (**expecting** and) in need of nothing. **

*In the beginning was the Word, and the Word was (as **expected**) with God, and the Word was God. He was in the beginning with God (according to **expectation**). All things were made through Him, and without Him was not anything made. **

---

* Footnotes: Section Two Worthy Words / *See Genesis 1:1-2, Colossians 1:16, 2 Corinthians 12:9, Philippians 4:6-7, Psalms 139:13-14, Hebrews 10:35-36, James 1:3-4, John 1:1–3 – all emphasis is mine and personal paraphrasing built on various translations and versions.

✧ WORTHY WORDS AS WE ENTER CHAPTER 5 ✧

*Your Word oh God... the Living Word... is a lamp unto my feet where Your Truth shines its way – Your Word is the Truth... guiding and leading me in my choices... my decisions (and **expectations**)... and it **m**akes my pathway clear... for it **c**arries clarity... **c**onfirmation... and is established in your **c**ovenant with **m**e.**

*For I know that You know the thoughts You think of me... the plans You have for me... plans for my good not **c**alamity... thoughts and plans of great hope (**expectancy**) and a bright (**expectant**) future. Because of You... how You **m**ake known to me the path of life... I taste and I see Your goodness **c**oupled with great joy – an abundance of joy... and it all in Your presence. For there, (oh the **expectancy**) at Your right hand... by Your right side... I encounter and experience the fullness of Your pleasures... even eternal pleasures for they are forever **m**ore.**

*Surely goodness and **m**ercy shall follow me all the days of my life. Come on goodness... come on **m**ercy... follow me in my life's journey (for indeed there is an **expectation**).**

*Your road led through the sea, Your pathway through the **m**ighty waters, a pathway no one knew (or **expected**) was there! Oh that You would teach us so that we would remember (**to expect**) such. For You **m**ake a way where there seems to be no way; You are the Way.**

*Thus says the Lord, who **m**akes a way in the sea and a path through the **m**ighty waters, who brings forth the **c**hariot and horse, the army and the power (they shall lie down together, they shall not rise; they are extinguished, they are quenched like a wick): 'Do not remember the former things, nor **c**onsider the things of old. Behold, (**expect** that) I will do a new thing, now it shall spring forth; shall you not know it? (Does not your **expectation** lie in it?) I will **m**ake a road in the wilderness and rivers in the desert.**

*Trust in **M**e... says the Lord...and with all your heart... that's **c**ompletely... and lean not – do not **c**ount or rely upon... your own understanding or opinions even your knowledge (that **c**an even include your **expectations**). In all (yep ALL), your ways submit, let go of, surrender and acknowledge Him – relying and **c**ounting on Him... and He will **m**ake your paths straight as He leads, guides, and directs you in all you do; through the decisions and **c**hoices you **m**ake... as He does.**

*I Your God... Your Lord, I go before you and will be with you; never leaving nor forsaking you for it is I who keeps you from all harm for I am watching over you night and day and for life. Indeed (so **expect**)... I the Lord, keep watch over you as you **c**ome and go both now and forever.* Hope (**expectation**) deferred **m**ake the heart sick... but, desire (**expectation**) fulfilled is a tree of life.**

---

*Footnotes: Chapter 5 Worthy Words / * See Psalm 119:105, Jeremiah 29:11, Psalm 16:11, 23:6, 77:19, Isaiah 43:16–19, Proverbs 3:5-6, Deuteronomy 31:8, Psalm 121:7-8, Proverbs 13:12 – all emphasis is mine and personal paraphrasing built on various translations and versions.

✧ CHAPTER 5 ✧

✧ *Establishing & Embracing... a journey with "Ee"*

"*Ahoy maties*", "*All board*", "*Bon Voyage*", "*Farewell*", *and* "*So long*" are all expressions associated with traveling and *journeying*. And, an exciting part of *our journey together*... and *together* with and in *Him*, is before us now with opportunities for a new kind of adventure and discovery.

Our *trip itinerary* suggests that we be certain we know the place we're departing from – yes, the *point of departure*... remember, it becomes as well a *point of access*. And, it's always good to know what is our *point of destination* when it comes to establishing and *embracing expectation*! Allowing both an *earthly* and a *heavenly* perspective to have its way.

So let's give *Him* access as we begin... inviting and allowing *Him* not just to be the *Author and Finisher*, but *Beginning and End* like we should... as you're encouraged to personally take into consideration the timeframe and pace you'd like to travel through the "*28 Day Journey*"... the pages of Chapters 5-8. For the engaging, embracing, and expansion of the establishing of "**e=mc3**" through *a journey* with *words of worth* now begins with "*e*", with "*m*", with "*c*", and with the pattern of "*3*" with their *encounters* and *experiences* they offer.

Holy Spirit, be the "GPS" that You are in our lives as we desire *God's* purposes, plans, and promises to position, posture and place us by *You, Holy Spirit*... the *Revealer* of all things, *Helper*, and *Teacher You* are.

There's a framework in place to assist you and it's created with flexibility and fluidity to offer a kind of *system* best for you when led by *His* leading:

> ➢ **28 days**... a **4 week journey** with **7 days** of *embracing and being empowered*... coupled with *expectancy* coming through e > m > and c *words of worth* all wrapping up in > 3... this is the "*original intent*" of the book for you to **encounter, engage in, and experience.**
> ➢ **Days**... a little here... a little there... a time of *His* leading at the pace of reading for the *process* He desires to meet you in.
> ➢ **With others**... there's a podcast opportunity to travel over 28+ weeks in the Appendices!

No matter the pace – *days, 28 weeks, months*... it's certainly **not** designated be a *formula* for winning a race or otherwise. But, designed *to build, grow, and enlarge* a new dimension and place of enriching the opportunity to develop and mature the establishing of our *relationship* that you... me... we have and are *expanding our expectancy* to have as we live more intentionally with and in *Him* in *expected* and un*expected* ways!

So *look, look again, to now look beyond* from where your *expectation* is presently ...into the place of where and how you desire to *embrace it and be empowered* by it. If uncertain... perhaps a "**ION**" word, remember the list of them, is trying to bring another *voice* into your place of decision? It might be worth revisiting that list and it's really a simple thing. Yet, it can be an interesting, even integral part, in how one of these **words** in the form and context of what it associates with and has attached to at this time in *your journey* and in *the process*.

Furthermore, a type of ac**tion** that has **e**ither happened, is attempting to happen, that will or needs to happen with *projection's* potential role at play. *Seek Him… He'll* be good to bring revelation to any needed attention given in any area addressing what's *hovering* there… as a direct or quite often subtle way of allowing *doubt, confusion, complacency* or **m**ore to have a place.

For **e**xample, in the path *He's* taken me in writing this… I've discovered in a very profound way the role "PROJECTION" plays in *expectation*. I found as I would attempt to determine what parts and pieces go where, let alone wondering who would **e**ver read this book… **m**uch got *projected* through doubt, fear, fear of man, intimidation, lack of **c**onfidence as a writer… into what would then arise with the potential of *influencing, directing or becoming* what I *did, would,* or *should expect* or give place to when I shouldn't. *God* is good in giving grace.

Expectancy indeed, is an *interesting* thing… but a **m**ost *fascinating* facet of the *process* of life… when you develop a greater awareness of its *potential, influence, and impact* in the **c**ontinualness of your life and life as *He* **expected** and planned it to be for us, for all.

God is good to help us. However, recognizing the way *hindrances* **m**ay try to stir up doubt or regret now, or in life in general is wise. It's no different over any part or any path as it attempts to become a portion of *our journey*; significant, insignificant, natural, or spiritual.

> ❖ *Perhaps*… you need to take a **m**inute here to invite *Him* in as the *Spirit of Truth, Revealer* and *Helper He* is? I'm **c**ertain *He'll* help you… me… us, unload anything that **m**ay have formed. Let us agree too, there's no **c**ondemnation, guilt, or shame in *Christ Jesus*… if it has, is, or is attempting to - just say NO. Recognizing it is key along with addressing it We only need the *suitcases* we're to take on this or any trip… not the excess "baggage"! Let's *journey* on now in a **c**onfident, **m**ore *hopeful expectancy*. And don't forget, *His expectancy* is there to join ours!

In this place I'm being reminded of how we **c**an sometimes see in a travel brochure a section where they share a **m**ore detailed *defining* of important aspects of where our travel is taking us to. Things that are important to **e**stablish and put into place before you go… so the foundation for a **m**ore *well-rounded* and *balanced* trip is grounded… and in such our defining of *expectancy* is set into place as well.

From simple *defining's, details, descriptions,* and *dimensions*… a loose, personal form of **e**xpressing **m**eaning has been released in these first **c**hapters, along with your own personal view that is arising. Let's now examine and discover a **m**ore formal view so we **m**ight broaden our *perspective, outlook,* and our *expectancy*… of what we will *expect and see* **m**anifest in the pages ahead. Taking a look now from an earthly perspective is in order.

Noah Webster 1828 dictionary on line shares this defining of *expectation*:

EXPECTA'TION, *noun* [Latin expectatio.] The act of *expecting* or looking forward to a future event with at least some reason to believe the event will happen. *Expectation* differs from hope. Hope originates in desire, and **m**ay exist with little or no ground of belief that the desired event will arrive. *Expectation* is founded on some reasons which render the event probable. Hope is directed to some good; *expectation* is directed to good or evil. The same weakness of **m**ind which indulges absurd *expectations,* produces petulance (**m**oodiness, sullenness, **c**rabbiness) in disappointment.

1. The state of *expecting*, either with hope or fear. **2.** Prospect of good to come. My soul, wait thou only on *God*, for my *expectation* is from him; . Psalms 62:5, **3.** The object of *expectation*; the *expected* Messiah. **4.** A state or qualities in a person which excite *expectations* in others of some future excellence; as a youth of *expectation*. We now more generally say, a youth of promise. **5.** In chances, *expectation* is applied to contingent events, and is reducible to computation (a formulating). A sum of money in *expectation* when an event happens, has a determinate value before that event happens. If the chances of receiving or not receiving a hundred dollars, when an event arrives, are equal; then, before the arrival of the event, the *expectation* is worth half the money.

Merriam-Webster on line dictionary shares a more current defining as:

Expectation / noun / ex·pec·ta·tion ˌek-spek-ˈtā-shən. 1: the act or state of *expecting*: anticipation in *expectation* of what would happen. 2a: something *expected,* not up to *expectations*, *expectations* for an economic recovery, 2b: basis for *expecting*: assurance they have every *expectation* of success, 2c: prospects of inheritance usually used in plural, 3: the state of being *expected*, 4a: **expectancy** sense to be, 4b: **expected** value.

Synonyms & Similar Words - relevance (relativity), anticipation, **expectancy, expectance,** *assurance, prospect, contemplation, alarm, apprehension, dread,* **misgiving,** *foreboding.* (Use of parenthesis and boldface mine in this defining.)

With these definitions comes clarity and connection regarding *expectation* as its arising to be *embraced*. Don't be afraid to go back to Chapter 4 that lays out what you may encounter and experience in the pages to remember the place and purpose of: ***words of worth*** and ***Worthy Words*** along with their, ***Meaning and Mission***… the connecting in our ***Meditation & Motivation***, along with how they create a place for ***Movement & Manifestation***

For within what they carry and release into your *expectancy* as we travel through this section, it is the intent in what is presented to enter into moments where there's an opportunity to reflect and write about what you: *Encounter & Experience… a Question or Challenge*, become more *Established & Empowered by The Word*, and be challenged to let it all come full circle, so to speak, into forming and birthing an: *Engaging & Embracing Expectation … a Decree or a Declaration.*

Yes, this book offers you choices – options for personalization and even expressions through your own writing as mentioned before. Just as it started off *in its beginnings* with a *telling* of pivotal personal *experiences* and *encounters* that played a role and were substantial valuable parts of my *life's journey*; *spiritually* especially. It's important you know my heart in suggesting and offering choices which is to help as you partner with <u>*His expectant* desire for you</u> and come to a place of knowing it's <u>ALL about what you'll *encounter* and *experience*</u> on this part of <u>YOUR *journey* and with YOUR *expectations* of, with, and in *Him*.</u>

❖ *Perhaps*… however it ends up looking… and in whatever way it unfolds and will become… what if for a moment anyway you imagine with me… could we even suppose it might turn out *He's* beginning the establishing of a part of your *telling* that's yet to come? *Oh heavenly expectancy of what He's has written about for you.*

Oh… the *"Tell them"* of *God*. It's not always about the way *I've*… *you've*… *we've* come… but the way we've *not* been before and *He's* drawing us into. I believe I'm hearing *His*, *"This is the* *way… walk ye in it… I am the Door, go through **Me** and **expecting to see** many doors to be before you. Their opening… closings… and the crossings of their thresholds that hold much beyond them." Come…enter and together with **Me**.*

Let's be open to and *expecting* the NEW, extending grace as we know the value and appreciation we feel when one honors and respects *the process* we're in… to the process they're in or any of us have been in – it's the stuff powerful testimonies are made of! And yes, let's *expect* that the **BEST IS YET AHEAD** for *you… me… us…* as we travel together with *expectancy* now and with *Him* on board… we'll have all we need!

Speaking of NEW things… I'm seeing a word, as if on a marquee made up of flashing neon lights – a long rectangular one with the letters **"P – I – L – G – R – I – M – A – G – E"**… *ahhh*, **"PILGRIMAGE"**. Yes, that's it, a NEW *word of worth being* highlighted and calling us into it because its more than a just a *word*… just *expect* and *see.*

It's what I believe *He's* eagerly desiring to reveal to us in a way to define and describe this *"kind"* of *journey* we're endeavoring and *expect* to enter into through a type of what could be called an eclectic energy… energy that's not fully of our own as it is fueled in part through those key components of our *expectant* **FAITH** and **HOPE** inwardly and towards *Him* because its fueled by an eternal *expecting* of **LOVE** – *receiving* it, *releasing* it, and *returning* it to *Him* for the essence of true *expectation* in the end is always about **HIM - who IS LOVE**.

There's an embedding of a form of extravagance that the *Father* lavishes on us… that will I believe be a most incredible part of this *3 fold cord* being woven in and through our *journey* since **HE – LOVE**, knows *He's* been invited in… or perhaps, *He* desires an awaited invitation to arrive? Don't worry, He'll RSVP favorably!

So… ♪*"What's love got to do with it?"* Everything as we will encounter and experience in pursuing this *adventure* together… and in some un*expected* ways. Particularly when this *telling* draws to an end and into the beyond of *expectancy!*

Oh… the *e=mc3*

e = *God **Eternal's Expectation*** in the   **m** = ***Mission*** of this voyage in *the journey of life* as **c** = ***Chartered*** by *covenant* love and purpose to the **3rd power** = ***Father, Son,*** and ***Holy Spirit*** in and with *you… me…* and for us as the *expectant* ones in *His family.*

✧ Day 1: The Journey of "e"... establish & E names

Let *expectations*... through this **word of worth's** part to *form, birth, and emerge in its* **meaning & mission** > *our meditation & motivation* > *as movement & manifestation* awake, arise and align in agreement with divine eternal *expectation!*

In considering the **meaning and mission** of the *word of worth* **establish**, let's explore together a few of the **E** names of significant beings **e**ternal and **e**arthly, **m**ale and female ... presented to us in the *Bible*, in the Christian faith, and beyond. Ones that *He* has highlighted to present and share about in a short summarized kind of **establishing** of them as ones with a **mission** connected to their **meaning** (eternal purpose), and it being **established** in *Him* and *His Word*.

> ❖ *Perhaps... He* will lead you to search them out **m**ore... possibly like being drawn to a *"tourist attraction"* in one's travels... presenting opportunities for the taking in of a special feature. **E**ven to **m**editate upon regarding who they are, what *God* did in and through them, and how that relates to where you are in life's **m**ission and *journey*. It's amazing how **His** drawing us to *"come look... stop for a moment over here..."* can open ways to add extended meaning, which often will **m**otivate us... bringing forth **m**ovement and **m**anifestation in an **expected...** or an **unexpected** pleasant and beneficial way. Not to **m**ention, in what it **establishes** in faith, for **expectancy** within our *foundations, functioning,* and *fellowship* with *God.**

El... **m**eaning *God – the one true God, power, mighty, goodly, great, idols, god, god-like one, false gods (demons, imaginations), might(y), mighty men of rank, mighty heroes, strength, power, Jehovah, Emmanuel.* So we can see where it is used for not only the true *God* we know but, false gods as well. *His* name is first **m**entioned indirectly in this scripture *"And Melchizedek king of Salem brought forth bread and wine: and he was the priest of the most high God (El)".** We will see *El* also in the next two names of *God*.

Elohim... *In the beginning God (Elohim) created by forming from nothing the heavens and the earth.**

El Shadai... *God Almighty* – our *Mighty God*... who is able to do and be what *He* says *He* is and will do in *His* overcoming power and all sufficient strength. First **m**entioning of *Him* as *Genesis* shares, *"When Abram was ninety-nine years old the LORD appeared to Abram and said to him, "I am God Almighty; walk before me, and be blameless."** Through the *journey* side of the setting of this book **m**ay we be, yes let us be... ones who are walking before *Him* blameless... **expecting** *Him* to be our *God* of the impossible who is faithful as we see *Him* **establishing** *Abram and Sari* in *Him* as such.

Take a **m**oment to take in who *He* is... and the **expectancy** that can arise in *Him*. In these three **E** names invite and allow *Him* to stir your **expectations** in the incredible, exceedingly powerful, **m**ajestic true, **c**reative, and **m**ighty *God He* is.

Eve... An **E** name from the beginning and of those **Elohim** first created in the expressed image and likeness of the fullness of *Him/Them*... and from *Him* in *Adam*. *Eve's* name finds its **m**eaning in *life* or *living*. *And Adam called his wife's name Eve; because she was the mother of* *all living.**   May we be like both ***Elohim*** and yes, *Adam* speaking words that conceive by *forming, bringing forth,* and *birthing* expressions filled with ***expectations…*** ultimately producing the manifestation of life and for living life as *He created, purposed,* and ***expected*** *in the beginning* and as *the Beginning He is…* and as *He* still ***expectantly*** does speak over us. *Oh* the power of speakings.

Elijah… who was a great prophet during the reign of *King Ahab* and whose name means "*my God is Jehovah*" or "*Yah(u) is God*".   A scripture with a key question regarding something *Elijah* asked comes to mind is, "*Elijah approached all the people and said,* "<u>How long will you hesitate between two opinions</u>? *If the Lord is God, follow Him; but if Baal, follow him.*" *But the people [of Israel] did not answer him [so much as] a word.*"*   What a question filled with an ***expected*** response which will **e**stablish **m**uch. Are we hesitating?

In **m**any places of ***expectancy*** in **m**y life, perhaps in yours too as ***expectations*** form, we discover the value of being wise to *look to see…* to recognize… and to acknowledge if there is a place of *hesita<u>ion</u>: a pause or wavering between two thoughts, mindsets, opinions, options?*   Remember our **ION** words?

As with the people *Elijah* was addressing, and just as *God* gave the power of choice to us in our free will in the beginning… choose with certainty and choose where you stand so you can move forward confidently… even courageously. May yours… mine… our choices be aligned with *His* for us and filled with ***expectancy*** they will bear good godly results.

Elisha whose name means "*God is salvation*" was a man of *God* who served the prophet ***Elijah*** and then succeeded him with the mantle of prophet continuing the prophetic ministry of the *Lord* and as well, performed the great miracles he did. Regarding ***Elisha***, this scripture shares a powerful principle, "*And when they had crossed over, Elijah said to Elisha,* "*Ask what I shall do for you before I am taken from you.*" *And Elisha said,* "*Please let a double portion of your spirit be upon me.*"*   Oh… the *double portion of God's spirit from Elijah to Elisha…* the **e=mc2!** May we ***expect*** double and more to come upon us by *His - Holy Spirit!*

Be encouraged to read in the books of *1* and *2 Kings* in the *Bible* the *rest of the story* of these two mighty men of *God* and discover more of the ***expectations*** they had in *God*, others had of *God* in them, and the evidence of such ***expectancy***!

Elisabeth… Now that's a familiar **E** name as it's mine, ***Elizabeth***, and means "*oath of God*", "*my God is my oath*"… a worshipper of *God*, and "*my God has sworn*". An *oath: pledge, promise, vow, assurance, your word.*   The wife of the priest *Zacharias*, mother of the prophet forerunner to *Jesus, John the Baptist*, and relative to *Mary*, the mother of *Jesus*.

My ***expectation*** always stirs and may yours too, when we read or remember this moment in *the journey* of the divine birth of *our Beloved Savior Yeshua Jesus* and in her life where… *At the moment her aunt heard Mary's voice, the baby within **Elizabeth's** womb jumped and kicked. And suddenly (in His **expectancy**), Elizabeth was filled to overflowing with the Holy Spirit! With a loud voice she prophesied (**expectantly**) with power:* "*Mary! You are a woman given the highest favor and privilege above all others, for your child is destined (as **expected**) to bring God great* delight. *How did I deserve such a remarkable honor to have the **m**other of **my** Lord? The **m**o**m**ent you ca**m**e in the door and greeted **m**e, **m**y baby danced excitedly inside **m**e with (**expectant**) joy! Great favor rests upon you, for you have believed (**expecting in**) every word spoken to you from the Lord."** **M**ay we *believe, encounter,* and *experience His Word* by *His Spirit Holy Spirit **establishing** His* purposes and plans within us… bringing favor and *God*-ordained ***expectancy*** for what *He* desires to birth and bring forth in the *earth*.

Enoch… *And Enoch… who walked with God… at the age of 365 years old, he was not - for God took him.** **M**entioned in the *Old* and *New Testaments* his name in both the *Hebrew* and *Greek* means *dedicated**. One **c**ould go in **m**any different ways when **c**onsidering ***Enoch…*** but, for the sake of the greater **m**eaning here it is interesting indeed, that his name's **m**eaning is established in being *dedicated… devoted… committed.* **M**ay we be like ***Enoch…*** *expecting* of ourselves a **c**omplete *dedication* in *our life's journey,* in all that lies beyond it, and in *His process* within our 24/7/365… so we'll be known as *one who walks with God*.

Esther… It's always good to take notice when *He* shows you a kind of picture or deeper **m**eaning and **m**ission ***established*** within a *word* – especially a *name*. For example, a fun one *He* showed **m**e was in ***Esther*** which means *star*. *He* revealed that within her names were two words: 'Est' 'her' and I heard, "*I **established** her and it was for such a time as this*"**… knowing it was for her to be a star in the **m**idst of a deep dark time where a spirit of death through annihilation was encroaching to wipe out the very existence *His* people – the Jews – much like today. There are indeed times where action is not only desired, but ***expected***. Yes, required when **c**onnected to and **e**ntwined in a greater eternal purpose *He* is or has ***established*** in *you… me… us*. **M**ay we be like ***Esther…*** *if I perish, I perish,* standing in *His* establishing.

Eistein… Although, not a biblical **E** name, it is a *Jewish* one and he was a *Jew*. Interestingly, within it ***Einstein*** the part ***ein*** in *Hebrew* **m**eans ***one*** and ***stein*** **m**eans ***stone***. Hmmm… ***one, stone…*** and that's *Yeshua… the Cornerstone… the Rock*. Remember, in that **m**iddle of the night **m**oment, I saw in *Albert's* eyes *His* eyes… and I've **c**ome to know just as *He* was drawing **m**e to *Him…* so did *He* draw him, but it is uncertain that he ever **c**ame to truly know *Him,* but did believe in *God*. **M**ay our **e**yes see as *He* sees… what is *relative* and the *relativity of it* in the foundations of the ***desired relationship He wants with us***. It was never at the **c**ore about a theory, let alone a formula. And, *the process* of it all being first *personal, intimate,* and *intentional…* then *purpose filled…* because we're ***established*** in our **c**onnecting, **c**onversing, and **c**ommuning in oneness with *Him* our *Rock* – the ***Eternal Expectant One***.

- ❖ *Perhaps… His **establishing*** within these **E** names of eternal and earthly beings there's been a form of *remembering, recalling… a recollection* of learning? **M**aybe recalling teachings that you've ***encountered*** or ***experienced*** that have been a blessing to you… benefitting and **c**reating an empowering building effect in the ***establishing*** of *Him, His* nature, **c**haracter, identity, authority, or *His Word*, will or ways in you? The ***establishing*** of *Him* in *you… me… us…* is of the utmost importance, particularly if we are *His*. For *His **expectancy expects*** in **e**arnest desire such fruit.

Establish… setting something firmly in place which confirms it as reliable and makes it stable – unchanging even… to found, start, begin, create, confirm, institute, prove, signify, inaugurate, authorize, form and more! *Oh* how the word more stirs much ~

This simple definition defines simply in words that mean the same… they *form, set in place,* and *confirm,* in and of themselves, so that we can start to *establish* the fact that they relate to *the process* or action of *establishing…* and, in an almost curious sort of uncanny way.

? So how important is that to understanding the need for our *expectancy* and *expectations* to be *established* beyond just knowing its meaning as a *word of worth* to embracing what we see as its *mission, job, assignment, or task* as it relates to our mission it reveals – the more?

Well, there's an overshadowing hovering as it sounds like something we read that's been said already… as it should just by virtue of its overall meaning being… *that which confirms and connects us* to why our focus now must be intentional to embrace this *word of worth*. To *establish* and consider *establishing* a foundational principle of what *God* desires to be… and must be, as a part of what *He* requires in *His Worthy Word* towards us always.

Yes, *establish* is a word that has been used already in these writings and will be throughout because it distinctly has taken on a place as a *word of worth* for grounding what we *expect* in the essential part of what *forms, starts, begins, creates,* and *emerges* giving life to our *expectancy* and beyond! What a place *establishing* and being *established…* has in *the process…. yours, mine… ours.*

Let's take a look now at this related verse regarding *Noah,* which also holds the place of being the *first mention* of this **"e"** word being used in the *Word of God*. It seems there's a degree of light *He* wants to shed about its value…so let's be wise to pursue and discover it.

*… But as for you, I will **establish** my covenant of friendship, and you will escape destruction by coming into the ark, you and your wife, your sons and their wives.**

Remember, firsts are important to *God…* as well as first mentioning. There were the **E** Names… but the *word* before us that *He* led to share first in *our journey with e* is **establish.**

A word that reveals *God* desiring, and not just in this case, to *establish* a covenant with *Noah* and equally with *you… me… us…* along with friendship. And not just any ole friendship… but, *covenant friendship*. The connecting of it to a promise and that such a relationship with *Him* can enable us with the ability to bring forth of a way to escape *destruction* and *death…* and some might say, *damnation…* because of *His* covenant with *Noah*. For those in this kind of relationship with *Him…* we have an eternal *establishment* of covenant promises as *He* is a covenant keeping *God.* Who is/has *He* placed in your life that you can help, through *Him*, escape destruction and death leading them to eternal life and friendship with *Him*?

Beginnings matter – *He* is the Beginning… and *He* still is moving to create an awareness that even though sin came and *He* had to flood the earth, *His* heart and original intent in covenant love with man over time remains, as it was, and is to be with *His family*. Did **He** not save *Noah's* family? That desire extends to save all and all families… and they be **born again** and return to be *His* sons and daughters… *family*. Can you imagine *His expectancy*?!

The *establishment* of what came in the beginning matters. And it came through words as *He* who is *the Word*... *He* spoke and released the essence of *Himself* and *His* creative power... revealing that were these words were **worthy words** and vitally important to know.

Establish*...** how could it not be in this underlying significant part of the start of this pivotal *pilgrimage* we've begun? It provides a way to seek *God* in *our journey* through special and holy times and places in the *ongoing process* of all *He* has, is, and will ***establish. It has the power to increase and enlarge *your* faith... *my* faith... *our* faith, as we potentially **embrace** and encounter spiritual growth. With it all being perceived and received by *Him*... as an intentional and genuine act of devotion dedicated to *His* and our mutual arising **expectancy** in many *facets*... and in the *forms* and *functions* that materialize in the *flow*!

*Thus saith the LORD the Maker thereof, the LORD that formed it, to **establish** it; the LORD is His name. Call (expectantly) unto Me, and I will answer you, and show you great and mighty things, which you do not know.* * Oh the *establishing* in a "Thus saith the Lord!" ~ Amen.

There's a hand-in-hand kind of *togethering He* does in *His **establishing***. A way *He* connects and confirms things... like how *He* reveals much within this *verse* mentioned... as it carries the essence for ***establishing*** life in it - in *His Words*. **Worthy Words** that tell us the importance of ***establishing*** the idea that *God* doesn't reveal everything clearly to us all the time. Sometimes *He* will conceal... keeping hidden something for an appointed time. Then... *He* draws and leads us into a seeking and searching of it ... uncovering it... for *His* revealing to us. To me and maybe for you too... it seems within the concealings and uncoverings ...there lies *His* desire for and an invitation always to *relationship*... and with a way to ***establish*** it.

He wants *you*... *me*... *us grounded, rooted* and ***established*** in the truth – in *Him, His Word*, in which *He* is the *Truth* and it is truth. Truth ***establishing*** us in our identity, what we believe our inheritance to be, as well as the authority we believe we have. and in *Him* who is *Truth*. Why? Covenant requires such... and, *He* desires and commands it and all in love.

*In the same way you received Jesus our Lord and Messiah by faith(**expecting**), continue your journey of faith (**expectancy**)... progressing further into your union with Him! Your spiritual roots go deeply into His life as you are continually infused with strength, encouraged in every way. For you are established in the faith you have absorbed and are enriched by your devotion to Him!*
* WOW!

All things are made for Him, in Him, by and from Him.* It is ***established***... for it is written. *As He is... so are we. Be ye holy for I am holy.** Now that's ***established*** and it's written in the New as a type of *echo*. But, a *very vital voice* in the new *He's* called and is drawing us into. *Oh the voice... His that **establishes***

As we approach the end to this day's part of our trip... let's go back to where it began - *Genesis 1-3*. For *He*, the *Author and Finisher, Beginning and End* who wants to ***establish*** a *fundamental formation* in our *foundation*. In *HIM* and in the fullness of *Them **established***.

Sometimes *He* reveals deep things you're not fully ready for. But... you grab ahold and hold on because you learn what's at the other end is really good. Yet... in the everything in between is a *very good* as well. So I've grabbed on and I'm still in the in-between... of the depths and dimensions unfolding in all *He* established in those first *three* chapters of *His Word* to us. Aren't you glad *He establishe*s and **m**akes **e**verything beautiful in its time!

Fundamentally, there was and remains an overall understanding of an invaluable vital and underlying powerful **c**oncept for ones who seek and search for deeper things, at least for me. When we **c**hoose to look **c**loser and in a broader sense… there seems to be an ***establishing** in the beginning* of ***our work is our worship and our worship is our work***. They are one and **m**eant to be one in *Him* – the *One*. Because in *common/ life union, communion* in *Him*, and with and in the partaking of the *Tree of Life* which is what *He* is… as it was in the beginning with *His* **c**reated ones *Adam and Eve*… where they were one, in *echad,* * with and in the fullness of *Him* who is **El.**

That's how *He* unfolded and revealed it for **m**e. *He* called it *His **www.** His **world wide web*** where **our *worship and work are one*.** A **c**hoosing of this kind of life as a *lifestyle* in and with *Him* and where all is as unto *Him* who has ***established*** and will ***establish*** us is in what *He* purposes and desires. Afterall, we're *His* family and the ones who *He* had and still has an *expectation* in and of to rule and reign in the **e**arth so *His* kingdom **c**an **c**ome and will be done as it is in heaven. In your *expectancy* is there an *expectation* of such?

May *He **establish*** it in you and **m**ore … in us, *His **established*** **c**ovenant ones in *His original intent*. Now *go, do, and be* by **c**ontinually becoming and being fully in *Him grounded, rooted*… and yes, exclusively **established in Him.**

e=mc3   e > establish = m > manifest My   c > covenant to the 3rd power with the **3 fold cord** of ***Them – Father, Son, Holy Spirit*** … what an *establishing* of a formula relative to an *eternal expectancy* of and *foundationally* in and through *relationship in sonship*… and because **covenant** love.

In light of this ***word of worth… establish & E Names*** and what's been shared:

- ❖ *Perhaps*… you **Encountered or Experienced a Question or Challenge**? Write it out…

- ❖ *Perhaps*… more has been **Established & Empowered by the Word?** Write what/which…

❖ *Perhaps...* it's time for **Engaging & Embracing your Expectations?**
Write what's forming...

Reminder: For *clarity, connection, and confirmation* regarding **expectancy** being stirred by this *word of worth*, seek *Him* and *His Word* first. To possibly assist you in *the process* the list of **ION** words is available in the Appendix.

*Footnotes: Chapter 5 Day 1 establish & E names / * See Genesis 6:18 TPT, I John 4:17, Jeremiah 33:2-4, Colossians 2:6-7 TPT, I Peter 1:15-16 and Leviticus 19:2, Genesis 1-3, Jeremiah 1:9, Strongs Concordance H259 echad, Genesis 5:24, Strongs Concordance H2585 hanok and G1802 henoch, Genesis 14:18, Strongs Concordance H410 el, Genesis 1:1, Strongs Concordance H430 elohim, I Kings 17:1, Strongs Concordance H452 eliya, II Kings 2:9, Strongs Concordance H477 elisa, Esther 4:14, Strongs H635 ester, Luke 1:41-45, Strongs Concordance G1665 elisabet, Genesis 3:20, 4:1, Strongs Concordance H2332 hauva - all emphasis is mine and personal paraphrasing built on various translations and versions.

✧ Day 2: The Journey of "e"... echad

*Let **expectations**... through this **word of worth's** part to form, birth, and emerge in its **meaning & mission**... our meditation & motivation... as movement & manifestation awake, arise and align in agreement with divine eternal **expectation**!*

In these first few days *He's* drawing some of the "e" words into an ordering. Will the days ahead always flow in a connected sense of ordering... or through a commonality of *themes* directly or indirectly that create an opportunity for such in the *words of worth* presented for us to explore?

No, not always... and that's such an empowering element to understand. It carries an ability to free us to extend and enlarge the potential in the possibilities for what we can or might *expect* as we travel experiencing *expectations* as they arise, change, dimmish, or are fulfilled.

There will be attempts to keep a flow in the adventure each day and what words offers. Additionally let us be eager to embrace that each *word of worth* has value in and of itself – just as *you... me... we* do. What we *expect* that attaches through the way it becomes associated in its meaning, mission, and more... and with any *expectation* forming. It's such a unique and wonderfully individual encounter that layering too much might create a kind of *forced relationship* or relativity that could hinder its exclusive place and purpose in the moment and the movement of *expectancy*.

As we begin it does seem appropriate... even beneficial, to draw from our previous word *establish* to do exactly what it means assisting us in *establishing... rooting and grounding* these chosen words as they are launched into *our journey*. Truly each plays a basic integral part that makes a way to enhance how our *expectations* can come *together*... in their building upon one another in how or what they naturally and spontaneously bring forth and into place.

Let's reflect back to the beginning revealed in the ending of *Day 1*... where in *Genesis* we were considering and reflecting on the eternal establishing that was being done then. Since our NEW *word of worth echad**, in its beautiful simplicity simply means *one / oneness*, we see a natural form of continuity and connection that wants to form. Additionally, it means *single, first, alone, unity, united*. We can also see how *echad*, in its effortlessness as *one,* truly moves to evoke a place for *oneness*.

There we read about an encounter where there was an unfolding... of an establishing. Its inter... and inner-connectedness with *God* was with *His* creation and within them. *He* spoke with *His* breathe and word creating which began a connection. In *His* created ones... human beings male & female... *He* was one with them and they were one with *Him*. Fashioned and formed in *His* image and likeness in *echad*; as one, unified, yet single, unique, whole ... in *Him*... the *One* comprised of *Them*... and in them.

An atmosphere and environment where a divinely designed pure form of unity was embedded in the very fabric and essence of *Him* as *Creator* and all creation and through an *expectancy* and *expectation* that *Father* had which manifested as a manifestation of *expectation* in us.

Never separated, but always intersected, entwined in *Him*, in *Them* whose image they and we were-are **m**ade in, as an **e**stablished work for *His* kingdom **e**stablishment on and in the **e**arth. *Original intent.* For the *work* entrusted to them and through them for the purpose of having dominion, being fruitful, **m**ultiplying, and replenishing the **e**arth. Their **work being their worship** in a **c**ommunion union life with *Him* which was the fullness of **all they did as unto Him**. So very simple, *extravagantly beautiful, purposefully powerful,* and *exclusively established* by *God*.

Sin **c**ame quickly to **e**stablish its hold in this **c**ommunion union. The life they had and became no **m**ore, after they opened the door to another form of union thru the intersection of their intentional interaction with **e**ating of *the Tree of the Knowledge of Good and Evil*.

The disruption of *echad* **e**stablished in **c**ommunion union with *life* **c**ame through *the Tree of Life* too as they were **e**ating of it. Interestingly **e**nough… it **c**ame in the disguise of a thought, of a greater *expectation* of *echad*; a deceived and perverted kind of oneness that said, *"Surely you will not die, but you will be like God."*. With such *expectancy* in the serpent's words, he allured and beguiled them into *expecting* **m**ore… causing them to forget what they already had – they were like *God* and **e**ven one *with Him*. They had everything they needed in *Him*… who was their *God*. Did they not know?

Since that time of *spirit to spirit* union in *echad*, where **e**verything in the spirit of **m**an - that which *He* knew and formed before *He* placed us in the womb of our **m**other*… and in which *He* placed in it an inner knowing **c**onnected to being and belonging through *echad* and it only in *Him*. It is likened unto that which the **e**arth is said to know as it groans and travails, along with all of **c**reation, and with an **e**arnest *expectation* for the **m**anifestation of the *Sons of God* again to arise and be **e**stablished as they were in the beginning.

A sign, I believe of such attempting to arise… will be when we *His* **c**reated ones, know again that ***our work is our worship and our worship is our work,*** as we're about our *Father's* business in our ***being one again through being born again***, and in living out of such **e**stablishing that **c**ame to *re*-**e**stablish the NEW **m**an in us! Only something *He* **c**an do.

Jesus walked in and **m**odeled this for us as *Son of God, Son of Man*. In **c**oming to serve, not to be served. In **c**oming to give *His* life as a ransom for **m**any as the *Lamb of God He* was… and, from *His* place of **c**ommunion union with *Father God*. *His* desire was to do the will and work *He* was purposed for. It was **e**stablished for *Him* and *Him* giving the purest form of *His* work as worship to the *Father* and for all the world *God* so loved.

Everything about *Him*, who *He* was, what *He* did in *His* life was and still is in obedience to *Father*. What *He* desired, required… for obedience is the better sacrifice; it's worship and it's work. It's where *Adam and Eve* lived from until they fell from the ***establishment*** of *God* in **e**arth in the garden into an ***unexpected***, ungodly ,and potentially ***eternal*** **e**vil ***establishing***. No longer one in the ***Established One.***

Father's heart was and is and will always be for ***echad***: one…*communion union – individually, collectively, corporately.* *Father's* ***establishing*** of a plan for such **c**ame from before the foundations of the world. It's the underlying essence in the foundation of *His* love for us. Or is it actually in its pureness... *union in communion*?

In giving them, *you...me... us...* free will to choose and to choose whether to be one with *Him*, who is *The Tree of Life*, He **established** that we could **expect,** in all certainty, that choice would be and still is available to us. In our choosing from where, from whom, and in any form of *oneness... echad,* of which we desire to encounter *body, soul,* and particularly in our *spirit...* it would be up to us. It remains, *His* divinely created design was and still is for **echad** with *Him, Them,* as one.

How would we settle for anything else? For a lesser form and source of *union communion* that's not in true aligning with *Him* as designed... where *our work is work and our worship is worship?* For it has separated us each from *Him* as our sacrifice due to sin goes to another god – the serpent (*Hasatan*)... and to the god of self. Both representing choices not of *Him* coming solely from an *establishing* in self over *God*, and in the *Tree of the Knowledge of Good and Evil.* For yes, there were two trees **established** and it was the other tree, *The Tree of Life* which is *Him,* as *He* **established** in the garden in the beginning... and remains in the garden of our lives to choose between today. Do not waiver; choose.

In the continualness of choosing that life presents **may** *you... me... we,* always remember *He* did what *He* did and does what *He* does because of LOVE... covenant love from *Him* who is LOVE. *He* loved and loves us *His* creation so abundantly, fully, purely, and wholly; like no other can love. Therefore, *He* out of the core essence of that love made a way to *reconcile, return,* and *set back* into place divine order so *His* perfect will to come on earth and in earthen vessels again... as it is in heaven. It is what *He* said to say when we pray.

Entwined in *original intent* is remaining in being **established** as the **echad** ones... in oneness in the *One*. Any disruption of that *communion union* intersection with *God* in **echad** – in heaven and earth coming in *Him* to them - has now been *redeemed, restored,* and *reconciled* to us through *Jesus the Firstborn Son* and the atoning work of the blood on the cross through *Father's* love in us *His* **established** ones.

- ❖ *Perhaps...* we're being empowered by an embedded **expectancy** that lies within the ordering of **words of worth,** *one upon and within the other* as He led in **Day 1** with **establish** and now in **Day 2** with **echad?** Let there be Lord, and be it so.

But wait... there's always a *beyond* as it continually unfolds through the *process* and in *our life journey* with *Him*. So let's look now at another side of *echad...* the side that connects and presents us with an opportunity to see the extra coming in the *addings* of *God*.

Let's extend this concept of being ones... who encountering **oneness** in *Him...* opens a door to consider and possibly include that idea that a form of divine eternal energy is produced within and a part of this '*being one - echad*' and form of **oneness**.

A divine exchange of sorts and by *His* spirit to us, to our *born again* new man... that new creature in *Him* as likened to when it all began... as the *Holy Spirit* hovered and brooded over the surface of our heart, our soul… and revealed truth – truth in love and through *Love* to us in *Him* powerfully calling and drawing us to reconcile us back to *God* – back to being **echad** in the *One*.

Remember, a fundamental element of our eternal purpose as set forth in the beginning, is that we have allowed and entered into an ***establishing*** as one could say where **our work is to be our worship… and our worship is to be our work** with all as unto *Him* the *One*. And, it should come from us being one in the *common union of our communion* Then we must enlarge the oneness formed in our ministry, which is our work/worship wholly being one too, not only in our ***expectations*** but our view… our perspective and all that makes it what it is.

Therefore, it is essential to include other portions of the ***meaning*** and ***mission*** of ***echad***… as revealed, portrayed, and displayed in and through the life and ministry on earth of *God as God the Son Jesus - Son of God, Son of Man* for *He* truly modeled it most excellently.

There was one who came before, however. The son of *Zacharius*, the priest and his wife *Elizabeth*, who had been barren… but *God*. And so was born, *John the Baptist* – the *Immerser*, whose ministry included making the way. The way from the old into the new in *the journey* of the progression and eternal timeline *of God's Holy Word*. The way he prepared for *Yeshua, The Word* with the message to repent… to turn and be baptized for the *kingdom of God* is at hand. His purpose becoming united with the greater cause and requirement for *Jesus* that *He* would ultimately fulfill as *Lamb of God* and in ***echad***… as *one, united, single, alone*, and as the *Firstborn and Only Begotten Son*.

Jesus knew *He* was to embrace this ***expectation***. After all, *He* was *God* incarnate – in the flesh. *He* embraced it for us the world *He* was sent to… and, for *Himself* as He desired to please *His Father, our Father*. As *Son of God He* undeniably was perfect, sinless… the blemish free sacrificial *Lamb*. But, in *His* humanity as *Son of Man, He* must be one with that role, partaking in all *Father* had ordered and aligned in this establishing of *His* kingdom to come on earth and what had been established in ***expectation*** before the foundation.

Down into the river… into the water of baptism *He Yeshua* went. In part a picture of the current old order of priesthood represented in *John*… only to come up out of the waters and into the rest of the picture presenting a new view of the *new priesthood* that was before them. Baptizing not just with water… but a baptizing in the *Spirit* as *Holy Spirit* descended ***expectantly*** upon *Him*… and as the *Father* spoke over *Him His* pure and holy pleasure.

For this was not just the new order, but a *royal eternal priesthood* ordering that we claim in our identity and inheritance in *Christ* today… a re-establishing of what came forth through *Abraham*… and back into the order of *Melchizedek**. It was and is who we are and for such a time. What **expectancy** stirs as we're just beginning to step into this portion of our eternal **kingdom identity** as *His chosen, peculiar people, a holy nation**. And as well…. *to Him who loved us and washed us from our sins in His own blood, and has made (as He **expected**) us kings and priests to His God and Father, to Him be glory and dominion (**expectantly**) forever and ever. Amen."**

He never desired nor does *He* desire for us to be separate from *Him*, but in **echad**; *oneness, unity, unified, aligned,* and in *agreement* with *His* divine design in its fullness. The fullness of *original intent*... the fullness of the **c**ommunion *He* **m**eant us to *encounter, experience, express,* and live from **c**ontinually and **c**onsistently. Remember, **c**reation is on its tiptoes waiting with *expectancy!* **M**ay we *expect* and **c**ome into greater *echad* with *Him* for *His* divine plan with our part and piece **expectantly.**

"*Shema Israel, Adonai eloheinu Adonai echad* ~ *Hear O Israel, the Lord is our God, the Lord is One*"* **M**ay those who have an **e**ar to hear what *He*... by *His Spirit, Holy Spirit*, is saying, and an **e**ye to see and respond knowing... for *to whom* **much** *is given – much is required.** And this *oneness* requires **m**uch ... *You shall (in all* **expectation***) love the Lord your God with all your heart and* **m**ind *and with all your soul and with all your strength... your entire being.** All... it **m**eans all.

When we surrender and submit, along with **c**onsecrating and dedicating ourselves fully to *Him* in the fullness of such **c**ommunion relationship... becoming... being one, *echad*... with *Him*, in *Him*, through and by *Him*... we see how it produces real true **c**hange in us... which yields a fruitfulness we **c**annot produce on our own... for an exchange has to happen and has. *Oneness* **c**omes as *reformation* through *restoration* turning the wheels of *reconciliation* so the ordering aligns in *echad*... and with **m**agnificent glorious *transformation*!

We exchange fully dying daily to our self; who we were in and of ourselves. For who we are now in *Him*, do you... am I... are we... living from that place and posture positioned in *echad* fully and wholly in *Him expecting* such of ourselves? Of **e**ach other? As *His Disciples, His Church* and *Bride, His Ekklesia, His kingdom governing ones* who are *His Family* of sons and daughters? For without *Him* we **c**an do nothing...

"*I am a true sprouting vine, and the farmer who tends the vine is My Father. He cares (with* **expectancy***) for the branches connected to Me by lifting and propping up the fruitless branches and pruning every fruitful branch to yield a greater (***expectant***) harvest. The words I have spoken over you have already cleansed you. So you* **must** *remain in (***expectancy** *of) life-union (echad) with Me, for I remain in life-union (echad) with you. For as a branch severed from the vine (***expectantly***) will not bear fruit, so your life will be fruitless unless you live your life intimately joined to Mine.*

"*I am the sprouting vine and you're My (***expecting***) branches. As you live in union with Me as your source, fruitfulness will stream from within you—but when you live separated from Me you are powerless. If a person is separated from Me, the is discarded; such branches are gathered up and thrown into the fire to be burned. But if you live in life-union with Me and if My words live powerfully within you (in His* **expectancy***) —then you can ask whatever you desire and it will be done. When your lives bear abundant fruit, you demonstrate that you are My mature (***expectant***) disciples who glorify My Father!**

"*I love each of you with the same love that the Father (with all* **expectancy***)loves Me. You* **must** *continually let My love nourish your hearts. If you keep My commands, you will live in My love, just as I have (***expectantly***) kept my Father's commands, for I continually live nourished and* *empowered by His love. My purpose for telling you these things is so that the joy that I experience will fill your hearts with overflowing gladness!**

How the *Worthy Word* **e**mpowers us as we **m**ove gladly into *our journey* together. But, at any point we are blessed that we **c**an start or begin anew… lining up **e**very aspect of our *expectations* in such, through such, and for such so good fruit… lasting, **m**ultiplying fruit… kingdom fruit **m**anifests that gives glory to *Him*! That's the fruit of ***echad!***

Jesus prayed *(from **e**xpectancy within)*… that all **m**ay be one *(echad)*; just as You, Father, are in Me and I in You, that they also **m**ay be one *(echad)* in Us, so that the world **m**ay believe *(in* ***expectation****) without doubt that You sent **M**e.** Will they believe *He* has sent us – that we are *His* let alone ***echad*** with *Him?*

Let our ***expectations*** *awaken, arise, and align* as one in the *One* and into what *He* has as *His* expected end for us..

e=mc3   ***echad = manifesting the completeness of Christ*** by **the 3rd power, Holy Spirit's** place… in **m**aking us one.

<u>In light of this **word of worth… echad** and what's been shared:</u>

- ❖ *Perhaps*… you **Encountered or Experienced a Question or Challenge**? Write it out…

- ❖ *Perhaps*… **m**ore has been **Established & Empowered by the Word**? Write what / which…

- ❖ *Perhaps*… it's time for **Engaging & Embracing your Expectations**? Write what's forming…

Reminder: For *clarity, connection, and confirmation* regarding ***expectancy*** being stirred by this *word of worth*, seek *Him* and *His Word* first. To possibly assist you in *the process* the list of **ION** words is available in the Appendix.

Footnotes Chapter 5 Day 2 echad / See Strongs Concordance H259 echad, Genesis 1-3, Deuteronomy 6:4, Luke 12:48, Genesis 14, Psalm 110, and Hebrews 7, I Peter 2:9, Revelation 1:5-6, John 15 and 17 - all emphasis is mine and personal paraphrasing built on various translations and versions.

✧ Day 3: The Journey of "e"... essence

Let *expectations*... through this **word of worth's** part to *form, birth,* and *emerge*
in its **meaning & mission**... **our meditation & motivation**... as **movement & manifestation**
awake, arise and align in agreement with
divine eternal *expectation*!

Although there can be a certain ordinary form of what we can **expect** via a *route, path, or way* designated to take on *a journey*... how it looks and presents itself, including what it offers or makes us aware of, how it can change more than we think, and how this can happen more often than we realize or desire... particularly if we've never been this way before. So it is, in a similar way, with a word... even our **words of worth.**

We assign certain **expectations** to them in *the process*... but must be aware of and open to what each unique *trip,* setting, and scenario offers and the way it influences or impacts what we **expect** related to that word. We can understand the foundation of a word. But, in its fuller meaning (like in a setting or scenario) as we gain revelation in the greater *depth, dimension,* and *demonstration* of it as a *noun, verb, adjective*... singularly or in plural... with a prefix or suffix added... or in its tense: *past, present, future.*

All bring us into a type of a *relationship* with that word that allows its *relativity* – how it is *relative* and its *relatability* – how it relates, and its *purpose* comes more alive to us. Not to mention what happens to it when we discover it in another language, such as in the *Bible* through these primary ones: *Hebrew, Greek, Aramaic* or *Latin*... and **English.**

Now take that word, put it within a sentence, and determine is it a *subject or noun* - the *person, place, or thing* it is about. Is it the *predicate* - simply what the subject is or does, which includes a *verb* - the word expressing action or a state of being? Or is it an *adjective* - a describing or modifying word? You *gotta* love the place for grammatical structure!

Not in an educational learning kind of way... but in a *practical life application* one, they really do all play a part within the dynamics of our knowledge and understanding of the word just like the formation of a word does. And... just like things along the *path, route, or road* we're traveling on are a part of the forming of it. What we **encounter or experience** through this *word of worth* in its fullness... most assuredly affects our **expectancy** and its overall effects within **expectations** that arise.

With that in mind... let's take a look at the word '*essence*' and what it embodies in its defining and see if we'll discover an interesting connection unfolding ~

Essence – *spirit of, core, substance, heart, embodiment, sum of, crux, beginning of a thing, bone/marrow, aspect of, odor, fragrance, characteristics, nature of, attributes, element of being or entity, existence/divine nature, the seed of*... a person or thing... and at times can be related to the describing of the *atmosphere or environment* of a place. Interesting ~

Let's take a more direct look at an example that connects it to the establishing of *echad* as we see in... *I and the Father are one (echad) established in essence and nature.** What a fascinating picture of our first *three* words of worth! Where essentially (the **essence** of) or basically we see that there is a connection both spiritually, naturally, and for our sake – as an example that shows a depth that the ***essence*** of **m**eaning and usage in a sentence **c**an *form, bring forth, and add* to our *process* and our ***expectancy*** therein !

Can we... do you suppose we **c**ould **e**ven see a **c**oming alive to the beginning of ***essence***... for does *He* not say... *in the beginning was the Word and the Word was God and the Word was with God**.... He is *the Word*. Therefore, just as we've **e**ncountered this **c**onnection in the word ***establish*** and the word ***echad,*** we see it again now in a layering that is **m**ost **c**ritical if we desire to know the ***essence*** of what **m**akes up... and **m**akes *us - yours... mine... **our expectations*** – is it, are they just of us... or of *Him?* Does a **c**onfirmation not **c**ome that brings the *Three* of them established in the echad of the ***essence*** *formed* and birthed... as well as the *manifestation* thereof in us... in the *process*... in the *journey?*

Let's **e**xplore a little further for some validation of this kind of underlying thought... remembering, thoughts with our beliefs and perspective are at the **c**ore and ***essence*** of what **m**akes up our ***expectations***!

In the *Word of God* we'll see in the *Greek* a word *ousia*. Translated into *English* it becomes the ***word of worth*** we're getting to know – ***essence***. And, *ousia* merely **m**eans, *that which makes something what it is considered to be; the essence of it.* You **c**ould **e**ven **c**ouple it with the *Greek* word *zoe* meaning *existence, as it exists* and also means *life – abundant life.* Encompassing it all in the natural or physical realm... and the spiritual realm which often refers to an eternal type of life. Sounds like something good to **c**onnect what we ***expect*** to!

Oh the determining... of what is and is not ***essential*** in what we bring together to **m**ake up what we ***expect,*** why we ***expect*** it, and all the other details that **m**ake it us. **C**reating a need for the ***essentialness*** of what lies in the ***essence***... the *foundation, attributes*, and very *core* of its nature where we **c**an actually sense a generating of a type of **e**nergy ideally good and godly... with all the *vigor, liveliness, and powerful potential* it **c**arries as the ***essence*** of the force/*Force* behind... within... and **c**oming from a source/ *Source*.

It **e**xemplifies... *representing, illustrating,* and *showing* the power not just of the ***essence*** this force and source of energy **c**arries, but perhaps what it is – and yes, **e**ven WHO it is or from? For if our ***expectation*** is a part of a new beginning that demonstrates the ***essence*** of our origins of our beginning... then the ***essence*** of our ***expectation*** **m**ust be in aligned in and by *Him*... He who is *Beginning & End, Alpha & Omega, First & Last... Author & Finisher... the Word* alive, full of life power in its divine ***essence***... and sharper than a two **e**dged sword!

Oh the **c**onfirmations that **c**an and will **c**ome in *the process* as *you... me... we... **expect*** such partnering together with *Him* and by/with *Holy Spirit*. What fruit will **c**ome from that trusting and abiding in the *Vine*... in the ***expectancy*** that will be established for the ***essence*** of this level of **c**ommitment and sincere devotion in *the process* going on is indeed of the utmost importance... because we know *God* has an ***essence*** as well... that which we will **c**all *the* or *His Divine **essence*** in *His* **exclusive** or godly *Divine Essence*. And, if you are *His* – a born again **c**hild of *God* – that divine ***essence*** *of the Divine Essence of Yahweh our God,* is alive and active in you. Be aware... yes, some use this name for ungodly sources and forces.

   ❖   *Perhaps*... it ***essence*** is essential in its part in linking us to *Him?* How... "*He knew us before He formed us and put us in our mother's womb!** *Oh*... that ***essence***... divine DNA ***essence* and *in His knowing!*** For did *He* not in and from the ***essence*** of *His* love for *He is*... **c**hose us in Christ... selecting us as *His* own and before the foundation of the world... so that we would be in *His* sight holy, **e**ven blameless, **c**onsecrated, and set apart for *His* purposes?* Yet, we would get to choose.* So stop right now, choose to receive from *Him, yours... mine... our Father, our God,* and *our Creator...* the **essence** of *His* **e**ndless redeeming ove for you. Feel it wrapping around you, **e**mbracing you... **e**ngulfing anything that is not of *Him* letting it **e**nfold you in becoming the **expectant one** *His* **essence** *in you* is **m**ade for and **m**eant to *be*.

Oh, the relativity and relatability which **c**omes in *the journey* and adventure of our *process* in relationship with *Him. Oh,* to **expect** to **see**! Remember, there **m**ay be some things that will attempt to *form* a perspective in *the process* that a relationship **m**ay or **m**ay not require. So indeed... the **essence** of the fruit such will produce and **e**ven reproduce is evidence of where **e**stablished oneness is **e**ither **e**vident or not.

*"And as **essence** of Christ Himself is seen for who He really is, who you really are (the **essence** of the true you) will also be revealed (as is **expected**), for you are now one with Him in His glory!"* * Where... *"the fundamental fact of (the **essence** of) existence is that this trust in God... this faith... it is the firm foundation under everything that **m**akes life (in the fullness of its **essence**) worth living – especially in Him who is Life (the ousia zoe **essence**). It's our handle on what we can't see."**

Oh... **m**ay we always **expect life**! May our **expectation** also be and become not just for the **essence** of such *individually*... but, *collectively* and *corporately* as the body of **Christ** – *His* **kingdom covenant family** and as His Ekklesia – His Church and ultimately His Beloved Bride.

Remember... He has spoken it therefore it is **e**minent and will... **m**ust become evident... as the glory evidence in *you... me... us...* the **m**anifestation of the *Sons of God*. Yes... we have **this power, this essence, this spirit...** *Holy Spirit*, in our earthen vessels. **His** power to the **third degree** which is <u>not</u> just a form of... and ONLY of and from *God* in us!

$e = mc3$... **essence** within **expressed** without = **m**atter **c**onstructed, **c**reated, **c**rafted by the **c**ircling in its fullness into and with the **3rd degree power** of *Holy Spirit* in *His* **c**reation...us.

$e = mc3$ ... will always draw you back as *Holy Spirit* **m**oves (full **c**ircle) to *Him...* where your **expectation** fully fulfilled **c**an only be *in Him*. That's what the energy of the **essence** of *Him* who is LOVE does – it draws and **c**alls... as it's the only thing entirely able to fill the empty void, the longing, and for belonging. *Oh yes,* **<u>It is a relationship... not a formula</u>**. Just as *He* said... as *He* spoke in an intimate intentional whisper to me and will to you.

Selah ~ Holy Spirit... in the fullness of *Your* **essence** hover and brood over us... as we reflect and pray... pour out and have Your way!

"Please, O Lord, let Your **e**ar be attentive to the (**expectant**) prayer of Your servant and the prayer of Your servants who delight to reverently fear Your Name of God... Your **essence**, Your nature, Your attributes, with awe... and **m**ake (as **expected**) Your servant successful this day and grant him compassion in the sight of this **m**an... the king. For I was **c**upbearer to the king of Persia."* - Joseph

*Meanwhile, Jesus was in Bethany at the home of Simon, a **m**an who had previously had leprosy. While He was eating, a woman came in with a beautiful alabaster jar of expensive perfume **m**ade from* **essence** *of nard. She broke open the jar (in* **expectancy***) and poured the perfume over His head... and she anointed Jesus' feet with it, wiping His feet with her hair. The house was filled* *with the (expectant) fragrance… of a most pure essence.** What an **example** in *Mary of Magdeline*.

Receive *oh God* out of and from the pure *essence* **of** our worship to You ~

In light of this **word of worth… ministry** and what's been shared:

- ❖ *Perhaps…* you **Encountered or Experienced a Question or Challenge**? Write it out…

- ❖ *Perhaps…* more has been **Established & Empowered by the Word**? Write what/which…

- ❖ *Perhaps…* it's time for **Engaging & Embracing your Expectations**? Write what's forming…

Reminder: For *clarity, connection, and confirmation* regarding *expectancy* being stirred by this *word of worth*, seek *Him* and *His Word* first. To possibly assist you in *the process* the list of **ION** words is available in the Appendix.

*Footnotes: Chapter 5 Day 3 essence / * See John 10:30, John 1/ Genesis 1, Strongs Concordance G3776 ousia and G2222 zoe, John 15, Jeremiah 1:5, Ephesians 1:4, Colossians 3:4, Hebrews 11:1, II Corinthians 4:7, Nehemiah 1:11, Mark 14:3 and John 12:3 - all emphasis is mine and personal paraphrasing built on various translations and versions.

✧ Day 4: The Journey of "e"... express

Let *expectations*... through this **word of worth's** part to *form, birth,* and *emerge* in its **meaning & mission**... **our meditation & motivation**... as **movement & manifestation** *awake, arise* and *align* in agreement with divine eternal **expectation**!

Oh... the cornucopia of words that *express* what *express* means! Especially as it enlarges into a word of action (a verb) *expressed* as the term *expression*. Yes... it's ok to use a word in and of itself to help define what it means as it places a type of emphasis on its meaning, the diversity within, and it emphasized! So let's explore a broader search into what this **word of worth** has for us.

Express... *to convey, state, speak, as in a voice speaking, to indicate, represent, communicate, demonstrate, reflect,* or *reveal what? A thought, emotion, message.* Remember... thoughts and emotions have an important role in *expectations* as they *form, reform,* or even in the *when, why, or how* one comes to an end... and, because of the *message* connected to or within them.

Express... it can also mean another form of action that describes (an adjective) such as in *fast, direct, prompt, speedy, with punctuality, non-stop* or *to squeeze out, to force out of something.* Plus, in the past tense of *expressed* it has already been *spoken, voiced, articulated, stated, uttered, displayed, communicated, declared* or *decreed*... and ideally clearly; not vaguely. And, it can be a *clear* or an *exact representation* or *close likeness, an image.*

Now let's examine an expanded form that ties nicely where we've been, we are, and where we're going ~

Expression... *the process of making known one's thoughts or emotions... an utterance, announcement, as to voice, declare, a declaration, a word or phrase.* Additionally, *an act, process,* or *instance of manifesting in representing something or someone.* It can be a *look or an appearance, countenance, manner, image, guise, face*... even a *mathematical or logical symbol or meaningful collection of symbols, to symbolize* and can include *a characteristic or detectable effect of our genetic makeup.* Such an eclectic blend of definings ~

Just by the meanings shared here that define the diverse connections to this **word of worth** - *express*... we start to see a great unfolding and with a layering of the importance it carries regarding its part in our *expectancy*. The emerging of what we *expect* as it comes forth in ours or other's *expectations*. For one could say with assuredness... an *expectation* is an *expression* of one's self. And, to the *good, bad,* or *indifferent* or the un*expected*... positive or negative, natural or spiritual – agree?

At its very core in the *Hebrew (H)* and *Greek (G)* we see an extension of depth come that I'll briefly share on as we progress in *this process* of laying foundations in beginning of this day. In *the Strongs Concordance* system of assigning words meanings, we encounter the *Greek* word **character** which has to do with *the process of engraving, carving, burning, marking or stamping an impression, an exact image or representation of a person or thing* for it to become in every respect *a replica, reproduction,* or *precise reproduction* of it.*

> ❖ Perhaps,... it's time to share an interesting note. In our English written form of the word **character**, it is <u>not</u> seen /*expressed* as that word in the *KJV* of *His Word*. Yet, we see *His*

character: His nature, characteristics, qualities, and attributes displayed... *expressed*... throughout *His Word*. And, we know we are to desire that character; *His,* and its fullness is to be shown, represented, displayed, portrayed... and demonstrated as an *expression* in us. This happens in a spiritual and even metaphorical way in the very nature and essence of *God* as revealed and released in *Jesus* and the image and likeness of *Jesus Christ* established in the essence of echad in us... *I would that they would be one (and an expression of that oneness) just as the Father and I are* one... remember? *Oh* what *expectancy ~*

In the *Hebrew* let's look now at two words. The word *express(ly)* is the word *naqab* which in short and for our usage means *to be designated as, specified or appointed as, as expressed with a name*. An *expressed* name matters as it appoints or designates the *person, place, or thing* as such that is, connected to, and is known by. The other *Hebrew* word *tselem*, is the word for *image* – a connecting word that appears often directly linked to *express* and to *expressly*. It's amazing how a name often invokes a *tselem –an image* associated with it.

Such associations with what we **expect** and our state of *expectancy*... they affect the outcome of our *expecting* a variety of ways. May we be aware and sensitive to these layers of meaning that add a depth in determining and designating what we're *expecting* and who or what it might *expressly* represent, associate with, or be an *image* or reproduction of. *He* will be good to help us when we seek and call upon *Him*.

Today let's look at this shared variety of *expressions* of meaning and context above for *express / expression* in *three different versions* of the same scripture which speak to a *Divine Expression...* containing **worthy words** from *His Worthy Word*... that carry within them an example of an interesting illustration of power and purpose *expressed* divinely.

*Who being the brightness of His glory, and the **express** image of his person, and upholding all things by the word of his power when He had by Himself purged our sins, sat down on the right hand of the Majesty on high (all as **expected**).** As seen in Hebrews 1:3 KJV.

*The Son is the dazzling radiance of God's splendor, the exact **expression** of God's true nature — His **mirror** image (as **expected**)! He holds the universe together and expands it by the mighty power of His spoken (**expectant**) word. He accomplished for us the complete cleansing of sins, and then took His seat (in all **expectancy**) on the highest throne at the right hand of the Majestic One.** As seen in Hebrews 1:3 TPT.

*The Son (filled with **expectancy**) is the radiance and only **expression** of the glory of [our awesome] God [reflecting God's Shekinah glory, the Light-being, the brilliant light of the Divine], and the exact representation and perfect imprint of His [Father's] essence, and upholding and maintaining and propelling all things [the entire physical and spiritual universe] by His powerful word [carrying the universe along to its predetermined goal]. When He [Himself and no other] had [by offering Himself on the cross as a sacrifice for sin] accomplished purification from sins and established our freedom from guilt, He sat down [revealing His completed work] at the right hand of the Majesty on high [revealing His Divine authority],* ** As seen in Hebrews 1:3 AMP.

What an *expressive* verse that *expresses* so much value to us through such a dynamic interplay between the words that are the same... and the ones that are different. Yet, all moving in alignment with the Divine essence and *expression* of it all... but, also adding to the depth of describing what *was, is,* and *has been* done. Truly it's how *He* has me sharing scriptures with the **m**erging and **c**onverging in a **m**ore **c**onversational relational way together!

Now this for **m**any… dare I say, and should be for **m**ost… works to stir a greater intensity for what we *expect* particularly as *born again* **c**hildren of *God*: *His sons and daughters.* In what we are believing for linked to our *expectations* and joined together with the *promises, plan, provision,* and *purposes* of *God* for us.

Here we observe a type of interchange of power in what *Christ* did on the **c**ross, what that work accomplished in atoning for our sin, *reconciling us back to God in right relationship,* and how it established a place for not just *Jesus's* positioning… but ours as well in our eternal *identity, inheritance,* and *purpose* in *Him.* My the *expectant* fruit – is it not too a birthright?

We now as *His*, are the righteousness of *God* in *Christ Jesus expressed*… which in its fullness allows us to be seated with *Jesus* in the **c**ompleted work in the full **m**anifestations of the *expression* of the *Son*, who is *Son of God, Son of Man* – an **e**xact representation of the **e**ssence of *Father.* Now within us arises phenomenal potential for being, to the fullest *expectancy, representative expressions*… yes, *representations* and *representatives* of *Him – Them.*

How our *Eternal God* transcends not only time and space surpassing the things of the natural in the spiritual **expressing** of *Himself* in us… through *His Son*… by *His Spirit* in its 3rd power! Now that **c**ertainly **c**reates an *expectancy* for what *we, you and me*, should *expect*… and *expect to see!*

- ❖ Perhaps… *expectation* is stirring in a new or greater way in you? It **m**ay be the effects or evidence of the *'earnest expectation'* since *He* paid the *earnest* – the legal price, that downpayment required for the atoning of our sin where the *expectation* (obligation) has been **m**et. A dowry for *His Bride!* It is done, finished – and the fruit thereof is good… very good *expressly* as it arises in *you… me… us* **m**anifesting in *who we are… what we do… how we live…* as *He* is, **m**ay we be *expressed!*

It's amazingly remarkable how the *Word of God* is there **c**onsistently revealing to us *Father's* heart throughout. Equally from *His* heart… as *expressions* that **e**stablish sure patterns and principles to form a firm foundations of truth within us. As we become acquainted and accustomed in alignment and agreement with *His Word* written and by *His Spirit*… how *He expresses Himself*… if we'll let it be there develops an establishing of some structure helpful for lining up our forming of *expectations*… which can produce the *echad* **e**ffect spoken of.

For example: *you reap what you sow.** A simple biblical principle to keep in **m**ind both in our *expressions, expectation,* and the **e**ffects they have on us and others. It all presents ways for incredible integral way for *life application* that illustrates the forming and joining together of what we *expect* to include not only things we need or want to *express* within them… but that *He expects* them to **c**ontain and encompass.

Bottom line… the *Word* **logos** - written out, *rhema* - coming alive, and *spoken expresses* what *Father* wants us to know that **m**atters, what *He* desires and requires in the what and how… and the *when, why,* and *where* we are to *express* things ourselves and to likewise let people know. Those things **c**onnected to us and yes… our *expectations.* And don't forget – it always goes two ways. Aware we **m**ust be of including and embracing, to one degree or another, the *expectancy* of others in the **m**ix of it all. I'm certain you know that **c**an change everything.

*Let the spoken word of Christ live... and have its home **expressing** itself within you dwelling in your heart and **m**ind... flooding you with all wisdom permeating (with His **expectancy**) every aspect of your being. Be sure to apply and **express** the scriptures purely and passionately as you teach and instruct spiritual things... as well as admonish and train one another with all wisdom (as **expected**). Even through the **expression** of singing of psalms, festive hymns, spiritual and prophetic songs given to you spontaneously (**expectantly**) by the Spirit...being sure to sing to God with all your hearts**

Moving forward now with our own ♪ song in our hearts... let's enter into concluding this part of *our journey* with the *word of worth express*... by taking a look at a few examples of the model of *Jesus* and the role of *Holy Spirit* for us as believers in and followers of *Him*.

Jesus Christ is as *Son of God,* the **express** image of *God* the *Father*... He adds that *He* and the *Father* are one... *and if you've seen Me (Jesus), then you've seen My Father*... and that is something we must be certain of. Especially if we truly believe that we were made also in the **expressed** image and likeness of *Them*... in the beginning. There's a *relationship* there and within it all. *Jesus* as the *Word He* is...well, without relationship this connection is just insincere attempting to be/become religious...ritualistic, not like *He* desired or designed, for us in authentic *relationship* where the oneness within is everything making all the difference.

There's also the fact of *Him* knowing us... implying some form of relationship is there in the 'before *He* formed us in our mother's womb'. How much more extraordinary is it then... when we come fully alive with *Him* in us as *His born again* children – as new creatures now living from our new man – from our spirit, which is **expressly** designed to live from an **expectancy** of a **Spirit to spirt** connection in echad relationship... like in *Eden* before sin?

Especially with *Holy Spirit* being sent to bring the **express** image of *God* as the *spirit of God He* is. The *Spirit* that hovered and brooded over the dark formless void in the beginning... now is in us once we are born again, and yet we are becoming being that new man we live from. And, it doesn't stop there because we need *Holy Spirit* **expressing** *Himself* as the *Helper Jesus* called *Him* before *He* departed telling us that *He* would endue us with power... plus, be our *Teacher, Comforter, Advocate*... the *Revealer* of all things. So *He* had to go.

When we're living from our *born again* nature... by our spirit because the *Spirit of God* is now alive in *you... me... us.* Our **spirit** is to now rule and reign; not our body or soul. So here's an interesting idea in light of that reality. There really is no **expression** of the *fruit of the Spirit* **expressed** as *self-control* for a *born again* child of God because our **spirit now overrules self**. Yes, we should exhibit self-control... but look what's **expressed** here.

Man changed some wording from the *original intent* words that said "**strength of the spirit/ spirit strength**" implying "**lordship**".* Now that can only come from the *Holy Spirit* being LORD in your life - not just *God the Father* and *Jesus the Son*, but the fullness of the **Three in One** as **LORD!** We can't muster up enough, let alone produce through "self" or "self -control" to manifest fruits "produced by the Spirit through love" and they last. That's why there are called **<u>fruit of the Spirit</u>** and **<u>*flow by the Spirit*</u>** as **expressions** of love established in the fullness and the essence of *God* in us... *glory!** Love so *Divinely* **expressed**!

Let us not forget however, how important the ways that we as humans who as believers / followers, which are *His* sons and daughters... the control we have through our *free will* to choose to **express** our *faith,* our *reverence,* and *devotion* to God in our worship through *prayer,* through our *communion* with *Him*, and *Him **m**oving* in us in it all and through truly giving **Him – Them, Lordship.** Which also includes and affect things like the *gifts of the Spirit* and *miracles, signs, and wonders* **m**anifesting in the **m**idst! AMEN!!!

When we are flowing, inviting and allowing the *Holy Spirit* to *"take the wheel"* too, to be *expressed* in and through as **m**entioned… a way opens for us to be *His kingdom* vessels… that are also *His kingdom* **c**arriers and **c**onduits as the *express* image of *God the Father, God the Son, and God the Holy* Spirit flow in and through bringing forth the fullness as we *GO… DO and BE* so *His kingdom* **c**an **c**ome – be *expressed*, on earth as it is in heaven!

*Now the Spirit – that is the Holy Spirit which is the Spirit of God… explicitly has revealed (what to **expect**)… speaking unmistakably **expressly** declaring, that in the latter times – the end of this time and age… some – perhaps **m**any, will depart turning away from the true faith, person after person… giving heed by paying attention and devoting themselves instead to **expressing** with the **expressions** manifesting through seducing spirits, deceitful spirits of deception, and doctrines of devils following demon-inspired revelations and doctrines of demons (discerningly **expected**).**

We are to *expect* it for the *Spirit* **expresses** *Truth*… and, *Truth* brings with it a **c**onfident assuredness that becomes a vital and essential influence in our *expectations* as they arise and we take heed of what *He* is *expressing*. For it helps, prepares, trains, empowers and enables us as we **m**ake ready with realistic … even strategic *expectations* that unfold *His* plans and purposes including *His provision, protection,* and *promises*.

Let's **m**ake every effort in it all to stay in the flow of what some **c**all, the *'unforced rhythms of His grace'** receiving from *Him* and *His* grace flowing through others to us… along with *you… me… us* releasing such *unforced rhythms of grace* to others to receive… particularly as we *create, give birth to,* and *release* *expressions* and *expectations*. The daily *rooting, grounding,* and *establishing* them in *His* truth in love and seasoned with grace… to those in our family and world around us we soon discover… or will, is needed, necessary… essential.

May it be evident in the evidence that we have *been with Him*… we are *His* – our *Father's* sons and daughters! What an *expression of expectancy* would that offer to and potentially influence to those who are not yet! Remember, *iron sharpens iron*… which we know, but don't always finish with the *rest of the verse* which truly **m**ust be *expressed* to complete it … *so sharpens the countenance of a friend**… as my precious sister friend *Karen* revealed to me **m**any years ago. *Christ* in her has surely partnered with *Him* and **m**anifested in the blessing of such to me in *the process* and *journey* of my life… which is truly an *expression* I value and honor in her… and in other **true brother, sister friends in Him**. Don't you too?

e = mc3
to *express* = ***m**aking **m**oving **m**anifesting of conveying character in communication* or *countenance* and to the **3rd power** > the *established echad essence* of the *Spirit of God*.

In light of this ***word of worth… express*** and what's been shared:

- ❖ *Perhaps…* you **Encountered or Experienced a Question or Challenge**? Write it out…

- ❖ *Perhaps…* **m**ore has been **Established & Empowered by the Word**? Write what/which…

- ❖ *Perhaps…* it's time for **Engaging & Embracing your Expectations**? Write what's forming…

Reminder: For *clarity, connection,* and *confirmation* regarding *expectancy* being stirred by this *word of worth*, seek *Him* and *His Word* first. To possibly assist you in *the process* the list of **ION** words is available in the Appendix.

*Footnotes: Chapter 5 Day 4 express / * See Strongs Concordance G5482 charakter, Strongs Concordance H5344 naqab, Hebrews 1:3, Galatians 6:7-9, I Timothy 4:1, Strongs Concordance G4490 retos, John 10:30,14:9, Mat 11:20-30 MSG – unforced grace, Colossians 3:6, Galatians 5:22-23 TPT and footnotes, Proverbs 27:17 - all emphasis is mine and personal paraphrasing built on various translations and versions.

✧ Day 5: The Journey of "e"... encounter

*Let **expectations**... through this **word of worth's** part to form, birth,
and emerge in its **meaning & mission**... our **meditation & motivation**...
as **movement & manifestation** awake, arise and align in agreement with
divine eternal **expectation**!*

We've seen before that sometimes there appears to be no need to define a **word of worth**, so to speak, because the word in and of itself seems to define itself... like with **"encounter"**. For the sake of *our journey* with **expectation**, let's start with laying a simple foundation to bring us all together into the common kind of framework of understanding... and possibly even expanding what we know it to **mean**.

Remember, in the defining of **words of worth** you'll **encounter** my choice to take the greater variety of meanings of the words, in this case **"encounter"**... in that eclectic sort of approach to bring *clarity*, *to enlarge* our knowledge, and *open* the door to the possibilities and potential the word carries in context to what we *expect* and the role it plays in our *expectancy*. Words again, are what *form our thoughts*, which along with our *emotions, and will*, work altogether to form **expectations** in general. **Encounters**, as we'll see, are a type of connected fruit.

To **encounter**... *a casual meeting, to come across, to meet up with or by chance, happenstance, to run into, a casual meeting and often not planned, a sudden unexpected meeting or experience that is challenging or difficult, to oppose, a conflict, struggle or fight as in or from the opposition or hostility, confrontation, an occasion, an eager conversation that's formed in anger or love... resentment or respect... bitterness or kindness and rejection or acceptance.*

Let's look as well... at a word that tends to often go hand in hand since an **encounter** which is a type of **experience**. **Experience** means *to be involved or engage with, something that has happened, a skill developed, to have knowledge that comes from life by use, practice, trials, or from a series of observations or encounters – either to the good or evil, suffering or enjoyment, and all depending on the circumstances and or the effects of it, an effort or attempt actively made to prove or do something.*

A few common characteristics or features in the context of both **encounters** or **experiences** play an important role which is good, necessary even... and to be understood we must consider the *setting and context*... along with the *atmosphere or present environment* things are happening in... and that of which is being created.

Personally, I tend to think of **encounter** and **experience** more often together than not. One happens – an **encounter**... and through it an **experience** begins to happen. Although ~ one might think just the opposite... because of this **experience** I am **encountering**. Either way, our realm of *expectancy* is always affected... and the effects influence what we *expect* and thus our **expectations** forming. Plus, the fact that **expectations**... in the reality of daily living are always there and ongoing as we've **established** already.

However we view the relationship between **encounter** and **experience**... and the relativity of it in *our journey*, they both offer individually or collectively an opportunity to *change, enhance, or grow* our perspective and beyond. Along with their undeniable connection to *expectancy* and the **expectations**... that do become a fruit of them.

Truly the importance and value we gain in *the process*... and the *processing* of these **encounters** and **experiences**... is obviously very intertwined and ongoing in the flow of life, *yours*... *mine*... *ours*. Together with the everyday parts and pieces manifesting that affect life, especially in the world around us... there's much happening within what we **expect** and they **expect**. So, as believers, we are in the ongoing progression of *becoming the being He's* made us to be, ideally in line with *His* **expectations** for us and of us... in the midst of it all.

Not long ago while reading a word entitled, *"Step Through the Door of More"* by *Tom Hamon* on a ministry site called *Elijah List,* I felt an increase of **expectancy** arise in me... the very title began to stir something. As I read on I came to this sentence... *"If we live in* **expectation** *and not* **intimidation** *and* **limitation** *this year, I believe this will* **position** *us for increase!** (boldface mine) He went on later to say, *"It's time for the door to* **more** *to swing wide for us this year, both in key "kairos" alignments and opportune moments of favor."*

Wow... now that's a powerful declaration of **expectation**... and it is certainly contingent upon what we would **encounter** and **experience**. But then, our awareness of such can help influence what our choices would be... to allow or not allow *intimidation* or *limitation*. Ah... those are **ION** words, which often come in to *disrupt, deter,* or *displace* us in *the process*... especially *the process* in us as *He's* growing and maturing us as *His* sons and daughters.

Our **expectations** for them to become the *catalytic* agents they can potentially be, when linked with an **encounter** and or an **experience** that *God* has ordained,... well, by *His Spirit*, who is the *Spirit of Truth*... things begins to happen. It's critical in these pivotal places... that we're sure we are NOT being driven by our soul or our flesh... tempting us to flow from our old motives, manners, methods... self. It's a challenge, but *God's* grace is there for us.

The cultivation of things **encountered** and **experienced** needs to be aligned and agreeing with the plumbline of *His Word* applied and activated in our **expectations** through the fact that we are living as a new creature now in *Christ Jesus*... with our **expectations** arising from that new *person, place,* and *posture* within us.

Holy Spirit helps us, *teaches* us, *leads, guides,* and *directs* us when we surrender... being submitted to *the process*. Where *He* is given **Lordship** over all things going on in our lives... so *His plans, promises,* and *purposes* can prevail. This provides for an opening of a door for the fulfilment of **expectations** which essentially is in our oneness with *His* **expectations**... there in that place... hope filled **encounters** can be produced and **more!**

- ❖ *Perhaps*... this is a good time to pause and examine whether *He* really is *Lord* in our lives... *yours*... *mine*. For me, I had to discover there was more behind *another door* so to speak. The *door of Lordship* is not just opening my life for *Him as God the Father* to be *Lord* and as *God the Son – Jesus, to be Lord*... but for the fullness of *Him* as well represented in the third person of **God the Holy Spirit being Lord**. The fullness of *Lordship* makes such a divinely defining difference in *the journey* of **expectancy**... as it makes way for the all-encompassing wrap around presence and power of *Him* to **move** in us... *minister* to us... and *manifest* through us... and in *His* **expected** end for us.

In all things **(expectantly)** *rejoice*... *do not despise the day of any* **encounter** *where you're* **experiencing** *a beginning or end*... *no matter how small*... *even if your grieved by various trials that arise. Let this testing (as* **expected***) of the genuineness of your faith you're* **encountering** *manifest what it will in the process. For it will be* **more** *precious than gold that perishes. And...*

*though it is tested by fire... let it be (**expectantly**) found encircled in praise and glory and honor at the revelation of Jesus Christ.**

Rooting, grounding, and *establishing* always and in all ways, what you **expect** to **encounter** and what you will **experience** in what the *Word of God* says. It will be fruit bearing... and this is fruit that tends to last, allowing us to *taste and see* that the *Lord* is indeed good!

The preparation unfolding in the nature of *the process*... it provides for what we're **encountering** and what we will **experience**, whether it's in a testing and trying way or an adventurous and exciting way... simply give it to *Him*. Remember, there's the simplicity of knowing **as He is so are we**... in Him we live, move, breathe and have our very being... with all being done as unto *Him* because we're for and with *Him* as *He's* truly for and with us. You **can expectantly** count on that in your **encounter!**

*In our lives may we let everything... any activity... any word that comes from our lips be done (as expected) in His name because of our intentional and intimate dependence on Him... in and through all **encounters** and **experiences** with and (**expectantly**) through Him. And in the core of it all... let thanksgiving filled with constant praise(and **expectancy**) from our hearts go up to God our Father... freely flowing from us... because of what He has done through Christ Jesus His son and His great love for us.**

In **c**ompleting this day of *our journey*... let's do a full **c**ircle as we allow the two forms of this defining of **encounter** present to us an interesting view. The word *paga* in the *Hebrew* and *symballo* in the *Greek*. Both have the **m**eaning: to **encounter**... within their layers of defining.

An example of *symballo* being expressed in *His Word* is seen in a kind of powerful intimate way as the layering displayed here reveals, "But Mary kept all these things, (**expectantly**) pondering (G4820 – symballo) them in her heart."* My, how that beautifully draws us into a kind of **connection**... and it being within a divine **encounter**.

Then in the word *paga* we see the **m**eaning of **encounter** being tied around a **m**eeting with a request expressed by *Ruth* when she says to *Naomi*, "*Entreat (paga) me not to leave you or to turn back from following after you; For wherever you go, (**expectantly**) I will go; And wherever you lodge, I will lodge; Your people shall be my people, And your God, my God.*"* He gives us so **m**any opportunities to see what *a* **word of worth** can truly **c**onvey when searched out in *His Word* through words expressed ***expectantly***. Along with ways to apply them in our lives too as Ruth did in her *entreating*... her **encounter** with Naomi.

Both giving us a glimpse of an intimate intentional inner **e**ngaging... and the relativity in *relationships* that **encounters** and **experiences** **c**an possess **c**onveying very strong and adamant expressions **c**ontaining ***expectancy*** with ***expectations*** that enlarge the potential and possibilities that **m**ay manifest when they are created and birthed from *Him* within us and we **embrace** them. Should we not add... carrying *His **expected end*** like we saw for Ruth?

Maybe you have an *"e = mc3" expression* for **encounter** forming?

In light of this ***word of worth… encounter*** and what's been shared:

- ❖ *Perhaps…* you **Encountered or Experienced a Question or Challenge?**
  Write it out…

- ❖ *Perhaps…* **m**ore has been **Established & Empowered by the Word?**
  Write what/which…

- ❖ *Perhaps…* it's time for **Engaging & Embracing your Expectations?**
  Write what's forming…

Reminder: For *clarity, connection, and confirmation* regarding *expectancy* being stirred by this *word of worth*, seek *Him* and *His Word* first. To possibly assist you in *the process* the list of **ION** words is available in the Appendix.

*Footnotes: Chapter 5 Day 5 encounter / * See Tom Hamon / Elijah List @elijahlist.com / February 9, 2024: Step Through the Door of More. * See 1 Peter 1:6-7, Colossians 3:17, Strongs Concordance H6293 paga, Strongs Concordance G4820 symballo, Luke 2:19 - all emphasis is mine and personal paraphrasing built on various translations and versions.

✧ Day 6: The Journey of "e"… encourage

Let *expectations*… through this *word of worth's* part to *form, birth, and emerge* in its **meaning & mission**… *our meditation & motivation*… *as movement & manifestation* awake, arise and align in agreement with divine eternal *expectation*!

Be *encouraged* by this *word of worth* and *His Worthy Word* today as it empowers us by reminding of the importance of being willing… being obedient. And, that because we are… there are benefits and blessings that become ours.

If you have a willing (expectant) obedient heart… to let Me help (encourage, exhort, edify, empower, equip) you… and, if you will obey Me… you will feast… eating like a king… on the blessings of an abundant harvest… yes, you shall eat good… of the very best part of the land.* He is so very good to us!

Did that *encourage* you? It should for it declares the power of *His* promise with provision attached. And,… that should always stir *expectation*, helping to keep us centered with our eyes focused on *Him*, moving forward into what *He* has said, the offered help *He* promises, and the provision *He* says is available. Those who respond with what *He* requires and *expects* soon discover at the very core is the *Father's* earnest and sincere desire to *bless, provide for*, and *protect us His* children… *His* family.

To *encourage* is to *inspire, cheer, reassure, comfort, strengthen, embolden, boost, hearten, nurture, motivate or quicken someone with the idea of raising one's confidence or filling them with a type of strength of purpose or hope for whatever they are encountering or experiencing in a given situation or within life's ever changing circumstances.*

This all a part of our daily disciplining that comes in *the journey*… that takes practice, per say and comes in the *process*. After all, it is said doctors are just *"practicing"* medicine. Therefore, this practicing of discipline regularly reflects our willingness to enter into a personal level of learning where the discipline can grow us… as it molds and makes us… shaping us … preferably and desirably, into becoming a being more like *Him*.

There's just something about this kind of *being transformed… not conformed…* 24/7/365… in the fresh daily surrendering and submitting of self, and in the desire for continual growing and giving of ourselves *spirit, soul,* and *body* to *Him*. Yes… for *His* reasonable service and purposes, which are *His* good and perfect will holy and acceptable to *Him*.* Beyond what we think, what seems to be, and what we really need to encounter in the moments.

Be ye holy as I am holy… As He is so are we… In Him we live, move, and have our very being… these are essential to secure in our knowing, our thinking, and in an intimate relational knowing as well in the *process* of growing into being what we're becoming. For they *encourage, edify,* and *empower* us especially in our identity. What we can *expect* of *Him* in us and us in *Him* is vital to <u>who</u> we believe we are… individually and corporately.

Those who are intent to be faithful in the little things will be given more… yet to those who are given the more, the greater… well, much is required. These all carry the essence of certain scriptures... as *words of worth* from *His Worthy Word* that need to just flow in us and through and from us... connecting us fundamentally to an *encounter* of some type because *He* is the *Word*... so we *experience Him* through them with **encouragement** as a fruit.

There's an acronym I learned that speaks so powerfully to this *over all process*... and to the need for us to have an *expectation* of ourselves for such. In walking out this growing and learning of a disciplined lifestyle *He* desires for and *expects* of us... an anointed man of *God* I honor and was blessed to know, *Apostle Dr. John Watson*, now in his eternal home, shared something I still find myself using as a kind of checkpoint and reminder.

He shared that we must always seek to be and keep ourselves "*FAT*"... and yes, everyone laughed. But when he revealed what it meant... a silence fell among us as the room became brighter from all the *light bulbs* going on with the awakening of *expectation* palatable in his revealing: **FAT** > always be **F**aithful, **A**vailable & **A**pproachable, and **T**eachable. What an empowering and truly embodied *expression* full of *Father's expectancy*. Just do it, be **FAT**!

FAT to who?... and Why? Ultimately *Him*, so that whatever *encounter* or *experience* we're having *He's* included... involved... and becomes *invested* because we are and that's who *He* is – **eternally invested in us.** *He* really wants to be and will be our **Expectant Encourager.**

Now that requires at the core a personal desire to yes, discipline yourself... which becomes easier if you value the blessing and the *process* of such. In which, or at least I have found, this kind of personal development to be highly beneficial discovering that it definitely connects you to and with a wider variety of *encounters* and *experiences*... particularly when embracing the action and application of such traits as they emerge, *encourage*, and *empower*.

Remember, *All Scripture is God-breathed, useful for teaching, rebuking, correcting, and training (experiences filled with His **expectancy**), in righteousness, so that the servant of God may be thoroughly equipped for every good work."**

Expectations that come within them, scripture, more often than not are formed and fashioned in ways that wouldn't have fully and fruitfully happened... let alone carry the relative and priceless life lessons they do. However, without this kind of self-*expectancy* that discipline holds... well, what we *expect* of our selves can diminish rather than enlarge through *Christ in us* which *encourages* and *empowers* causing enlargement in *Him*... an *expected* end.

Perhaps... a *journey* that is *encouraged, edified, and empowered* in a way not known, encountered, or experienced before being based not just on who we are... but by the *expectation* we put before us of WHO *HE* IS, WHO *HE* IS IN you, me, and IN others is CHRIST IN US... which He says connect us to HOPE. In the GREATER of life HOPE matters... <u>is it not</u> **greater is He that is in you... me.. us...** than he that is in the world... posturing and positioning us in another type of *encouraging* and *empowering expectation?* A way that manifests a fruit of kingdom *expectancy*... for the distinct certain HOPE we have of **CHRIST IN US...** *it is* **the HOPE of GLORY!**

Got *encouragement*? Got *edification*? Got *empowerment*? You should ~ but let's be real, sometimes we discover we're giving place to... or possibly have already gotten into a form of *stagnation, indecision, self-pity, woe is me...* or *self-sabotage*. In the battle remember, the war over our **expectation** started in the beginning. The **e**nemy does nothing new.

*Rise up out of the ashes... out of the pity pit... out of the **m**iry clay... out of any place of stagnation... degradation... limitation...* holding you back from how *He'll* faithfully **e**xhort you **encouragingly** to arise! Get *awakened*! Get into being *accepted* for you are in *Him*... and, get *aligned*! Get into *expectancy* for what *He's* assigned!

*Don't give up, don't lose heart when encountering comes disappointment, discouragement, or despair. Even though our outward **m**an is wasting away, perishing, and gradually wearing out... our inward **m**an little by little (in its **expectancy**)is surely progressively being renewed by His loving* **encouragement**, *bold* **empowerment** *and gracious* **enablement** *day by day.**

Grab hold we **m**ust of this ability to **e**nter into where we are and into what is ongoing and going on... for it **c**omes as we *walk by faith and not by sight* and from *faith to faith*... **embracing** our *carpe diem's*... the *expectant* seizing of **m**oments!

For the door of opportunity before us is to **c**ome out better by **c**oming through *looking... and looking again*, <u>not</u> to *look back* at just our *expectation*... but remembering what it **c**arries within. The potential and possibilities for the beyond. *Engage* with what is being revealed... allowing the fruit of it to play its part and piece in the formation and the *process of expecting*... all while being *encouraged, edified, empowered* IF giving *Him* a place. There is an **emboldening** *Holy Spirit* will produce that will arise as *His* fruit in our *expectancy*.

Hazaq is a word for *encourage* in *Hebrew* with layers of **m**eaning including: strong *repair, hold, strengthened, strengthen, harden, prevail,* **encourage**, *take, courage, caught, stronger, hold, misc.** We see the use of this word in these *worthy words* of scripture, *And David was greatly distressed; for the people (were **expectant**) as they spoke of stoning him, because the soul of all the people was grieved, every **m**an for his sons and for his daughters: but David* **encouraged** *(hazaqed) himself in the LORD his God.**

A *Greek* word used with part of its **m**eaning within our *word of worth* **encourage,** is *paramytheomai,* **m**eaning *to comfort, console, or encourage.* Here's a perfect example in these words unfolding... *We pray you have known how we've sincerely* **encouraged, exhorted,** *comforted and affectionately treated and charged every one of you, like a loving father caring for his own children.**

So now advance... **encouraged** by these words released knowing *He* loves and **c**ares for us always **encouraging** us as in *His Worthy Words* expressed. Let us be intentional to reflect on these thoughts as we **c**ontinue *this journey expectantly*... positioning ourselves to receive by *His Spirit* from them and their **encouraging** potential and power.

$e = mc3$ **encouragement** = **mission** and **message moving** in the **comforting consultation** of **courageous counsel** through **the 3rd power** of the fullness of *God* and beyond!

In light of this ***word of worth... encourage*** and what's been shared:

- ❖ *Perhaps*... you **Encountered or Experienced a Question or Challenge**? Write it out...

- ❖ *Perhaps*... more has been **Established & Empowered by the Word?** Write what/which...

- ❖ *Perhaps*... it's time for **Engaging & Embracing your Expectations?** Write what's forming

Reminder: For *clarity, connection, and confirmation* regarding *expectancy* being stirred by this *word of worth*, seek *Him* and *His Word* first. To possibly assist you in *the process* the list of **ION** words is available in the Appendix.

*Footnotes: Chapter 5 Day 6 encourage / * See Isaiah 1:19, Romans 121-2, 2 Corinthians 4:16, 2 Timothy 3:16-17, Strongs Concordance H2388 hazaq, 1 Samuel 30:5, Strongs Concordance G3888 paramytheomai, I Thessalonians 2:11 - all emphasis is mine and personal paraphrasing built on various translations and versions.

✧ Day 7: The Journey of "e"… eternal

Let **expectations**… through this **word of worth's** part to *form, birth,* and *emerge* in its **meaning & mission**… **our meditation & motivation**… as **movement & manifestation** *awake, arise and align* in agreement with divine eternal **expectation**!

It's always good to **e**njoy the *journey* in our time spent with **words of worth** and with *Him* who is The *Word*, and to find ourselves laughing in the **m**idst. You know how scripture says it's good for the soul to be cheerful, laugh… **m**aking our hearts **m**erry, as it works like a **m**edicine. Yes, **e**ven… "*The* **Eternal** *One enthroned who rules in heavens laughs.*"*

Did you know *He* will **e**ven fill our **m**ouths with laughter and our lips with shouting?! *And, the Lord delights in, enjoys, and takes pleasure in those who fear the Lord and place their hope in His steadfast* **eternal everlasting** *love.** My how these stir a kind of **expectancy** for just how truly amazing, authentically relational, and ready to enjoy life our *Abba Papa*… the **Eternal One** is.

My **expectation** is that you've actually encountered *Him* in similar ways… or *Him* doing such things… perhaps as you're encountering *Him* as *we journey* together in these pages on this **pilgrimage** with **expectation**. So, the actual **m**anifestation of my… your, **expectations** have come **m**ost likely and yet are coming. You, me… well, we *gotta learn to love* that about **expectancy**… and *the yet comings.* To me, it's a good kind of *child-like faith* thing to learn to love the "*gotta's*" in life!

Not only in some ways have our **expectations m**anifested… but because of *His* inclusion… and in *His* **eternalness** He, the One *who was and is and is to come*… will do and be just that *continually… consistently… constantly.* It's who *He* is and how *He has, is,* and *will* faithfully **m**ove taking *His* place and do when invited and permitted to. Remember, *His* part in the **m**ovement really is needed for *forming, creating,* and *birthing* what we **expect.** This allows for a *God* connection with *His* **eternal** ordering to become a part of our *process* and *journey* while we're on earth. Yes… bringing **m**ore of heaven and *His* kingdom to… and on earth!

The door that opened to our *journey with "e"* which began six days ago… if you're traveling through the book in that order, is now **c**oming to an end as we enter in to receive from what our last "e" word in day seven's **word of worth** presents and offers to us. Actually… we **c**an see this word *"eternal"* in some of its forms has already been revealing insight in the unfolding of our beginning. Let us continue believing to *finish well* in the **c**ompleting of this first week!

Eternal in its *Latin* foundation is the word *aeternus* and its **m**eaning in the broader perspective is connected to the idea *of an age* because it's root **m**eans *age*. As we extend the defining we learn that it **m**eans things like *eternity, lasting, permanent, enduring, perpetual, unending, everlasting, endless, of life and long life, or a vital force.*

In its origins in the *Hebrew* **eternal c**onnects **m**ainly in **m**eaning to the word ne•*tzach / netsach* and indirectly in the word *olam*. Ne'tzach's **m**eaning being established in *eternal, everlasting, eternity or an everlasting time span,* along with *forever, eternity, splendor, enduring,* and *perpetual.*

"*And also the* **Eternal One** *of Israel will not lie nor change His* **m**ind*; for He is not a man, that He should change His* **m**ind*.*"* and "*You will show* **m**e *the path of life; in Your presence (***expectancy*** knows) is fullness of joy… at Your right hand there are pleasures for evermore*"*

Olam being connected to *eternal* in it meaning: *long duration, forever and ever, everlasting, evermore, perpetual, old ancient world or time, continuous, perpetual existence, eternity (eternal).* We see this used in *God's* name as *El Olam* and is first mentioned in this verse... *"And Abraham planted a grove in Beersheba, and called there on the name of the LORD, the everlasting God."** *God's* names are important... and knowing who *He* is and how *He* is being portrayed when you read the word name *'God'*... can shed great light and bring a depth to our understanding for who *He* wants to be to *you... me... us, His* people.

We've had two of *His* names revealed regarding the usage of our **word of worth**... *God* as our **Everlasting God** and the **Eternal One of Israel**. Knowing these two essential dimensions of who *He* is presents information to help us to know what to **expect** of *Him*... as well as what to **expect** in context to scriptures that identify *Him* in this side of *His* nature... the side connected with *Him* being **eternal.**

Perhaps for you, like me... this endearing and enduring kind of unending quality certainly builds a foundation of **expectation** that carries within it a perpetual aspect of *hope*, an assurance that speaks to *faithfulness*... and that truly makes a way for our developing of a confident *trust* in *Him*. And those things, well what *He* wants to involved in dimension of our **expectation**... they – *hope, faithfulness,* and *trust* thrive when *He* is.

God's **eternal** nature reflects **expectantly** too, in the capacity for *His* promises to manifest. The conditions or truths to be kept in *Him* being a covenant keeping *God* and the essence of it all being grounded and established are not just in truth, hope, and faithfulness... but in who *He* is as love and how *His* love is most assuredly and **eternally** at work.

To further explore this dynamic of *His* **eternalness** let's look a bit further. For one, it's good to know that just from a perspective of time... understanding that in our *born again* identity and relationship with *God*... we inherit a life that transcends time and even circumstances. How do we know this and what can we stand on as we add this dynamic into what we can reasonably **expect**? This ~

*And this is **eternal** life, that they may know You, the only true supreme and sovereign God, and Jesus Christ... in the same manner... whom You have sent. Now Jesus was saying this to Father because the **expected** appointed time had come... a time to unveil the glorious splendor of Him as God's Son... enabling Him to magnify and glorify the Father. Especially through all those whom He had given Him to be His - permanently and forever. He also had completed the work fulfilling and manifesting the **expectation** of Him... and Him/Christ in them... what He was sent to do.**

Think with me for a moment how such powerful truths shared in these words from *His Worthy Word* of this **eternal** relationship between *Father* and *Son* transfers, evolving into *His* relationship with us as *Father's* children, sons and daughters of *God*... whom *Jesus* lives in... and, for whom the *Father* has plans of hope... a bright future and an **eternal** purpose for. Does that not create an **expectancy** for *eternity* we know of? But, also for the **expectancy** for such while we're here on earth walking and living it out being about our *Father's* kingdom business... and partnering with *Him* for *His* on earth as it is in heaven ~ *His* **expected** end.

*For what we have is the living... active... full of power Word of God – which is The Word in Spirit and in Truth... and is full of perpetual energy... making it operative... energizing... and, all effective as should be **expected**... especially as a vital force for here and now... and **eternally** !"**

Remember, *He* is the *Word*... and as such the divine and vital energy essence of *Him* within us who believe... that's some potential creating all kinds of possibilities that will jump start a heart with **expectancy**! That energy is **eternal** for *He* is **eternal,** not new age. And, in *Him* we have **eterna**l life…that *Divine* godly energy is by *His Spirit*… for *He is Spirit*. In and as the *born again* ones we are those who are now predominately a spirit living in a body with a soul rather than a soul living in a body with a spirit. <u>**As *He* is so we are**</u>.

What tops it off exceedingly, abundantly, and profoundly is that the essence of that **eternal** energy in our spirits is LOVE! For *GOD is a Spirit,* and the essence of *GOD IS LOVE*. And He so loved the world, you… me… us… others, that He gave. Oh yes… He gave freely His Only Begotten Son – the Firstborn One… that whoever believes… putting their **expectations**… each and every… in Him – only Him. They're not going to perish… but have the **eternal everlasting forever and ever** kind of life.* Just as *He* promises and **expectantly** desires to give us… should we of our own free will **c**hoose to… *expecting* that everything *He* has said *He* will do, *He* will do… and that all *He* says *He* will be, *He* will be – cling to that. So we too **c**an go… do… and be! Oh the **expectancy** in the perpetual goodness and faithfulness of our *God* – the **Eternal One El Olam**!

- ❖ *Perhaps*… it is time for you to rest in the **c**ertainty and **c**onfidence that *He* is not a **m**an that would lie. Therefore, let's take a **m**oment to examine the depths of our hearts and to know for **c**ertain we are resting and trusting in this promise of eternal life available to us through the work of the cross. When we turned, repenting of our sin, receiving *His* forgiveness, and in turning giving our life to Him - we were truly *born again* of and in *Him*. For IF there is any doubt NOW is the time to seek *Him*, pray, and find out. If there is any kind of hesitancy that if you'd die right now, are you confident that to your **eternal** home in heaven with *Him* is where you'd go?

  Beloved friends ~ no need to wonder… read these truths and take a **m**oment with *Him* ~ "Listen to this **eternal** truth: Before a person can even perceive God's kingdom, they **must** first experience a rebirth and be born again. For I speak an **eternal** truth: Unless you are born of water and the Spirit, you will never enter God's kingdom. For the natural realm (as **expected**) only gives birth to things that are natural, but the spiritual realm… it gives birth (**expectantly**) to supernatural life! You shouldn't be amazed by My statement, 'You all **must** be born from above!' For the Spirit-Wind blows as it chooses. You can hear its sound, but you don't know where it came from or where it's going. So it is the same with those who are Spirit-born!"*

  "I am the Resurrection, and I am **Life Eternal**. Anyone who clings to believing in Me in faith in **earnest expectation**, even though he dies, he will live forever. And the one who lives by believing in Me as their Savior, will never die.* Do you believe this? My **expectation** is in and for your **eternal life** in your "*I believe*" that I am hearing.

Our final place of adventure in the end of *this journey* with "e" **c**alls out for us to uncover and discover **m**ore about *eternity*. There's a *Greek word of worth aion*, which **m**eans *forever, of an unbroken age, perpetuity of time,* **eternity** *as in eternal, of the worlds, a universe period of time, or age.* Oh the layering of **m**eaning. Interesting to, it has an ION in it!

*According to the **eternal purpose** which He purposed **expectingly** in Christ Jesus our Lord… as He gave unto them… us… **eternal life**; and the **expectation** that can stand on and walk in… is knowing that they… we… shall never perish, neither shall any **m**an pluck them… us… out of My hand.** Nothing like *His* **expected** end for us wrapped in *His* love.

$e = mc^3$ eternal life = mission of *Christ* to the 3rd **power** perpetually

The simplicity of *eternity* gives a picture to allow us to taste and see down here in the *earthly* with hearts of *expectancy*... as they **expect to see eternally**. Father, Your kingdom come, Your will be done in our earthen vessels and in *our expectations*!

<u>In light of this **word of worth...eternal** and what's been shared:</u>

- *Perhaps... you **Encountered or Experienced a Question or Challenge?***
  Write it out...

- *Perhaps... more has been **Established & Empowered by the Word?***
  Write what/which...

- *Perhaps... it's time for **Engaging & Embracing your Expectations?***
  Write what's forming...

Reminder: For *clarity, connection, and confirmation* regarding *expectancy* being stirred by this *word of worth*, seek *Him* and *His Word* first. To possibly assist you in *the process* the list of **ION** words is available in the Appendix.

*Footnotes: Chapter 5 Day 7 eternal / * See Proverb's 17:22, Psalm 2:4, Job 8:21, Psalm 147:11, Strongs Concordance H5331 netsach, Psalms 16:11, I Samuel 15:29, Strongs Concordance H5769 olam, Genesis 21:33, John 17:1-5, Hebrews 4:12, John 3:16, Strongs Concordance G165 aion, Eph 3:11, John 10:28 - all emphasis is mine and personal paraphrasing built on various translations and versions.

✧ Expectancy's Look Again... at the end of the Journey of "e"
~ Brenda

*He will (in all **expectancy**) achieve infinitely **m**ore than your greatest request,*
*your **m**ost unbelievable dream, and exceed your wildest imagination.*
Ephesians 3:20 (TPT)

Expectations Reflection: Now that's some **Words of Worth** full of **expectancy** and **expectations**! I first **m**et *Beth* several years ago. I noticed right away - *"there is a woman of words."* She has a unique way of *stringing words together* that increases understanding: **c**onnecting them and **c**hallenging a line of thought. I have **c**ome to know her not only as a woman of **words of worth**, but of *the Word*... **c**oming out of **m**any years hidden away with *Him* as the *Word, as Holy Spirit*... and now through a pouring out that **e**ncourages and **e**mpowers others to do the same.

When she approached me about joining a *"Book Ministry Support Group"* through a **c**onference **c**all, **c**oncerning a book she was writing, I was pleasantly surprised... intrigued. Over the last two years, our group discussions have **m**ore than raised my *expectations of expectation.* Through her story of how she **c**ame to the **e=mc3**... I have also **c**ome to a deeper knowing of *it is not as a formula... but a relationship* with my *God* experiencing *His* goodness to me... *His* faithfulness in ways that have **e**levated my *expectations* for the NEW.

Over time... throughout the hours of **c**onversation on our **c**onference **c**alls... I have **c**ome to a new awareness of what *He* has already **e**stablished in me over the 60 years of walking with *Him.* But now, looking beyond with **expectation** for how *He* is reestablishing *His* ways, purposes, **c**allings, and anointing in the *journey* and *process* of my life as *Divine Eternal.*
May you too...

*He will (with all **expectancy**) achieve infinitely **m**ore than your greatest request,*
*your **m**ost unbelievable dream, and exceed your wildest imagination.*
Ephesians 3:20 (TPT)

Prayer of Expectancy: *Father God, **m**ay we partner with Your Spirit of **expectancy** in us to allow Your seeds of "unbelievable dreams" and "wild godly imaginations" filled with Your **expectations**... germinate and grow in us... being fruitful in all things as we **c**ontinue on our journey and in the process with You.*

Expectation's Declaration: I declare we will *experience... encounter... embrace*... and enjoy the *ongoing journey* of *expectancy* for **the MORE**!

✧ WORTHY WORDS AS WE ENTER CHAPTER 6...

*What comes into our minds when we think about God
is the most important thing about us.* A.W. Tozer

*When I gaze... see and consider, Your heavens... the moon and Your stars in them mounted like jewels in their settings... through the work of Your fingers as would be **expected**. I know You are the Fascinating Artist who fashioned and established it all! But I (**expectantly**) ask this question desiring to know Your response: Why would You bother with mortal earthbound man or care about humans being mindful of him? Yet what honor You have given to men, created only a little lower than Elohim, crowned with glory and magnificence. Yet You have made him a little lower than God, (as **expected**) and You have crowned him with glory and honor. You have delegated to them rulership... dominion over all You have made, with everything under their authority, placing earth itself under the feet of Your (**expectant**) image-bearers. All the created order and every living thing of the earth, sky, and sea— the wildest beasts and all that move in the paths of the sea — everything is in submission to Adam's (**expectant**) sons. Yahweh, our Sovereign God, Your glory streams from the heavens above, filling the earth with the majesty of Your name! O Lord, our Lord, indeed... how majestic and glorious and excellent is Your name in all the earth! People everywhere see your splendor and **expectancy** arises!**

*Seek the Lord Yahweh our God... while you sense He is present and **expect** that He may be found making Himself approachable; call on Him **expectantly** [for salvation] while He is near. Let the wicked leave behind and abandon their ways and the sinful unrighteous ones banish every thought; and let him return to the Lord, and He will have compassion on him and they will experience His mercies that are new every day... and to Yahweh our God, for He will abundantly pardon lavishing His forgiveness upon you all - you can **expect** it. "For My thoughts are not your thoughts, and My ways are different from your ways." declares the Lord. "For as high as the heavens are... yes, higher than the earth, so are My ways higher than your ways and My thoughts higher than your thoughts."**

*Be sober-minded; be watchful – **expectant**. For your adversary the devil prowls around like a roaring lion, seeking and **expecting** someone to devour. Resist him, standing in **expectancy** firm in your faith, knowing that the same kinds of suffering are being experienced by your brotherhood throughout the world.**

*There's an **expectancy** for a grinding wheel to sharpen a blade because iron sharpens iron. And so, it is **expected** that one person sharpens the character of another; even his very countenance.**

---

*Footnotes: Chapter 6 Worthy Words / *See Psalms 8:3-9, Isaiah 55:6-8, 1 Peter 5:8-9, Proverbs 27:17 – all emphasis is mine and personal paraphrasing built on various translations and versions.

✧ CHAPTER 6 ✧

✧ ESTABLISHING & EMBRACING ... A JOURNEY WITH "M"

As we enter into *Chapter 6* which begins *our journey* with **"m,"** let's recall and reflect on the framework for times of **c**ontemplation, **c**onnection, **c**onfirmation, and **c**reation... and sometimes **c**orrection... as we advance into these next seven days.

Remember, these are the **m**ain *'attractions'* that we are being presented... and happen within the encounters and experiences we have on this *pilgrimage* with *Him* and together. As we are lead to examine to enlarge our place, posture, and positioning with our *expectations*... along with *His* for us... there are key facts and features... parts and pieces... and vital aspects that will help align us so we **m**ake a place and a way for agreement to **c**ome in our *expectancy* – with ourselves, others ... *Him*... enabling us to **engage, embrace,** and be **empowered** by what we expect and believe to **m**anifest.

With **m**ost *words of worth*, as we saw with **C**hapter 5 in our *journey* with **"e"**, these elements were laid out for us NOT by being labeled as such necessarily... but, within the **c**ontext of information shared as we discovered them in their unique, yet unifying purpose as they unfolded... and will **c**ontinue to as we press forward enjoying the *process* within each day ... each week with what it offers.

Remember, **words of worth** presented include: the **Meaning and Mission** of them and how they **c**onnect us to an opportunity for **Meditation and Motivation,** along with how they **c**reate a place for **Movement and Manifestation.** Not in an outright *titling* or obvious presentation that one **m**ight look for in a structured framework of traditional types of daily 'devotionals'... **c**ontaining a type of repeated ordering within them. But, an intertwined flowing that includes an interchange and interplay in and through **e**ach day and *word of worth*... as the *Spirit* leads, builds upon, and keeps before us a bigger purpose... needed or desired in the *process*.

We are looking for and at these elements... examining them... in the **e**stablishing of *thoughts, perspectives,* and **m**ore being released so our *expectations* **c**an form, being **c**reated, and then birthed out of fresh *revelation, impartation,* and *application* that **m**anifests presenting a suggested activation of such and uniquely to *you... me... us,* as **expectancy,** one could say, forms its own place positioning itself within the personality or temperament within us **e**ach.

So do not yield or give place to fear, for I am with you always near; do not be dismayed, for you can expect Me to be what I am – your faithful God. Be expectant knowing I will infuse and help you with My strength as you count on it expectantly; I will uphold you firmly with My victorious righteous right hand.*

As previously **m**entioned, the days in each week do build... but not always directly as one upon the other. So be encouraged to be open to just receiving in the **m**oments especially from *His infusing* from a word... and the words together with it bringing to us information and illustrations... while we're reading and taking it all in. As well as the developing of what you **expect** from them.

So let's *"get on the road"*. There's **m**uch to anticipate as we explore what's now before us. And *oh,* how hopeful anticipation tied together with our desired *expectation*... will work to form a **c**onnection that **c**an *grow great faith* in us!

With that in **m**ind... *whatever you do, do it in the **m**easure of faith you have and with all of your heart... as working for and unto the **(expectancy** of the) Lord and not unto the **expectancy** of **m**en.** Remember, *faith* is one of our greatest acts of obedience and **m**easures of our belief in *Him, His Word* and what we ***expect*** from *Him... for without it – faith, it's impossible to please God.**

*Footnotes: See Isaiah 41:10, Colossians 3:23-24, Hebrews 11:6 - all emphasis is mine and personal paraphrasing built on various translations and versions.

✧ Day 1: The Journey of "m"... man

Let *expectations*... through this *word of worth's* part to *form, birth, and emerge* in its **meaning & mission... our meditation & motivation... as movement & manifestation** awake, arise and align in agreement with divine eternal *expectation*!

There's just something about knowing... **experiencing** and **encountering** that you're a part of something greater than yourself. A greater adventure too, if you will, where the greatness of it all comes from a far superior plan than that of **man** or the world. A plan that contains and establishes a purpose... and conveys within such purpose promises in which all of it carries a form of *power, presence,* and *provision* intertwined with the source of it all that *you've... we've* discovered *Adonai Yahweh* as our *Source* and *Elohim... Creator God.* Amen.

The above is what perhaps *you and I... we* sense in essence... when we contemplate and receive from the fullness of the truth and revelation that we are indeed *His* Creation. But beyond that.... a far exceedingly more incredible, almost unbelievable purpose arises when *you... me...we*, as born again *children of God...* know we are now a part of *His* family – *the family of God* which is also the *Body of Christ..*

Now... the identity of the *Source* has *enlarged, expanded,* and *enrichingly* unfolds to reveal *Elohim* is and desires to be our *Father God – God our Father,* as well... which affects everything mentioned above in that it's not just about creating the earth and all therein – creation and creatures... or even created ones... living – human beings... but *Him* embedding in *His* masterful eternal plan that it all would be exclusively relative to their absolute connectivity – and it in *Him...* the - our *Creator... Yahweh... God... the Sovereign One.*

Certainly that will stir an *expectancy* and not just momentarily, but for and in a continual kind of way... that is released in what we ongoingly *expect* and all it entails... coming forth because... well, hasn't it always? That inner knowing and sense of our *expectations* being connected to so much more than we can, could or ever will think or imagine... because He who created us first divinely imagined and thought of us in *His* forming and birthing of *His expectation*... yes, that "*In the beginning...*".

Let's take a look at a relative and essential part of this '*in the beginning*' where we see what appears to be the '***mission***' of *God* being to create out of the *dark, formless,* and *void* nothingness the earth by *His Spirit* hovering and brooding over the face of the water. The work included the creative task of *Him* going beyond this initial reveal... to revealing *Himself* in what *He* was creating. And, it building on anything presented so far and what we know.

Then God said, "Let Us - Father, Son, Holy Spirit / Them, the Three in One, the Holy Trinity, make **man** *– human/mankind... in Our express image... after and according to Our likeness not physical, but a spiritual, personality and moral likeness... So God created* **man** *and* **woman** *(expectantly) fashioning... forming... shaping and establishing them in His own beautiful image... and with His image inside of them... so they were (with all expectancy)made in the image and likeness of God as His created ones... His masterpieces... male and female He created them (filled with His* **expectancy**)*. **

And, this manifestation of *His expectation* was carrying... and still is as we know by the revealing and unfolding of *His Word*... a greater *expectancy* in that of *man*... a family... *His*. And yes... the power of the potential of *His expectation* being transferred through the expressed *image, likeness, fashioned and formed* of *Him – Them*, in us... **m**an. This leaves a powerful place for believing and positioning our belief in that the very **e**ssence and viability of *His Divine DNA*... was now in these **c**reated ones... these living beings.

Let's recall for a **m**oment that science has discovered a *double helix structure* in that which **m**akes up *man*... with the very **c**ore of it being **m**ade of *DNA - deoxyribonucleic acid*. This **c**omplimentary two stranded **m**olecule forms a double helix kind of spiral staircase... and is a self-replicating **m**aterial passed on in bloodlines being **c**onnected to what is inherited. It is *expected* to be found in our genetic **m**akeup... that which is hereditary being passed from our parents (father **m**ale and **m**other female) to a child... and that which is present in *living organisms – beings,* as seen in ***man***.

It's the **c**arrier for all genetic information possessing within it **c**hromosomes which determine the **c**haracteristics and qualities that are distinctive in **e**ach person they're housed in. And, it is responsible for the development and functioning of living... life... as a *human organism*. Often it is referred to as the *"molecule" of life*! What *expectancy* lies in it!

But through *Him* in us now... for me, perhaps for you too... there's something hovering out there in the 'spirit' realm **c**onnected to *Him* that **c**auses a curiosity in me... **c**reating a deep **e**ternal form of *expectancy* ... that there's **m**ore to the two strands of *DNA* than is obviously seen. Especially in the fullness of *Him*... where the *divine essence* in 'Them' as the *Holy Trinity*... which is *the Three*... **c**omes by our invitation to dwell in us **e**qually.

Remember, the glory of God is to conceal a matter; the glory of kings(us), is to search it out.* Although spiritual in its foundations... when we give our searching to *Him* and what we **expect** or desire to find *in the process*, we discover that the principles of *God*... and yes, this one, **c**an apply to all things in life. When our lifestyle is one lived in *Him* and *His* purposes in us, we see this at work often... and in our searching,

It didn't surprise me in my searching... to discover there's a form of *three cord* structure of non-**c**oding DNA *called H-DNA*. Immediately there was an *"Aha..."* that arose in me as I sensed in my spirit the '**H**' stood for '*His - His Heart*' *DNA*... with it forming a *triple helix* or also known as *Triplex DNA*. Interestingly it is seen in what is **c**alled *Satellite DNA*... either between two different *DNA* strands (inter) or within the same DNA strand (intra)... with the *intra-molecular* being formed by a ***mirror*** sequence that **c**auses a type of repeating within the single strand! Hmmm... gotta love what *He* will reveal, **e**ven symbolically in it all, when *He's* invited and included in the searching.

Oh yes... I **m**arvel at these kind of things because all <u>true science points to *God*</u> and *God* is the *pure Source/Force* that is *behind* and essential *within* the *science of God*. Immediately two scriptures **c**ame to **m**ind... with one being to how we are *woven or knitted together by Him in our mother's womb individually* as *His created ones**. The other speaks to how *love* is what *knits together believers in love**... which **c**an be said is the *pure essence* of who *God* is – *God is love,* therefore it is in and is *His DNA*... one **c**ould say and *H-DNA*.

We **c**arry this treasure in the earthen vessels we are. But, when **c**hoosing to also be *His* – a *born again child of God*... are we not now likened to that of *Jesus – Son of God, Son of Man*... as we activate the fullness of the *treasure, power, presence, purpose, provision... glory of Him – Them,* in us? For it is <u>not</u> of us... **it is of *Him!***

And, there in and of itself is a beginning that began the *'in the beginning'*... before the *Genesis 1 In the beginning.* If *He* is *the Word* that we treasure and find worth in, as it is encapsulated here in *the Word... for in the beginning was the Word and the Word was God, and the Word was with God*!* Oh my... again, what a perspective with an exclusive kind of divine **expectation** connection for the more of *God* all over it!

In the first chapter of *God's Worthy Word* we see a beginning... and in this *word of worth* **man** come forth... as a word written and as what it represents in a living being with the revelation of *Him*. All along... *expecting* His fullness to manifest in and through this **man**... this **woman**... and **them** being made in the express image and likeness of *'Them'* – the *'Us'* of Father, Son, Holy Spirit.

His **expectation** for the manifestation of what *He... They...* the expressed trinity of *Godhead* were *expecting* to do happened... and it produced man... and within them – **man** and **woman**, a **male** and *female* – was *Them*... and in the fullness of the expression of oneness in Him, *The One* – *Adonai, Yahweh*... our *God*.

And *God* blessed them with the seal of *His* love bearing *His* approval and agreement through the alignment in the breath of *His Word* speaking forth... bringing a binding of them together into their *mission* which became now a *'mandate'*... saying, "Reproduce and be fruitful! Populate the earth and subdue it!"* Which also was releasing a **commissioning** and a **co-mission** to them into their earthly mission full of power and purpose to manifest *His* kingdom in communion in echad... aligned with *Him* on earth as it is in heaven.

Remember, we call that *'original intent'* (OI)... before **man** sinning came confusing, causing crisis, opening a door to chaos (enmity), and changing the authenticity of their oneness status... in their *spirit to spirit* communion in the garden with *Him*. There and then **expectation** was tied to **motivation** driven by a *personal, intentional,* and *intimate relationship* as He had *designed, designated* to them, *desired* for and with them... and, was *distinctive* with **man** being cultivated in their *ongoing process* of relativity and relevancy being attached to and contingent upon the communion covenant relationship they had.

Who **man** was and was created to be had no limitations as long as they remained living in the **expectation** of echad, that unity of being one... eating of all the trees ... even the *Tree of Life - He* didn't tell them they couldn't eat of it. Just not of the *Tree of the Knowledge of Good and Evil* – the tree that held within in it an imitation... a counterfeit... and a death to the fullness of what and how *He* made them to *be... go... do.* Oh... to know and obey *the process His* way. It really is the only way... as *He's* the Only Way.

But *His* covenant with *His* creation demanded that just as it was driven by and written in *His* heart first... the giving of *free will* to man... *Adam, Eve, us*... with there never be a forcing of them or us to *honor, serve, worship,* and *work* together partnering with and in *Him*... for true pure LOVE cannot... will not.

In bringing things all together into a place of closure with our *word of worth* **man**... it's interesting it appear 2,614 times in the *KJV(King James Version)* of the *Bible*.* Just a side note here... s13 is the total of these numbers added together. In *Hebrew* the number 13 is connected to LOVE which has everything to do with it and man! Check I Corinthians 13 ♥

We see later that it is spoken of *Yeshua, Jesus*… whom *God* sent because *He* so **loved** the world – us… that came through the *expectation* of *Him* in *His* **m**andate and **m**ission to represent and **m**anifest in/on the earth as it is in heaven… in and as *Him* coming not just as *Son of God*, but together with *Him* as *Son of Man*… born through the virgin womb of a *woman* – Mary… as the *Holy Spirit* hovered and brooded over her implanting in her *His* spirit seed of life bringing forth what *He* **expected** to accomplish through a work done already and before the foundation of the earth.

He carried both the *DNA* of *God* and of **man** through *woman* in whom the *DNA* of *God* was already in for *He* knew and formed her, Mary, before placing her in her **m**other's womb… just like *you*… **m**e… **u**s. With that in **m**ind let's look briefly and in a simple way at **H-DNA**. Remember, it's a *three* stranded *triple helix* structure of *DNA* that adds another dimension which can come in two forms. From my simple defining it has the potential to **return** and **regulate gene expression** and depends on location and **sequence** in *proximity*… selah ~

> ❖ *Perhaps*…. If you can, just set aside your intellect for a **m**oment imagining through that *God* sanctified imagination we possess in *Him*… the spiritual possibilities of what this scientific structure and working paints in a *picture* presenting the potential of an **e=mc3** type of understanding… in the power of *Father, Son, and Holy Spirit*… **m**oving and **m**anifesting in us. Be encouraged right now to invite *Holy Spirit* to help and teach you to see in a beyond kind of way, trusting *Jesus* in *the process*. Be willing to allow the fullness to have a place to **m**anifest in any *expectations* of what this can **m**ean… particularly in connecting with our being *born again* (taking us back into an aligning with *His original intent*) which truly realigns us back to and into *Him* who is the *Hope of Glory* arising and shining! We are… or can be both a "son of **man**" and a "*son of God*" with *Christ* in us… in **man**. And, in being filled - endued with the **expecting** power of *His Spirit* to do in us and through us as it did in *Yeshua* while *He* walked the earth in *His* **m**inistry, the early church in its first hundred years, and continues to in those yielded *expectant* ones!

…but He emptied Himself [without renouncing or diminishing His deity, but only with the **expectation** of temporarily giving up the outward expression of divine equality and His rightful dignity] by assuming the form of a bond-servant, and being made in the likeness of **men** [He became completely **human** but was without sin, being fully God and fully **man**].*

We can further see this in the words and **m**odeling of *Jesus* while on the earth. *He* told them and tells us in *John*… *If you have seen Me… you have seen the Father.* As *He* is *so are we* to be… especially in *echad* oneness…unity. *It's good for you to be one as I and the Father are one**… as *Yeshua* also adamantly spoke and revealed in **m**ultiple ways.

Now our natural **m**inds create a narrative contrary to **m**ind of *Christ*…. but we're now new creatures; a new **man** in *Christ Jesus*. And, *Jesus* told *His* disciples… which *He* speaks also to us… that it was important to not only do what you see the *Father* doing and say what you hear *Him* saying… but just as *He* did when on earth as *Son of God, Son of Man*.

This aligning in *Him* came from an abiding of *Him* and *Him* be a dwelling place for *God* alone. *Him* being so aligned in oneness that *He* would not be conformed… but continually living *transformed*… for this would bring forth a renewing of the **m**ind necessary to carry out *God's* purposes and plans… as it was in the beginning. *He* **m**odeled it all for *He* knew the *expectancy* and its *expectations*. *Father expected to see* and *Jesus expected to see*… and *expectations* were *formed, fulfilled,* and ***manifested***. They **c**an be in us as we remain *in Him spirit, soul, and body* as well. He is ***Emmanuel***... *God* with us and because *He's* in us.

*"I will bestow upon them within **My** household both an honored place and an honored name, even better than the **(expected)** honor that comes from having children. I bestow upon them **My** everlasting favor; you will never be forgotten."* *

Oh... the honor of being given *His* name... not just *'son of **man'*** like **Son of Man**... but *'son of God'* as a **Son of God** like *Jesus*. We do not have to remain as just a ***man***. As *His* **c**hildren **c**arrying *His* name in its fullness we are royalty... as *Yeshua* is. For *He* is *King of Kings* and *Lord of Lords*. *He* speaks over us as well, that we are *His* Kings and Priests... who are seated with *Him* at the right hand of *God the Father* in heavenly places through the righteousness of *God* in *Christ Jesus*. How *He* **c**rowned **c**reation on the sixth day through **c**reating **man**.

We have additionally been given a seat at *His*, the *Lord's* table... where we fellowship and dine with *Him* regularly having **c**lose and personal **c**onversations where *He* reveals *His* heart, plans... and even *His* **m**ysteries as we sit ***expectantly*** for what *He'll* release for us to receive... **expecting** to see as we believe. Plus, partake of the **c**ovenant remembrance **m**eal.

He wants *you*... *me*... *us* – **man**, to know we **c**an belong to *Him* and eternally no longer *longing to belong, hoping to, or wandering* if we **e**ver will. As a part of *His* family we have every good and perfect gift that our *Abba Papa – our Father*, desires and **expects** to give us for *He* never lies. What we need to thrive not just survive... for we shall not want. And, all because *He* **c**herishes and values us as *His* beloved **c**hosen ones... **c**onnected to *His* eternal purpose, **c**onfirmed by *His* everlasting love, forgiven and received through *His Firstborn Son*... so let us stand embracing and being empowered with all **expectancy** of ~ *For He has set **eternity** in the hearts of men.*

e=mc3   *eternal* ones = *manifested* **man** *created* **c**onnected **c**ovenantally ***c**onfirmed* through the fullness of **Them** the ***3 in 1***... in **man**...by the **3rd power!**

<u>In light of this **word of worth... man** and what's been shared:</u>

- ❖ *Perhaps*... you ***Encountered or Experienced a Question or Challenge?***
  Write it out...

- ❖ *Perhaps*... more has been ***Established & Empowered by the Word?***
  Write what/which...

❖ *Perhaps...* it's time for **Engaging & Embracing your Expectations?**
   Write what's forming...

Reminder: For *clarity, connection, and confirmation* regarding **expectancy** being stirred by this *word of worth*, seek *Him* and *His Word* first. To possibly assist you in the process the list of **ION** words is available in the Appendix.

*Footnotes: Chapter 6 Day 1 man / * See Genesis 1 /1:26, Strongs Concordance H120 adam, John 14:9, John 17:21-23, I John 4:17, Genesis 1:28 – in TPT be sure to see footnotes, Proverbs 25:2, Phil 2:7, Psalm 139:13, Colossians 2:2, Isaiah 56:5, Ecclesiastes 3:11, Philippians 2:7 - all emphasis is mine and personal paraphrasing built on various translations and versions.

❖ Day 2: The Journey of "m"... M names

Let **expectations**... through this **word of worth's** part to *form, birth,* and *emerge* in its **meaning & mission**... our **meditation & motivation**... as **movement & manifestation** *awake, arise and align* in agreement with divine eternal **expectation**!

The *words of worth* we'll explore together as we continue in this *journey* with together in *the process* of growing, expanding and enlarging us to **expect** more, being more like *Him*... and entering into receiving from what *He* reveals. We'll discover a few of the *"M" names* of significant beings: eternal and earthly, male and female... presented to us in the *Bible*, in the *Christian* faith, and beyond from reliable sources in this part of our *pilgrimage*. Ones that *He* has highlighted to present and share about in a short summarized kind of establishing of them as ones with a **mission** connected to their **meaning** (purpose) and it being established in *Him* and *His Word*... with life and relevancy arising.

May what you encounter and experience through each produce a greater **expectancy** and further ground you in the **expectations** from the *past, present,* and that are *yet to come* relevant to *you... me... us,* because of what they were called and chosen for, engaged in, **embraced**, and were **empowered** by through their **expectation** in *God* and *His* in them... and ultimately in us as we partner with *Him* **expectantly**.

- ❖ *Perhaps*... you have a good foundation of knowledge and understanding regarding some or all of the *"M Names"* shared. So, this time in our *journey* will serve as a good time for *remembering, reflecting,* and *inviting Him* to reveal more with the principle of *Him* delighting in our seeking *Him* as we... *look, look again (not to look back),* and *look beyond* from the here and now. There's something powerful when that happens in the *ongoing process*... of a kind of expansion of revelation that arises influencing our **expectancy**. The part that can play in the **expectations** we currently have or have not had before. For now is a time to stretch out our ropes, drive down the tent peg, and receive... positioned to make a way for the NEW! *

    If some or all of these *M Names* are new to you... then in them there lies a door waiting to be opened... just like an opportunity to pull aside at an attraction that appears on a trip as if curiosity calls inviting you to come and see... come and discover more... to *expect* **and see!**

    In either case... it's good to *expect* to take at least a moment. *He* will lead you in the length of time... and meet you there when you are open to explore the how and why... as what's shared may relate to where you are in *the process* within your life's mission and journey.

    What *He* will bring forth always creates a personal kind of place for *mediation, motivation, movement, and manifestation* to offer up an *expected*... or even an **unexpected**, but beneficial way for *expectant* filled *encounter* and *experience*. Not to mention what it all can *establish* toward growing and maturing us in our faith... in our **expectancy** within the *foundations, functioning,* and *fellowship* we have in a life of relationship with *God.**

***Melchizedek*...** is revealed with his first **m**ention in the book of *Genesis Chapter* 14 as *Abraham* is returning from a battle where victory arose. He is a priest... a royal one and he rules over *Salem (Shalem)*, which we know to be a part of the word *Jerusalem*. And, it is the **c**ity that becomes **c**entral biblically as the **c**ity of *God's dwelling place... the temple*. It is also **m**ade known that he knows *Yahweh*, the *God of Israel*... who is our **c**ovenant *God* *... with *His* positioning dual in nature as a *King-Priest*.

When ***Melchizedek*** is presented or brought up in study or discussion... often attached to his name, let alone his role and purpose... arise questions filled with uncertainty regarding who he truly is. Yet, when you **c**ontinue to search for the **m**ore in the *New Testament* of the *Bible* where he is **m**entioned through an unveiling of him representing the royal priesthood. This **c**ovenant **c**onnection serves as a **m**odel... a foreshadow or type of *Jesus*. Therefore, a **m**odel for us. *Hebrews* **C**hapter 7 promises to arouse **m**uch *expectancy*... as it is dedicated to the revealing of important truths to receive... and to believe for the fuller **m**easure. So take some time if not now then soon to **e**nter in... and with ***expectation***!

What is written is important to **c**onsider and **c**ontemplate as it presents a kind of **m**ilk to **m**eat to **m**ysteries **m**essage... for does not *His Word* connect in an interesting way when it says ...*Yahweh has taken a solemn oath and will never back away from it, saying, "You are a priest for eternity, after the manner of **Melchizedek**!"** That beckons **c**alling up the ***expectations*** we are forming, **c**reating, and giving any kind of birth to in walking in and walking out our divinely assigned role as *His Ekklesia* who are to be *His 'kings and priests'* in the earth. Not to **m**ention we're **c**alled... even commissioned to as well, as *His royal priesthood* unto and into such an ordering.

My *personal journey* of discovery in ***Melchizedek*** has been *intriguing, rewarding,* and *provided for*... and still is, a **m**ost wonderful layering of revelation with **c**onnection to the truth of *His Worthy Word* in a foundation laid for now and **m**ost **expectantly** for the future. **M**ay your searching be so too. By the way... ***Melchizedek*** **m**eans, '*king of righteousness, king of Salem, king of peace'*.

***Moses & Miriam*...** the *deliverer* and his sister in which **m**ost who are familiar with the *Word of God* know them and their story in the *Book of Exodus*. Let's take this opportunity to recall them and their lives in part shared in a timeline kind of way... as we go about seeking and searching out what *He's* saying and wants us to see now in this time we are in.

His name **Moses m**eans *to be drawn out or taken out of water*... which speaks to what took place at the beginning of his life as a *Hebrew* baby when he was put in basket, adrift in the *Nile River* to preserve his life, and was discovered by *Pharoh's* daughter... who takes him in and raises him as her son; as a prince in *Pharoh's* house. After a **c**risis **c**omes... which always disrupts ***expectations*** and un*expected expectations* ... where he **m**urders an *Egyptian* fleeing as a fugitive to the land of *Midian*. He becomes a **m**eek **m**an who shepherds, **m**arries, has two sons, and begins his life of worshipping and serving *Yahweh* where he learns patience, trust, and so much more about *Him* and himself.

This all **m**aking the way for God ***expectations*** of him grounded in *His* eternal purpose for him. God has ***Moses*** approach *Pharoh* to "*let His people go to worship Him*", uses him to be an instrument of authority in the ten plagues that break out, along with the passing over of death through the blood of the *Lamb* on the doorposts establishing the *Lord's Feast of Passover,* and then as a '*Deliverer*' of *God's* people out of *Egypt*, breaking away from their *bondage, oppression and slavery*.

*Oh... the **encounters** and **experiences** **Moses** and even the people had as their God Yahweh used him to lead them in the parting of and **m**aking a way through the Red Sea... which no one **expected**. Nothing like the un**expected** He also provides! Then they entered into the wilderness with its almost 40 years of adventures like quail and **m**anna, the pillar of **c**loud by day and fire by night, the burning bush, the giving of the Ten Commandments, and all thereafter. To the **c**oming out of the wilderness to **c**ross over the Jordan River and into a new place... as the Promise Land was now before them. The power of God and His greater purposes **m**oving in their **m**idst, in their process... and always with His expectation ultimately ordering His **c**ovenant inheritance for them whether their **expectation** fully aligned with His or not.*

We see this in **Moses'** sister **Miriam**... a supportive sister who's role began as a strategic **c**arrier of precious **c**argo... her brother as a baby in basket... helping to save his life when firstborn sons were being killed. Now let's look at what **Miriam m**eans... *to be rebellious or bitter*... which we see later in her life, after the *Exodus*, becomes an actual trait that arises **c**louding her *perception and perspective* in delusion leading her in a direction producing an action that goes against not just her brothers leadership, but her true worship of *Yahweh*, their... her *God*. She had just led the people, if you'll recall, in a *new song of celebration* rejoicing in their victory of **c**rossing the *Red Sea God* had parted... along with the destruction of *Pharoh's* army. They **c**ould now **m**ove *expectantly* forward in new freedom!

Later upon **Moses** returning from the **M**ountain of *God* with the *Ten Commandments* he received from *God* to give to the people, he discovers they have **c**ried out for '*a god*' to worship. His brother *Aaron* and **Miriam** questioning **Moses'** leading too... gave place to and partnered with this rebelliousness as it **c**ulminated in **c**reating and worshipping the idol of the golden **c**alf they had **m**ade. *God* help us when we give place to ungodliness and idolatry.

Remember, we also saw her rebellion and bitter spirit during the *Exodus journey* in her **c**omplaining about Moses. The fruit of her rebellious pride in putting her *expectation* above that which Moses – whom *God* had **c**hosen to lead and direct them... **c**ausing leprosy to **c**ome upon her and her being set out of the **c**amp for seven days... not sure she *expected* that.

Yet, in **c**ompassion and through the loving **m**ercy of *God*... which is the *Hebrew* word *chesed*... she is allowed to later return to the **c**amp. Her return to them and to *Yahweh* redeems and restores her to being the anointed *worshipper, dancer,* and *prophetic minstrel of the Lord He* had purposed her to be as one of His *female prophets* and *Torah* teachers of women she was. **M**ay we *expect* such *chesed* to **c**ome to us from *Him*, even others, and to extend it as well as *He* freely does.

My how we see the role of some **ION** words influencing *expectation* in theses ones and their life stories and examples to us. May they help us grow our *expectancy* and **m**aturity as we are *continually* in *the process* of aligning all *in Him*. The **ION** list is there in the *Appendices* for you to *review and reflect* as *He* leads.

Mordecai, Micah & Malachi... these three **m**en of *God* were instrumental in **m**uch that happens during their time and their *expectation* of standing aligning with *Yahweh* and with being utilized by *Him* to accomplish *His* purposes. We see them *embracing* where they are, although difficult, and who they are as **m**en of *God*. Let's look briefly at each through a scripture linked to them.

Mordecai... not always known as a prophet, but he was... for he is better known as the adoptive family **m**ember of *Esther* after her parents death. He was a leader of *Israel* when they arose the potential annihilation by the wicked *Haman's* decree for the death of all *Jews*. However, it was also during a time when *Esther*… who was concealing she was a *Jew* after being chosen by the *King* to be his queen.

Which leads us to the power of words spoken like his… and at the leading of *God* that carry in them bringing forth an *expectation* that stirs conviction through connection and confirmation… along with an inner persuasion as were released by *Mordecai* to her, *"Do not imagine that you in the king's palace can (***expect** *to) escape any more than all the Jews. For if you remain silent at this time, (a greater ***expectation***) that liberation and rescue will arise for the Jews from another place, and you and your father's house will perish… since you did not ***expect*** *to help when you had the chance. And, who knows whether you have attained royalty* **for such a time as this** *and in* **expectation** *of this very purpose?** stirring deep in her his words called up a spirit of determination… through an intense inner *expectancy* of… *"If I perish, I perish."** May we **expect** modern *Mordecai's* to arise and *Esther's* too and be ones who will *pray* and *fast* for the revelation and strategy of *God*.

Michah… as a prophet of <u>God</u> he speaks to *Israel* at a critical time *telling them* that *God*, like a good *Shepherd* will regather rescuing them to *Him* as *His* people encouraging them… and us… with this promise filled word giving them hope, *"The breaker… the Messiah, who opens the way,* **expect** *Him to for indeed He shall… go up before them liberating them. They will (and can* **expect** *to) break out, pass through the gate and go out; So their King goes on before them, The LORD at their head."** Such words are wonderful to hear when *Micah* had also been correcting and warning them too – just as *He* lovingly does us… so our *expectancy* can shift… readjust… and realign to partner with *Him*.

Malachi… comes to Israel releasing the word of the *Lord* indicting them regarding their rebellion during their exile… yet, assures them that *He* will move to defeat evil never abandoning them as we see in the book of the *Bible* written by him. And, I'm sure there's been a time or two… when we've needed or appreciated such a word either through *His Worthy Word* or a personal word of the *Lord* to us. Here's one that brought great hope and should to *you… me… us*, when **Malachi** writes in the final words of his *telling*, *"Behold, I am going to send you (so* **expect** *it) Elijah the prophet before the coming of the great and terrible day of the Lord. He will turn the hearts of the fathers (***expectantly***) to their children, and the hearts of the children to their fathers (oh the* **expectancy***)… a reconciliation produced by repentance, so that I will not come and strike the land with a curse of complete destruction."** *Father*, help our *expectancy* to **expect to see** this manifest fully as is written by your faithful prophet **Malachi**.

Michael… the only angel in the *Bible* given the title of archangel… a chief messenger of *Yahweh* and we know from the book of *Daniel* he is the one who stands guard over *Israel*. When reading in the *Bible* book of *Jude*…it is a time we see it recorded of him speaking to *Satan* himself, *"The Lord rebuke you."** May our *expectancy* always be in the *Lord* to move on our behalf allowing our words to be the same as *Michael's*. Let our *expectancy* arise for *He* indeed is for us not against us.*

Matthew & Mark… two of the 12 disciples/apostles of *Jesus*, who were also authors of books in *His Worthy Word* for the purpose of spreading *Jesus'* gospel – the *Good News* and both share a commissioning to all who believe in and are followers of *His*. Because their writings have much in common with each other… along with *Luke*, and are called *"synoptic gospels"* meaning they can be seen or intertwined together. May these common scriptures carry a deeply devoted sense of knowing *His expectation* as *He* was hanging on the cross in the ninth hour and cries out… *"Eli, Eli, lema sabaktanei?"* that is, *"My God, My God, why have You forsaken Me?"* In His divinity as *Son of God* He **expected** knowing this **m**oment would **c**ome... but laying *His* deity aside as *Son of Man*... that is an agonizing but **expectant cry** of **expectation** that only *He* alone will ever know because of *Father's* and *His* great **eternal expectant love**. **Matthew** and **Mark** both chose to share this **m**oment of **expectancy**.

Mary the **Mother of Yeshua our Messiah**... highly favored of *God* and a young virgin, yet by the power of *Holy Spirit*, she... not **expectant** to give birth as divinely orchestrated by *God* or **expecting** to become an unmarried **m**other... let alone the **m**other of *Yeshua*, the prophesied long awaited **M**essiah of *God's* people. To encapsulate and exemplify her genuine **c**ommitment to her being **c**hosen and **c**alled by *Yahweh* for such... let's recall her words to the *angel of the Lord* and the **m**essage he had just delivered... allowing them to stir **expectantly** as a response we **m**ight want to **c**onsider. *"Yes! I will be a mother for the Lord! As His servant, I accept (with great* **expectancy**) *whatever He has for me. May everything you have told me come to pass."** Your **expected** end oh *God*. Selah ~

Martha & Mary... simply said, in our asking of *Him* that we **m**ay always know who we are and what we're **c**alled to be and do, like these two anointed women of *God* and sister friends of *Yeshua's* did and discovered **m**ore. **M**ay we honor what this word picture of *Yeshua* speaking to them and us, reveals... *"***Martha, My beloved Martha.*** Why are you upset and troubled, pulled away by all these* **m***any distractions (things you* **expect** *you are to be doing)? Mary has discovered the one thing most important by (in* **expectancy** *to please and delight Me) choosing to sit at My feet. She is undistracted (aligned in her* **expectation***), and I won't take this privilege from her."** Let such a devotion and desire **expectantly** arise in us!

What are some **M** names that *He's* **m**ade **m**eaningful to you, have become a **m**odel to you, and have **m**ade greater the potential in the possibilities and **expectations** in *His* ability to **m**eet you in *the process* **m**anifesting **expectantly**? Or they have helped you deal with the un**expected** in your life?

<u>In light of this **word of worth... M names** and what's been shared:</u>

- ❖ *Perhaps*... you **Encountered or Experienced a Question or Challenge?**
  Write it out...

- ❖ *Perhaps*... more has been **Established & Empowered by the Word?**
  Write what/which...

❖ *Perhaps*... it's time for **Engaging & Embracing your Expectations?**
   Write what's forming...

Reminder: For *clarity, connection, and confirmation* regarding **expectancy** being stirred by this *word of worth*, seek *Him* and *His Word* first. To possibly assist you in the process the list of **ION** words is available in the Appendix.

*Footnotes: Chapter 6 Day 2 M names / * See Isaiah 54:1-3, Genesis 14:17-20, Psalm 110:4, Exodus 3:12-15, Hebrews 7 – if TPT see footnotes, Book of Exodus, Micah 2:13, Malachi 4, Jude 9, I Samuel 17:47, Romans 8:31, Luke 1:38, Luke 10:41-42 - all emphasis is mine and personal paraphrasing built on various translations and versions. * See the Bible Project video teaching: *Abraham, Melchizedek, and Jesus* / bibleproject.com

✧ Day 3: The Journey of "m"... mountains

Let *expectations*... through this **word of worth's** part to *form, birth, and emerge* in its **meaning & mission... our meditation & motivation... as movement & manifestation** *awake, arise and align* in agreement with divine eternal **expectation**!

As we travel together in this *journey* of **expectation**... in the world we live in all around us in various ways and through a variety of **m**eans... which is **c**ontinually attempting to fashion, shape, **m**old, and **m**ake our **c**ulture through influencing, promoting, and flooding our daily living environments and atmospheres with ideas, beliefs, attitudes, and values... that go vehemently against the ordering, design, plans, and purposes of *God* for us, others... for all.

So let's adventure into a place where we **c**an **encounter** and **experience** a way, to discover and consider just how we... as we live out our lives in *Him* **c**an become ***influencers*** and examples of a better way... *His*. Remember... on this type of *pilgrimage* we're on, the exploration attached to **expectation** should begin to be a reverential one is some ways, respectful, and yes, enjoyable overall as we enter into the *process* in such and in *everything, everywhere*, and with **everyone**... especially with *Him*. Grace... extend it to all and yourself.

We **c**an invite and allow *Him* to visit and sometimes suggest *new things, thoughts, or ideas* to us. But, when we intentionally join together in a **c**onsistent partnering with *Him*... let us ***expect*** that a **c**onstant relationship holds within it always providing for greater potential and possibilities. Well, that opens a door **m**aking a way to **c**ounter the influences of the world in *yours, mine*... our lives and those around us so we **c**an be and bring forth a ***counter culture***... that of *God's – His kingdom will, ways*, and aligns with the eternal worth *His Word*.

There... in that kind of place... arises an ability for others to receive from our anointed authentic and sincere releasing in the **c**omings and **g**oings of everyday life as *He* is **m**oving in us reflecting and releasing hope, peace, joy, **c**ompassion, **m**ercy, kindness, grace... and **m**ore... and it's all *real... raw... pure...* filled with truth... because it's *rooted, grounded, established* in us... through the essence of *Him* and *His* love shed abroad in us.

It's *organic... relevant, relative, related*... to all being encountered and experienced in life in the world. *But God...* who *He* is in and through us... and how *He's* **m**oving and working in the **m**idst of it all... holds a powerful purposeful opportunity for an invitation to authentic relationship and fellowship... beyond how we, *you*... me influence and **m**odel... but as *He* **m**oves as their *Maker* to become their *Messiah*.

Do you suppose there's a way it... we really **c**ould? And, should we discover it to be so... would we? **C**ome... let's follow a purposeful path that leads us to a ***mountain***... actually ***mountains*** I've seen and have **c**ome to identify with... through a discovering uncovering an ongoing unfolding in and through this **word of worth mountain** and an ***expectancy*** that ***expects to see*** such happen and **m**ore ~

*In the last days it will come to pass... (so with great **expectation** we await knowing) the **mountain** of Yahweh's temple – the House of the Lord... will be raised up firmly established as the head – the highest of all the **mountains**... exalted and towering over all the hills. A sparkling stream of every nation (in **expectancy**) will flow into it. Many peoples will come (**expectantly**) saying,*

"Everyone, come! Let's go up higher to Yahweh's **mountain**, *to the house of Jacob's God; where we know (and* **expect**) *that He can... and will... teach us His ways. Then... we can and will walk (as His* **expectant** *ones) in his paths!"* This **mountain**... also known as the realm of *'Zion'*... Mt. Zion... where Yahweh is enthroned... there in the center where the ones... who in **expectation embrace** and are **empowered** by the instruction and the all wise word of Yahweh(and **expectancy** they contain)... and that goes out from there... into Jerusalem... and unto all the world... the nations... who will see His light, know His truth, and be changed... transformed... blessed.*

Oh... the continual *ebb* and *flow* of *the process* of change, transformation... can you see it... can you sense it... will you **embrace** it, even apprehend it? The ascending and descending of the **mountain of the Lord**... only to ascend and descend *again* and *again* and *again*... *receiving... reflecting... releasing...* and again... *receiving, reflecting, and releasing.* This manifesting of a form of *ladder,* like *Jacob* saw... in a regular daily form of encountering that connects us to a part of our *eternal purpose identity*... which can link us with a portion of the **expectation** of manifestation that comes as we move in obedience and in our authority in *Him* with *His* mandate to us... for *His* mission through us... in *His* commission for us... as *He* remains seated on *His* **Mountain** above all others.

An interesting side note... when we look back at the time *Jesus* was in the testing place of the wilderness on *a journey* where *the process* was preparing *Him* for *His* ministry, the devil took *Him* up to an exceedingly high *mountain* showing *Him* all the kingdoms... their *mountains* within the nations of the world and their glory... trying to convince *Yeshua* to worship him and in exchange he'd give *Him* all of them. But *He* knew they belonged to *Him* through the *Father* already... for they were a part of *His* inheritance the *Father* had promised *Him.** This is one of many *mountain* encounters in *the Word.* Mountains are important to *Him*... for *He* is LORD of the **Mountains**.

By the way... did you know that the top of the *mountain* can be referred to as the *'table'* - the flat part. The part where we're invited to meet and sit with *Him*... yet, we know now we're already *seated* in heavenly places with *Him* in the righteousness of *God in Christ Jesus*...should we choose to be. So let's purposefully, *expectantly* see ourselves there in *the process*. It's work produced not by might... nor by power... but by *His Spirit*... in our new man (our spirit) arising to *go...do... and be* from a place of intimacy and intentionality where divine **expectancy** is *formed, created, birthed,* made ready to manifest from there.

Either way... beside and with *Him* seated at the right hand of the *Father*... or at *His* table seated... the table of *His* **mountain**, *His* communion table *'doing this in remembrance'*... or at *His* banqueting table partaking of all *He* has for us to receive now. It's all with *Him*... in *Him*, and by *Him* for in our **expectations** we come to learn ***it's all unto Him, about Him,*** and ***for Him***.

With that in mind, let's travel a bit further to where we can take a look at and learn about the 'other' **mountains**. Already... as I *expect,* some might, have a basic or working level of knowledge and understanding related to these often called the **Seven Mountains** or the **Seven Mountain Mandate,** which include these cultural spheres of influence in society: *Government, Family, Religion, Education, Economy/Business, Media,* and *Arts & Entertainment/Celebration.*

For the sake of this day's journey let's move forward with the idea and **expectation** that we know it's good to form a common foundation establishing basic information that will create a type of illustration through a representation connected to the *meaning, identity, purpose,* and *functioning* related to the seven... particularly based on the above sharing, scripture, and strategy *He* has led me to present bringing us to this point.

Just a reminder... a *Point of Departure*; we've departed into this part of the *journey* regarding our *word of worth* **mountains**, **c**an also be a *Point of Access*. So this **m**ay stretch you a bit in your thinking or **c**hallenge you to see the point or its relevancy. I encourage you to sincerely invite and allow *Him* to bring forth what *He* wants you to know... and what this has to do with a relative place of **encounter** *He'll* **m**eet you in to **experience** something new or extend what you know. Along with, how your... our **expectations** are linked, related... even relative especially to the world *He* has set us in and those *He's* sent us to.

Let's begin in identifying what the **seven mountains** are and what they each represent... in the simple way I've discovered and as they have unfolded in my *personal, professional, and spiritual life* **experiences, encounters**, and by putting an **expectation** out there as *He* opened the door for me to be aware of them, allowing them to hold a viable place in the lifestyle of *worship /work /ministry I am, you are... we are* **c**alled to in the world; the **m**arketplace. This is just as we saw *Jesus* **m**odel out living, **moving, ministering to, and meeting** people in the world of their everyday lives... and for a reason. *He'll* be good to show you for you. We **m**ust remember however, *we are in the world, but not of it.**

The *Seven Mountains*... as we **e**nter into a brief defining and delegating some forms of **c**haracteristics attached to **e**ach of the **mountains**... receive from these *Worthy Words* from *His* for yourself. Let them be spoken and released over the **mountains** as they are presented and **c**onsidered linked to their relationship with or to the place of **expectancy** within us **c**oncerning them for *you... me... us... His* church ... *His* people... our place in *the process* of *life's journey* to influence the **mountains** with our part or piece **c**onnected to *Him* and *His* kingdom purposes... and beyond.

"Can't you hear the voice of Wisdom(her **expectancy***)? From the top of the* **mountains** *of influence she speaks (***expectantly***) into the gateways of the glorious city. All the places where pathways* **merge***, at the entrance of every portal (of* **expectation***), there she stands, ready(***expecting***) to impart understanding, shouting aloud to all who enter, preaching her sermon to those who will listen. I'm calling (in holy* **expectation***) to you, sons of Adam, yes and to you daughters as well."**

The Mountain of GOVERNMENT... indeed it is time we, for *His* righteous **c**ause, **m**ust be praying at **m**inimum, seeking *Him* to know our part and or piece to begin to take and take back this **c**ultural sphere influencing it through our involvement according to *His will and ways for truth, justice, law* and *order, mercy, peace, and more*. Through humble service based on **c**allings and giftings in the ones of integrity and honesty *He* sends to and sets in this political institution and structure that rules over and in the land and its people *administrating, legislating, and judicating civil righteousness* at all levels. I've heard it said, "All government starts with self-government."... which is **c**rucial of us to take ownership and stewardship for. Remember, this **mountain** establishes a legal form of *authority, control, and ordering* within/over ALL other **mountains**. And, *His* government rests upon *His* shoulders ultimately.

*When the righteous lovers of God are in authority flourishing everyone (***expectantly***) rejoices, but when the wicked ungodly ones rise to power ruling the people groan.** Does this not speak to an **expectation** of us to influence and be involved? Seek *Him* for *His* **expectations** for you regarding **government**.

***The* Mountain of FAMILY**... in the foundation of *family* as a *God* designed created 'unit' we can start with looking at the fullness of the *Godhead* as *Father and Son*, and then the *Holy Spirit's* role within. The *family* unit... as an institution created by *God* is particularly under attack now. Just as in the beginning, any UNGODLY form of worship seriously puts the *family* at risk... continually attempting to *destroy, redefine, and undermine God's* plan for family, in the attempt we'll depart from *His* plan giving access to the enemy to usher in his.

The **family** is very near and dear to *Father's* heart as *His **earnest expectation*** of and for a *family – **His,*** is reflected throughout *His Word*, *"... He will turn the heart of the fathers to the children, and the hearts of the children to the fathers..."* which speaks of *His* heart to us within *the process* of our lives, from the beginning when *God created male and female He made them* to procreate blessing them to do so by speaking over them to multiply replenishing.* *God* says, *He* is *our Father setting solidarity into **families****. *He* says when we pray to *Him* to pray, *"Our Father, who art in heaven..."** and then later we see that we're *adopted into the family of God.** Know our heavenly *Father* has **great expectancy** for us desiring us as *His **family*** to partner with *His **expectations*** so *He* can release our inheritance of *blessing, promise,* and *provision*.

The *Mountain* of EDUCATION... as believers we know it is essential and *God* has an ***expectation*** of us to *train up our children in the way they should go so when they are old (we can expect that) they will not depart from it.** It's key to know this training starts with and is primarily the role of their parents... and in the home... teaching them of *God's Word, will, and ways* for their life so they will live righteously with rational clear thinking and the ability to *process* their knowledge with understanding applying it to life through wise and productive means and methods. Any additional training is meant to supplement that of the parents (within the family structure) as *education* coming from the church and how *He* orders... so together they work in agreement and alignment with godliness. ***Education*** is said to be *skills or knowledge developed or obtained through learning and the ongoing process of it in our lives*. With the majority of **education** coming from outside the home and through others today, we can see why it is vital we have an ***expectation*** to influence this ***mountain***... plus, also return the importance of its role through parents within the family and home... as well as the church. May this ***expectancy*** be awakened in all these forms of educators and education

The *Mountain* of RELIGION... *oh* the deluge of gods and spirits inundating the world today also with the god of self, self-righteousness, and all forms of idolatry, immorality, and ungodliness right in there too. Certainly that fact alone reveals the great necessity for influencing this ***mountain*** to godly and righteous ways under *Yahweh* – the *God of Abraham, Isaac and Jacob*... and for calling them all to fully come under the '***mountain of the Lord** and let Him teach us His ways.*'* This battle over influencing the ***mountains*** goes back into time and before earth as we know it... to where *Lucifer* fell thinking he could be like *God*. The war is and remains over *who we will worship*... as we saw it start in the garden and the enemy ***expects*** to continue not letting up. May our ***expectations*** tied together with *His* as the set apart influencing sent ones we are... draw us to impact this arena of society.

Let's continue on remembering what *He* has told us to do... *"Trust in the LORD **(expectantly)** and do good; dwell in the land and cultivate faithfulness. Delight your-self **(with expectancy)** in the LORD; And He will give you the desires of your heart. Commit your ways (daily **expectingly)** to the LORD, Trust also in Him, and He will do it... and help you to do it"* *... as *He's* there in ***expectancy*** with us too!

The *Mountain* of ECONOMY / BUSINESS... work is a divine **m**andate from when life began in the garden through *Adam and Eve*. Therefore,... we would be wise to start with the **m**odel Jesus exemplified when *He* said and did what *He* said... and did regarding such even as a boy. *"I must (His **earnest expectation**) be about My Father's in My Father's house... and, be about My Father's business."** To the point of where later *He* was flipping the tables set up by the merchants and **m**oney **c**hangers there... because it was a blatant disregard for the holiness of where they were: the temple... which was **c**onsidered *God's* temple – *His*, our Father's house. It was not the **m**arketplace... but in the **m**arketplace... so we **c**an't help but view the **c**onstant influence and powerful part **m**oney... the spirit of *Mammon* plays in **e**very sphere of society where ***Business*** is an integral piece in each. Godly **c**ouncil and strategies are vital to bring forth... as well as encouraging those gifted **c**alled ones to *Him*. To arise so they **c**an discover that part of their life *process* which is linked together with their eternal purpose/destiny and it *expectantly* in *Him* for *He's* written of the place they are positioned.

With this all in **m**ind... a simple but important aspect in our perspective when forming *expectations* should be that we too be about our *Father's* ***business***... as *He* **c**alls us to take our influence out of *His* house of prayer/the **c**hurch... and be *His* '*temples*' going to the people in the **m**arketplace to be salt and light sharing *Him* with them. Let us partner with what *He **expects*** in the **c**alling them to *come back to God*... and to do all as unto *Him* with the ***expectation*** of knowing their *work is their worship is their work* unto *Him* with *His* purpose-filled ***expectancy*** linked through *His* loving faithful provision for all they, we need.

The *Mountain* of MEDIA... is indeed one of the **m**ost **c**urrent extreme societal arena's for influencing and influencers of our time, particularly when it comes to the *Good News*. Yet... the **m**ajority of the time it **c**an appear to be influenced by **e**veryone and **e**verything but that. *God* help us and **m**ake a way for *Your* plumbline of truth to be restored for *You* have said... *How beautiful upon the **mountains** are the feet of him who comes to bring and announce (**expectantly**) the good refreshing news... publishing peace... carrying the wonderful good news of happiness... publishing salvation to Zion, "Your God (as **expected**) reigns."* For it is not a blessing and it doesn't really benefit us to call evil good and good evil replacing darkness with light and light with darkness or the bitter with sweet and the sweet with bitter.* It is a time for those to arise and shine who will *tell them His* truth so it **c**an establish an ***expected*** foundation and framework through the power of words that **c**ontinually **c**arry ***expectancy***... *His*!

The *Mountain* of ARTS & ENTERTAINMENT / CELEBRATION... probably the **m**ost **c**ontroversial of all the ***mountains***... yet the idea of ***celebration*** in its pure and unadulterated form is *God's*. We see its beauty all around us... yet beauty is in the **e**ye of the beholder says the world. *He* says beauty **c**omes from our inner being – who we are and are in *Him*. Therefore, what we are beholding affects what we **c**all or see as pure and beautiful or otherwise. And... this ***mountain*** is very diverse including all forms of ***entertainment***, *music, drama, art, sports, dance, fashion,* and all the other variety of ways we **e**njoy life... and **e**nter into receiving from and through the ways of ***celebrating*** life that are godly...in godly forms.

This ***mountain*** especially attracts and targets **c**hildren, youth and young people because *God* is the Creator, **c**reative, and takes pleasure in **c**reating in and through all *His* **c**reation. So... *He* who is in them and how *He* **m**oves through them is something the enemy, with evil forces wants to **c**apture, kidnap, and **c**ontrol in the *journey* of their life's *process*. And, as soon as possible he begins drawing them away from the pure form of *God* to the **c**ounterfeit he offers... versus the innate essence of their godly *DNA* producing in them a pure *desire, gifting,* and *talent* stirring ***expectation*** for such expressions and ***celebration***. Due to time we **c**an't explore this in depth, but recognize the need to address that the church hasn't done the best with teaching stewardship... let alone ownership through lordship in these areas and others. To birth and bring forth a *godly counter culture'* of influence and interaction with godly guided **expectancy** is therefore, of **e**xtreme importance to *Father*.

As we **c**lose... let's look at a part of the **m**eaning our *word of worth* **mountain** in its roots as *har* in *Hebrew*. One portion of it paints a type of picture compared to what happens in or with a *promotion*. Hmmm... so who/what is being *promoted*... elevated... now within the ongoing *process* in the **mountains**. Who will *promote* what *He* desires and **e**ven requires *His* ones to *promote His* **m**ission/**c**ommission to us within the seven... and how **c**an the ones... you, me, we... who are to *promote Him, His gospel of salvation* in its fullness as the *gospel of His kingdom* too... do so within them and in the marketplace of the world? Only by *His Worthy Word, will,* and *ways leading, guiding, and directing* us with all *expectation* of knowing we're to grow becoming influencers for His kingdom's sake. *With God all things are possible* ~ so let's **expect!**

> ❖ *Perhaps*... if or when we **c**an begin to... learn to... fully **embrace expectantly** doing such beginning with our **expectations** in our daily lives giving an intentional place of **c**onsideration to the potential of all the opportunities... filled with the **e**xceeding abundancy of possibilities and that *Holy Spirit* will help us. Help us understand how the **c**oncept and action of this kind of *'promotion'*... and as an act of bringing someone into a place where **more** is now required and **expected** of them (us) in their (our) position. Remember, we are **c**alled to be **m**inisters with the **m**inistry of reconciliation... to **c**all people *back to Father... to God*. This type of *His promoting* of us **c**alls for a greater level of responsibility... which opens a door for greater prominence... which **c**arries within it an **e**nlarged realm of distinction for theirs and our influence to **m**ove, be a work... and by *Christ* in us. For *His* grace and gifts, nature and attributes within us are to rise and shine in *the process* of the **expectancy** to live and do life in this way. It starts **m**erging together with *His* desiring and **e**nabling us to be the salt and light *He* has **c**alled us to be. We move as ones then who *follow, serve, worship,* and through love in all we do and it being done as unto *Him*. Interestingly, we're given an incredible opportunity to believe to see now how *He's* brought forth a way where it's tied to being wrapped in **expectancy**... and yes, in this *word of worth* **mountain - *har***. Oh... **expect and see** that the *Lord* is good!

Let us never forget no **m**atter where we are at... presently in our **expectations** and how they **m**ight... could... should align with the prospect of what's been shared with you regarding the *word of worth* **mountain**... and in what these words from *His Worthy Word* tell us... "*For behold, He who forms the* **mountains** *and creates the wind and declares (****expectantly****) to man what is His expectant thought... Who makes the dawn turn to darkness and treads on the heights of the earth... yes, the* **mountains** *of it —the* **Lord, the God of hosts, is His name**".* The **mountains** are *His*... these belong to *Yeshua, Jesus our King,* and *His kingdom*! *His* house is at the top of them. We, in our **expectancy**... will see this day **c**ome. Amen.

And *He* has spoken it... *You Yahweh will (in all* **earnest expectation***) bring them into the land of promise, and plant them in the* **mountain** *of Your inheritance... the place, O LORD, which You have made for Your dwelling place (the* **mountain** *of the Lord), in Your Sanctuary, O Lord, which Your hands have established. For all who join themselves to Yahweh to worship Him (our work is our worship and our worship is our work)... those who want to be His servants and love His name... honoring the Sabbath and not disregarding it... remaining true to My covenant... I make this promise... 'I will welcome you into* **My holy mountain** *and make you joyful in* **My house of** *prayer*. *I will accept every sacrifice and offering that you place on **My** altar, for **My** house will be known as a house of prayer for all people.* *

Let us *imagine, hope* and *believe* for… with boundless *expectation*… such places… houses… altars… within and in all *seven **mountains*** that are under the established ***mountain of the Lord*** and for the establishing of *His* kingdom where are all in echad… in the One… as it was in the beginning… and will forever be.

And we say ***expectantly***, "Not by might, nor by power, but by My Spirit says the Lord … Who are you… what are you, great adversarial ***mountain*** of unbelief… what are you religious obstacles and ***mindsets***… hindrances or deterrents of any kind… before us the sons and daughters of God… His ambassadorial apostolic sent ones… His empowering equipping edifying *Ekklesia made* of *His* kingly priests. You will become a plain (for we ***expect*** it)… flattened… of no affect or ungodly authority… as the ***mountains*** will arise under the ***mountain of the Lord*** as they are being and will be influenced by the infiltrating of *Christ* in us and *His* kingdom plans with *His* purposes arising and with confident ***expectant*** loud shouts of "Grace, grace to it!" In Yeshua's Name – amen. Now that's ***expectancy***!!!

e=mc3   eternity = all ***mountains*** under the ***mountain*** of the *Lord* with *His*.   **created** ones ***covenantally committed*** to *Him* and *His **commissioning continually celebrating** Creator God* to and in the **3**rd **power** fullness of *Him* as *Father, Son, Holy Spirit*.

<u>In light of this **word of worth**… **mountains** and what's been shared:</u>

- ❖ *Perhaps*… you **Encountered or Experienced a Question or Challenge?**
   Write it out…

- ❖ *Perhaps*… more has been **Established & Empowered by the Word?**
   Write what/which…

- ❖ *Perhaps*… it's time for **Engaging & Embracing your Expectations?**
   Write what's forming…

Reminder: For *clarity, connection, and confirmation* regarding **expectancy** being stirred by this *word of worth*, seek *Him* and *His Word* first. To possibly assist you in the process the list of **ION** words is available in the Appendix.

*Footnotes: Chapter 6 Day 3 mountains / *See Isaiah 2, John 17:16, Proverbs 8:1-4, Proverbs 29:2, Gospels of Matthew, Mark and Luke re: Jesus wilderness testing, Strongs Concordance H2022 *har*, Amos 4:13, Exodus 15:17, Isaiah 56:6-8, Proverbs 29:2 Government, Genesis 1, Psalm 68:5-6, Matthew 6:13, Ephesians 1:5, Malachi 4:5-6 Family, Proverbs 22:6, Ephesians 6:5 Education, Proverbs 3:5-6 Religion, Psalm 37:3-5, Matthew 21, Mark 11, Luke 19, John 2 Economy/Business, Isaiah 52:7, 5:20 Media, Psalm 16:11, 2 Chronicles 5:11-14 Arts & Entertainment / Celebration, Isaiah 56, Zechariah 4 - all emphasis is mine and personal paraphrasing built on various translations and versions. * See The Seven Mountain Prophecy Quick Reference Chart / Johnny Enlow Bk: The Seven Mountain Prophecy – Unveiling the Coming Elijah Revolution / Appendix and www.restore7.org.

✧ Day 4: The Journey of "m"... message

*Let **expectations**... through this **word of worth's** part to form, birth, and emerge in its **meaning & mission**... our meditation & motivation... as movement & manifestation awake, arise and align in agreement with divine eternal **expectation**!*

Moving through our *journey* with "**m**"... let us set our **expectations** both for the natural and spiritual revelation we are being presented with that creates an **expectancy** ... and especially for MORE! What a great "**m**" word that is... MORE! Particularly as these first days in this 28 day 'pilgrimage' have presented much in their messages for us to *meditate* on as we in this ongoing process. May our **expectations** and the **mission** they are connected to by what they carry, be expanded, enlarged... tried and tested... exceedingly presenting to us and ultimately leading us to embracing and being empowered more by their connectedness, relativity, and relationship to *Him* and to *His*.

In this **word of worth - message**... much will open up to challenge us in *our looking, looking again,* and *looking beyond* into the what lies within and past the typical perspective, attitudes, or outlook we take once we've read, heard, or received a **message** and its contents... let alone its purpose, along with the **mission** it may contain and convey to *you... me... us*.

A **message** can be simply defined in these words... *note, letter, memo, memorandum, conversation ... a form of communication*. And, they can be *written or spoken*... even perceived... with the idea that information is being *shared, conveyed, transmitted, conducted, even implied*... between/from one person or party to another.

Often within a **message** is contained a **mission** attached to its purpose. The meaning of **mission** is *a task, job, assignment, kind of work or undertaking to be accomplished or achieved* related to a goal or purpose that requires or is attached to some form of action.

The first **message** that came forth in the earth perhaps can be seen in the words of *Elohim* as He spoke... "*Let there be...*".* These words were extended in their substance of *His* essence into *His* creating of and breathing *His* creative power – the same power within the words that created all of creation... was also at work in the fashioning, forming, and bringing forth mankind on the sixth day... as *His* created ones. Here we immediately read discovering a **mission** attached to and aligned within what *He* defines as a most essential part of their (our) purpose... *to be fruitful, reproduce, multiply, replenish* and *populate, filling, subduing and taking dominion over every living thing in the earth.*

With many, many hundreds of years passing... we see a **message** with a divine and eternal **mission** come through *God*, in *His* fullness coming to the earth in and through *Jesus His First Born Begotten Son, as Son of God, Son of Man* – our *Messiah* and *Redeemer*... sent to *save, deliver, heal,* and *reconcile* us back to *God* as *His* 'born again' created ones – "sons". Those who choose to believe in *Him*, repent, turn away from the world and their old man/self to *Him*, and live a life of *loving, following, serving,* and *worshipping Him*.

Along with coming through the fullness of *Him* as *Holy Spirit*... whose **mission** in large part is within the **messages** and assistance *He* gives and makes available to us continually as the *Spirit of God* being our *Helper, Teacher, Comforter, Advocate, Revealer of Truth,* and as the *Source* of power we are endued with. This encompasses *God's* **message** and equally the **mission** given to us so *His* kingdom can come with *His* will being done on earth as it is in heaven. What *a process* and **expectancy** that all *contains, conveys, and carries.**

Truly *the Word of God* in *Jesus* – I am *The Word*... and the *Holy Spirit's* **message** and **mission** are divinely connected in covenant through *a marrying of Them... them, together* that cannot be separated. Try as ones may... you cannot have one without the other. That's the way *He* designed and desires it to be... us connected by the *Truth* and the *Spirit*... in and to the fullness of *Him* as one in "*Them*"- one in the *Father, Son, and Holy Spirit*. When you have one you get all three. For in actuality... try as you ma, *you... me... we,* cannot separate Them.

Reflecting upon the above and the **expectations** that may be surfacing because of the **expectancy** that's associated to the content of what came forth within the overall **message**... and the related **missional** assigning... let's meditate for a moment in the *meaning and motivation* attached to the simplicity of this *word of worth message* and its linking to **mission**. By bringing together a foundational perspective and functioning within their joined framework and with that which *spoken words* can carry... these messages and the role they play and in some profound ways... if we'll **expect** it and enter into it all too.

Here's a few reminders about the power and purpose of spoken words – the **messages** we carry and release when we speak. Our words, *yours... mine,* must be... which is only by *His* grace... aligned with what *He* has spoken. Because words transport and release what's within them each and together. That's God's principle of sowing and reaping... along with the vital importance of them being aligned in *His truth, life,* and *love*... which is who and what *He* is. Therefore, they deposit seeds of *Him* who is *the Word* and in all kinds of soil.

In a kind of abstract way, let's not forget to consider closely examining beyond what *He* is saying... like when *He* said... *"Ask, and it – anything, a gift or otherwise (***expect***) it will be given to you; seek, and (***expect***) you will find discovering more... answers even; knock (***expectantly***), and it – the door, I am the Door... eagerly waiting to and will be opened to you."** May an **expectancy** for such arise more fully... and may it be carried out manifesting in the **message** and **mission** of our words aligning with *His* having a profound influence and impact not just on us and our **expectations,** but on others and theirs... and in our world.

For... *the tongue... with words being released... spoken... are so powerful they can... yes (we can* **expect** *they) will, bring death or life; those who love to talk... indulging it... will (should* **expect** *to) eat its fruit... and (expect to) reap the consequences of their words."**

For remember as well... *by your very words yours...mine... ours – reflecting our spiritual condition, will (***expect to***) be justified, and acquitted being sentenced as innocent (the* **earnest expectation** *of the blood), or by your words you... me... we will (can* **expect to***) be condemned (***expectantly*** if rejecting Him-Truth) guilty."** What power words hold... and what fruit unfolds in and through them. Truly we must weigh with fervent **expectancy**... the **message** and **mission** within them.

He is the **Word**. *He* is the **message**... as *graphe*: the written word of *God* in the scriptures, and yes as *logos*: the totality of *His Word* revealed. The written and the spoken word coming forth... ultimately is alive with personal meaning and holding enormous purpose revealed to us... and within us by *His Spirit* – *rhema: revelation*. Therefore, we can extend this to *Him* fully as *He* was and is. The *One* who is the **Message**, the **Messenger** of the **Message,** and the **Commissioner** of the **mission** within it all and in which *He* has **expectantly** purposed a releasing of it in the ways

He did while on earth. And... in its commissioning to us and beyond... in what we carry connected to the *eternal expectation* dimension of *expectancy.*

These forms of *Him* as *The Word* in *His Word* and words... come to us in *the process* of life as *manna**... that daily bread *He* provides as the "*Bread of Life*"* *He* is. In its most basic level of sustenance, *this Bread*... it contains all that *He* speaks of and says it does. *He* offers it to us to freely partake of in *His* written *Word,* when *He* meets relationally with us through it *individually, collectively,* and *corporately* in *communion, conversation,* and *connection,* and when *He,* as manna is joined by the spirit to us through *Holy Spirit.* Any level of our *expectancy* makes way for *His manna messages* to *root, ground,* and *establish* us in *Him.*

Additionally, there's a simple form of it called *milk** that's growing us as we develop and progress with a revelation that manna and milk *messages* are good... but, there's often a hunger within for more. This opens a door to being established in *the meat messages* in the *process* of becoming more mature disciplined ones who regularly partake of, meditate upon, and chew on it; *His Word* and related *messages* of words that align, agree, and as *meat*... the essence or main heartier substance it is made up of and what *He* reveals to partakers.*

Not to mention... the multifaceted, beautiful, powerful ways that *He* chooses... at times *He* determines... to reveal in the depths of *this growing process His* mysteries... things hidden being unveiled to those earnestly searching deeper because their hunger puts a demand out there... for a boundless *expecting* has been awakened. Those, who won't relent until through this level of partnering produces *encounters* and *experiences* where the manifestation of *His* more becomes the norm of their *expectancy.* Those... *perhaps us*... who are indeed becoming like *Him. Messengers* who as *His* conduits contain and carry the *Message*... *His* holy kingdom one where the *expectancy* within it amazingly brings a form of heaven to earth.

One thing for certain about our *expectations.* We can *imagine, meditate on,* and *devise* much within them. However, if *you... me... we* are *in Him*... knowing as *He* is so are we to be... and that *in Him* we are to *live, move, breathe* and have our very being... then the *expectation* that is formed by *His* words that are formed in *the Word*... and that word *to, in* and *through* us... that all creates the greater *message* of *His.* A *message* we can now partner with in the *mission* we're in on earth... *His.* Involving us and influencing others as it invites *His* presence, power, and *glory* which *saturates* and *permeates expectancy* into atmospheres where *mission expectations* always and in all ways *move* and *manfiest.* Selah ~

*"Once your life was full of sin's darkness, but now you have the very light of our Lord shining through you (**expectantly**) because of your union with Him. Your **mission** is to live (in **expectancy**) as children flooded with His revelation-light! And the supernatural fruits of His light (**carrying expectancy**) will be seen in you—goodness, righteousness, and truth (**expectantly**). Then you will learn to (**expect** and) choose what is beautiful to our Lord."* *

❖ *Perhaps*... this is a time to pause and let what you've read be heard through your "*spirit ears*"? You know... *having an ear to hear what the Spirit is saying**... unfolding in this *message* with a *mission* allowing that to hover and brood. *He* will be good to present a type of emphasis on that which *He* knows *you... me... we* need to focus on at this time... place.. and season of *the journey* we're each uniquely in. *He* will bring before us the needful *message He* desires us to hear... to listen to... to receive from so the *mission* is clear... and *His* greater commission connected to it starts to be imparted and embedded in our *expectations* as well. Oh... what *messages* the *Father* has for us to hear and by *His*

Spirit… and with not just our *spirit ears*, but our hearts fully aligned with *His*. The **expectancy** of the *Father's* heart, *His* **expected e**nd, and **e**verything in between *He* has for us and **c**alled us to.

Let's turn now to what *He's* revealed in *His* **Message** in *His Worthy Word*… to us through two versions of a special kind of *message* that is actually a *commission* that tells about our **m**inistry **m**ission as the *Body of Christ – as Believers, Followers, Disciples.* Ones aligned with and **c**onnected to *Him* are to partner and **c**o-labor with the bigger spectrum of *His Kingdom* **m**andate to **go, taking** and **telling** the "*Good News of the Gospel of Jesus Christ*" *message* to others… all the world – *tongues, tribes, nations…* and *generations.*

We see these two *commission* variations in **Matthew 28** and **Mark 16**. They both release to us a **c**ommon **m**ission with **m**andates that reveal strategies for *the process.* As well, each **c**ontains and **c**arries distinctives that **m**atter and **m**ake a difference in our ability to understand the fullness of what we actually are being *commissioned* for and to.

There's a **c**ouple key words we're going to take the time to define in simple terms before we go further. A **mission** is *an assignment, undertaking, kind of task or job and they all involve a type of work.* Ours is a **<u>co-mission</u>** **m**eaning we're partnering with someone else… in this **c**ase it is God… and it is in and through *His* fulness as *Father, Son, and Holy Spirit*. That's why above it is **m**entioned about *co-laboring* with *Him;* not just partnering… there is a difference. And it's good to note, *commission* is an **ION** word **m**eaning some type of *action* is involved or required in part to what the word **m**eans.

The *Good News of Gospel of Jesus Christ* actually has two **c**omponents. One aspect that is typically taught as the **m**ost essential dynamic of this *mission* and where the **m**ajority of the church is putting its *expectancy,* if it is actively following this biblical directive at all. It speaks to our **c**all to the "**Gospel of (or unto) Salvation**". **E**qually as important and vital is the inclusion of the whole **message**… not just from the first **c**omponent of salvation – which is the door… but to the overall **m**aximized **e**ssence and *expectation* within… regarding the crossing over the threshold into it also being a *"Gospel of the Kingdom of God / Heaven".*

Both of these sets of scripture are shared below with a very brief summary pointing out their similarities and differences. Then a **c**oncluding view point on why it's **c**ritical the **c**hurch be *preaching, teaching,* and *equipping* all for the work of this **m**inistry according to both the **messages**… *what He has written. Father* has an *expectancy* for this and we should too… *His* Kingdom **m**anifesting on **e**arth as it is in heaven. Please note… these are as written in the KJV with no personal paraphrasing or no author additions. The **m**ost ancient **m**anuscripts of **Mark c**onclude with verse 16:8. Later **m**anuscripts add verses to form an **e**nding, **c**omplimentary to what's been said. Verse 15-18 are what is shared in both sets of scripture.

MATTHEW 28 … And Jesus came and spake unto them, saying, All power is given unto me in heaven and in earth. Go ye therefore, and teach all nations, baptizing them in the name of the Father, and of the Son, and of the Holy Ghost: Teaching them to observe all things whatsoever I have commanded you: and, lo, I am with you always, even unto the end of the world. Amen. (KJV)

MARK 16 … And he said unto them, Go ye into all the world, and preach the gospel to every creature. He believeth and is baptized shall be saved; but he that believeth not shall be damned. And these signs shall follow them that believe; In my name shall they cast out devils; they shall speak with new tongues; They shall take up serpents; and if they drink any deadly thing, it shall not hurt them; they shall lay hands on the sick, and they shall recover. (KJV)

To summarize in general, let's start off by pointing out... these two versions of the *"Great Commission"* are not opposing each other for both have their valuable and much needed place. We become and do all mentioned as we *go, do, and be* in the earth according to what *He's* called, chosen, and commissioned us to... and according to what both *messages* require.

Dutch Sheets, a type of *apostolic watchman prophet* whose call is mainly in the area of government in our nation of America... and to *edify, empower, and equip* the church corporately in the sphere *He's* assigned him to. I have chosen to listen to and receive from regularly from his anointed ministry holding it all before the *Lord*. I was particularly blessed by some strategic revelation that he shared about within both sets of scripture... their commonalities and differences, why they matter, and putting them into context with both *Gospel's* components in mind. Additionally, where the church is headed apostolically and as *His* kingdom ones – some call the *His* ekklesia in the earth to nations and generations. So check the footnotes for links should *He* lead you to.*

For what are *you... me... we* to *tell them*? There's a *message* connected to the commission *He's* given to us... and within that good news *message*, there's a type of increased larger *telling He's* given in our individually unique testimonies that speak to the hope we have, the light we carry, and the *Father's* love we've personally *encountered* and *experienced*... we are... and He desires us and all to be continually.

Someone is waiting... actually *expecting* for something is stirring deep within them a knowing there's more yet be revealed and fulfilled in life... and it's more than a need they have; it's a *longing*. A *longing* to hear an answer in *the place of the process* they are in... *what is this that is drawing and attempting to lead me through a door that's I sense is there before me?* Oh the inviting that leads into a *belonging fulfilling the longing*. And that *message*... well,... you, me, we **carry it!** Lay down any form of fear quickly so your faith *expectingly* can arise to GO & TELL!

Many are in the valley of decision... and NOW is the time to **GO** in *expectancy*... yes even **TAKE** *expectantly* what *He's* given you to take or take back... and then **TELL** *expecting Him* to move toward them with arms open wide waiting to receive them. And, *tell well* so NEW *expectations* in them... and even in you... can *form, birth,* and *manifest* in salvations, healings, deliverances, and more! What a *message* we *messengers* get to take and tell!

e=mc3   eternal life = the **Man's** and **man's mandate mission motive** manners in the *message* **manifesting** through **Christ's continual constant communion commitment** in **covenant catapulted** outwardly inwardly by 3rd **power** propelled by the *eternal essence of purpose* and *love*.

No greater love has this... than we lay down our life for Him our Friend, our friends... and as friends to be in **expectancy**!

<u>In light of this *word of worth… message* and what's been shared:</u>

- ❖ *Perhaps…* you **Encountered or Experienced a Question or Challenge?**
  Write it out…

- ❖ *Perhaps…* more has been **Established & Empowered by the Word?**
  Write what/which…

- ❖ *Perhaps…* it's time for **Engaging & Embracing your Expectations?**
  Write what's forming…

Reminder: For *clarity, connection, and confirmation* regarding *expectancy* being stirred by this *word of worth*, seek *Him* and *His Word* first. To possibly assist you in the process the list of **ION** words is available in the Appendix.

*Footnotes: Chapter 6 Day 4 message / * See Genesis 1:26-28, John 3, I Peter 1, Ezekiel 36:26, the four Gospels – Matthew, Mark, Luke, John, Matthew 7:7, Proverbs 18:21, Matthew 12:37, Deuteronomy 8:3, John 6:36-51, I Peter 2:2, Hebrews 5:13-14, Colossians 3:4, Revelation 2 and 3, John 15:13 - all emphasis is mine and personal paraphrasing built on various translations and versions. * See Dutch Sheets Ministry official link @dutchsheets.org > The Two Commissions/ 2017
https://dutchsheets.mybigcommerce.com/the-two-commissions-mp3 download/?searchid=71099&search_query=two+commissions

✧ Day 5: The Journy of "m"... ministry

Let *expectations*... through this **word of worth's** part to *form, birth,* and *emerge* in its **meaning & mission**... *our meditation & motivation*... *as movement & manifestation* awake, arise and align in agreement with divine eternal *expectation*!

Our **ministry** as a Believer... as a son or daughter of *God* is to *Him* first and foremost as *He* is the Most Worthy One we are to give ourselves freely to in *the process*... the *journey*. This is evidenced in the fullness of our yielded surrendered life we offer continually through our *sincere love, adoration, devotion, worship, service*... given with all *our heart, soul, strength,* and *mind* which is all a form of what can be called and seen as our *personal* **ministry** expression to *Him*. And yes... our *expectancy* within it all must equally be offered up to *Him*... as I hope and believe you're discovering in this quest we are on together. That together which is in *Him*... and as *His*.

Never forget... one of the main desires of *Father's* heart was to create ones – *you, me*... *us*, to be *His* beloved family on the earth With us... those created beloved ones *He* desired... and desires. *His* personal '**ministry**' to us was designed to be through *authentic personal one-on-one relationship* with *Him* as our heavenly loving *Father*, not just our *God* and *Creator*. That *communion union* – *that oneness, echad* we've spoken of that *He* had with humankind in the beginning... and as it was modeled later to us in the life and union between *Father and Son*... and is what *Jesus* earnestly exhorts us to pursue.

For each of us it is intended to be a *genuine, intentional*... even *intimate* coming together that *He* pursues with us continually in the ebb and flow of life. Yet, it is unique in that *He* meets us each in ways *He* knows are special to us helping us to **embrace** and **be empowered** through *His* **ministry** to us... and by the **expectations** that stir a knowing, let alone the **encountering** and **experiencing** of such **ministering**. Remember... *He* is the *Author* of *expectancy*... and yes, the *Finisher* too!

Oh the beautiful, powerful, and personal.. yet collective **ministry** *of being one... yes, you... me... us in and with Him, our Father, the Son, Jesus, and by His Spirit Holy Spirit... where we're living fully in (expectancy in) Him as He lives, moves, breathes, and is our being as He manifests fully in us. And from such a posture and place we position ourselves so that the (expectant) words of my mouth and the meditation – those thoughts of my heart in its every movement, be always pure, pleasing, acceptable before Your eyes in Your (expectant) sight, Yahweh, my Lord, my firm, immovable Rock, my Protector, and my Redeemer.**

Yes... this goes back to and connects with the idea that in the *original intent* of what came forth in the beginning... and as seen even in the words used and the essence of their fuller **meaning**... *our work is our worship is our work*. ALL that *we are, do,* and *become* in part is the very essence then of the fuller meaning of our personal **ministry** that's to others... when being done for *Him* and as unto *Him*... is essentially through and by *Him* in us.

Ministry that should be and truly is best when it is our life; a "*lifestyle*"... because it's easy when we know why we are here... align our **expectancy** accordingly with our **expectations**... establishing all in *Him*. Where *His* heart displayed is seen in and toward every needful, essential element of our connectedness to *Him* that truly and eternally matters... and is expressed in our ongoing mutual **ministering**.

Ministry where as our *word of worth* it is, can simply be defined in a few ways as *holy orders for service, work, a holy call, vocation, a religious occupation for some, a part of our worship*... yet, it can be a structure such as *an agency or department of government.* These all involve various types and levels of service – work one to another, to or for some group, to or for someone; in which for the *Believer* it is to *God*, and it emanates from a fully devoted commitment to such a call, to such work… in and with one's life… one's purpose even.

Hence it ultimately becomes a type of driving force affecting what we or others **expect**… with all the related and varying **expectations** and *impact, influence,* and *interconnecting* in the adventure and *process* of one's life! And,… we can certainly see where it helps to connect the fuller meaning through the root word **minister**: which at its core simply means *to serve…* Its primary focus established in the foundation of the idea that the *service* in the way one is *serving, working* and potentially within their *calling…* is where what they are offering is **primarily to and for others.**

This is key for *you… me… us* to understand and **embrace** for the *connections, interplay, and interchange* that takes place within our *expectancy…* and thus our **expectations** is and can be enormously impacting. Actually it has the potential to be… and truly is at its core… **eternally impacting** for those who **minister**. Devoted **ministering** ones who grab ahold of this understanding, walk in, and are intentional about *our lives* being the '*platform*' of and for our '*ministry*'… to the ones we have, are, and will **minister** to in a variety of ways.

Let's explore some of what *Yeshua* says regarding this…. *a person who loves his life and pampers himself will eventually (can* **expect** *to) miss out on… even lose out on encountering and experiencing true life! But the one who detaches his life from this world… hating his life in this world because he is concerned with (establishing His* **expectancy** *in) pleasing God… and abandons himself to Me, will keep it, finding true life… yes, eternal life and (fervently, earnestly, expectantly) enjoy it forever! If you want to be My disciple, follow Me – without hesitancy holding steadfast to Me… conforming to My example in living… and if need be suffering – perhaps, even dying because of your faith in Me… you will go where I am going. And if you truly… continually faithfully serve and follow Me (as He* **expects** *- positioned in His great love and desire) as My devoted disciple… for there you as My servant will be also (the manifesting of mutual* **expectancy***)… for the Father will (expectantly) honor you and shower His favor (an* **expectant** *form of His kindness and goodness) upon your life.* *

My… what *a process* with layers of **expectancy** and all the attached **expectations** that *He* has shared with us and modeled for us regarding this life of **ministry**… being *His* **ministers**… **ministering** from the *relativity, relevancy,* and *relationship* we must always… yes, even out of necessity… have with *Him*. It flowing from *Him* in and through us so all remains as unto *Him*, for *Him* where *His* purposes and plans are aligned rightly to flow to others as *expected* … for theirs and our sake. So, the ultimate *benefits, blessings and promises* attached **expectantly** manifest glorifying *Him* and reflect *His* heart for *His* purposes here on the earth.

Our willingness to consider these things in our **expectancy** aligning first in *His*… requires we – as *His* **ministers** represent *Him* well. Within you there is a plumbline… most certainly if *He* is in you… to not just represent *Him* well, but to model *Him* as *He* is in what is good and right in *His* sight… what is just and true, honorable, of the highest integrity… reflecting *His* attributes as well as *His* example as *He* did to us in and through *Him* as '*Son of God'* and as '*Son of Man'*.

An alignment/accountability assessment tool that *He* connected me with in a season where there came a great shifting in the course of my *life's journey*… propelled me into a deeper level of commitment and personal spiritual development by providing a type of means and a way to measure as it were, key areas/things in our personal lives that truly do matter. Particularly in view of our life's *ministry* and a way to *view, discern* the plumbline, and *obtain* an overall state or condition of any *minister*... even *ministries* in general.

The 10 M's for Maturing and Maintaining Ministries was a tool created by *Bishop Bill Hamon,* founder of *Christian International,* in what God revealed as vital to ministry life and includes the following ten "M's" – *Manhood, Ministry, Message, Maturity, Marriage, Methods, Manners, Money, Morality, and Motives.** They still provide life scale for me.

> ❖   *Perhaps*... for you as for me, once I heard mention of these I knew immediately within me it was *Him* answering prayer providing me with direction and strategy for godly growth... for developing the depth of my 'being' and character... to be and become all *He* was... is establishing in me in becoming more like *Him.* For a passionate *expectation* was *budding, blossoming,* and *blooming with* me... the real me. And, I believe within you, there hovers a similar *expectancy He* has placed there in you like in me... and for us as *His* family. For *He* met me in that place of longing not just for belonging... but the belonging of aligning in, with, and to what is true, pure, just, good, godly, and fully by and of *Him*... *His* eternal purpose and destiny for me, my life, my *ministry*... as for you and yours too.

How you might ask and why? He taught me to let the list be a working kind of framework providing a solid biblical structure and godly moral foundation... to look at and evaluate... that is to say, myself and where I was in what I desired. Each of the ten began to have *expectations* within them undeniably intertwined in this *ongoing process* of life – particularly life *in Him.* Their connectivity within them all contained and carried the ability to assist with the creating of a foundation of *expectancy* for aligning my life... the *ministry I am, you are, we are called to* in a fuller measure with the power and purposes of *God's Word, will, ways* and as did and does *His* character, nature, and example for life and living.

This continual ongoing *process* in varying ways and types of *stages*... within the *process* of life's greater adventurous *journey*... not to mention the influence and impact such opportunities for intentional and meaningful self-examination these ten provide. Which makes a godly, positive, and trustworthy way for guiding our *expectancy*... our *expectations* forming, adjustments needed and necessary in *the process*... the forming, *creating, birthing and manifesting* that is ongoing as well. Truly... should it not be what we *expect* of ourselves... and each other as the body of *Christ* and as the *family of God*?

Remember, first these characteristics and attributes... and beyond into *the methods, manners, and motives*... are well modeled for us in the *ministry* of God the Father, God the Son – Yeshua/Jesus, and God the Holy Spirit to us. Yes, it is *His ministry* to us by *His Spirit* – *Holy Spirit,* that is what originally draws and calls us to *Him*... which begins *the process* then that opens the door to our lives becoming *His*... as we become *His* born again children... and live our lives in service, worship, and living for *Him* with all that we are... and all being done unto and for *Him.* Remember... as *He* is so are we to be ~ oh the *expectancy.*

Additionally it's important we recognize that foundationally the mission/commission of the *ministry* we've been called and assigned to is divinely described as being a *ministry of reconciliation.* At its core in the idea that to *reconcile* means to – to *return, reunite, resolve, restore* back to original intent or purpose, bring back into unity that which was broken by separation, disagreement, or as expressed in the word of God, through man's sin – which links *reconciliation* to the atonement that *Jesus's* sacrifice of *His* life brought forth to remove the barrier sin created between humanity – us and *God*.

We see this in what *His Worthy Word* reveals to us in this way about such **ministry**…

But all these things are a gift from God, who **m**ade *all things new and reconciled us… bringing us back to Himself through Christ…* **m**aking *us acceptable to Him… for He* **expected** *to do this before the foundations and gave us the* **ministry of reconciliation** *– reconciling others to God, so that by our* **(expected)** *example we* **m**ight *bring others to Him – we* **m**ight **(expectantly)** *call them pleading with them to "Come back to God…", that is, that God was in Christ – the Anointed One - reconciling the world to Himself, not counting people's sins against them - but canceling them – not even keeping records of their transgressions. And He has committed to us* **(expecting** *us to carry and release)* *the* **message of reconciliation**… *that is, restoration to favor with God. So we are ambassadors for Christ, as though God were* **m**aking *His appeal (in* **expectancy**) *through us; we - as Christ's representatives – His* **ministers**, *minister…pleading with you on behalf of Christ to be reconciled to God. He* **m**ade *Christ who knew no sin to… judicially… legally… be sin on our behalf, so that in Him we would become the righteousness of God… that is, we would be* **m**ade *acceptable to Him and placed in a right relationship… our reconciled reunion of oneness/echad, with Him by His gracious lovingkindness.**

My what a **ministry**… of *Him*, the *One*, who **m**inisters so those *He* **m**inisters to can **m**inister… and with **expectancy** that *His* pure, sure eternal love "energizes" … driving it so the **m**otivation is *holy aligned* with *His* heart; the returning of the *Father's* heart to the children and the children to the *Father* – as *He* **expects**.

Meditating on the fullness of *His Word* as expressed above and in general as well… inviting and allowing it to take *you*… *me*… *us*, into the beyond of *His* **m**odel and example. Indeed, it does have a way of **m**aking a way for us to begin to *embrace, adopt, and settle* within us what are the good and right ways to *worship, serve,* and *go* about the work – the **ministry** God has called us to.

With *Him* assisting us in aligning our **manhood, motives, manners, methods, message, ministry**… our **money** too and the **managing** of all ten of the "**M's**"… in all truth and godliness withing what *He originally intended…* all we had need of was provided through the *Tree of Life* and *Living Word* (which *He* is) for producing such in and through them then… and as it can and should be for us in *Him*… what *He designed, planned, purposed*… **expected.**

Therefore, these **m**entioned above along with the **m**any other dynamics of **ministry**… plus, within *the process* of **expectancy** producing godly **expectations**… it will all come **m**ore naturally as we *grow, develop,* and *mature.* Yet, let us not forget, these aspects dynamically *require a kind of intentionality* that comes with an *investment of time and effort* grounded in *genuine desire* and always over time. Thus, we will see their overall role *influencing, directing,* and *impacting* us in life and in our **ministry** – the **lifestyle of ministry** where *our work is our worship and our worship is our work*… and **m**ore than we think… as it should – agree? And… it does please Father.

For both in the ongoing unfolding potential within the beauty and power of the *depth and complexity*… as well in the possibilities of *practicality and simplicity* offered… we come to know we are **m**ade for **m**ore… and that **m**ore in part **m**anifests in the **expectancy** and **expectations** we receive in *His* revealing as *He* does and for *His* **ministry** we're called and created for! Imagine… He desires to use us in this way ~

In this place of *ministry* in all its godly potential budding, let's take a **m**oment to look at the realm of **m**ore that is available as our visit with this *word of worth ministry* draws to an end... and, extend what's being presented to include a **m**ost vital and necessary *threefold structure* within His divine design for *ministry*. Hmmm... *threefold*... is there a *third power principle* yet for us to see?

We began this day in our *journey* with **"m"** in the importance of our personal *ministry* of *adoration, devotion, worship, service*... *giving our very all, our lives to Him*... and a glimpse of our good, good *Father & Creator's ministry* to us. And, we cannot complete this time without recognizing the fullness of *His ministry* to and through us in these three distinct *ministry* forms, particularly in the course of our lives spiritually and our relationship with *Him* including the role of *expectancy*.

In *His Worthy Word* we see expressions revealed to us in a variety of ways. The t*hree* we'll touch very briefly on are identified as *The Ministry of the Father* - given to us in what **m**any **c**all or recognize as the *"Motivational or Redemptive Gifts of God"**... *The Ministry of the Holy Spirit* - given to us in what are referred to as the *"Gifts of the Holy Spirit or Spiritual Gifts"**... and, *The Ministry of Jesus; the Son*– given to us in what are called *"The Ascension or Five-Fold Ministry Gifts"*.*

My heart is to **e**xpound more on each of these *ministries* for they are full of such incredible benefits that have **m**anifested in varying unbelievable blessings and beyond to those who honor His **m**oving in and through them. Not to **m**ention... how *He* has designed in it all for us to partner with *Him in His - this ministry* – be it to us personally, to others around us, or it being *you... me... us, ministering* out of these graces as *He* gives **m**easure and **m**akes a way for. Wherever we are... as *He* shows up and **m**oves as only *He* can in *His process* and within ours to **minister** to the needs at hand by *His Spirit* and stirring **m**uch *expectancy*... this **m**eeting of *expectations* creates a place for new *expectations* to arise filled with *faith, hope,* and indescribable anticipation and hope as *His power, presence,* and *glory* are present.

The *gifts* are worthy of recognition beyond just being foundational and functioning as the needful and necessary areas of *ministry* they are. For imperatively, we should deem them established as required for *He* has seen to set them into place **m**odeling them in the *ministry* of *Jesus* while on earth, *His* disciples/apostles, *His* church that was birthed, and now in us. Through the birth and examples within *His* early church, and **m**aking them available *to, in,* and *through* us... He designed and designated them to be essential parts of *teaching, discipling, equipping, actively applied in all ministry, building up,* and *uniting* the *Body of Christ* as we reach oneness in faith, in one accord, as **m**ature *Believers* with our gifts active.

Fundamentally, is it a form of requiring of us as the *Father's* said to be like *Jesus*, who was about our *Father's* business *receiving from Him and Holy Spirit operating in, and releasing* to others. The gifts are particularly **e**videnced operating in those who are willing to **embrace** and be ***empowered*** by the *Spirit*, and their **c**onnectedness to the ***ministering*** not just of the *Gospel of Salvation*... but, the *Gospel of the Kingdom,* and to all who will receive.

There is no greater time or reason than to obey and please *Him* now. Not just by who you are and what you do, but in full surrender and devotion in the ***ministry*** *He's* called YOU to.

Passionately and adamantly I now **e**ncourage and **e**ntreat you to pursue not just knowledge and understanding... but equipping beyond just teaching. That which releases *impartation* with opportunity for *application* and *activation*… as part of *your process* in becoming well *grounded, rounded,* and *established* for/in **ministry**! That is *my hope and expectation* for and of you! I believe I **c**an have such **c**onfident *expectation…* as it's *His* too!

e = mc3   *establishing* of *eternal expectancy* = *manifestation* of *man's ministry* in its *methods, manners, motives, messages,* and *more* in the **mutually constant communion** and **continuity** of ***Christ*** in you… me… us as ***covenant commission carriers & conduits*** to the **3rd power** by ***His Spirit*** – the fullness of *Father, Son, Holy Spirit*.

In light of this ***word of worth… ministry*** and what's been shared:

- ❖ *Perhaps…* you ***Encountered or Experienced a Question or Challenge?***
  Write it out…

- ❖ *Perhaps…* more has been ***Established & Empowered by the Word?***
  Write what/which…

- ❖ *Perhaps…* it's time for ***Engaging & Embracing your Expectations?***
  Write what's forming…

Reminder: For *clarity, connection, and confirmation* regarding **expectancy** being stirred by this *word of worth*, seek *Him* and *His Word* first. To possibly assist you in *the process* the list of **ION** words is available in the Appendix.

*Footnotes: Chapter 6 Day 5 ministry / * See John 17, Psalm 19:14, John 12:25-26, 2 Corinthians 5:11-21, Romans 12:3-21 The Ministry Gifts of Father – The Motivational Redemptive Gifts, I Corinthians 12 The Ministry Gifts of Holy Spirit -The Gifts of the Spirit or Spiritual Gifts, Ephesians 4:11-12 The Ministry Ascension Gifts of Jesus – The Fivefold Ministry Gifts - all emphasis is mine and personal paraphrasing built on various translations and versions.   * See The 10 M's for Maturing and Maintaining Ministry by Bishop Bill Hamon / Excerpted from Dr. Bill Hamon's book, "Prophets, Pitfalls and Principles" by Destiny Image 1991 / Appendix.

✧ Day 6: The Journey of "m"... maturity

*Let **expectations**... through this **word of worth's** part to form, birth, and emerge in its **meaning & mission**... our **meditation & motivation**... as **movement & manifestation** awake, arise and align in agreement with divine eternal **expectation**!*

*... and he will be standing firm (in **expectancy**) like a flourishing tree planted by God's design, deeply rooted and fed by streams of water – brooks of bliss... bearing and yielding its fruit in every season of life... for its leaves don't wither or dry... and, in whatever you... me... we do, never fainting... we(**expectantly**) come to **maturity**.**

Maturity means simply the state of or quality of being ***mature***... and so ***mature*** means *having come to or attained a desired state or condition of full development, exhibiting well balanced and responsible behavior, an adult who is older, or the state of reaching the most advanced stage in a process.* Oh the *process*... is it not in and a part of everything?

Telios is the word used in the *Greek* for our *word of worth **maturity***. *It means perfected, complete, mature.** It is often seen and should be... in the character of a son or daughter of *God* reflecting *Christ* likeness... and can connect with being developed spiritually beyond just character and moral perfecting, into the manifesting of one's faith. Just as we mature so should our *faith;* a fruit of ***maturity.***

So as we continue advancing into this *journey* and *the process* of our encountering more of *Him* and *Him* within our ***expectancy***...where ***maturity*** will be something that plays an important role regarding much... in the subtlest and weightiest of ways as one's commitment and discipline of *heart, soul,* and *body* to it. Along with the willingness of recognizing ***maturing***... it all comes with its own kind of cost requiring an intentionality always... and in all ways, to produce results that are fruitful related to ***expectations*** of ours, others, *His*.

In *His Worthy Word* we are told that... *through Him we also have access by faith (**expectancy**) into this remarkable state of grace... which we encounter as an expression of His marvelous kindness in which we firmly, safely, and securely stand (**expectantly**). Let us rejoice in our (**expectant**) hope and the confident assurance of experiencing and enjoying the glory of our great God... in the fullness of the manifestation of His excellence and power and not only this... but in confident joy let us rest in our sufferings, and rejoice in our hardships, knowing (and **expecting**) that hardship... distress, pressure, trouble... which produces patient endurance; and endurance, refined and proven character - spiritual **maturity**; and proven character, hope and confident assurance of eternal salvation. Such (**expectant**) hope in God's promises never disappoints us for it is not a disappointing fantasy, because we experience the endless love of God... which has been abundantly poured out cascading into and within our hearts by the Holy Spirit who was given to and (with **expectancy**) lives in us.**

Much in *the process* within this *journey of life* and all attached ***expectancy***... over and over *again* we are fined we're given opportunities to *distinguish and determine* what is good and right versus what is not good and not right in the area of our growth and development. These determining distinctions can be seen functioning and manifesting *physically, emotionally, cognitively, relationally*... and yes, *spiritually*... thus affecting every area and arena of our lives.

One could say *maturity* is *the journey of the process* of *maturing* over one's lifetime. As we *mature, grow,* and *develop*… get *grounded, settled in,* and become *established*… what we **expect** and the connected **expectations** progress and mature in *this process* likewise and in an interconnective way.

Along the way… *His* part in it all begins to sharpen and shape us. For we learn… *The plans of the heart belong to a man… but the answer of the tongue is from the Lord. For all the ways of a man are clean (expectantly so) in his own sight… and, we may think we're right all the time, but God thoroughly examines and weighs our motives. And, the living Word of God is full of (expectant) energy… so like a two mouthed sword it will penetrate to the very core of our being where soul and spirit… bone and marrow meet (as expected). It even truthfully interprets and reveals the thoughts (expectations) and secret motives of (tied to the expectancy) our hearts.**

CAUTION: Often as a way to appear *mature* or convince ourselves or others regarding our *maturity*… within us - our soul, we can be challenged in this *process* and in what will attempt to influence and direct ours or other's *expectations*. For example… when we desire certain results or responses seeking to impress or convince, we can be tempted to manipulate. Unfortunately… this can open a door that lends itself to the ignoring or the opposite in the manipulation of *His Word* – what it says, means, and in context of what *He* is revealing and any connected requirement.

Again, motives and methods determine much in our forming of *expectations* and they are a driving force that works to creating a way for what is truly in the abundance of our heart to flow out… good, bad, or indifferent.

> ❖ *Perhaps*… it is within such times our *true manhood, motives, message, manners, ministry*… those 10 **M's** as previously mentioned… matter most in what then forms for what we and others **expect** *of* us… *from* us… *for* us. But, more importantly is what we **expect** of ourselves and within the context of *His expectation* of and for us. *His* overrides any others… and must be allowed to have the role and place that helps readjust us so the reestablishing of what is good and grounded in *Him* by *His Word, will,* and *ways* can prevail providing for us a sure and firm foundation that *the process* of our *maturing* has been setting into place and securing. Remember, our **expectations** can come to a point of expiration. Be sure to seek *Him* regarding timing - *His*… for what is being reset. And here's a thought… perhaps a *mentor, pastor, prayer partner, godly spiritual life coach, counselor, teacher, or another* person who represents a type of mature *Believer*… is something *He'll* open a door of relational connection for in *this process*. This can truly add many benefits and blessings when we're open and willing to explore such with realistic and mutually aligned **expectations.**

All of this within the topic of **maturing… maturity**… requires we acknowledge why we should *willingly, sincerely,* and *seriously* to take a look at the role our *soul* plays in the **maturating** *process*. Because **expectancy** will certainly be affected by our soul and the aspects and effects of what we **expect** will undoubtedly be working to some degree or another… whether through our part or the part of another or others. Let us not forget to consider and call upon the **expectant** role of the *Holy Spirit – our Helper, Teacher, Advocate, Revealer*… the *Spirit of Truth* for all that *He* is and does to aid in the *processing of* our *soul* in *maturing*… and what that looks like in spiritual development and **maturity.**

As you'll recall… the *soul* is composed of the *mind, will,* and *emotions* and is a **m**ajor influencer of the flesh in all its varying facets and features… **c**reating a type of **e**ntwining that often projects things into the arena of our *expecting.* Remember too… a **m**ajor way the soul works is through **projection** and **perception**. Two of those key **ION** words that **c**an tend to be up at the *top of the list* for having some form of bearing or impact within or upon what we *expect* and why or why not/

This is a topic I believe we **c**an all totally relate to… in how the broad spectrum of the *soul*… with its **e**ngaging fluctuating **e**motions, the deciding and determining role of our *will*, along with the intellectual rationalizing and reasoning realm of our *mind*… **e**ach in the extensive roles these *three* dimensions of the *soul* respectively, yet **c**onnectively play… and what they produce in the larger overall picture here is not only relative, but **e**qually relevant.

From producing feelings of *love, faith, joy, hope, patience, happiness, acceptance, assuredness* and **m**ore… to *unbelief, sadness, weariness, displeasure, rejection, discouragement, doubt, skepticism*… just to identify a few. **E**ach **e**ither help or hinder where we are and desire to be in *the process* and undeniably within our *expectations* and our life.

One beautiful and powerful perspective and outlook **e**ssential and productive for *you… me… us* to tap into… that brings forth strategy and ways for the good fruit of our *expecting* to arise… is to remember and respond by and out of the **new creature of Christ in us**… and in faith: that *fervent hope filled expectancy*. Believing that *He* made our soul, it is good… and as we grow in *Him* it is **c**oming up and into its refining… sanctifying… *maturing*… being **m**ade **m**ore and **m**ore like *Him*! The **expectancy** that unfolded in the old things has passed away… **behold all things are new – yes YOU**!

For… *we all, with unveiled face* – because that happens the **m**oment we **(expectantly)** turn to the Lord with an open heart. *We draw close to Him with the veil removed from our faces*… **m**aking us become like **m**irrors *who brightly reflect the glory of Him who we are***(expectantly)** *beholding as in a mirror the glory of the Lord* – which is the Holy Spirit being referenced here… *for wherever* **He** *is Lord* (now that's *His* **expectancy** so *He* **c**an help **e**mpower ours in *Him* to arise)… *there is freedom*… *as we are being transfigured and transformed (in all* **expectation***) into His very image… the same image from glory to glory, just as by the (***expectancy*** of the) Spirit of the Lord.***

What we *see* **m**anifest from *maturing* unfolding is every time *you… me… we* **m**ove aligned in *Him*… in giving the fullness of *Him* full **Lordship**… so the glory in us that **c**omes from such in *Him*…it gets brighter as the blessings overflow **m**ore abundantly and readily.

Oh… the value in these **m**irror **m**oments looking at the **m**an or the woman in the **m**irror is required. Examining one's self, particularly in what we *expect* of ourselves… it will **m**ake all the difference in what we see. Is it through a lens of reality or a lens bearing an image influenced by the world, self, rejection, trauma, deception, or other hindrances keeping *Chris*t from arising and shining in *you… me… us* with *His light, life, and love* in which we are created and *expected* to do?

*The mind of sinful man is (***expected** *to produce) death, but the mind… when controlled by the Spirit is (***expectantly yields***) life and peace; the sinful mind is hostile to God (you can* **expect** *this). It does not submit to God's law* – which in *Him* is out of love and for our good… *nor can it do so. Those controlled by the sinful nature cannot please God (an accurate* **expectation***).** Our **expectancy** is to please *Him* with all our *soul* – *mind, will, emotions*… right?

*For... All that He does in us is designed with an **expectancy** to **m**ake us a **mature** Church for His pleasure, until we become a source of praise (**expectantly**) to Him—glorious and radiant, beautiful and holy, without fault or flaw... His white, spotless, pure, and holy Bride.**

Don't forget, part of the preparation in **m**aturing **c**omes in all *three* of these: the **m**anna, **m**ilk, **m**eat portions... with **e**ach having a part in the *progress* and *process* of our development... **c**oming to us in the *Word of God,* through *Jesus's* wise *worthy words,* and by *His Spirit.* Therefore, they all play a part in our **maturity**... why we are, where we are... due to what we are... or aren't partaking of. *He* is the *Word*... these are all forms of *the Word* alive **m**oving, and **m**anifesting for those who partake... remember?

Valuing, acknowledging and *prioritizing God's Worthy Word* is vital for **maturity**... as **e**ach of us in our own unique way and within *the ongoing process* are taking in varying **m**easures of it. Undoubtedly, in our relationships with *Him* and others... and within the **m**inistry of our lives *He's* **c**alling and drawing us to and **c**hosen for *you... me... us.* We need *His anointed Word sharpening, refining, and perfecting* us into *His* **m**ature sons... daughters... *His* fruitful **c**hurch... and radiant *Bride* in the **expectant m**aking and shaping going on!

Character, along with *integrity* is a byproduct of it all. So let's reflect now on a few general thoughts that **m**ay have *transpired* in *this journey*. Character is what you do when nobody is watching. Character is also how you treat people who **c**an do absolutely nothing for you. Character is how you react when the pressure is on. Character is deciding beforehand that you are going to do the right thing. Just a few **e**xamples of **m**any defining words I've recollected that speak to the important value of **c**haracter.

We **m**ay not see the dividends immediately of what *good godly character* produces -- but be assured that *God sees, knows, and recognizes* the fruit of all our **c**haracter **c**hoices. And, *He* will **m**ake good on what *He* determines and desires. For again... as *He* is, so are we to be... and the work of that **expectancy** is at work in us **c**ontinually. It's up to us to whether we partner with it... allowing the **manifestation** of what it will produce to arise and demonstrate *Him* in an *honorable, just,* and *godly righteous* way to the world around us.

My brethren, **(expectantly)** *consider it nothing... counting it all joy whenever you fall into various trials, knowing* **(expecting)** *that the testing of your faith through experience produces patience – endurance leading to spiritual* **maturity** *and inner peace. But let enduring patience have its perfect work with its result doing a thorough work, that you* **m**ay *be perfect, complete, and developed in your faith lacking nothing.**

In **c**losing let us examine and **e**valuate some things ~ Has your **expectancy c**ome to a place where you are **e**xperiencing hard times, unusual **c**ircumstances, un**expected** or drastic **c**hanges... trials, testing, or **e**ven familiar patterns of warfare arising again? It's a part of **maturing** so don't feel alone; you are not. And... this too will pass so be it well in your soul.

Stay **c**onnected to *Him* to stay strong. Keep your **e**yes and **m**ind on *Him* ... as your thoughts influence **m**uch... having great potential to become what you then perceive thus believe. Watch when they **c**ontradict what *He* says in *His Word* and has **m**ade known to you. Once again, the **ION** word list is a source to assist you in uncovering what **m**ay be hindering your *development, growth,* and **maturity** in an area, with an issue, **c**haracter trait, or **e**ven in your relationships or **m**inistry. Identifying it does help in **m**aking a way for development to advance your progress... and possibilities to open up.

Sometimes you'll hear exactly what you need to expand the possibilities that open up... and in a moment where a mature response is needed to bring forth an effective solution. In a teaching by a man of *God* I admire, *Ed Watts*, he shared something along the lines that we must be sure to *"Take God's pill of the gospel as a remedy."* It made a way in my particular situation for the *Lord* to remind... we are subject to the whole of the *Word of God* as *His* sons and daughters. Let *His Word* have its perfect work and work *His perfecting grace* in you.

Remember, in every matter we must always look at and examine things asking of ourselves first. Are *you... me... we* rooted at the very core of us in the fullness of the gospel and those principles? Remember, it is a *gospel of salvation* Then... we can look at others, what is transpiring, being questioned, or otherwise. Particularly to help determine any further need for any kind of examination.

Mature ones make intentional efforts daily to do this and do so in *acknowledging, recognizing and acting upon God's Word* which reveals *His* will and reflects *His* heart... in its authority and place in all aspects of one's life. *God's* wisdom and guidance are presented to us through it so we can align our desires with *His* plans and purposes.

This helps us to follow *His* teachings and commandments actively, sincerely... in the continualness of life, because we're committed to obeying *Him* as *His* sons and daughters and beyond! It also helps in *the process* of a *truer transforming*... that comes from *His power* at work in us. That power is connected to and proceeds from a *surrendering, rendering,* and *releasing,...* that eventually enables us to enter into encountering a *thriving*... not just a *surviving* kind of life primarily in times where growth is important and imperative to *form, birth,* and *manifest* the optimal... even impossible in our *expectations.*

Here's another thought I'll share by *Jane Hamon,* an anointed prophetic woman of *God,* to encourage and empower us in this place of *the journey* of **maturing**... *"Your setback is only a setup for your mighty comeback!"** Agreeing with that decree over you... me... us! For *He* is so very good to meet us right where we are and *work all things together for our good when we love Him and are living in the call of His purposes for our lives.**

Press fully into what *He* is revealing... saying... leading and directing. Remember, **maturity** is the byproduct of the *process* in many ways and in all areas of our lives. Typically these kind of setback moments come at *"thresholds"*... times where something that is in *transition* is now ready or soon to shift... to be birthed... to come forth, cross over and into a time to manifest. The enemy works hard to stop it... but greater is *He* in you so let *God* arise!

Brethren, I do not count myself to have apprehended; but one thing I **(expect** *to)* *do, forgetting those things which are behind and reaching forward to those things which are ahead, I press* **(expectantly)** *toward the goal for the prize of the upward call of God in Christ Jesus.**

Our own **expectations** or lack of do not sway the *Lord,* they do not influence or change *His* character, or faithfulness towards us or others. *He* remains *holy, good, just,* **merciful,** *powerful, faithful, gracious,* and *loving* and **m**ore.. for that is who/what *He* is.

We however... are *growing, developing,* and **maturing** in these ways. All the while, *He* is consistently constant, unshakably unchangeable, and dependably dedicated and devoted to who *He* is and *His* purposes within all things no matter what happens to convince us otherwise. As we become more grounded and established in *Him*... in this *lifelong process* of **maturing** to be more like *Him*... our **expectancy** and the **expectations** that we have toward ourselves, others, and in life will begin to adjust and align increasingly, reflecting and revealing **Christ in you... me... us which is indeed the hope of glory!*** Gotta love that!

Is there an **e=mc3** *He's* revealing to be written out by you regarding ***maturity***?

<u>In light of this ***word of worth… maturity*** and what's been shared:</u>

- ❖ *Perhaps…* you **Encountered or Experienced a Question or Challenge?** Write it out…

- ❖ *Perhaps…* more has been **Established & Empowered by the Word?** Write what/which…

- ❖ *Perhaps…* it's time for **Engaging & Embracing your Expectations?** Write what's forming…

Reminder: For *clarity, connection, and confirmation* regarding **expectancy** being stirred by this *word of worth*, seek *Him* and *His Word* first. To possibly assist you in the process the list of **ION** words is available in the Appendix

*Footnotes: Chapter 6 Day 6 maturity / * See Psalm 1:3, Strongs Concordance G5046 *telios*, Romans 5:2-5, Proverbs 16:1-2, 21:2, Romans 8:6-8, Ephesians 5:27, 2 Corinthians 5:17, 3:17-18, James 1:2-4, Philippians 3:13-14, Romans 8:28, Colossians 1:27 - all emphasis is mine and personal paraphrasing built on various translations and versions. * See Ed Watts / Zion Gate Ministries Gateway HOPE Center in Flint, Michigan @ziongateministries.com. * See Jane Hamon / Christian International, Vision Church, Santa Rosa Beach, FL @visionchurchci.org.

✧ Day 7 / *The Journy of "m"... manifest*

*Let **expectations**... through this **word of worth's** part to form, birth, and emerge in its **meaning & mission**... our meditation & motivation... as movement & manifestation awake, arise and align in agreement with divine eternal **expectation**!*

When we *look... to look again* at the **"m"** *words of worth* that have been presented in this portion of our *expectation* adventure: **man, 'M' names – Melchizedek, Moses & Miriam, Mordecai, Micah & Malachi, Michael, Matthew & Mark, Mary,** and **Martha & Mary, mountains, message, ministry,** and **maturity**... and, *to look beyond*... let your *expectancy* stir for how *He'll* now conclude this time with the **word of worth manifest.**

Like with *expectation*... you can't really run or hide from things **manifesting** as things continually are and have been since before *"In the beginning..."*. So let's lay out a basic defining for this *word of worth* **manifest**: *to show, display, demonstrate exhibit, present, or by one's actions revealing a quality or feeling. Also, to be in the eye or mind in such an obvious or clear way* which connects to being or making something clear, apparent, evident, notable, or noticeable. And, can connect to mean *to purify or cleanse out one's self*

Now let's look at how turning to some key scriptures in *His Worthy Word* can help to ground us... you, me... in the establishing of a core of *expectancy*... and even for this book. Yet, room has been left for an *enlarging, stretching,* and *expanding* for spiritually based revelation and related *manifestations* to begin to arise displaying in clear and creative ways, showing and demonstrating much to me in my life and I believe have or will in yours. Both spiritually and relationally with *Him* and most amazingly in more of the fullness of who *He* is.

Our *word of worth* **manifest** has and continues to stir *expectation* as it speaks most often to me and possibly you, of an *inner process* where an inward work creates and bears a kind of fruit outwardly, with an end product of some type from *the process*... or some connected result that becomes *evident, obvious, present*. And, it tends to be often attached to some very deep kind of thoughts... that we come to know are not our own... but come from *Him*. Thoughts that carry much *expectancy* to one degree or the other and definitely stretch us to come up into a realm of knowledge and understanding that only *He* can reveal, make clear, and release anything that we are to receive as *you, me... we,* align *expectantly* as *He* releases.

Typically a part or portion of revelation given broods within... and often remains hovering there until it's time for it to become **more**. More than just a *logos written word*... but a significant *rhema coming alive* word with **expectation** embedded in its very **multifaceted** core. For what it says will be *exhibited, demonstrated, and obviously displayed* in or through me... or to with whom or what it is joined together or associated.

These types of discovery are uncovered over time... as it is with the foundations *He* laid through the writings of *Paul* as expressed in *Romans* 8 and actually the whole chapter overall in my life. But, in this place... and relevant to the word **manifest**... here's an encounter of an interesting sort and the development of understanding, through what started to happen as *He* will often have us look broadly... in an eclectic extensive mixture of translations and versions... and there begins a honing in of sorts, on different aspects which to some degree has been acknowledged already. **Expectancy** many times includes for me, knowing there will be the searching out of a matter. Perhaps, you understand and appreciate what I'm sharing because you can relate to being informed and it containing keys that build our confidence in what we come to *expect*. Let's experience together a portion of its fruit and a taste of its unfolding in searching out of these couple of verses shedding light on our *word of worth* **manifest.**

The entire universe is standing on tiptoe anxious and eagerly awaiting... ***expecting****, yearning to see the unveiling* **manifestation** *revealing God's glorious sons and daughters – His children, His family (that includes you... me... us)! For creation, in frustration and ineffectiveness... not willingly, but against its will due to a fault of the universe... creation itself... there has been an enduring of the empty futility of purposelessness in all its frustration including chaos... resulting from the consequences of human sin – to what it became subjected. But now, with an eager,* ***earnest*** *... yes, a persistent* **expectation** *where all creation longs for freedom to* **manifest***... propelling it out of the state of slavery it is in with its decay and degeneration... to experience and enjoy with us the wonderful freedom accompanying the glory* ***expectantly*** *coming to God's children.*

And all *God's* children say – "YES and AMEN." Be it so and so be it and all for *His* glory! And yes, these scriptures may sound familiar as they were shared in the introducing as we began entering into the **encountering** and **experiencing manifesting** within this quest of **expectancy** and within what I was sharing about mine.

Just as there remains a *waiting* of the earth as it groans and travails *expecting*... there remains as well a type of *progressional waiting* we **encounter**... with its own type of **expectations**... considering the last parts of this *pilgrimage* through our next *upcoming journeys* with "**c**" and "**3**" which lie ahead awaiting us.

One way we can **embrace expectation** and **be empowered** as we continue on this quest... is to appreciate and value where we are enjoying the process and **expecting** to finish well while here (a good biblical life principle). This requires a pressing into the growing comprehensive continuation that moves *you... me... us* forward, not just as a movement because of **expectation...** but with opportunities that seem to hold promising potential and growth.

Attached to that potential and together with the revelation that comes through *impartation,* when coupled with *application and activation*... we can experience the creating of potential for **mobilization** and **multiplication** which typically produces and yields a **manifesting** of varying fruit, which can make way for a harvest, and a tangible presence of *His* power and purposes at work ***moving in the midst*** of it all.

So here at this point, be encouraged. Remember, it's NOT about entering each *day* with the idea of reaching a destination or an ultimate goal of completing a *word of worth*. For within this framework *He's* laid out to *"tell them"*... you, remains my invitation as the author and your sister in *Christ*... but more significantly is ***His*** desire for and invitation to you to *build, nurture, and develop* a more *intentional, authentic,* and *intimate* relationship with *Him* our *Creator*... our *Father*... just as I am in writing this and experiencing it with you.

> ❖ *Perhaps...* making and taking time to reflect, to respond to what *He's* saying, revealing, desiring, and requiring... which all makes the way for a meaningful realigning and reestablishing of ourselves... *spirit, soul and body...* as He increase and we decrease. Yes, somewhat in a diligent and discipled way... yet yielding to *Holy Spirit's* moving and guidance that carries in it a special kind of spontaneity that is priceless... as it infiltrates and saturates *the process*... especially as our usual

expectancy becomes increasingly entrenched into echad oneness... and with *His*. Now, may the fruit of the *Spirit*, which is *love*... in all its varied *expressions* and beyond*... find a place to join *His* heart's pure intent in us and **manifest**!

Remember... *He* speaks in multiple ways and dimensions to us revealing things in layers which takes us through many types of *processes*. And so... in all the **moments** spiritually and together in the intertwining with the natural of this way of **moving** and **movement** *you*... *me*... *we*, are establishing a solid foundation of and for *God's* character and nature to have its proper and providential place... and to **manifest**. And we know...repetition can be a part.

That moving moves to create a knowing beyond our head knowledge regarding who *He* is, what *He* is, why *He* is that way, why such matters to *Him* and should to us, where we need to be in *the process* of this developing in us by *Holy Spirit* in our spirit too. You get the idea... as these are just a few of the facets in *His* **multifaceted** dimensions that will **manifest**, potentially reconciling us back to and with *His original intent* and in a spirit kind of way.

For they are essential and necessary characteristics...dynamics... traits. The fruit of them... of *His* nature (*His Spirit*) in us are not only the result of an *expectancy* within our *Divine* DNA... but our personal *expecting*... especially since it has come alive in our salvation as the *born again spirit* we are now living in a body with a soul. Yes, there's always the positive yet negative aspects at work in this all; it's part of the nature of *expecting*.

And, there's the result that comes from the *expectation* of our free will and our willingness to surrender... *fully submitting ourselves to Him for His reasonable service – that which is His good and perfect will as we're being transformed in the renewing of our mind and more*... as well as *being not conformed to this world* *... or our old man **manifesting** anymore.

We can rest in knowing that transformation works to redeem our past, not erase it. Yet... the blood of *Jesus* and the work of the cross have atoned for our past sin erasing it making way for the **manifestation** of the transforming work and power of *His* great redeeming love full of *expectancy* for us to receive it wholly, as we become *His* fully, and will be *His* eternally!

The eternalness of it all truly contains and carries a unique kind of *expectancy* that certainly works to stir in us an exceedingly powerful and prevailing kind of hopefulness...as the only conforming that needs to be taking place as we put our confidence in and **expect** *Him* to arise in us. Oh, the **manifestation** of the conformation of *Him* continually in *us*... *you*... *me*, becoming increasingly like *Him*... *His* possessions you could say... because we are *His*.

Each **encounter** and **experience** made up of moments where our **expectations** are in the *divine dance* of being *formed, birthed*... and yes **manifesting**. In these times... especially appointed ones... and in these seasons we find ourselves in a type of '*coming into*' a *momentum* that's been and is being created as the catalyst of *expectancy* thrives when associated and aligned with *His*... and how He's actually moving in the midst of all things in our live even when we're not fully aware or where we're to be.

This is stirring the remembrance of *His* heart released in *His Worthy Word* that tells us as *He* was telling *Israel* ... "*For just a brief moment I deserted you, but with tender feelings of love I will gather you back to Me (expect it). In a surge of anger, for just the briefest moment, I hid My face from you, but with (and expectantly because of) My everlasting kindness, I will show you My cherishing love,*" *says Yahweh, your Kinsman-Redeemer (The Ever Expectant One).* *

We come in our continual, even in our own way consistent comings... in this apparent *ebb and flow* and *process* in our *life journey* to *threshold moments* where we find we're at a 'door'. Oh the doors in life... where we're in a place that can in some ways, be likened unto what the Word speaks of as the *valley of decision.** Does the door before us open, or close... if it's slightly open or remains closed? Either way... we go through it, a door in some form, if not the one before us than another or the next that appears due to *His* ordering not anothers.

That's when it's good to recall and always grab hold of *Him* being **The Door**... *the Only Way*. The way we access our spiritual salvation which then presents to us the way to go forward in and together with *Him* in relationship, experiencing the abundant life that is ours in *Him*, and through *His* lordship*. *For His ways are not our ways... they're better than ours and His thoughts are better and higher than ours**... bringing forth light, producing life, and engraining *His* constant *expressing, exhibiting,* and *evidence* of love.

Because when *He* is... or at minimum we're seeking *Him* to be in *His* presence and counsel with us at these doors; which ultimately is with Him *The Door*... what **manifests** will be encircled in *His* faithfulness that is always working to present to us the fruit of *His working all things together for our good*. Gotta love that! What a place in *the process*... where we **expectantly**... yes, intentionally enter into *acquiring* and *inquiring* that's embedded in ours and in *His desiring*, requiring... that transpires **emerging** with *His* divine energy from the incessant merging and converging propelling us over the threshold, out of any transitioning, and into appointed, anointed places filled with purpose.

Amazingly... yet, a bit funny, is how then *the process* begins **again** filled with **expectancy**! For, *He* is at the door too as our *Shepherd* and as the *Gate*... the *Spirit* of *Revelation and Truth*... and more. There where as our *Source, He* in all *His* varied dimensions that can **manifest,** provides through not just *moments, movement,* and *momentum,* but by *His Spirit* because it's *not by might nor power... but by His Spirit**. There where there is a *grace, grace... a grace upon grace* that moves us as we've recognized before from *faith to faith, strength to strength,* and *glory to glory*. Amen. So let nothing move or stop you... not even what forms in our *expecting* when confronted with a mountain.

Moving on... not long ago in my time with *Him* I encountered one of those *'signs'* He gives to me in the form of a type of marquee neon sign with the letters spelling a word. This time the word formed was "**SOUL**". Then I saw the **U** drop down and the other letters come together flashing and forming **SOL**. In my spirit I knew SOUL to be our soul – comprised as we know and was recently shared of our *mind, will,* and *emotions*.

Upon seeking *Him*, He revealed how the **U** had to be dropped because it stood for *'you'* and *you* don't have the same role now in *His* moving and working by *His Spirit* in our *born again man*... which is a spirit. The soul still having a place... an important place as it is fearfully and wonderfully made like the rest of us. However, the *soul* is no longer in the *driver's seat* like in our life before being *born again*. *His Spirit Holy Spirit* now *leads, guides,* and *directs* our spirit so it is *driving* through being led by *Him*, And, by our partnering by keeping ourselves *'fueled'* too by eating of the *Tree of Life* for *He* as it is our *Source*.

In pressing and pursuing *Him* more of it was revealed as *He* connected the 3 letters to 3 words *He* had been emphasizing to me. With **SOL** representing: **S** > *stewardship,* **O** > *ownership,* and **L** > *Lordship*. How it all unfolded was a full circle kind of presentation of meaning **manifesting** in... the importance of *stewardship* and *ownership* that are required in and if *He* has been given true

Lordship in our lives. Thus... *Lordship* when truly given to the fullness of *Him* as *God the Father, God the Son*, and <u>*God the Holy Spirit*</u> **manifests** in us giving *Him* **total ownership Lordship**... as we are now *His*; *His alone*... *His only*.

In our partnering and co-laboring with *Him,* we must take hold of our realm of responsibility in this type of *ownership* which **manifests** displaying and presenting in multiple ways – through our rights, which <u>we now give totally to *Him* all rights</u> as we *love, serve* and *worship Him*. Our possessions are *His*. Our title is that we're *stewards* now of what *He's* given and blessed us with. This impacts enormously our relationship with *Him* so true peace and freedom **manifest** being offered to **us in *Him* as *His* solely**. The importance and value of our good and righteous *stewardship*... whether it is seeing all that we have and are as *His* or any other varying portions of *stewarding*... the maturing should **manifest** in all things being done well in our stewarding all as *His* in which *He* provides and bestows to and on us.

Let's also look at another interesting definition of *sol* as *sol/sola/solus/soli* meaning in Latin, 'alone' or 'only' – a *solitary state, single person, or unique thing*. It is often associated in a religious type of connotation as exhibited in the **5 *Sola's* of Reformation**: *1) Sola Scriptura by Scripture alone, 2) Sola Fide through Faith alone, 3) Sola Gratia through Grace alone, 4) Solus Christus in Christ alone, and 5) Soli Deo Gloria with Glory to God alone.**

These tenants summarize the doctrinal revelation released by a *German Priest* and *Theologian Martin Luther* which **manifested** in a shifting moment full of NEW *expectations* that changed the establishment for a portion of the church's foundation in the 1500's. It led to what is known as the *Protestant Reformation* movement creating a way for the **manifesting** of *Protestantism*. Here the *sol* obviously established an ultimate pointing to it being *Him alone* and *Him only* which is *expected* from us regarding *Him* too.

He is continually and constantly desiring to be in *His* rightful place of dwelling occupying the foundation of what we believe... like that fundamental revelation of truth which has **manifested** in the truths above, there will always be things that will **manifest** in the *ongoing processing* and *expecting* within life. Be aware as sometimes so called *truths* present in other areas a removing or change to the solid sure foundation *He* has established in *His Word*.

Remain stable, remain steady, remain faithful and committed...to study and show yourself approved... remembering the whole Message. For one part of Luther's message gave place to somethings that weren't truth in a replacing. Messages we carry and share and should be intertwined with fully in TRUTH in our testimony, praise, worship, adoration, hope, joy... and love for *Him* and *Him* moving as the fullness of TRUTH... and TRUTH **manifesting** in our lives. At this time I'll not address the replacement theology *Luther* shared too.

Here's a testimony I'll share now to encourage you to **embrace** being **empowered** as your *expectations* either discover a new view and portion of this SOL revelation and beyond. Or the revelation *He's* made known is stirred, uncovered if it became hidden... moving to bring a fresh commitment to the **manifesting** of *stewardship, ownership,* and **Lordship** and more which are important *words of worth* too in the *journey* and through the *process*.

THE SHIP ...

A message with a type of prophetic word within it came forth connected to a global ministry I'm blessed to be a part, *Aglow International*, as the word to them was it's time to *"Turn the ship"*.*

There was a *reset, realigning,* and *reestablishing He* was beginning in general across the board for *His Church*... and **m**any were hearing and speaking it at that time and still are in ways. After hearing this timely strategic **m**essage to *Aglow* and having recently seen a picture of a small tugboat pulling a huge ship into a harbor; an **e**xtreme difference in size being displayed... I recalled thinking *how odd* and *extremely unusual,* at least in a presumed kind of **expectancy**... that such a *little boat could carry out* and *accomplish* such a huge task as it did towing that larger ship.

Within what was shared, I also heard it aligning with the fact that *His Kingdom* is **c**oming forth in the **e**arth which I **e**quated to being **His Ship**... *for the earth is the Lord's and the fullness thereof... declaring God's ownership and dominion over all creation.** I likened it to also being spoken and released to *you, me... us,* as the *Body of Christ, His Family, Church, Ekklesia, Righteous Remnant of Sons, His Army, Kings and Priests, Chosen and Called*... all those powerful ways we are described and defined by *Him* through *His Worthy Word*. And yes... it was to us as *His* Bride.

Hearing it as a **c**orporate word to all, overall... I anticipated with *expectancy* a stirring for the **m**ore *He* wanted to reveal in what was **c**oming together. Yet, it's important that I share I was interestingly **c**onvicted within and **c**onvinced that at the **c**ore and heart of it... there needed to be a hearing and receiving of it first *individually,* then *collectively*... so it **c**ould be heard and received *corporately.* Directing my e**x**pectation in that way... it all further pointed to how *embracing* this word would be accompanied with great potential for an *empowering* to *manifest* through it.

Now all of these descriptions of *who we are as His*... with the definitions that define them... **m**ake for a wonderful **m**ixture of ways for us to visualize and to look at **His Ship.** As well... **His Ship** with its own type of **kingdom fleet of ships** in all the varying styles of ships there are. For it is said that any type of vehicle or **m**ode of transportation **c**an symbolically or prophetically represent *ministry.*

After seeing the above **m**entioned picture of the little tugboat pulling the very large ship... well, as stated it all started to stir in me. I heard within a **m**essage I tend to hear a lot from *Him* through the *Holy Spirit* prompting me to *discover more... search it out... look deeper... look, look again and look beyond* to what you know about the **m**ain subject of this... <u>**ship**</u>.

Searching I went and here's a bit of *the process* it lead me into. **M**ost importantly it *opened a door* for some incredible, **e**ven fun, **c**onversation as I **c**ommuned with *Him* in this initial and ongoing searching which for turned into a type of *treasure hunt* with the laying out of a kind of **m**ap and a *sharing* of *words* where within was *hidden treasure.*

From a variety of online sources, the definition of **ship** was defined to **m**ean things like: *a large boat, to cause to go or be taken from one place to another, as in to send something somewhere, or to cause to go as in to be sent.* The word *apostolic*; simply as *kingdom sent ones*, instantly **c**ame to my **m**ind.

Immediately I discovered another treasure in this variety of dictionary definings... that when **ship** is added to a noun: a person, place, or thing, as a **suffix**, it **c**reates a new noun by 1) further signifying the **c**ondition or state of being in something or someone the position, 2) the status or duties of something/someone, 3) the skill or ability as someone/something, 4) the people in a particular group, and 5) a specialized union. I knew that in basic way – you know as well because we learned about *suffixes* in school – right?. But now knowing it, **c**arried a *new* **expectancy** with *expectations* swirling.

He then prompted the **c**reating of a list of vital **ship** words - *words of worth* I'd now **c**all some of them, that represent a type of relevant 'role', part, piece, or purpose in advancing the kingdom in the *earth* and for the ministry in its **turning of the ship** so to give way to her appointed ***rebirth***. Or, in *ship* language you **m**ight think of *berth – a sleeping place on a ship/boat/train*. Yet, the birth of a *place, a portion,* and a *purpose* for this **m**inistry was certainly awakening and for such a time… and as we've seen in *His Church*.

As the *captain* is known for saying… *"ALL aboard"*… **c**ome along with me on this *fantastic voyage of the word ship*! **M**ay it stir the waters and waves of ***expectation*** in you as it did me… and still is as *He* keeps **e**xpounding on these **e**ssential **e**lements in a *Believer*'s life. For example, in **SOL***: Lordship from ownership and in stewardship of and in the process of you… me… us,* turning. *Particularly our turning to, in, and through Him in all things, all ways, and always. So - full steam ahead!*

The Ship… *a casting of a modern day type of word parable*

We know **Kingship** and **Lordship** are at the helm of the heart of *relationship* with *His* **Messiahship** in our lives as we're no longer on a *slave ship* because we're now in *sonship*, secured in *His* redemptive ***kinsmanship*** and reigning ***rulership***, grounded in intimate *friendship* leading to **c**ovenant *courtship* flowing from loving *fellowship* as a fruit rendered through our divine ***heirship***.

With **servantship**, as *Jesus* so beautifully **m**odeled and powerfully defined, laying the foundation for **m**inistry and leadership of any kind. And, **c**o-laboring ***partnership*** prominent part of what *He* desires from out of *His lordship* with us, yet *in and with Him as Father, as Son, and as Holy Spirit – the three in one* **m**aking us one in the three as such unity flows from *His* **headship** down as its fire takes us higher. Oh… the *expectancy* for the **c**ommanded blessing that *He* says will **manifests** there!

Good ***sportsmanship*** certainly is required when you're on *His* team in **m**inistry. It's an important trait too in being a part of *His* family. Because we're never riding alone in a kayak or adrift in a sailboat out in the sea. Together is best as *He's designed* in all things; *His threefold* **c**ord in you and me.

For as we embrace that true ***worship*** in *Spirit and Truth* is our life, we **c**ome to know it's also our warfare ***warship*** helping overcome **c**ontention and strife. But remember we **m**ust, that we're living in a ***citizenship*** not of this world. Which offers an ***ambassadorship***, along with ***landownership,*** and all that is our *identity, inheritance, and authority*… oh how that **m**akes our enemies swirl.

Discipleship, mentorship, comradeship, companionship, and ***partnership*** all bring about a spirit of *kingdom* ***championship*** in *His* daughters and sons that arise.

But ultimately, every ship **m**ust be *rooted, grounded and established* in personal ***ownership*** with accountability for ***stewardship*** and ***dominionship*** with truth in its **c**ore and flowing from its lips.

His excellent ***workmanship*** evidenced in such will glorify *His* **m**agnificent ***craftsmanship*** in the beauty and reflection of *Him* in the ***flagship*** with its fleet of *sent ships* in **c**ovenant alignment with the fullness of *Him* and under *His* heavenly host angelic ***guardianship***.

Among the fleet *He's* gathered and is gathering, you will see **battleships, cruise ships, cargo ships, and transport ships. Passenger ships, hospital ships, icebreaker ships** and even **lightships** – you know the ones that are anchored like a lighthouse in the bay. Providing a steady source of light for all to see and navigate through by their *seamanship* in the midst of the calm, the waves or the storms, making the way.

Every *ship* and *shipmate* matters with their special *part, piece, and place*, so that we don't sink the ship, as we try to avoid *hardships*, as we desire to encourage ones not to *abandon ship* because we don't want any *ship* wrecks as we press in this race through our *heirship.*

I AM calls, surely you hear *His* voice drawing, *"Ahoy. All hands on deck shipmates*! *I'm the Captain at the helm and it's not too late, for indeed you've not missed your calling.* **I AM** *the* **Ship** *Owner,* **Ship Master,** *and a* **Shipmate** *with you too, helping keep all things shipshape by My compass. Drop anchor in Me and you will see how I will carry you through."*

Ship builders, **ship** buyers, and **ship** owners are in the *shipyard* about the *Captain's* business too, along with all those who are in the docks awaiting their place on our future *ship crews.*

In the skies above as the *ship* proceeds, our spirit filled prayers like *rocket ships* are continually arising, over and in all the nations and with all *He's* commissioned us to do… and, with no compromising

Then I heard the *Captain's* passionate cry arise in the midst of a *manifesting* moment … *"Anchors aweigh, oh ships of My glorious fleet… afloat and turning. For I love you My Ekklesia, My Church… My Bride of original intent for whom My heart is yearning and My Love Boat's course is set for returning."*

♥   ♥   ♥

> ❖ *Perhaps… the process of it all filled with the electricity that* **expectancy** *can create. So maybe in your reading within yourself there may have been a* **manifestation** *of a ♪ song with its tune arising through a humming or singing (out loud or in your head) to the tune of the theme song possibly recalled from the old TV show (and I'm probably dating myself),* **"The Love Boat"** *(aired 1977-1986) after our little excursion with* **"ship".** *With the idea of a song in mind, it seems a good time to share a kind of fun fact also related to* **sol.** *One of its other meanings reveals it is the fifth (5) note of the musical scale when its sung and is usually pronounced "so" – you know… ♪ "Do, re, mi, fa, sol (so), la, ti, do"! Only the* **expectancy** *for His more… and how it can* **manifest** *in fun ways like in songs that He knows are a special way to speak to me… actually to each of us… as He does tell us He ♪ "… rejoices and sings over us"!**

Let's find the end in our completing this day of *our journey* with m by examining willingly where *you.. me*… *we* are, in this current *place, posture,* and *positioning* of *the process* and in the area of obedience to what *He* requires and desires… so we're compelled into greater *Christ* likeness too… and yet only by our free will.

Remember… at this *Point of Departure* there is also a *Point of Access*… that place where either quick surrender and submission come to *His* leading and direction OR… resistance comes entering to prevent revelation received from presenting itself. Let alone it being released in this moment as our flesh or the enemy arises to *kill, steal, and destroy* * keeping these doors of *expectation* and any attached **manifestation** from fully being aligned with and in *Him*. We've already identified this before.... that *"war is always at the door."* So, let the *battle be the Lord's** as *His Lordship* enables us to breakthrough with *Him* as *the Door* and at the door *expecting* the best is ahead and to come with *Him* as *Captain* of the ship too!

Let your **expectancy** *manifest* from the **expectations** forming and birthing from what *He's* been ordering...not yours, or ones others have had for you. *Be strong, courageous, and empowered** to press in for the *manifested* breakthrough *the process* is producing and awaits. Let it propel you forward so the **m**ore of *Him* in you **c**an **manifest** as a **c**atalyst **m**oving *you*... *me*... *us*, into the next adventure **c**ontained in the *manifestations* that will **c**ome as *expectations* arise for **"c"**.

E=mc3 eternal energy = mass of **multifaceted moments, movement, multiplying,** and **mobilizing** the **myriad** of **manifestations** that have **constantly come**, will **continually come,** as **Christ** in us **catapults** us by *His Spirit* into the 3rd **power!**

<u>In light of this *word of worth... manifest* and what's been shared:</u>

❖ *Perhaps...* you **Encountered or Experienced a Question or Challenge?**
  Write it out...

❖ *Perhaps...* more has been **Established & Empowered by the Word?**
  Write what/which...

❖ *Perhaps...* it's time for **Engaging & Embracing your Expectations?**
  Write what's forming...

Reminder: For *clarity, connection, and confirmation* regarding **expectancy** being stirred by this *word of worth*, seek *Him* and *His Word* first. To possibly assist you in *the process* the list of **ION** words is available in the Appendix.

*Footnotes: Chapter 6 Day 7 manifest *See Romans 8:19-21, Proverbs 25:2, Galatians 5:22-23, Romans 12:1-2, John 10:7-9, Isaiah 54:7-8, Joel 3:14, Isaiah 55:8-9, Zechariah 4:6-7, Psalm 24, John 10:10, 2 Chronicles 20:15, I Samual 17:47, Joshua 1: 6-9, Zephaniah 3:17 - all emphasis is mine and personal paraphrasing built on various translations and versions.

*See Turning the Ship. This re-telling of the "wordship" word voyage has a few modifications from the original way it was written to Aglow. This was done out of my love for and desire to please Him through enhancing and enlarging through the power, purposes, and promises in His Word a broader scope and spectrum of biblical principles and *kingdom bridal strategy* in this prophetic message/word parable to the church at large in its growing and flowing for now and beyond to reflect and reinforce how His kingdom must and will go forth on earth as it is in heaven through His will being done *individually, collectively, and corporately*. Make us glorious to glorify You.

* See Aglow International @aglow.org. > Identity Statement /Aglow is an international organization of women and men in more than 170 nations of the world, presenting Biblical principles as solutions to the challenging issues of our time. Every heart touched… every nation changed.

✧ *Expectancy's Look Again... at the end of the Journey of "m"*
~ *Ted & Lynette*

*When I was a child, I spoke about childish matters (as **expected**), for I saw things like a child and reasoned like a child. But the day came when I (**expectantly**) matured, and I set aside my childish ways. 1 Corinthians 13:11 TPT*

Expectancy's Reflection: *When we got **married** we had **many expectations**. Several of which were based out of the selfishness of what the world says a **marriage** should look like... even what our parents demonstrated. Through counseling... **mentoring**... and finding God's wisdom about **marriage**... we began to **mature** as individuals and as a couple. Childish ways sometimes try to block our growth. We have to choose wisely in the process... to put them away. We have to live in and through the **expectations** of who He says we are; not what we were.*

*Rise up in (**expectant**) splendor... and be radiant, for your light has dawned, and YAHWEH's glory now streams (**expectantly**) from you! Isaiah 60:1 TPT*

Expectation's Extended Reflection: The prophet *Isaiah,* one of the **m**ost quoted in the scriptures, unveils a **m**ystery... a **m**andate... a **c**all for each of us as the body of **C**hrist. As we encountered *Him* through the **"m"** words of worth, we now hold **expectations** of a greater radiance and extended spectrum... along with a new way of perceiving and thinking as we seek to **m**ature in *the process*. Where are we in this **expectation** and **e**ndeavor?

As *Isaiah* speaks of great darkness **c**overing the earth, he says through the *Holy Spirt,* "but YAHWEH arises upon you and the brightness of His glory appears over you!"... BUT YAHWEH arises! What a vision for us as we **expect** and seek to **m**ature in *Him,* yielding ourselves so that *His* very glory **c**an now stream from *you... me... us.* As we encounter the *Most High...* we rise up in splendor with *His Light* dawning in us... to us... and through us. As we long for freedom, *perhaps* this is a **c**hallenge... a **c**all to be *Mighty Warriors* for our *Lord... Warriors* of *Truth... Hope...* and **m**ost importantly, Love.

The **m**ighty *Spirit of Lord* YAHWEH is wrapped around us because *He* has anointed us as **messengers**... to share *His Light, His* glory redemption with those we **e**ncounter, both in our families and **c**ommunity... at work and play. As shared in the **"m"** word of worth **ministry**, a **ministry** of reconciliation, both in ourselves to *Him* and for others... partnering to reunite the heart of our *Redeemer* to *His* **c**hildren... and us *His* **c**hildren to *Him*... and with one another.

This returns us to the *Garden*, a garden of **c**ommunion and oneness as the *Lord* intended... and as shared in this *telling*. We are to treat one another as fellow heirs of the grace of *God*... each as powerful vessels of *God*... with *His* glory streaming from us.

We are being prepared as brides of *Christ*... yet, the *Bride of Christ*.
May we set our focus to be and **c**reate with *Him* a ready bride, sanctified and **c**leansed by the washing of the water of *the word*... so that we **m**ight present ourselves in splendor... *without spot or wrinkle, holy and without blemish.** This is only accomplished in union with our **M**aker as we yield ourselves to *Him* **maturing** day by day as *He* imparts to us the riches *His Spirit of wisdom* and *Spirit of revelation* to know *Him* through our deepening intimacy with *Him.**

It is truly in the yielding, the submitting… along with the prioritization of all that we are individually and as a **c**ouple… giving all that we have and are to *Him*.

*"Rise up in **(expectant)** splendor… and be radiant, for your light has dawned, and YAHWEH's glory now **(expectantly)** streams from you."**

Expectation's Prayerful Considerations:

As we **m**editate on the words of the prophet… are our words, our thoughts, our **m**inds and wills and **e**motions radiant, rising in splendor, reflecting the heart of our *Kinsman-Redeemer* in **e**very aspect? What stirs our hearts? What does *He* speak to us in it?

Do we prioritize our time, our **m**arriages, our relationships, our work, our **m**inistry… what is it that we nurture… prioritize?
Do we *invite and allow Him* into *this process*?
To what or who do we lift our **e**yes and our focus as we go about the day?
Is our speech, our reasoning, and our desires set above?

Are we to war in prayer for the land as we learn to **c**ommune with the *Lord* and yield ourselves to *Him* that *His Light* **m**ay dawn in us permeating atmospheres, **e**nvironments… **e**verywhere?

As we look in the ***mirror***, not understanding or not **c**omprehending
…do we trust our **M**aker?
What stirs in our hearts as we read these verses, this reflecting,
on *this journey,* and in *the process* we're **e**xperiencing
in this book of *expectant* encounters?

Expectation's Declaration: $e=mc^3$ encounter = mature communion created through **Christ** in us rising up in the *splendor, radiance, and light dawning*… streaming from us in the **power^3** of the **Trinity!**

*Footnotes: See 1 Corinthians 13:11 TPT, Isaiah 60:1 TPT, Ephesians 1:17, Ephesians 5:25-27, Revelation 19:7 TPT.

✧ WORTHY WORDS AS WE ENTER CHAPTER 7…

*He is the divine portrait, the true likeness of the invisible God,
and the firstborn heir of all creation (according to **expectation**). For in Him was created the
universe of things, both in the heavenly realm and on the earth (as **expected**), all that is seen and
all that is unseen. Every seat of power, realm of government, principality, and authority - it all
exists through Him and for His purpose (**expectantly**)! He existed before anything was made,
and now everything (**expects** to) finds completion in Him.**

*By faith we (**expect** and) understand that the universe was created
by the (**expectant** filled) word of God, so that what is seen was not
made out of things that are visible. **

*For His invisible attributes, namely, His (**expectant**) eternal power and (**expectant**) divine nature,
have been clearly perceived, ever since the (**expectancy** for) the creation of the world, in the
things that have been made. So they're without excuse (in their **expectancy**).**

*Know therefore that the Lord your God is God; He is the faithful God, keeping
His covenant of love to a thousand generations of those who love Him and
keep His commandments (**expect** it).**

*For God wanted (**expects**)them to know that the riches and glory of Christ are
for you Gentiles, too. And this is the (**expectant**) secret: Christ lives in you
(with all **expectancy**) – you are a carrier of Him. This gives you (**expectant**)
assurance of sharing His glory."*

*Don't you realize that all of you together are (**expected** to be) the temple
of God and that the (**expectant**) Spirit of God lives (ever expecting) in you?*
So we, the many, are one body in Christ (as **expected**), and each
one of us is (**expected** to be) a part of it.**

*Yes, I am the vine; you are the branches. Those who remain in Me (**expectantly**), and I in them (as
I **expect** to), will produce much fruit.
For apart from Me you can (**expect** to) do nothing.**

*Be eager (**expecting**) to maintain the unity of the Spirit
by the bond of (**expectancy** in)peace.*
Come… draw (**expectantly**) close to God, and God
will come (as you've **expected**) close to you.**

*(So **expect** to) Arise… Let your light shine (in **expectation**) for all to see.
For the glory of the Lord rises to shine (with **expectancy**) on you. Darkness
as black as night covers all the nations of the earth, but the (all powerful **expectant**) glory of the
Lord rises (**expectantly**) appearing over you.**

*Footnotes: Chapter 7 Worthy Words / * See Colossians 1:15-17, Hebrews 11:3, Romans 1:20, Deuteronomy 7:9, Colossians 1:27, I Corinthians 3:16, Romans 12:5, John 15:5, Ephesians 4:3, James 4:8, Isaiah 60: 1-2 – all emphasis is mine and personal paraphrasing built on various translations and versions.

✧ CHAPTER 7 ✧
✧ ESTABLISHING & EMBRACING … A JOURNEY WITH "C"

The **c**ontinuing of this adventure we've entered into and together in *Him*… and *Him* **m**oving in the **m**idst of *you… me… us,* in and of itself produces an underlying *expectancy*. If we're sincerely pursuing through a fuller **m**easure of **c**onsideration with **c**ontemplation, along with reflective observation of all the varying aspects happening and their unique elements they bring… certainly our *expecting* will become about **m**ore than just the rudimentary **c**ourse of things evolving… if we desire and allow it to.

What we **e**ncounter **c**arries such hopeful potential and possibilities as we're learning in this ongoing **c**ontinuum of the *forming, creating,* and *birthing* of not just what we *expecting*… but, a personal opportunity for enhanced enlightenment that arises often producing a deeper place of *rest, trust,* and *peace* as *expectations* **m**anifest in part or in full along the way.

Don't worry or let apprehension to *"what is this really all about"* encumber progress. The how and why within where we are for what is unfolding will be revealed. Like it is with so **m**any things, it is over time… not in one **c**omplete deposit of revelation that bears within it **c**omplete understanding, a full solution, or an automatic outcome we've desired or *expected*.

Remember, we're **c**ontinually day to day… week to week… in *the process* life is wrapped in and are experiencing in some way *transition*… either from *something to something*… or *somewhere to somewhere*… because in *some way at some time somehow* we will. Yes, we **c**an *expect* that eventually we get to a type or place of *destination*… the end point of it all.

If the end appears to remain somewhat hidden, uncertain or starting to disappoint… it's ok. He's **m**oving in it all and because you… me… we, are **c**alled according to *His* purposes and we love *Him*. It is *His Word*… as *He* promises it works together for our good.* *He* who began it will **c**omplete it.* Keep tucked within your heart… there is *God's expected* end.

To stir *expectant* hope as we press forward… let's look at what the *words of worth* we will be discovering and allowing *expectancy* to have its work in through what we discover in… ***create > communion > covenant > C Names > carriers > connect >*** and ***celebrate.***

As you'll recall… in this *process* we're desiring to take a **c**loser and deeper look at the **Meaning and Mission** of *words of worth* and how they **c**onnect us to an opportunity for **Meditation and Motivation** … along with how they **c**reate a place for **Movement and Manifestation**. Let these *Worthy Words* linger to inspire and remind us of essentials as we begin our *journey* now with "**c**".

In each and every sunrise… the beginning of each new day continuing (expectancy) that each plays in a week… I know You will hear my voice as I prepare my sacrifice of prayer to You and in my time with You. Every morning of every day… I lay out the pieces of my life (with all the attached expectations)… on the altar and wait for Your fire (containing Your expectations) to fall upon my heart.*

For You oh Lord are waiting (expecting) to be gracious, compassionate, just, faithful… keeping Your promises…as your goodness overwhelms me. So I entwine my heart to Yours as I wait longing (expectantly) for Your goodness will not fail me.*

*Footnotes: Chapter 7 / * See Romans 8:28, Philippians 1:6, Psalm 5:3, Isaiah 30:18 – all emphasis is mine and personal paraphrasing built on various translations and versions.

✧ Day 1: The Journey of "c"… create

Let *expectations*… through this **word of worth's** part to *form, birth, and emerge* in its **meaning & mission**… **our meditation & motivation**… **as movement & manifestation** *awake, arise and align* in agreement with divine eternal **expectation**!

By faith… which (**expectantly**) empowers us to see… we understand that the universe… the very worlds were created, beautifully coordinated, and framed by the (eternally **expectant**) power in and of the word of God – God's words that He spoke (with earnest **expectation**), so that the invisible realm (of **expectancy**) gave birth to all things which are seen – as they were not **m**ade of things which are visible.* Be it so….

As we **m**ove into a place of *looking, looking again…* and *looking beyond* in our journey – particularly now with our "**c**" *words of worth* and the *processing* that will **c**ome into *the process* we're in after "**e**" and "**m**". He's led to begin with the *word of worth* "**create**" which seems logical to me with it being a word attached to a beginning… an *"In the beginning…"*.

Some revelation with information has been shared in the *ebb and flow* of this *telling* speaking to the word **create** and its various forms: ***creating, creation, created, Creator, creative, creatively,*** and ***creativity.*** Yes, all of it is **c**onnected with and to the foundation of the portions that have been released already. Let us build upon it now, yet be open to what will **c**ome forth inviting and allowing *His* leading to take us into the **m**ore as ***expectancy*** hovers.

The above layering of words through this opening scripture imparted a sense that it is to provide a type of *image* for us link together *faith's* role in **creating**… and in *His* **creating** of **creation**. **M**ay we **embrace** it and be **empowered**… as it says, *to see in a greater capacity*… and **expect** a *greater measure* then we have… **c**oming into greater understanding in and through what we will **encounter** and **experience** by doing so.

He's reminding of how *His Word* parallels this by saying, *We walk full of* (**expectant**) *courage in a manner consistent with our confident faith in God's promises… therefore, it is walking by faith… and not by sight – what we* (**expect** *or not to*) *see with just our eyes, calling into the beyond… speaking words aligned and in agreement with His faith filled Word…* and the **creative** power within those words coming together as our words become one with them… to address calling out (in all **expectancy**) those things that are not to come forth!*

This is a time where we **c**annot, **m**ust not… let the *familiarity* of these verses steal from what *He*, as the/our **Creator** is freshly releasing to us… *His* **created** ones. What *He* is saying intending for it to propel us forward in taking the *unseen faith steps* that are *required* and *desired* by *Him*. Because in *the process*… there is *fruit*, along with **expectancy** *forming* and *birthing*…full of **creative** power ready for **m**anifesting by what's been **creatively** stirring… in the **creativity** of *Him* and as **Creator** in us… with its incredible infusing.

Just as *Holy Spirit*… full of *His* **creative** *faith filled power* **expectantly** hovered and brooded over the darkness, which was formless and void. All the while… the stirring of *God's* divine essence filled energy **creating** its own kind of *circle* and *cycle* at work within it all to…. *"Let there be…"* and there was… and it was good. The state of *"tohu bohu"* which in *Hebrew* **m**eans *without form, formless, in chaos, void, or empty*. It was done… finished, as the power of *His Spirit* breathed releasing **expectancy** for life!

There's a beckoning type of ***clarion call* sounding an alarm** as a present day type of *tohu bohu* is attempting to infiltrate life with *self... **c**reating* an **e**mptiness and **v**oid designed for our ***Creator*** and *His* life giving *DNA*, breath, and eternal purpose in us. And I believe that it in part, is arising today as a warning to *tell us* to NOT let *His* divine power... *the **creative** Source and Force of Him* in us... lay dormant any longer! We **m**ust have the power thereof!

Arise! Let this **e**ternally **e**nergized foundation and framework of *expectancy* be released through the ***creative*** *power* of words... *written* words... *logos and rhema* words... turning into *powerful life and light filled spoken words*... **c**arrying the *telling* to *whomever, whatever, wherever, however, whenever,* and *whyever He defines, determines*, and *directs*. Truly an *embrace it and be empowered* time! For *His* **m**ultifaceted, **m**ulti-dimensional ***creative*** *power* is needful... and it **m**ust at work by *Holy Spirit* and through *His gifts* in *you... me... us*.

It is *His* way of ordering... like in the *missional mandate in the message* given **c**ontaining *His original intent*, given to the ***created*** ones – **m**an/humanity *in the beginning*. Oh... the returning as *He* orders such for such times. Releasing what will bring forth ***earthly*** and ***heavenly*** strategies and blueprints to the **m**any *challenges, issues,* and *problems* we are facing today... and need to begin to **c**onfront and **m**ust in the days ahead. And yes... it is in part is about *dominion*... as *He* intended in the beginning and has redeemed and reconciled us back into *Him* to restore and renew as we're partnering with *Him* **now** on/in the **e**arth... to be as it was to be. *His* timing for *His* as it is in heaven be it so on **e**arth. Kingdom **c**ome... our *expectancy* lies in *Your* will being done oh *God*.

Our undeterred faith is required of us all to turn and turn back to being *rooted, grounded, and established* in place with all *expectations* aligned in *Him; His Word*. The *Word He* is and the Word that goes forth and has it perfect work. For indeed there is something right now... in *yours, mine, our* lives that would *'behoove'* us to let this ***creative*** hope filled ***expectant*** faith arise. For even if the **e**nemy has tried or is trying to put it out... huffing and puffing like he does... **e**ven roaring *like a lion* seeking whom he **MAY** devour*... as the *Lion of the Tribe of Judah* is roaring and *His* banner of love is over us.

*Now glory be to God, who (**expectantly**) by His mighty **creative** power at work **creatively** within us – you and me... is able to do far **m**ore than we would ever (**expect** or) dare to ask or even dream of... infinitely beyond our highest prayers, desires, thoughts, or hopes.*

This is who *He* is, this is what *He* does. Our ***Creator*** God who lives in us. The *One* in whom *He* spoke expressing through ***expectant*** filled words *His **creative*** power and it **m**anifested in physical realities as we are being reminded of. And *oh*... the ways of *His **creative*** power in the present at work, along with the power of the unending testimonies of how it has worked, operating with *His* divine agenda in the **e**ssence of *His* divine love distinctly driving it.

Truly different from all other powers and principalities... is *He* in *His expectancy*... with *His **expectations.*** Unlike any other *gods*... or **m**an. Especially after **m**an's: *Adam* and *Eve's*, turning from their primary *Source* in the *Tree of Life* and all other trees in the garden...to the forbidden *Tree of the Knowledge of Good and Evil*... where it **m**ight appear things turned out to un***expectedly*** be. Ah... let us not forget however, *He* gave and still gives free will. And, *His* greater plan we know had a strategy in place to deal with that latter **c**hoosing of what was prohibited. No other *god* has ever... or **e**ver will exhibit such *extravagant love*... let alone such genuine **e**ndearing **c**are and in an **e**nduring **c**ovenant **c**ommitment.

Remember and *trust* in this... in *the journey* and steady flowing *process* is His **expectancy** which always reveals and reflects the fullness of *His heart, character, nature,* and *intentions* which are always good... grounded and established **expectantly** in love... everlasting eternal divine love which is God because *God is love.* However... counterfeits come.

Regardless... He **m**ade them, us... and still is **making His created** humanity as the authentic *male and female* in the image and likeness of *Them/Him* as He **created** them. A *man* from the dust of the **e**arth... and a *woman* – in which she in part was out of the **m**an He **m**ade her. And, as a gift from *God to Adam* as an **e**qual **c**ompanion and helpmate for him... for *He* gave to them together His **expectant** plan. A **m**andate with a **m**ission including being *fruitful, replenishing, multiplying, subduing,* and *having dominion* in the earth and over creation.

So one can understand why an **e**nemy would quickly **c**ome to deceive... drawing them into deception that **created** a place for the **c**onception of identity **c**onfusion turning into *identity crisis, creating chaos* which **e**nded up in *identity theft.* He is still doing the same today as he does nothing new. Oh, the enemy **expected** that he had won and still thinks he **c**an. But, the greater love plan is still at work as from the start... in the blood of the *Son,* the *Lamb of God,* slain before the foundations.

Let *His Word* arise and **create** for a **c**ompleting of that which *He* has begun in **expectation**.... For we are His workmanship... likened unto His poetry (written with great **expectancy**), created in *Christ Jesus for good works to fulfill* (**expectantly**) *the destiny He has given each of us...* for we are joined to Jesus – the Anointed One. Even before we were born... God (in **expectation**) planned in advance our eternal purpose, preparing beforehand that we should walk in doing the good works He's ordered we would do fulfilling them... which (as **expected**) achieves it.*

Therefore if anyone is *enfolded into Christ*... that is, *grafted in, joined to Him by faith* (**expectantly**) in Him as Savior], he is an entirely new **creature** – person, that is reborn and renewed by the Holy Spirit... where the old things... the previous **m**oral and spiritual condition have passed away. Behold, everything is fresh (and **expecting**)... new things have come... because spiritual awakening brings a new life (and all its **expectancy**).*

... and, all these things are from God, who in **making** all things new,... reconciled us to Himself (**expectantly**) through Christ... **making** us acceptable to Him... and gave us the **ministry of** reconciliation... so that by our example we **m**ight bring others (in **expectation**) to Him... that is, in other words... that God was in Christ – the Anointed One, reconciling and shepherding the world to Himself, not **c**ounting people's sins or keeping records of their transgressions against them... but **c**anceling them (through a greater **earnest expectation**). And He has committed to us... entrusting (and **expecting**) us to enter into the **m**inistry of opening the door with the (**expectant**) **m**essage of reconciliation... that is, restoration to favor with God (His hearts **expectancy** fulfilled).*

Come, if you haven't already... and *as you are.* **C**ome to your loving *Father* and *Creator* who **created** the universe and **c**hose to **create** you... me... us, His **c**hildren, *His family of sons and daughters.* As we know and are growing in our knowing in *this process*... as *He is so shall we be.* It's His expectation connection

So... don't back away, back up, or back out... draw *closer*... and *closer* still. *He* longs... along with all of **creation** for the *manifestation of the sons of God* to arise... to **m**anifest in and through what *He's* already **created**...written. The **m**aking a way for *His* **expectations** to **create**, to initiate, *and to activate* a NEW **expectancy** and its **c**oming **NOW** for we are in the beyond!

e=mc3   **expectancy's energy** = our *Maker moving* in the *midst* of *mankind* with *the Master's eternally expected end embedded* in the *3rd power* by *His Spirit!*

<u>In light of this *word of worth ... create* and what's been shared:</u>

- ❖ *Perhaps... you **Encountered or Experienced a Question or Challenge**?*
  Write it out...

- ❖ *Perhaps... more has been **Established & Empowered by the Word**?*
  Write what/which...

- ❖ *Perhaps... it's time for **Engaging & Embracing your Expectations**?*
  Write what's forming...

Reminder: For *clarity, connection, and confirmation* regarding *expectancy* being stirred by this *word of worth*, seek *Him* and *His Word* first. To possibly assist you in the process the list of **ION** words is available in the Appendix.

*Footnotes: Chapter 7 Day 1 create / * See Hebrews 11:3, 2 Corinthians 5:7, Genesis 1, I Peter 5:8, Ephesians 3:20, 2 Corinthians 5:17-19 - all emphasis is mine and personal paraphrasing built on various translations and versions.

✧ Day 2: The Journey of "c"... communion

Let *expectations*... through this **word of worth's** part to *form, birth,* and *emerge* in its **meaning & mission**... *our meditation & motivation*... *as movement & manifestation awake, arise and align* in agreement with divine eternal **expectation**!

To **commune** and be in continual **communion** with *Him*... how it is the desire of *His* heart. What exactly does that **m**ean and why is it so important? An **e**ssential **e**lement **e**ven in our *life's journey* and *the process* of living life... as well as doing life with and in *Him*?

Let's start off by taking a look at our *word of worth* **communion** in a simply stated definition of its **m**eaning: *intimate fellowship, friendship, or deep and personal relationship with another or with God.* When with *God, Jesus, Holy Spirit...Them,* in a **communion** style of relationships includes that we recognize and honor *His* desire equally, actually **m**ore so for the **m**eanings as listed... as *He's* **e**ven drawing and wooing us by *His Spirit* into such things that are emphasized.

For indeed *He* is the *Author* and *Finisher,* the *Beginning* and *End*... **e**ven when it **c**omes to our **communion** with *Him*. So responding in obedience is key... it's better than sacrifice. Yet, uniquely from us it renders a fragrance sweet unto *Him* who is **expectantly** **c**alling.

His Worthy Word is always so very good to **c**onnect us to a bigger picture... yet, draw us into an opportunity to sometimes **e**ncounter an intimate invitation from *Him*. Let us be those with *eyes to see, ears to hear... and a spirit that chooses to respond* sincerely to *His* revealing and anything *He* is offering.

Draw near to **M**e *moving your heart (in* **expectancy***) closer to Mine and I will draw nearer to You. Since we know in fact and we have this (***expectant***) confidence that we have in Him, we can also exhibit great boldness going before Him knowing (and* **expecting***) that if we ask anything according to His will, He listens to us and He hears us (we can* **expect** *Him to). And if we have settled it and know that He hears us in whatever we (***expectantly***) ask, we know that we have the petitions and requests that we have asked (in* **expectation***) of Him.**

While we're there **communing** in quietness adoration and affection or in *mutual dialog and discussion... conversation*... that's **m**ore than just a **c**ommon **m**ode of **communication**... we learn, glean, and grow. Honestly... this is the best place in *the process* to be... in the *continual constancy of* **communing** *and* **communicating** with *Him*... especially when we invite and allow it to be respectfully reciprocal. As these *divine daily deposits* of *His* love, peace, rest, joy, along with *speakings, hearings, receivings,* and **m**ore taking their place in this genuinely **m**utual **common – union... communion.**

It's all about the fact that fundamentally it's a kind of a loosely designated time given to a type of a *divine design dynamic* where in this *devoted time He speaks and listens, you speak and listen. He deposits His* goodness into you and you yours toward *Him*. And, you begin to recognize and benefit from the ongoing two way *circle* that *creates* a kind of *cycle* in it all... in all *seasons of life*... and **e**ventually ongoing in time within our *daily rhythm of life*.

That my friends... is of **precious worth**... filled with some *powerful revelatory capacity*... as **presence** becomes increasingly **m**ore of what is *propelling* it – you **e**njoying *His* and *Him* **e**njoying yours. *He* **e**njoys and is blessed by your times of **communing** and through **e**ncountering

Him in ***prayer, worship,*** and ***service*** as unto *Him*... which are acts of ***communing*** with *Him* too. Just as prayer is a partnering with *God* to release *His* will in the earth. Truly *He* is worth the costly investment of your time for surely it is more costly not to. Our focused genuinely desired attention to discovering this amazing manner of the *ebb and flow*... may we find ourselves adjusting our *expectations* to value and prioritize it.

Expectancy will overflow when it comes to being your ***expectant*** intentional pursuit of *Him* and *His* of you, for this needful necessity called ***communion*** in the quest we're on with *Him*.

*For I know the thoughts that I think toward you, the (**expectant**) plans I have for you all about your marvelous destiny, declares Adonai, the Lord... Thoughts and plans of peace – shalom, your well-being, and not of calamity or evil, surrounding you with prosperity, to give you a beautiful future glistening with hope. If you reach out to Me (**expectantly**), you will find Me (as **expected**) when you search for Me with all (the **expectancy** in) your heart.* Selah ~*

A good way to inclusively view our *communing* with *God* is shared in both the *Old* and *New Testaments* of *His Word*. It has been mentioned briefly before, as it holds great worth. Therefore, it is a good thing to share it *again* for what it *contains* and *carries* within the message of its words... and the ***continual*** and ***constant*** underlying place it makes for the importance of creating a sincere lasting establishing of our *intentional, intimate **communion*** with *Him*. And... *you shall love the Lord your God, Yahweh, (**expectantly** doing so) with all your heart (**expecting**) and with all your soul (**expecting**) and with all your mind (**expecting**) and with all your strength(**expecting**) which is all your entire being (including your **expectations**).**

This powerfully provides a means in *the process* for what *Yeshua* calls us to in multiple ways and times as *He* admonishes us to pursue *being one (**common union** – unity, echad)* with the *Father*... just as *He* and the *Father* are one. It provides opportunity for sincere and meaningful ***encounters*** and ***experiences*** in small and large ways... and in all the in between ways of daily life *communing* with *Him* and in *Him*... and can't be emphasized enough.

A concept that's been highlighted and stressed multiple times in this *telling* too, as I've certainly found... and believe you have or are discovering the vast *benefits* and *blessings* wrapped in a *beauty* that *manifests* touching one *deeply, profoundly,* and *influencing personal **expectancy*** in needful way that really... nothing or no one else can.

Now, let's turn our attention to another form of ***communion*** that requires a new defining. Here let's enter into a simple examination together as to the meaning and purpose of the *Lord's Supper*... also known as *Holy Communion or the Remembrance Meal*... and it's correlation and connectivity to ***expectancy***. And *perhaps* your ***expectations*** were possibly headed there with this *word of worth* with it bringing up a more common kind of meaning.

In *His Worthy Word* there are a couple places where ***communion*** is written about. But let's look first, at a symbolic, yet measurable way, that it was revealed in a type of *first mention* of it shared in the *Word of God*. We see it early in *Genesis* 14 where *Abraham* encounters *Melchizedek*, king of *Salem* (peace) and priest of the *Most High God, Yahweh*. There he chooses to *fellowship* first blessing *Abraham* with ***wine and bread***: the two elements offered in the ***communion*** meal we know. However, with *fellowship* being first, what a wonderful illustration and expression of the other form of ***communion*** being essential.

The blessing of him in this significant way represents a type of weighty *authority from* and in *relationship to God* that *Melchizedek* possessed. Because *Abraham* recognizes this about him and in the blessing releases honor through giving him a tithe. Therefore, this **m**eaningful *kingly priestly* example is a foreshadow of *Yeshua* to us as a *three-fold* depiction of the **e**ssentiality of ***fellowship, communion,*** and ***giving*** togethering in ***common-union***

Later... we see *Yeshua* with *His* disciples gathering in an *upper room* to **c**elebrate the *Lord's Feast of Passover/Unleavened Bread.** It was a feast that required a **m**eal... a *Seder* **m**eal which is an *ordered* **m**eal with a *telling*... actually a re-*telling* in an *ordered remembrance* of *God* **m**oving to bring *His* people *Israel* out of the bondage of *Pharoh* freeing them from slavery and **m**aking a way of **e**scape from *Egypt* and is **c**onnected to the blood of a lamb.

A particular part of this *telling* highlights *God* requiring them to select and slay a *firstborn spotless lamb*, apply its blood to the *lintel* and *doorposts* of their home, and prepare to exit *Egypt* once the *Lord's Angel of Death 'passes over'* their homes seeing the blood applied. It was the *tenth* and final plague *God* would *release* and *execute* upon *Egypt* – the *plague of death* where firstborn sons and firstborn animals die. He was a *Son* and a *Lamb* ~

In this... we so powerfully see in their obedient actions to *remember* and *honor* the *Lord's Feast of Passover*... in a *"look, look again* with it not being a *looking again* to just *look back*, but... *let's look beyond"*... and now, into here where we are and what this **m**eans for such a time. They had no **c**lue in full what was also being revealed... a **m**ystery, per say, being brought into the light... in what would **e**merge to disclose the **m**eal it was becoming.

*Worthy Word... speak to us as You're **communing** with us in this significant part of the telling... The cup of blessing which you... me... we bless, is it not the **communion** of the blood of Christ – Mine, says the Lord? The bread which we break, is it not the **communion** of the body of Christ – which is Mine, says the Lord?"* The *Passover Lamb*... in the *Passover Unleavened Bread feast meal*... now revealed in *One* the way was prepared for... the *Lamb of God* – who is *Son of God*, *Son of Man*... the *Lamb* slain before the foundations.

For did *He* not set it all into order then and now? Indeed... *He* did. In an inviting to a *Come away come in moment*. A... we **m**ust go into our houses and shut ourselves in for we have done what *He* said applying the blood of the *Lamb* on our doors. They waited... and death did pass over. So now the taking them away, in *His* **m**aking of a way truly came through the *Lamb* who is the *Door*, and is the *Way*. Taking them out – yes, there were other *taking outs*... out the garden, out of *Sodom, out of your father's land*... for in the beyond it would **c**ome to a **c**omplete **m**easure of an **e**ternally ***earnest expectation***.

To the now... in Yeshua's ***we must go*** to *His* disciples... and to the house where there is an upper room prepared for us. All the while they're thinking it was a time to *honor* and *remember* the appointed time of *Passover*... and it was. However, **m**ore hovered in time and awaited them in the beyond.

Ah, yes... there's by and of itself a *relativity* and *relevance* in the **communing** He calls us to in *His* divine and **e**ternal, perpetually **c**elebrated and appointed (*moedim*) times... aligned in what *Yahweh* had *ordered, done,* and would *reveal* in the fullness to be in a *Lamb* – their/our *Deliverer*... as they all knew it was the time of *Passover*.

But first... a shift had to happen as *Yeshua* met them upon entering the room prepared... with *His*, *"Let Me serve you as My guests... let Me wash your feet"* kind of serving, before you take your seat at *My* table in which I've prepared for you... and in which a greater preparation was occurring. *His "Come sit now and fellowship with Me... "* for you are freely welcome to come to.. and always will be welcomed at, *My* table ~ it was all unfolding.

For *He* had not come to be served... but to give *His* life as ransom for many – *His ministry, mission, mandate...* as *He* came actually to serve. There is a serving in **communing** that *He* calls us to... and at a *cost* He knew all too well... do we? Let us go low... *expectantly* in an *unselfish loving...* serving as *He* did - the *Suffering Servant* yet as a servant leader.

Oh... the better revealing that now *emerged...* at the table... in the *telling* of the meal with new and different words spoken... *"This is My body – take eat of it. This is My blood – take drink of it..."* not to mention, *"...and when you do this, do it in remembrance of Me."**

That invitation *Jesus* offered then... to come to the table, *His* table and partake freely of *His* body given... *His* blood shed... it is still open and *He* is always inviting us to come. It's a table of fellowship where *His love, grace,* mercy and more are served. Because **He** who loved us first and is Love, awaits us as *Jehovah Rapha our Healer, Jehovah Jirah our Provider, Jehovah Tsidkanu our Righteousness...* and all that *He* is as *I AM that I AM*, and all that *He* has done. What an unimaginable laying out of *His* **expected** end.

Victory and triumph are within the meal that heals being served at the table. For it is also a *covenant table*. Where the power of the blood which is sufficient and has spoken a better word... yes, the best and whole word of the *Word...* has *enabled, fulfilled,* and *completed activating* the authority and power of *covenant* with *God*. A **new better covenant** of *God* with us for now... and for all *eternity*. It's been *His* **expected** end all along.

Oh yes... we see clearly a *process* in *His* life's *journey He willingly* and *knowingly* entering into, has gone through, and is presently seated at the right hand of the *Father* - now willing and available to us... as we're going through what *He's* ordered and is calling us to. A part of *the process* that when in **communion** and in actively **communing** with and in *Him...* requires a dying to and crucifying of self... the old man... the old creature, in its nature and flesh*... and all the **expectations** attached for a **common-union** to form in the NEW!

That's why it's so very good that *He* said... when you do this –a matter of fact, as **often** as you do this... do it in remembrance of *Me*. Not lightly or with malice... but with sincere hearts filled with the deepest depth of gratitude knowing *I am not, you are not, we are not worthy...* of what's been done in the blood of the *Firstborn Begotten One – the Lamb of God*.

And, *He* through the *done, completed, finished* atoning work of the cross, which has made all things NEW... and through *His* great love manifesting and at the table of **communion**... bringing **common union** in a meal... a remembrance covenant meal with a *telling*. It carries within it the power of *redemption, restoration, forgiveness, healing, wholeness...* and more, reconciling us back into right standing in the righteousness of *God* in *Christ Jesus* from where our *worthiness* comes. You... me... we, can count on that **expectation manifestation** and beyond us... for our *family, bloodlines,* and *generations...* and even *nations*.

How my heart it turns back in *His Word* also to that moment so very, very long ago when *Abraham* was requested to give the life of his son... the son in whom he *loved* – remember?

And... it's the first *m*ention of the word *love* there in *Genesis 22*. Where he placed him on a *table* - which was an *altar*... which was a place of sacrificing. But, love came down, intervening because of the obedience of a *man*... a *father*... to trust in a greater purpose and *His God*. For *greater love has no man than this then that he lays down his life for a friend**... nothing like a picture within a picture connected to and fulfilling **expectations.**

Remember... in this *telling* we've discovered within the *journey*, there is an offering of opportunity always for examining and assessing our life and in our *process*. For in it is the *ongoing processing* of our **expectancy** *forming*... *birthing*... *creating*... and *m*anifesting **expectations** continually in order to help us **embrace** a greater fuller *m*easure. Don't forget, it's never just our **expectancy,** but that of others too... and *His*. *m*ore importantly and intentionally, so we can receive from *Him* and truly be **empowered**!

Such a recap at this point is being presented because there can come a peripheral subtle form of **communion** – as one way to describe it... that attempts to arise within us... *within self*... with only our **expectations**. So it's important to *recognize* and *remind* of how passionately... even zealously... *He* desires any **cultivating** of **communion** – especially in the **garden of our heart...soul... life**... to **be with *Him* first** *and* **foremost**. Let's allow that to linger as we head into looking at our final aspect connected to our *word of worth* **communion**.

Community is an essential part of what we are called to partake in and it is connected to our **communing** with *Him*, which primarily is a type of *personal intimate intentional fellowship*. When extended from our personal individual fellowship with *Him* to others...*He* has an **expectation** there for us to involve *His* family, our family of *God*, as it becomes a collective connecting, and in a larger way with the *Body of Christ* – the greater corporate Church body.

Let's start with looking at this last piece we'll connect to our *word of worth* **communion** in an opposite spectrum kind of way... by looking at what *He* tells us in the form of a warning...

Do not be or continue to team up with mismatched alliances unequally yoked together with unbelievers (set your **expectations** *accordingly): for what fellowship or partnership is there between righteousness with unrighteousness or rebellion? And... what* **communion..** *or who could even imagine light joining together with darkness? For what harmony can there be between Christ and Satan? Or what does a believer have in common with an unbeliever? What friendship does God's temple have with demons? For indeed, we are the temple of the living God, just as God has said: I will make my home in them and walk among them. I will be their God, and they will be my people**... *His* **community** of Believers.

With this warning in *m*ind... let's allow some insight to come into the picture so the opposite spectrum as to what then *m*akes up the definition or criteria of those we are to partner or align ourselves with, in a godly yoke joining us and bringing us together in *Him*. Where such a teaming comes in *encouraging, empowering,* and *edifying* one another in *fellowship*... with a common emphasis on the honoring of *His heart, His purposes, His plans,* and to the greater degree *His kingdom's cause* – which potentially *m*akes way for *His* kingdom to come and will to be done on earth as it is in heaven.

He tells us that... *Behold... how good truly wonderful and delightful it is to see brothers and sisters – remember, we're His family (oh the* **expectancy***)... to live and dwell together in sweet unity. That kind of unity is as (***expectantly***) precious as the sacred scented oil flowing down from the head of the high priest Aaron... it even dripping down (as* **expected***) onto his beard and* *running all the way down to the hem of his priestly robes – consecrating (in godly **expectation**) his whole body. This united kind of harmony can be compared (**expectantly**) to the dew dripping from Mount Hermon, which flows down upon the hills of Zion. Indeed, that is where Yahweh has decreed His (**expectant**) blessings will be found, the promised (**expectancy**) of life forevermore!**

Wow… what an ***expectant*** description of what true unified ***community – common unity*** grounded in the ***common union communion*** of and with *Him…* and how it should be established and flowing. Yes, it is an older **m**ore religious kind of *image* presented to us. But, I'm reminded that we today are *His kings and priests** in the earth… so perhaps there's something in it we've yet to see? It's *His process* in it all overall for us… so let's **expect**!

Expect the importance of understanding what *He* is attempting to present… and how it **c**an sometimes be presented in what I write. Yet, there are definitely times *He* drops something before you… opening the door to **c**onnection, **e**ven **c**onfirmation, and you **m**arvel at *His* timing. Not that long ago, that happened through a short but empowering type of teaching in an **e**mail I received, and with its underlying theme: **community.** *Expectation* arose and a few things were highlighted to share as we draw into **c**losure for this day of *our journey.*

Over the years I've been aligned with the **m**inistry ***community*** of *Glory of Zion* as a *House of Zion* and with their *Kingdom Harvest Alliance* that is led by apostolic leaders *Dr. Chuck Pierce* and *Dr. Robert Heidler*. An **e**xtended blessing has **c**ome additionally by **c**onnecting to ones **c**onnected to them. In this **c**ase it is *Word Alive International Outreach* with *Kent* and *Beverly Mattox* who shared the **m**entioned teaching regarding ***community.***

Within it there were three overall areas **c**oncerning ***community***: *The Laws of Nature & Community* with topics like: Human Biology & **C**onnect, Neuroscience & Belonging, Physics & Interdependence. *The Laws of Man & Community* with topics: Legal & Social **C**ontracts and **E**conomics & Prosperity. And **c**oncluding with *God's Design for Community*. It was very revealing, informative, and **c**reated a place for some new thoughts… which of **c**ourse **c**an open a new potential place for ***expectancy*** to stir and ***expectations*** to form… and **e**ven by the very title of the topics, along with their brief summary.

It **c**ertainly **c**alled me up and out of the box of the familiar to broaden my perspective and view of just how dynamically diverse the topic of ***community*** is. For the sake of time my sharing will be limited but I do want to leave you will some really key thoughts I **c**ame out with.

Nothing in **c**reation **e**xists in isolation as *He* **c**reated it. *He* **c**reated it to be *interwoven, interconnected*, and ultimately flourishing through some type and level of *relationship*. Wow, there it was… the word *relationship*…remember? *He* was good to reveal as **e=mc3** started to unfold… that at the **c**ore *He* was wanting me to fully understand in *the journey* and the *process* in life… **It's not about a formula… but about a relationship.**

Bringing together what I *read, discovered, and learned…* in all simplicity it **c**omes to this.. there **c**an't be ***community*** let alone ***communion,*** without some form of ***relationship***. So any repetition you've been hearing is **c**oming out of a place of the **c**ontinualness of **c**ommuning yet in new ways. For *He* is good to again remind how this actually takes us back to "*in the beginning…*" when *He* **c**reated and why *He* **c**reated… how *He* wanted a *family* and relationship with them – us. Ultimately… a kingdom ***community - His***… and essentially for all forms of ***communion*** to be *real, relative,* and *relevant* established in *relationship* with *Him first…* and with others in *His* **c**reation.

Just as there's an *interwoven, interconnected longing in us for belonging*... remember, it came from the fruit of the **e**ssence of who *He* is as *Love* and *His* longing for us to willingly not just **c**hoose **communing** with *Him* so we **c**ould live in *His* love, from *His* love, and out of *His* love... but the **c**omplete ***manifestation*** of *love in His* sons as an ***expectation*** in **communion** releasing *mutual love* to *Him*, for *Him* and from the fullness of *Him*. Selah ~

May the grace of our Lord Jesus Christ, and the love of God, and the **communion** *of the Holy Spirit, be with you and fill you completely. Amen.*

<u>In light of this **word of worth ... communion** and what's been shared:</u>

- ❖ *Perhaps...* you **Encountered or Experienced a Question or Challenge**?
  Write it out...

- ❖ *Perhaps...* more has been **Established & Empowered by the Word?**
  Write what/which...

- ❖ *Perhaps... it's time for* **Engaging & Embracing your Expectations**?
  Write what's forming...

*Footnotes: Chapter 7 Day 2 communion / * See James 4:8, 1 John 5:14-15 Jeremiah 29:11-13, Deuteronomy 6:5 Mark 12:30, Exodus 12, Leviticus 23, 1 Corinthians 10:16, Matthew 26, Mark 14, Luke 22, Matthew 20:28, Mark 10:45, Galatians 5:24-25, 2 Corinthians 6:14-16, Revelation 1:5-6, 5:10, and 1 Peter 2:9, 2 Corinthians 13:14 - all emphasis is mine and personal paraphrasing built on various translations and versions. * See *Kent and Beverly Mattox* / Word Alive International Outreach Center @waio.org / A portion from their daily email Thursday, March 27, 2025.

✧ Day 3: The Journey of "c"... connect

*Let **expectations**... through this **word of worth's** part to form, birth, and emerge in its **meaning & mission**... our **meditation & motivation**... as **movement & manifestation** awake, arise and align in agreement with divine eternal **expectation**!*

There's nothing like *hearts of ones set out* on a *journey*... *expecting* and *willing* because they are *desiring*... perhaps even *hungering*... to take in all that's a part of *the process* as they travel. From the everyday life kind of things that *develop, unfold, and come* about...to the things that are revealed and now noticed. *Oh,* the **connections**... because they are connected in some way. Yet, there is yet to be things *uncovered, discovered,* and **connected** to a more *distinctly driven desire.* Linked to some extent of a *required expectancy* by what or who is being pursued... especially when their adventurous quest is one that has been discerned to be and designated as a type of *spiritual pilgrimage.* We see in our most recent **word or worth** that *communion* or *communing* is part of *His* **expectation connection**.

By clarifying all this alone... we can perceive how there opens the potential for the revealing of a greater depth of *meaning and purpose*... along with the **confirming** of any essential elements, which when linked together, bring opportunity for a profound type of **connection**. A joining that calls us up higher into the becoming more like *Him*... and onto a separated type of path aiding us in being more *holy as He is holy* as we purpose to live more from, *as He is so are we.* The **expecting** of a **connecting** together of what one's heart is *set out for* and to whom one's heart is *set towards*. *His Word* speaks in wonderful words about such.

*How enriched and blessed are they whose (**expected**) strength, empowerment in grace filled enablement, is (**expectantly**) in You... those who within (the **expectations** of) their hearts there are forming highways of holiness... for their hearts are longingly set on a (**expected**) pilgrimage... unwavering... focused with holy determination (all **expectation**) as their faces are set as flint... to do His good and perfect will... not being disgraced or disconnected as they press, pursue and prevail.**

Oh, to press to **connect**! Our *word of worth* **connect** can surely conjure up much! And... at its core it means *to join together, to tie, link, clip to or attach*... as each creates a type/place of **connection**. *Chabar* is a *Hebrew** word for **connect** or *joining*, along with being *linked* to the idea of **connection**, *coupling together,* or *joint(ly)* in the roots of its defining. We see it as *harmos:** *a joint,* **connection**, or a *fitting together,* in the *Greek.*

In *harmos* there's an opening here to share a delightful kind of **connection** I've discovered. For in its core meaning, there is a coming together with the idea of *harmony.* It is seen in the *Greek* word *harmonia*. Two others related words are: *sunphoneo:** *to agree, be of one mind, to be in harmony* and *sunphonia:** *agreement, in harmony...* with all of them being words that carry in them meanings which associate with a role they play to bring about preferred outcomes within all of our **connections** and them joining together. I can't help but hear music all over this. We know *He* sings rejoicingly over us. Is it **expectancy's** song?

He presented this connecting to me once as *His* **togethering**. What's done with multiple layers unfold **connecting** and **corroborating** as they *converge*... because it's what *He* does as only *He* can. *Holy Spirit* works together with our great *Master Connector Father God*, who is our *"Maestro"* the **Master Conductor** too! *"Let's take it from the top... instruments up..."*

Expectation has awakened and its time for *His harmonia* and *sunphonia* to come forth in the *song He* is forming through ***expectancy*** in our lives.

Let's *linger* here… in a *likening* unto the *lingering* of *the Spirit-His*, over the *dark, formless and void* at the beginning… therein lies divine ***expectancy*** for the ***connectivity*** He'll bring together in this *telling* through the writing of what *He* wants revealed… released… and to be received in "c". A conceiving one could say because there is a *forming…creating a birthing*… for a ***manifesting*** of some things ***expected.*** Which at times has a surprisingly sweet un***expectancy*** in our being ones who are unquestionably ***connected.*** Ones who *listen* and *hear things in the unheard* and *notice things in the unnoticed*… sensing by our *spirit* and responding in delightful pleasure filled *obedience* because we know there's a joining.

Yes, let it be settled now. *Vertically, horizontally, diagonally… individually, collectively, corporately*… there's a ***connectivity*** in the ***connectedness*** we are designed for. And, it is *divinely* linked in OI (not to be mistaken with AI)… *His original intent.*

Now unfolding in the defining above… if we are willing to ***expect*** and *see* in what was said… therein lies a marvelous kind of *imagery* that can be figuratively described as a type of *harmonious symphony* conceived and made of ***multifaceted*** and ***multidimensional melodies*** that exist… waiting to be heard throughout the earth. As written in *His Worthy Word*, all things were created by and for *Him* for they *started in* and *through Him*… including *humanity.*

And… they possess a ***connection expectation*** placed in their *DNA*… which for us, it's been there since *His knowing* and *forming* of us… *togethering us in Him*… before *His* placement of us in our mother's womb and then brought forth in our birth. Oh… what complexity holding *eternal* ***expectancy!***

Let's linger a bit more and imagine for another moment.. you know, with our *God designed, defined,* and *sanctified imaginations*… that before us now is a set of *keys*… like those on a *piano*. All 88 of them both black (36)and white (52)… you can decide what kind of piano it is: *acoustic or digital-electronic,* and *upright, electric, baby or concert grand.* Because the image you ***connect*** it with means something to you and affects with all certainty your ***expectancy.*** So… maybe at first mention of the word *'keys'* you started to imagine *keys* – like locking and unlocking ones? This ***confirms*** that with every word there's usually a couple of ***connections*** that could arise to have a place… thus *clarity* is key.

Continuing on with *keys*… the piano kind, take a look with me at something important you should know about center of the keyboard: everything flows from out of it to the right up the keyboard with sounds releasing becoming higher and higher… or to the left down the keyboard with sounds being released becoming lower and lower. That note is called "*middle C*". And, it will always be a C and in the middle on an 88 key piano.

Interestingly, a lot, but not all tuning forks are tuned to C – that same C representing the middle of the range in comparison to the notes(keys) on each side. It is good to know who or what we are "*tuned into*". Once I read something related expressed by a man that went something like this as he struck a tuning fork releasing a sound… "*That's middle C! It was middle C yesterday. It will be middle C tomorrow. And, it will be middle C many, many years from now.*" One might say it's an *absolute.*

Here middle C presents a constancy in its ***connectedness*** to its continual consistent place of positioning and releasing of the same sound. Hmmm… this is all leading to share how *He* was revealing to me a *piano player*, how *He* like middle C would like to be the center and the central ONLY *One God* in my life… keeping *Him* and *His Word, will,* and *ways*, along with *His plans*, *promises*, and *purpose(s)* which are truth, at the **c**ore of what and who I am *tuned into*… and as the plumbline of all things in my life. Letting *Him* be the *Absolute* to me – yes there are absolutes… and what a difference that **m**akes in *life's process*.

Not only would the *process* in and of my life's *journey*, with all its diverse everyday kind of life **connections**… flow in *greater harmony*, but it all would **c**reate a wonderful form of repertoire of **encounters** and **experiences c**omposed of **m**any genres to bring all sorts of benefits, blessings, and beauty He desired me to *enjoy, grow through*, and *know Him* and *His* love **m**ore personally by. Wow!!! How **c**ould I say no… so I welcomed *His* invitation and have been **e**njoying *growing in knowing Him* in this **m**ore *inclusively, intentional, intimate,* and *individual* kind of way. It's actually an invitation to you too.

- ❖ *Perhaps*… you are seeing how *He's* **c**onnected it all to something I was personally **connected** with and passionate about? *He'll* do that… for *He* is an 'up **c**lose and personal' relational kind of *God*. And, I'm sure you've encountered some kind of similar **connections** with *Him* before. Now's the time if you haven't… or, you want to **m**ore. It's an individual kind of thing… yet, there are ways *He* **connects** (or wants to) in general with everyone. *He's steady, stable, constant, solid, faithful*… and yes, *trustworthy*. So go ahead… enter in. Yes… **expectantly** enter into such times and ways of **connection** to and with *Him* that often open a way and enable a part of the *process* for us to experience greater *unity, alignment* and *agreement* with *Him*… which spiritually **c**reates a place for the **expectancy** *He* has for us to be of one **m**ind (*His*) and in one accord in *Him*, our *Lord*. Having the same love, thinking the same way, and being filled with *His* ever present and available *joy* throughout it all!

Joy is truly a fruit of the *Spirit* as an **e**xpression flowing out of love* that **m**anifests when the love of *God* in us is shed abroad in our hearts* as we *come together connecting* in *unity*. Just like the **c**ombining of **m**usical notes in a 1-3-5 pattern together which orders the notes to produce a harmonious sound released that's **c**alled a *chord* – kind of like *one accord*… the sound of *the three* becoming one… **c**an't **m**ake these kind of **connections** up!

The notes are *agreeable, unified*… therefore, in *harmony* as they **c**ome together, A *chord*… in accord, because **m**usically a kind of *jointly fitting together* has happened. I believe we **c**an see in it all the vivid expressive imagery that **c**omes as *He* speaks it *of*… *to*… and *over* the *body of Christ* because it is as it should be… **m**ust be… aligning with *His* **expectancy**.

In *His Worthy Word* the **c**oncept of **connecting**, being **connected**, or being joined together is revealed in several references it suggests. One **c**oming to **m**ind is that in *Christ*… we are all *joined or built up together* becoming a dwelling place spiritually for *God* to **c**ome, to rest, to have a place where *He* is welcomed and honored as it in its **e**ssence should always be a place distinction… and where *His* presence by *His Spirit* **c**an hover and brood… which is so vital.

Let's **e**nter into what *His* words present, "…*you are citizens as God's people… members of God's household who are rising (in* **expectancy**) *to be like the perfectly fitted stones of the temple… and your lives have been built up together upon the foundation laid by the apostles and prophets (as* **expected**), *and best of all, you are connected to the Jesus Christ – the Head Cornerstone of the building… the Anointed One Himself. This entire building in all its structure is under construction and is continually (***expectantly***) growing increasingly under His supervision… until it rises up completed (as* **expected**) *as the holy temple of the Lord Himself. Which means… that God (through His* **expectation**) *is transforming each one of you into the Holy of Holies, His dwelling place, through the (***expectant***) power of the Holy Spirit (pregnant with* **expectancy**) *living in you!**

And then, as we ~ *speak the truth in love (as He **expects** us to), we will in all things grow up into Christ Himself, who is the head. From Him the whole body, fitted and held together - **connected** by every supporting ligament, (**expectantly**) grows and builds itself up in unselfish love (as **expected**) through the work of each individual part.**

Our lives joined together in *Him*, in *Them*. The fullness in the perfection of the completion of *Him* who is *Author and Finisher – Alpha Omega – Beginning and End* **in us**. As *His Body*, … as a part of *His* **C**hurch… a **c**ongregation… but in the **expectancy** of *His* heart… the family of God… His.

*For those who are planted – rooted, grounded, established, connected… in the house of the Lord shall flourish in the courts of our God. They shall still bear (as **expected**) fruit in their old age… and they shall be fresh and flourishing out of that **connection**.**

What **c**onfident **c**ourage **c**omes and arises as we **connect** with what *He's saying, revealing, directing*… and how that speaks into our **expectations** that are forming or have formed. Amazingly… *He* often **m**oves in a way of **confirming, comparing,** and **contrasting,** and ultimately bringing greater **clarity** which opens the door for *His* **m**ore, including *His* **expectations**… to be **m**ade known which helps us in tremendous ways as we seek to *remain in faith* and *stay steady* in the *ongoing process* in the *journey*.

Yes… there's a **connection, confirmation,** and **clarity** that **c**an **c**ome through **m**an –*family, friends,* **c**o-*workers, spiritual leaders*… and others in your life. But, there's a **c**onnecting which only **c**omes *from Him to you* through a **m**eans and in a way **m**an **c**annot *orchestrate*. **E**ven if and as *He* uses **m**an in all the ways *He* does – *you know that you know that you know He* is speaking revealing to you *personally* and *directly* in a way only *He* **c**an and **m**ost often they are not aware of.

Again… there is this *togethering* in which *He* brings together as *He's always working it all together for our good*. Often it is in these **m**oments when we've **e**ncountered perhaps, a type of tension **e**specially in transitions. Where our natural *sensing, sight, insight*… and our spiritual *sensing, sight, insight* - that which rises believing in our spirit through faith by *His Spirit*… **m**ay *experience conflict, confusion*, a kind of *chaos* or **e**ven a **c**risis attempting to **e**nter in.

Our sense of *logic, rationale,* and *reasoning* produced out of our soul (or flesh) will sometimes **m**ove in a **c**ontrary reaction or response to what *He's* been *showing, developing,* and *maturing* in you in the *process*. And, occasionally you'll know or discover it is linked to a vision or strategy *He's* given you.

A *remembering* that is key in such times is being grounded and rooted in knowing *you have the mind of Christ**… along with *power, love,* and *a sound mind*.* Together with a *mind that is renewed daily and not conformed to this world, but transformed as it submits itself to God, His good and perfect will and for His reasonable service.** And that all reminds and **e**mpowers us to remain in the **connectedness** of *Him* in us that **m**akes us *more than conquerors* because *His grace to us, in,* and *through us is sufficient*.

The victory is already won for *you… me… us* in, with, and through *Him* who **m**akes all things possible. So in *the process* don't be deterred, no **m**atter what it looks like – *He* is **m**oving in the **m**idst and things are **connecting,** **c**oming together. And, if you're not **e**ntering into that **e**stablished kind of response or **expectation**… then you **c**an always *pause… take a selah*. Seek *Him, His Word*… and *pray* – pray in the spirit if you do, allowing the *Spirit* to *help, reveal, teach*… Holy Spirit to your spirit. All that *He does, will do,* and *divinely downloads* to increase the potential for your good and success that can be contained in these moments... and, the momentum created in *the process.*

For *then* there comes an opportunity to move or quit – by letting something just end or cease, by waiting on the timing in it all, or moving forward in the *reestablishing, reset or recalibration* that happens as we give place to new or different ways – *His* ways. Ways that work as we take it all in... *assess, interpret,* and *respond* to it all as He is *leading, guiding, and directing.* Remember, all of this is to the *positive or negative...* to *the good, bad, or indifferent...* to the what is good and right in *His* sight or not.

There remains the necessity for *fluidity* and *flexibility* in the *formability* within what we **expect.** Before completion comes in its varying forms of manifestation in and through our **expectations**... there are **connections, confirmations,** and even **confessions** that are *critical, valuable,* and *essential.*

Again, there is the consistency of *as He is, so are we** manifesting in the midst. For when we draw back to or upon it... it signifies that we as Believers are really becoming like *Jesus*, who was *perfected in love*, which ultimately **connects** us to what comes in our *reformation for transformation*. Watch for connections trying to happen vying to create any comparison.

"Comparison, at its root, isn't always bad. Comparison notices similarities and differences. It can become a slippery slope. However, when our comparison is tainted by judgment, it sounds like "this is better," or "this is worse," or "this is the same."" shares *Sara Whiten*.

She goes on to say, *"Those judgments not only can be incorrect (as we are ill-equipped to be judge), but they tend to feed into our predictions of what we think the Lord is going to do. We compare with what we know or what we've experienced, because we don't know how to compare with what we have yet to see. The Lord, however, is trying to do what "no eye has seen, no ear has heard, and no mind has imagined"* (1 Corinthians 2:9 NLT).*

As we finish up this day... it can *seem like* to **connect** with *Him* and with others, well... that all requires *effort, time*, and at time *resources*. I cannot lie... it does. It like all that *He* calls and draws us to... there are types of required things and there is undeniably some kind of cost. I'm believing *you... me...* we've grown (and are still growing) to know this and accept this. And, as ones who know or want to know what it takes to be **connected** to *Him*, to the *Body of Christ, the Church,* and to the others *He* leads us too and aligns us... will we be willing to obey following *His* lead whatever the commitment and cost? It's all *His* anyway... right? And... all is unto *Him* too... right?

For have we not discovered **connection** in such a way... wherever we are in the *process*... that it is worth it, especially when it is together in *Him*? And, in any other directing of togethering *He* makes way for... just do it! If you've not discovered what lies within what I'm sharing... perhaps, therein lies the simple entering into the beginning of *expecting* such... and in the forming of an *expectation*?

He is with us in all things and *His* yoke is easy and *His* burden in light. Even the **connecting** in our confessing is that we're commissioned to pursue the sharing of the *Good News of the Gospel of Jesus Christ* – of *His* love to all. A sharing that points to *His* incredible desire and pursuit of **connecting** with us that required *Jesus* giving of *His* life freely... to the point of death to cleanse and redeem us from our sin. That completed work makes a **connection** for *His* resurrection to bring forth life again... eternal life. Now that's contains some *expectancy*! What hope amazingly lies within that sharing that is *connecting* them to the open door of being *born again*; an ***eternal expectation***!

So we… *stand fast therefore in the **(expected)** liberty by which Christ has **m**ade us free, and do not **(expect** to) be entangled with any yoke… especially those that put you in bondage. To the weak I became weak, that I **m**ight gain in **(expectancy** for) winning the weak to Him; I have become all things to all people, so that I **m**ay by all means by His **(expectant)** grace save some. I do all things becoming God's partner in (His **expectations** of) this connection with Him, for the sake of the gospel so that I **m**ay as well, become a fellow partaker of it.**

This is *His* faithful **connected** servant *Paul* – our *brother in the Lord* in whom we are **connected** to, speaking. And yet, we certainly see the **m**odel of *Jesus* in these words and the *desire, dedication,* and *daily pursuit* of this as something that prepares a way for an authentic type of **connection** *He* came to bring to all**.**

The diverse **connections** shared in this *word of worth connect*… may we **embrace** the reminder that we **m**ust be linked together in what *He* the **Master Conductor** and **Connector** communicated to us… ***as He is, so are we to be***. As we **connect** to *Father* through *Jesus* and the *Holy Spirit* foundationally, it will then be in our *functioning* and *fellowshipping* enabling us to **connect** to others from out of that **connection**. For we know, *the journey* was never **m**eant to be alone, but with *Him* and with each other. Let our earnest *expectation* arise!

What's your **e=mc3** that's forming:

<u>In light of this **words of worth … connect** and what's been shared:</u>

- ❖ *Perhaps… you* **Encountered or Experienced a Question or Challenge**? Write it out…

- ❖ *Perhaps… more has been* **Established & Empowered by the Word?** Write what/which…

- ❖ *Perhaps… it's time for* **Engaging & Embracing your Expectations?** Write what's forming…

Reminder: For **c**larity, **c**onnection, and **c**onfirmation regarding *expectancy* being stirred by this **word of worth**, seek *Him* and *His Word* first. To possibly assist you in the process the list of **ION** words is available in the Appendix.

*Footnotes: Chapter 7 Day 3 connect / * See Psalm 84:5, Zephaniah 3:17, Isaiah 50:7, I John 4:17, I Peter 1:15-16/Leviticus 11:44, 20:7, Galatians 5:22-23 – in TPT see important footnotes, Romans 5:5, 1 Corinthians 2:16, 2 Timothy 1:7, Romans 12:1-2, I John 4:17, Philippians 2:2, Ephesians 2:22, 4:15-16, Psalms 92:13,14 - all emphasis is mine and personal paraphrasing built on various translations and versions. * See Strongs Concordance H2266 *chabar*, G719 *harmos*, G4857 harmonia, G4805 sunphoneo, G4857 sunphonia. * See *Sara Whitten* / Elijah List / May 25, 2025 Prophetic Word.

✧ Day 4: The Journey of "c"… covenant

Let **expectations**… through this **word of worth's** part to *form, birth, and emerge* in its **meaning & mission**… *our* **meditation & motivation**… *as* **movement & manifestation** *awake, arise and align* in agreement with divine eternal **expectation**!

He is giving **c**ontagious **c**ourage with **c**ommitment attached and **c**ommuning is an active part in what *He's* revealed in the value and importance of *His* **c**onnecting with us and us with *Him*… in all the ways *He* has, does, is… and attempts to *vertically, horizontally, diagonally*… *individually, collectively, corporately.* Let's not waste any taking and **m**aking of **m**oments in our daily *walk* with *Him* and as we enter in to receive from what *He'll* release to us in *our journey* today with "**c**" through the *word of worth "covenant".*

This scripture, **m**ay it help prepare our way… *As for Me, this is My covenant (filled with **expectancy**) with them, says The Lord: My Spirit who is on you, and My words that I have put in your mouth, (you can expect that they) shall not depart from your mouth, or from the mouth of your offspring, or from the mouth of your children's offspring, says The Lord (zealously **expectant**), from now on and forever."* *

Oh, the **expectancy** of the **c**ontinualness and **c**onstancy that **covenant** brings to *the process*… to *the journey* of our relationship with *God*… who is to become and be not just *our God, Yahweh*… but our <u>only</u> *God* and of our *children*, their *children*, and their *children*… and the *generations* now and forever. *Know (**expect** that) the Lord your God is God; He is the faithful God, keeping His **covenant of love** to a thousand (**expectant**) generations of those who love (it's their **expectation** to) Him and keep His commandments (as **expected**).** Amen

The underlying **c**ertainty of *God* is seen in *Him* being a **covenant** *God*… and, **e**ven greater *He* is defined and **c**onfirmed that *He* is a **covenant keeping God.** **C**learly in *His Word* we see this over and over again that *He* is a god – unlike any others, who never lies, always doing as *He* promises.* If *He's* not a **c**ovenant keeping *God*, what good then is *His* with us?

Indeed, **covenant** is truly one of the **m**ost significant and imperative *words of worth* from *His Worthy Word He* has highlighted to me, rooted in me as foundational for me and my life, and life in general. It was **e**stablished and sealed when *He* imparted revelation awakening me to the needful and necessary understanding and grounding that ***His love*** - the love it is, because it is **covenant love… pure, holy, just, true…** it is <u>not</u> like the love that others, the world, or as an emotion **c**an or will **e**ver offer like *He* does.

Covenant is a word that requires we *absolutely, purposefully,* and *intentionally* know… not just in the *intellectually, ritually,* and *religiously* knowing of it and of it with *Him*. But in and through… spiritual heart knowing *Him* as our **covenant** God… a knowing that is better still as its *real, raw,* and *made relative* in our continual **m**utually intentional and intimate *keeping* of relationship, yours… mine, with *Him* our **covenant** keeping *God of love*.

It's the **"keeping"** part that shifted everything in my *covenantal paradigm*… and **m**aybe for you too. In my life, my view of *Him* as one living in **covenant** with *Him* first and foremost… and then in a godly defined ordained **covenant** marriage, as one woman and one **m**an, in which for me is my one and only husband *Greg* of 34 years and I know will be beyond by *His* sufficient grace and our **expected** **m**utual **c**ommitment. The boldness and courage *He's* **c**onnected me to for standing with *Him* in this truth… is being displayed now in a spirit of my heart speaking through the filter of *truth in love*... as I realize just in stating this, some of you reading **m**ay disagree. **M**ay you seek *Him* and step into what *He'll* reveal ~

As always on *this journey... our life journey*, we **c**an *agree to disagree* **c**ontinuing to remain together through this *telling* with an ***expectation*** to ***embrace*** it and be ***empowered*** respecting that it's ok to allow the **e**xpression of differences. Or... it **m**ight be (put I pray not) this is your end... only you know. But, my ***expectancy*** lies in *Him* to you and within you to help you know the direction of any defining in this place of ***covenant*** deciding.

Our **c**onnection with the word ***covenant*** **m**ust **c**ome and **m**ust occupy its *absolute truth filled required foundational place* as it does in the *life of God* revealed to , the *Word of* God given to us, and should be seen in the life of **e**very *Believer* who is a true *born again child of God*. This **m**ust happen in order to identify and dismantle anything... and yes, deter anyone attempting to infiltrate our *knowledge* and *understanding*, as well as *life application* of what **covenant** is defined to be in the fullness of its ***expectant*** **m**eaning to *Him*. This is critical in the **c**onfused **c**ulture, state of the world, along with some churches and the **m**any gods offered.

A **c**loser look at the definition for our *word of worth **covenant*** will help us begin to discern **m**ore **m**eaningfully why *He* is starting off this day with this word in this way. Biblically we see its **m**eaning **e**volving around this summary of defining: *a type of sacred bond through a solemn, legal, binding agreement, which is built upon or through relationship between two or more persons or parties, where conditions are established through promises made with the sincere intent of keeping them*. These **c**onditions include *mutual obligations* and *responsibilities*, as well as *blessings* and *benefits* to all who've agreed and entered in. For *Believers*; you and me, it would be between *Yahweh Adonai* - our ***covenant*** keeping God and us who are *His*. For at its **c**ore, ***covenant*** **m**eans a **c**oming together...hmmm *togethering*.

In **m**any ways a ***covenant*** is often defined as *a treaty, an agreement, a promise or pledge* because it involves *promises* and *commitments,* as well as *restrictions* where one obliges their self to with another or others. Plus, it **m**ight **e**voke **c**ontrol of things additionally by including the setting of *limitations, boundaries*, **e**ven *borders* or otherwise. We see this in our world.

A ***covenant*** is <u>not</u> exactly that same as what we **c**all a in today's world a *contract or deed* – particularly biblically. Yet, **c**ontracts/deeds will include or **m**ention **c**ovenant structures within them. This differentiation is essential to know and honor. Therefore, **e**ach parties responsibility in the formation of it, acceptance, and **m**utual intent is important in it all. ***Expectancy*** is **c**onsiderably embedded in the **c**ore of ***covenant*** and should be known fully to all involved. For you get one **e**xperience if it's just a **c**ontract... and a whole other **e**xperience when you know it's a **covenant**.

Like **e**verything with our *God Yahweh*, *He* gives us **c**hoice as *He* always has and always will in all things and in all ways... including joining together with *Him* and being aligned in ***covenant***. Being *His* requires that we **m**ust choose and rely solely on the *Word of God* and it being absolute inherent *God* breathed truth, by *His* Spirit *Holy Spirit* conceived truth regarding ***covenant*** and all *related, included,* or *attached* requirements.

We are in the world, but not of it. We are to be *holy, separated,* and *set apart* for *Him* and *His* purpose for us. Yet, we are living a life which is to be **m**odeling to the world as the kingdom influencers we are. We are to walk out our purpose and **c**alling, sharing the *Good News* revealing and reflecting *His character* and *heart* – which is seen in *His Word, will, and ways*.

THE JOURNEY OF EXPECTATION... EMBRACE IT AND BE EMPOWERED!

The time spent *considering* and *reviewing* in this *revealing* and *reflecting* on just how important the *foundations* and *grounding* in **covenant** are to *Him*... and should be obvious to us. In reality and actuality, our place and posture in *Him* in our *covenant* with *Him*, will be witnessed to the degree it is established in us. Its vital part of the core and essence of who we are does represents if our *expectancy is* aligned or not in *Him*... our **covenant keeping God**.

❖ *Perhaps*... it is as simple as in our choosing life in *Him*, the door opened to pursuing and entering into our **covenant** and **covenant relationship** with *Him*. Yet, as *His born again* ones it is required that *He* be the <u>only</u> God we're in **covenant** and *relationship* with. It's good to remember that God doesn't **expect** *perfection* from us... just our **expectation** to pursue all that is *good, right,* and *required* by *Him*. Through the *Son – His Son Christ Jesus Yeshua* our *Messiah*... is how that *perfection* comes. By the *Firstborn Son,* and *Holy Spirit* at work in us... *He* is molding and making us... helping and teaching us. You know... *the process* as we make our choices and establish our **expectancy** accordingly. Now... as we move forward into more on **covenant**... let's just take a moment to ask *Him*, our **covenant** heavenly Father to create in *you*... *me*... *us*, a clean heart and renew in us a right spirit so we can come with clean hands and a pure heart into this reminder, but **expectancy** filled remainder of fresh, even extended, and possibly new revelation and understanding of why *recognizing* and *reestablishing* if led, the *remaining in*... our **covenant** with *Him*.

It's amazing how the very *process* of **expectation** stirs starting a *forming, creating,* and *birthing* for a manifesting within me just in hearing the word **covenant**. It re-minds me so very much of *Father's* heart and faithfulness to be who *He* says *He* is and do what *He* says *He'll* do. Remember, in the *Bible* the heart of a **covenant** with someone... at its core, at the center... there is a **RELATIONSHIP** between two or more people. It has to have its place here too. Just like *He* said through e=mc3... *"It's not about a formula... it's about a relationship"* where we know with all **expectant** certainty it's in the *journey and process*.

For once *again*, in the *foundations* set and our genuine connecting through fellowship in our relationship with *God*... lies a *mutually binding agreement* called a **covenant** that is *formed* with *His promises, commitments,* and *obligations* to us, and all in the context and **expectation** of a partnering and working together through love, benefitting and blessing each other – that's the **covenant mutuality** needed for a *righteous kingdom outcome* which *glorifies Him*.

One way this happens in this *telling*... is to not assume what you the reader know regarding this topic. For we know, *assumption* can take us into *presumption* which is a sin. And, *He* tends to direct us, if were willing receive, a requiring to keep secure and shored up our foundations as is shared by *His* leading. Plus, these are powerful action required "**ION**" words. Pay attention... *He* may lead to look again at the list.

Simply... in this we start to see that <u>**covenant with God is a form of partnership with God**</u>. It brings out the power of the full potential and purpose of what *He* created us for. We know originally... in the *garden* through *Adam* and *Eve's* sin, their **partnership relationship** became broken as a *rift* formed a *breach* which created a *shift* in their *communion connection* with *Him*. Now *division* came carrying its **corrupted seed of expectancy** for they had chosen to eat of the ONLY tree they were told not to; the *Tree of the Knowledge of Good and Evil,* instead of the all other trees which included the *Tree of Life*.

The un*expected* came for them. They didn't *expect*, after being deceived which led them to eat of the *forbidden tree*... to suddenly having an *awareness of their nakedness*... to ending their *communion connection* with **God,** which at its core essence is ***covenant***. Not to mention how now… they'd be removed from dwelling with *Him* and *Him* with them in Eden

But *Yahweh* in *His* all-knowing and eternal **covenant love**… *He* stepped in, took over, and *His* **covenant keeping covering** kind of plan, set into place before the foundations of the world; should such happen and did, it was in place. The ***covenant*** *He* had with them was as long as they honored and followed the directives of it, along with the restrictions it required. Those consequences went into action – they had to for covenant requires. Yet, within the covenant was His covering as He covered them. But in the beyond there was the redeeming… and atoning portion of His reconciling them… which was yet to be seen.

He has remained faithful to *His* part of the **covenant** and still is praise God! And, *He* is loyal to it with us who are *His*. In still giving to us free will - choice… even after their choosing against what *He* had ordered and said, which brought forth the need for *His* redemptive heart and purposes within *His* **covenant** plan to begin the restoring order to the disorder that was no longer aligned with *His original intent.*

We see this pattern of *His **covenant promising*** to do certain things **if** *His **covenant*** people, us, will obey so they/we can partner with *Him* as *it is written.* Commit to doing things required as outlined and we should settled within. It was and is a **covenant** partnership… based on *agreement, commitment, being trust worthy,* and *loyal*… to death. Each ***expects*** the other to fulfill their part. Each ***expects*** a circumcising of the heart to totally commit.

An interesting note to add here from biblical times, and some still do today, covenant ordering called for an entering into a *"cutting of covenant",* which actually was represented in the seriousness of the act. It involved the cutting or shedding of blood to seal a binding oath or solemn agreement. It could be done with the slaughtering of animals by the people making the ***covenant*** and them laying out the cut up pieces on the ground and walking together between them. It served as a sign of their willing pledge to fulfill their parts. It is rare, but sometimes… the cutting of ***covenant*** is actually each person cutting themselves and then joining their blood together as a sign and doing so seals their oath.

Overall, there are ***five key covenants*** shared in the *Word of God* between *God and Noah, God and Abraham, God and Israel,* and *God and David* which are all *Old Testament* examples. The final one is revealed to us in the *New Testament* where *God* forms the *New **Covenant*** through *Jesus* with us. Overall, a ***covenant*** was initiated and formed by *God* in each of these… to restore *His* family back to *Him* with the ultimate idea of things returning to how it was in the beginning and was always to be. Central to *His **covenant*** is that it was and has originated from *His* heart for ALL people being restored and reconciled back to *Him.*

It's a wonderful discovery where ***expectation*** grows in the unfolding the layers of revelation, meaning, and the unique aspects and importance in each **covenant**… should *He* lead you to or you decide to search and study them out further. Quickly you realize that *God* incredibly is… *yes,* unbelievably is faithful and true to always ***keep His part*** in the partnership. That facet alone moved me deeply. *Oh* the ***keeping of covenant***, so near and dear to my heart too.

Covenant is the foundation of the way *God* chooses, uses, to enter back into rightly restored partnership relationship with *His* created ones – us, human kind, after sin because *He* created us to be *His* family… and through ***covenant*** with us *He* can provide a reliable way we can partner again. However, *God's **expectation*** for man was that he would choose to be and remain faithful to ***covenant*** and in ***covenant*** with *Him*. Man… *you, me… us,* we continually fail and break our part of the ***covenant***. But *God*… doesn't back down nor will *He* ever, from *His* part.

Yahweh our **Covenant** God through *Yeshua* comes to *His* people – us, as *Son of God, Son of Man* to fulfill by *restoring, redeeming,* and *providing what is required* in the **covenant** for once and for all. This reconciled **m**an in *Him*… is a result of *Him* putting things back into right order so our **covenant** rights **c**an legally be given to us through the *better fuller measure completed and fulfilled* in *Yeshua – the Lamb of God's* blood shed securing our **covenant** and the way to **e**nter back into a *renewed covenant relational partnership* with *God*.

Explore now **m**ore about **covenant** through this profoundly truthful defining in *His Word*… *The ministry Jesus has received is as (expectantly) superior to theirs as the **covenant** of which He is Mediator is superior to the old one (as **expected**), since the new **covenant** is established on better (an **earnest expectation**) promises.* For this reason Christ (**expectantly** so) is the Mediator of a new **covenant**, that those who are called (in their **expectation**)may receive the promised eternal inheritance—now that He has died as a ransom to set them free from the sins committed under the first **covenant**.**

Thank You, thank You, thank You Jesus!!! Here we are now a *New* **Covenant** family **c**onnected and **c**ommuning in our partnering with *God*… in a renewed relationship and partnership now formed out of a *new beginning - He* is our *Beginning*… for that was what *He* intended in the *original in-the-beginning… in His original intent.*

Let us understand, *Jesus* was beyond just being *committed, dedicated, or obligated*. *He* was **submitted, surrendered fully to completion**… to the **willing point of His own death** and *the journey and process* **before** *Him*… in *His crucifixion, death, burial, resurrection, and ascension*… in **c**oming as *God* to the **e**arth to bring all *His* family…us, back to *Him* our *Father* in our new beginning. Grab hold and hold on tight to these words: *We focus our attention and* **expectation** *onto Jesus… who birthed faith within us… leading us forward into faith's perfection… for He was the perfect example (as **expected**). Because His heart was focused on the (**expectingly** exuberant) joy of knowing that you… me… we, would be His, so He endured the agony of the cross and conquered its humiliation and now sits exalted at the right hand of the throne of God.**

And praise *God*… don't forget, part of our **covenant** with and in *Yeshua* secures the fact that *He* isn't just seated at the right hand of *God the Father Almighty*… but, *we are seated* next to where *He's* seated in heavenly places at *Father's* right hand through the righteousness of *God in Christ Jesus*. That's what **covenant** will do… has done for you – us!

Overall… in this part of the *journey of expectation* we should find ourselves **e**ven **m**ore bold and **c**onfident as suggested at the start of our day and within… knowing and trusting that **He keeps covenant** never breaking it. That is an assuredness needed and appreciated in these days and times we're living in and beyond. For there is a **c**olliding and great **c**lashing that's **expectantly** and increasingly **m**anifesting in the **e**arth today. And in part… it's due to that fact not only is *He* a **Covenant** Keeping God – but the <u>ONLY **covenant** keeping god</u> and *Yahweh Adonai* is *His* name.

Yahweh… who is the also the *God of Abraham, Isaac, and Jacob,* honors us in the fullness of the **covenant** *He* made with them. Particularly because of our *grafted in* identity as adopted "sons" who are not just in *His family*… but are joined with *His people Israel – the Jews,* becoming a **one new man humanity**. For if *He* doesn't keep *His* **c**ovenant with them how **c**an we ever *expect Him* to with us? And yes, in the *New Testament -Covenant* too… since *Yeshua Jesus* was a *Jew* and the *early church* was birthed by *Jews*. We **c**an see and I pray you know… we have a *deeply rich and vast inheritance* in which we get all that our *Father* has for us. What *benefits* and *blessings* **c**ome in our **sonship and one new man identity**.

For indeed the very essence of who our *covenant* God is… is a good, good loving **covenant** keeping *Father* generationally, eternally. *Again…* *His* heart is and will always be for family and unquestionably *His.* **E**specially with the *covenant* pure, white, and spotless *Bride* who's **c**oming forth from within *His Church* (us) being **m**ade ready with such *longing* and **expectancy**… for *His Son* our *Bride-Groom.*

In **c**losing, *for sure and for certain…* let's just settle it now. He <u>does not</u> break *His* **covenant**. If *He* did not keep it by breaking it… then what good are *His* promises to us in our salvation with our new **m**an/humanity new life,… let alone eternal life? *For though a thousand generations may pass away, He is still (as **expected** to be) true to His Word (**expect** it He said it) which He commanded and established in truth… He remembers keeping (by His **expectation**) His **covenant** forever.** Amen.

> ❖ *Perhaps…* the best **e**nding in this significant part of our *pilgrimage…* and, for this day with the *word of worth* **covenant** would be**,** if led and you are able, partake of the *covenant* victory **m**eal that heals… the *Lord's Supper.* It would be good, I believe… if *you… me… we,* heed the **c**all in the invitation I'm hearing to, *"Come… freely come and receive at My table and do this in remembrance of Me and with great **expectancy** for Me to meet with you there… as you experience a fresh **covenant** consecration,"*
> … *Now as they were eating Jesus took bread, and after blessing it, He broke it and gave it to the disciples, and said, "Take, eat; this is My body." Then He took a cup, and when He had given thanks, He gave it to them, saying, "Drink from it, all of you. This is My blood of the **covenant**, which is poured out for many for the forgiveness of sins."*

What **covenant expectancy** for *the journey* that lies yet ahead of us!

e=mc3   *God's* **essence energy** of *earnest expectation* = manifestation in a *mandated mutual message* in a *covenantally committed communion connection* and the *crucified contents of communion catapulting* us into the *3rd power expressed by the Spirit* in the voice of the blood which has spoken a better word and is sufficient.

<u>In light of this **word of worth … covenant** and what's been shared:</u>

❖ *Perhaps…* you **Encountered or Experienced a Question or Challenge**?
  Write it out…

❖ *Perhaps…* more has been **Established & Empowered by the Word**?
  Write what/which…

❖ *Perhaps… it's time for* **Engaging & Embracing your Expectations?**
Write what's forming…

Reminder: For *clarity, connection, and confirmation* regarding **expectancy** being stirred by this **word of worth**, seek *Him* and *His Word* first. To possibly assist you in the process the list of **ION** words are in the Appendix.

*Footnotes: Chapter 7 Day 4 covenant / * See Is. 59:21 Deuteronomy 7:9, Number 23:19 KJV, Titus 1:2, Hebrews 8:5, 9:15, 12:2, Psalm 105:8, Matthew 26:27-28 - all emphasis is mine and personal paraphrasing built on various translations and versions. * See *The Bible Project* / Part of the writing regarding covenant was influenced by solid biblical teaching available by The Bible Project: The Five Key Covenants God Makes With Humans in the Bible/ Partnerships Between God and People by Whitney Woollard. @Bibleproject.com or their channel on YouTube

✧ Day 5: The Journey of "c"… C Names

*Let expectations… through this **word of worth's** part to form, birth, and emerge in its **meaning & mission**… **our meditation & motivation**… as **movement & manifestation** awake, arise and align in agreement with divine eternal expectation!*

When it was determined that within *our journey* with "**c**" it would be good to start with a selection of names beginning with "**C**"… some immediately **c**ame to **m**ind. In seeking *Him* and *His Word* regarding any others to be **c**onsidered… these ten names were the *words (names) of worth* I discerned to include. These names offer to us some interesting relevant information in who they are, what they are known for biblically, and why that **m**atters to us as we pursue through this *process* of life and its needed inclusion of the role of *expectancy.*

Christ… Starting with the **m**ighty **m**atchless name, *His* name of **Christ**, which **m**eans the *Anointed or Chosen One*, and is a name given to *Jesus, Yeshua* our *Savior* and *Messiah*, as we begin because *He* should be first. However, the plan was for these names to be in the order of how they appear in the *Bible*. Now you **m**ight be thinking **Christ** doesn't appear until later… shouldn't **Cain** be first? Actually there are references where scholars say it's in *Genesis 16* when the "*Angel of the Lord*" appears… for **m**any believe that is *Jesus*.

If you want a kind of *mystery factor* that lies within the not so obvious being revealed through what *types* and *shadows*, like this answer offers.. let's push it a bit further to *Genesis 1* and back to "*In the beginning*". Even when things began before the foundations of the world *He* would be the *Anointed Chosen One*… the *Beginning* After all, *He* is referred to as the *Beginning* and not just in the beginning of the *Bible*. But, also in the **e**nd chapter where in *Revelation 22* in the Greek *He* is **c**alled *Alpha – First*… **m**eaning *first*, to *begin*, to *start* with.

What a powerful *full circle* as we begin this *quest* to let these names speak and reveal to us and give us a a reason to *celebrate* because *He* is such for us. The *Beginning, Alpha - First, and the End – Omega, Last*. There and everywhere in between *He* is *Author* and *Finisher* of all things and things in our lives too. Which we see in *His crucifixion, death, and burial*… the *finishing work* of *atoning for our sins* on the **c**ross unto death @*Calvary*.

It all **m**ade the way for our *new beginning* as *new creatures* in *Christ Jesus* since it was **c**ompleted in *His resurrection* and *ascension* into heaven back to the *Father*. What *expectancy* arises in knowing and being reminded of all of this. Plus, receiving from the everlasting **c**ovenant connection that *Christ* offers to us in our salvation. *His* vital and **e**ssential role has a divinely purposed place in the lives of all who **c**hoose it. *He* does have an *expectation* that ones will because *He* is and *eternally* will be the *Beginning* and the *End*. Go searching and **e**nlarge your *expectation* of knowing *Him* as these.

One last provoking thought about **Christ,** "*The revelation of Yeshua as the Word made flesh anchors our understanding of life, identity, and creation itself. From "Let there be light" to "The Word became flesh," this message invites us to see the unity of Scripture and to stand firm in the truth of the One who spoke all things into being.*". *Ariel Blumenthal* I believe has **c**aptured a profound expression of *expectancy* pointing to and **m**anifesting in *Christ*. Amen.

Cain… the *firstborn* son of *Adam and Eve*, that **c**ame after they had been set out of the garden into the world for their **c**ommitting of sin – the breaking of **c**ovenant directions given to them regarding the eating or not, of the trees *God* planted there and distinguished between. **Cain's** name **m**eans to *acquire, obtain, an acquisition* – in the deeper *Hebrew* roots it **m**eans *to forge or fit together*. In *Genesis 4* we see in his *life's journey* a *process* at work developing his **c**haracter, where his **c**arnality affected his **c**hoices, and led to **c**onsequences… like it does in our lives. That *ongoing process* of being and becoming as we are… and should be in *Him*, it's the - *as He is so we are to be*. And… attitudes, they do lead to action that joins together with the *forming, creating, birthing,* and *manifesting* of what we **expect** specific or general.

The **e**ating from the *Tree of the Knowledge of Good and Evil* that his parents partook of with its *process* now at work in their bloodline and the generation of *Cain*. It was producing a fruit that did not **c**ome from the *Tree of Life*… for remember, they were outside of the garden now and **c**ould not partake any longer of it. *Cain* was born and living in the world… their world – which is our world… and *sin was crouching* at the door because it was the fruit of sin now in the **c**hildren, from the *confusion, crisis,* and *chaos* that **c**ame through the *identity theft* his parents experienced… as it, **sin** continually is, for the **e**nemy continues to **c**ome seeking *access expecting* to find any legitimate reason to *accuse* as well as *kill, steal,* and *destroy* and always presenting a **c**ounterfeit **expectation** that appears good.

Yahweh offered a door to *Cain*… a way to **e**scape to **e**xit that which was invading his soul – *mind, will,* and *emotions*. But, he turned inwards towards the *evil inclination* within him… not away from it. And, the blood of *his brother Abel* that he **m**urdered in **c**old blood over the giving of an offering where it produced a deep deadly jealousy within the **c**ore of *Cain*. The innocent blood of *Abel* – who brought a better sacrifice… it fell to the ground **c**rying out to be heard. It was… by *God*. Innocent bloodshed *always cries out*. *He* hears it – do we? And what is our **expectation** in regard to doing something about it? For it remains as it was then… an *offering to other gods* **e**specially and unfortunately… the god of *self*. Like the gods of *Molech or Ishtar* who often attach to *self as god*, requiring either a blood or **c**hild sacrifice.

Truly our *Father God Yahweh*… in *His* **m**ercy and justice within *His* sovereignty… had already **m**ade a way before the *foundations of the world* for another *Firstborn Son – His*… to *reverse the curse* of the sin **c**ycle which had begun. An **eternal expectation** filled with righteous rectification and restitution as it was **expected** to **m**anifest in *restoration, redemption,* and *reconciliation* and it did.

- ❖ *Perhaps*… actually for sure, we're to pause a **m**inute here. As I'm writing this portion I ask for grace as I sense *Holy Spirit* leading me in a spontaneous type of sharing, what I'm physically dealing with at this place in the *telling*. Not what I **expected**… but I will follow *His* leading with **expectancy**. Presently, a deep wound on my left **c**alf has formed and is now inflamed and infected to some degree. It **c**ame from bumping up against something un**expectedly** and that I was unaware was there. For some reason *He* is leading me to *compare and contrast* this physical *experience* I've **e**ncountered to what happened to *Cain* in an *emotional soul* kind of way. *Perhaps*, we **c**ould say… he bumped up against something in himself, and so did *Abel* in someone else - *Cain*. It **c**reated a place for a '*wound*' to develop. In *Cain* the wound became infected and inflamed by what was at the **c**ore of *Cain's* soul affecting his spirit and his **expectancy** as it **m**anifested negatively in <u>ungodly</u> *anger, rage, contention,* and *strife* taking root. In *Abel*, the wound became the source and force of the **m**otive and **m**urderous **m**ethod in his un**expected** death. Yet, **expected** in its premeditated **m**anner for *Cain* because he **c**hose not to turn his heart toward the *good inclination of God* in him. Rejecting *His* desiring to help him to direct his **expectancy** toward godly good so *He* **c**ould bless him as *He* received from **Cain's** offering of obedience, which **expectedly** so is better than sacrifice... and meant to bless the heart of *Father God* too. Hmmm... Selah....

It seems like a good time to freely enter into this special **m**oment *He's* ordered... going boldly to *His Throne of Grace*, if led in this **c**rafted prayer *He's* help form ~ *Father* in heaven, *You* know where **e**ach of us are and what/who we are **c**onfronting or is **c**onfronting us. We recognize if it is a *who*, that we wrestle not against flesh and blood. Only *You* know if it is a **m**ajor or **m**inor kind of wound *You* **m**ay want to reveal to us. We invite and willingly allow *You* too, because we know *You* love us wanting what is best for us. We *thank You* for **m**oving in the **m**idst of it all to be who *You* are and do what *You* will do when we **expect,** so we do, **c**hoose to respond obeying *You*. *Thank You Jesus, You* are interceding with us and for us. Have *Your* way *Holy Spirit* in *this process* that needs to happen right now. Help us to let go of any *aught, angst, or anger* we **m**ight have in us toward anyone, releasing and forgiving them as *You* have forgiven and released us for we don't want any foxes, little or big, to spoil the *Vine of You* in us. We praise *You* oh *God* for *Your* **c**onstant *love*, amazing *grace*, **c**ontinual *goodness*, and faithful **m**ercy *You* extend and execute on our behalf in *Jesus's shed blood* and *His Name* that we **c**ome in and through. We repent for any sin knowingly or unknowingly, willingly or unwillingly. *Forgive us... selah ~* Now we receive *Your* forgiveness and any forgiveness You **expect** us to possibly extend as we **expect** the *humility, courage, grace, and opportunity* to offer it. *Thank You* now for restoring us back into godly right alignment with *You*. And, for helping us overcome and experience *healing delivering breakthrough* that's all **e**stablished in *Your constant eternal covenant love* **c**overing. We love *You* and decree *You* alone are worthy of all glory. In *Yeshua's* name – amen.

Caleb... A **m**ighty **m**an of *God* who was truly a ***man of expectancy***... even described as having a *"different spirit"* as he was filled with hope in his belief to *see and receive* what he **expected** based on *God* place in his *life's process* and due to what *God* said. Now, from right there... we can assuredly *glean a valuable* and *irreplaceable* lesson for *life's journey*. Place your **expectancy** in what *He* said, what is written, and **expect to see**! Seems to be a pattern forming.

With that in **m**ind, let's recall where we first see **Caleb** appear in the *Word of God*. In the *Book of Numbers 13/14*, he is presented to us as *Moses* is sending out ones into the *Promise Land* to spy and scout it out. *Canan* was the place... that is the land flowing with *milk and honey as God* had promised them, after being delivered from *Egyptian* bondage. He sent *tribal leaders, one from each of the tribes,* **m**ore commonly known as the *12 spies*. **Caleb,** representing the tribe of *Judah* (*praise*) –the tribe that *goes first* for it *plows* being the *lawgiver* (ruler) and holding a *scepter* (the ruler's royalty staff) as part of the blessings of *identity* and *inheritance Jacob* spoke over *Judah*. **Caleb** believed for his portion as the blessings that were spoken were a prophetic announcement for the *sons* and *their tribes*.

Upon their return to give the report to *Moses* and *the people*... he, along with *Joshua* from the tribe of *Ephriam* (fruitfulness), were the only two out of the 12 that reported from a *place of faith* within them that aligned with what *Yahweh* had said... as it contained within it a... *let's go up and take the land as it's flowing with milk and honey and God will be with us as the battle is His*.* They **expected** it and they saw it... even bringing physical evidence of the **m**agnificent fruit and more from what the land was producing creating an **expectancy** in them and for all to **expect and see**.

However, the other ten spies... from the *expectancy* of what their *eyes* saw a report was released that was encircled in *unbelief, fear,* and with *terror* forming... because as *Yahweh* also said, there were *giants* in the land. They, as could be **expected** out of such a place... released a *bad report* filled with words spoken from out of a *positioning* and *posturing* arising from *their souls*. Yet, remember... they ALL knew ALL *God* had told them. So what is our report saying? Where are and what are *yours*... *mine*... our *expectations* in it? Eventually some, not all, of the people did go into the *Promise Land*, after 40 years of *a process* of *wandering* and *wondering in the wilderness*. **Caleb** arose in that same *spirit of faith* and called out for *God* to now *"Give me my mountain!"** And, as he **expected**, *God* did. We should in like spirit arise and call out!

Cyrus... a *pagan Persian King* that was used by *God*, although he did not "believe" in *Him*. **Cyrus** is mentioned in the *Books of Isaiah, Ezra,* and *2 Chronicles* and is such a powerful representation as to how *God Himself* will use whomever *He* desires to partner with *Him* in *His* purposes and plans for *His* people and for the land. From issuing his *royal decree* of *written words* that went forth as *spoken words* to work in the *releasing of God's people* (the *Jews*) from *Babylonian* captivity to return to their land allowing them to rebuild *Jerusalem*... and, all in a *sincere spirit of benevolence* that included giving them the provision to do it – now that's *God*! All of this attributed to his being called a type of *Messiah*... a *Shepherd* to the people... a *type and shadow* of their... our *Messiah and Shepherd Yeshua* - who we know has come... but the *Jews* then and still now, await for *Him* to come unless *Messianic*.

As with *King* **Cyrus**... *He does hold the hearts of kings* (**expectantly**) *in His hand, turning them* (*for His* **expectations**) *as He pleases*.* And, again – we are *His kings and priests* now.* So... how are we doing with letting *Him* turn our hearts? Do we have an *expectancy* along with a willingness to let *Him*? What decrees are being written and spoken by us in words that align with *His* **expectations** for us, others, and all *He* has *assigned* and *purposed* us to do? Remember, there is a writing of the vision, making it plain so those that receive it can run *publishing* and *pronouncing* it in its *appointed time*.* Just like it was for **Cyrus**... we have *God's appointed times* for our lives filled with **expectancy and expectations** for us.

Caiaphas... a respected *High Priest* of *Israel* and is mentioned in the *Word of God* in *Matthew, Luke,* and *John* and becomes an important person in connection within the journey and *process* of the death of *Jesus Christ – Yeshua*. He actually was the organizer. What a look at **expectation** gone wrong and enabling what it did. Yet, with all certainty we can determine that he believed in what he was doing and that it was what was best to address the threat *Jesus* had become to "*Rabbinic Judaism*" and all it stood for. In a majority of ways it was what *Jesus* opposed too. Additionally, he was very concerned with the influence *Yeshua* had on *His* disciples and all who were following *Him*. Plus, the fact that some of what *He* was teaching went against their ideas and religious way of life.

Caiaphas was the highest leader within the *Sanhedrin*, which he presided over, so you can imagine the pressure to deal with *Jesus*. Let's examine several other key roles he engaged in and unfortunately created... and not just determined to fill the **expectation** of his part... but he too, like *Jesus* influenced people... to the point of persuading other religious and government leaders to agree with and participate in what was decided and he **expected** to see through. He was instrumental in interrogating *Jesus* personally, created a scene where *Jesus* could be charged with committing blasphemy, condemning *Jesus,* and handing *Him* over. If that's not enough, the mocking and beating of *Jesus* actually took place at **Caiaphas's** house.

In searching, a critical piece of relative revelation conveyed that **Caiaphas** also embodied the idea that *'The good of the many outweighs the good of the one.'* This idea is of course wholly contradicted by the gospel, which asserts that *the good of the many derives solely from the good of the one.* He, with others, were threatened *Yeshua* could be the "One".*

There is a responsibility and accountability we must have with our ***expectancy*** and in our ***expectations*** and it first and foremost is to *God,* to ourselves, and to others. All the more reason *His* **expectations** must be what lines up ours, overriding ours when uncertain, and by the teaching and guidance of *Holy Spirit* we must access and draw from *His* help so we know the truth and ***expect*** all we do to flow out of it.

Cana & Corinth... biblical cities highlighted in the *Worthy Word of God* and worth a mention as we continue in our moving forward together ***encountering*** and ***experiencing*** what *He's* unfolding and revealing to us. In looking at **Cana** – a town in *Galilee* mentioned primarily in the *Book of John,* we discover or may recall, it is the city that *Jesus* entered into after coming out of the wilderness encounter *He* had for 40 days. There, *He* went to a wedding that *His* mother was invited too and she, along with *His* disciples attended. Little did those attending know the greater reason of why *He* was there... as even *He* did not fully appear to, until the appointed time came and *Mary, His "imma"-* mother, from *em* in Hebrew,* told the servants who were there to assist Him with the urgent need of the moment saying, *"Whatever He (Jesus) tells you, do it."**

These words that carried great ***expectation*** within them became a type of catalyst for *Jesus* displaying what is seen and spoken of as *His* first ministry act and miracle in the miraculous *turning of water into wine*... for they had run out at the wedding. Let's imagine for a moment... the possibilities of and potential for miracles that may have happened had *you*... *me*... *we,* **just done whatever** *He* **said to do?** Those spoken words that contained *His* ***expectation.*** What might have, could have, should have, and would have come forth from the ***expectant*** obedience of our actions... *His* servants? Now there's no *shame, guilt,* or *condemnation* here... *grace, grace.* We're all in the *process* of being and becoming such *honoring, compliant obedient ones – His*.... especially in what we ***expect.***

Within this moment is an opening for us as personally led by *Him*... and, you'll know if *He* is stirring a conviction in you... to *repent, turn,* and *return* into or just freshly commit to a greater commitment of intentional devotion like *Jesus* to willfully obeying *Him*... allowing *Him*... especially through *Holy Spirit*; the/our *Helper* and *Teacher* to aid in the establishing of and moving us into that posture where our ***expectations*** are enabled more easily to be one with *His.* Who knows, may it be what we hear ones expressing lately that... **Expectancy is the breeding ground for miracles!** *Yes Lord*... so be it and be it so!

Lastly... this **Cana** moment reminds us of how important weddings are, as the *God* ordained *two become one covenant* ceremonies and celebrations they are. He knew this then... yet, an extension of knowing came in this chosen city and setting to connect with an ***expectancy*** that was before *Him.* Maybe... the fullness of *Him* as *Father, Son,* and *Holy Spirit* in the longing within for the *ultimate final wedding* where the *Bridegroom Yeshua Jesus* is, *He* will experience the miracle that's been in the making of *His Bride pure, white, spotless,* and *holy* in *His Church*... miraculously manifests! For the *Spirit* and the *Bride* have, are, and will be ***expectantly*** saying *"Come..."* Till that time comes... ***whatever He says just do it!***

Corinth*...** now **m**oving forward out of ***Cana into the **m**ore... we see how the **c**ultural hub of ***Corinth***, a **c**ity in ***Greece***, arising into its divine destiny as a **c**ity where the **e**arly **c**hurch began to **m**ove out and into **e**stablishing roots **c**reating an incredibly influential **c**enter for promoting and advancing the *Gospel of the Good News* through *Salvation* and the *Gospel of the Kingdom*, particularly since it was inclusive of non-*Jews*, *Gentiles*... **e**ven though it was to the *Jew* first.

An added blessing **c**ame **c**onnected to ***Corinth***, in the two needful and beneficial letters found in the *Books of 1 & 2 Corinthians* that *Paul* strategically, lovingly, yet passionately and with a vast amount of ***expectancy***, wrote to the **c**hurch there. They truly bless and benefit us as *His Church* yet today. For me personally, I **c**an't fathom my life without the ***expectations*** spelled out from *His* heart to *you*... *me*... *us*, in the writings within 1 *Corinthians* 13 and as *The Passion Translation* (TPT) titles it: *Love, the Motivation of Our Lives*. There's no denying how **m**uch I need the love foundation it lays in the **c**onsistent **e**mbracing of and **e**mpowering it **c**alls me up and into. And, the **c**urrent **e**ternal relative blueprint it is with the relational framework it provides, full of actions and attributes we are to be *receiving, reflecting,* and *releasing*... for its filled and overflowing with *Father's* love based ***expectancy*** for *you*... *me*... *us*, and what undoubtedly ***expect.***

With these letters to this **c**ity *Corinth* and its people, I sense *Him* forming an "*ask*" for us in this... What is our **c**ity's purpose for *God's* kingdom **c**oming forth in the **e**arth? How is *He* revealing *His **expectancy*** to you and others there to partner with *Him* in *His **expectancy*** for it? For **m**uch is written in *His Word* already that tells us in a general **c**ohesive way. As well, there's *His* unique designing and appointing of times that are key to the fulfillment of *His* greater ***expectancy*** for *yours*... *mine*... and all our **c**ities and in all nations, through all tribes, tongues, and generations as we ***expect*** to *awaken, align,* and *advance* as *His* **C**hurch and for *His* **K**ingdom ***expectancy*** to **c**ome on **e**arth as in heaven and in our time!

***Cornelius & Chloe*...** let's **e**xplore two *non-Jews* who became *Believers, Followers*...

Cornelius... a *Roman Centurion,* a *Gentile* who became a devout, God-fearing **m**an, **c**haritable, and generous as he, along with his house believed in and served the *Lord*. He was the first *non-Jew* to **e**xperience receiving the *Holy Spirit* after being water baptized since the death of *Jesus* had happened **m**aking a way for the **e**nlarging of an area where *Christianity* was **e**xpanding into. In the *Book of Acts*, **C**hapter 10, we read learning about how ***Cornelius*** **e**ncountered a vision *God* gave through an angel that lead him to the *Apostle Peter* to learn about *Yeshua* which became the ***expected*** **m**oment of his **c**onversion – oh, the ***expectation*** within such times as it *forms, creating,* and *birthing* in the ***born again*** process with all its ***expectancy*** as it **m**anifests! What **c**ultural, not to **m**ention religious barriers were there. Yet, we see the *Spirit of God* with the *Truth* in love break through! Let us ***expect*** barriers to be **m**oved so *God* **c**an **m**ove partnering with *Him* like *Cornelius* did and as was revealed in his *character, serving,* and the *catalytic part* he played in the ***expectation*** for the *Gospel* to go to the uttermost parts as it did.

Chloe*...** whose name **m**eans *tender verdure, green blooming.** She lived in the **c**ity of *Corinth* as a pagan *Greek*, who became a "*Christian*", was well known in her **c**ommunity, and active in the **c**hurch *He* was birthing and planting there. She was instrumental as a homeowner who offered her house to the service of the *Lord*... actively leading and participating as one of the house **c**hurches in *Corinth*. That's right – **c**hurches in houses. ***Chloe, as a reputable servant leader, was perceived as humble and wise in her pursuing of the *Apostle Paul's* **c**ounsel and advice regarding a spirit of quarrelling and disagreement happening at their gatherings. She's **m**entioned in the *Book* of *1 Corinthians* in Chapter 11. **M**ay we find ourselves with such *willingness, well doing,* and *wisdom*, in the *process* and our **expectancy** as we serve *Him*... in our homes... and yes, in our **c**ities as *He* leads.

In **c**losing, probably the *Christian* word **m**ost used and often heard after that of *Christ*... is the *word (name) of worth* we will wrap up this day as it draws to a place of **c**losure. And actually, it is **m**ore **c**hallenging to me than all the other "c" names to write and tell about. But *Lord, You* know... my **expectancy** lies in *You,* for what *You* offer **c**ontains **m**uch... in part, leading and guiding that provides direction, **e**ven **c**orrection, in the *process*.

Christian... a name given to a person who believes in *Jesus Christ* as their *Savior and Lord* because they are a *follower* of *His*, **Christ's**... and so in **e**ssence they *identify with belonging to a group of people who believe in and seek to be like Him*... and *truly follow Him daily in their lives,* therefore they are known as "**Christians**" sometimes referred to as "*Believers*"... ones who have been "*Saved*" and unto eternal life. The word **Christian** appears according to some versions/translations in three places in the *New Testament*.* This was my brief summary from searching out the *Biblical* defining of **Christian** and what time permits.

Here I've **c**reated a brief summary utilizing a few worldly dictionary based definitions of **Christian.** *A person who professes to be a Believer and who puts their faith in Christianity: adhering to, following, and trusting the teachings of Jesus Christ and Him as their Lord and Savior, along with receiving through* **Christian** *baptism which has a foundational connection to the* **Chrisitan** *salvation process.*

One **c**ould go on to **m**ore specific *defining* that includes a few of these dimensions which include things like... how this belief in and following of is of ones who believe they are saved, these believing ones accepting *Jesus Christ, Yeshua Ha Mashiach* alone based on the requirement that *He* is the ONLY way to salvation. And... through **Christ's** divine **c**onnection to and relationship with *God,* the *Father* **c**omes as well... and it all leading to everlasting life promised by *Him*.

Although *saved* is a good word... it is found in scripture but *once*. **M**any argue it is **m**ore than *just being saved*... it is in the fact that you are required to be *born again* because *His Word* says you **m**ust be. Some will **e**ven say there's a requirement to be water baptized and some as well, that you need to be filled and baptized in the *Holy Spirit*. I believe you know what I'm referring to. If not... be encouraged to study these kind of *positions, beliefs, and thoughts* out as *He* leads. Start with *His Word* and with **expectancy** to *learn, grow, know*.

These above defining **m**eanings, particularly the ones with greater requirements within their specifics that are so very **c**ontrary to what **m**uch of the world today believes and we see **m**anifesting. There has **c**ome now, in my humble opinion, a growing alarming acceptance that just by saying **c**ommon things like: *"I believe in God, I'm a good person, I do good things, I go to church, I read the Bible, I believe in the Bible, I watch* **Christian** *shows and ministry teachings on TV"*... any **c**ombination of these **m**ight sound good and or **m**ake you feel good for within them there **m**ay be a partial way they **c**onnect to true *Christianity*.

However, we **m**ust examine their relationship to the ***fullness of required truth***. We **m**ust see the *red alarm* lights flashing and warning signs appearing... in any or all of these tolerated and received by **m**any as acceptable kinds of definitions for a **Christian.** Please know, I respect and honor wherever you are in your place of defining or *process*. But, it's what *He* knows and thinks about where you are and in your defining that **m**atters. So don't forget, required is the **expected end He has**... and what *He* establishes it takes to get there.

For the sake of time and even what truly is behind the *expectation* I have and I believe *He* has prompted in my sharing of this *word of worth* in the name/title **Chrisitan**... is the greater accountability and purer refining in the defining that *He* is calling true *Believers, Followers, ...Christians...* up and into. *As you believe you become.* So taking responsibility for our *expectancy* to not just know of *Him*, but to *know, accept, follow, and live* by ALL of *His Word* as the *Absolute Truth* it is. The *Word of God* as presented to us in the *Holy Bible* and by *His Spirit Holy Spirit* as the *Spirit of Truth* and *Revelation H*e is.

Unfortunately... there has been the ever changing, rearranging, and watering down of *His Word*. Some of you, I realize, may think or say this of the informal relational type of sharing I present in this *telling* through the way of writing I use. Remember... as previously stated this book it is not a theological teaching or exegesis of scripture. It is a *telling of my journey* represented by what *He's* revealed... and still is to me in the *ongoing maturing process*. It is *intentionally worded* to be very *invitational, conservational,* and *intimately relational.*

It seems pretty true that the bottom line of *His expectancy*...lies in the end which says we're each individually accountable to *Him*. And, because of *His* great covenant eternal love for us, *His* plans of hope, and a purpose for us, and so much more... *He* knows right where *you... me... we* are in the *process* of our defining and what we've accepted as truth that is or isn't truth. There is no gray with *Him*... no lukewarm... you're either hot or cold*... not wavering between two opinions.* May we allow a maturity to develop in applying such to living life *His* way. *Father God, Holy Spirit* help us, and *Jesus* intercede and intervene as *You* all do and only can.

Let's just pause here... as I hear a question I believe *He* wants to move in and through to move us from wherever we are to where *you...me... we,* need to be. Even if we've got a good foundation for knowing who we are and whose we are... there's still growth before us, yet to happen in us, and in the *process* of this *journey* of life in the kind of relationship *He* offers us with *Him*... and together in *Him* in *yours... mine...* and all of *our expectancy* and *expectations* arising, attempting to stir in this and *His togethering* of it all.

By *His Spirit* I hear *Him* releasing a familiar kind of asking in this critical question... **"Who do you say I am? What do you say I am?"** *Oh,* the wealth lying within the treasure of knowing *who and what you say I am/He is*... as it opens a lid like that of a treasure chest. Where in our searching for and receiving truthful truth filled knowing that are *gems* given to us *in His Worthy Word* – what it contains and by *His Spirit*. How we determine and realize their worth is priceless... as they pave the path for what to say, when you say *who you are and what you are* assuredly to *Him* first, to yourself, and to others in your response to <u>your defining by who/what you are as a **Christian** in *Him*</u> and living out of *Him* in you unashamedly, unquestionably in *His expectations* alone. The critical need is for the fruit of this *process* to manifest *His expectancy* aligned in *His end*.

It's time... go ahead put your **expectation** out there. *He's* waiting... *He'll* meet you, *lead, guide,* and *direct* you from right where you are and all because *He* loves *you... me... us...* and, first as *His* created ones in a world *He* created with us in *His* heart and design... as *His family, His* sons and daughters...then *in what He defines as and is a **Christian**...* if that's even what *He'd* call us? For historical references, in *His* early church they were established in the person being described as a *devout "follower of Christ"* and *Jesus Christ of Nazareth*. a *Jew, Yeshua Ha Mashiach* as *Lord of Lords, King of Kings* <u>alone</u>. Alone means alone.

Spirit of Truth... manifest Truth in all things to us.

Let's remember now, in our ending of this day… what *He* said in this verse which **c**arries a kind of universal expression **c**ontaining *His* **expectation** any and all true *Followers* of *Christ* **embrace** and are **empowered** by… *For God so loved the world, that He gave His only Begotten Son, that whoever believes in Him shall not perish, but have everlasting life.* *

Therein lies the spirit of *original intent* in the fullness of *His* **expectancy**… first in that *He* so loves us as a part of the world *He* spoke **c**reating it and *His* **c**reation and as *His* desired divinely designed ones… **m**ale and female, **m**ade in *His* image and likeness **c**reated ones – *His* family - humanity. **C**an you feel now what's at the **c**ore of *His* defining in *His* heart beating with **expectan**c**y**… that we know, are sure, we are *His* and will be **expectantly,** eternally that **C** name… ***Child of God! Child of the One True God.***

There **m**ay be an **e=mc3** in all this for you so don't hesitate to release it ~

<u>In light of this **words of worth** … **C Names** and what's been shared:</u>

- ❖ *Perhaps… you **Encountered or Experienced a Question or Challenge**?*
  Write it out…

- ❖ *Perhaps… more has been **Established & Empowered by the Word**?*
  Write what/which…

- ❖ *Perhaps… it's time for **Engaging & Embracing your Expectations**?*
  Write what's forming…

Reminder: For *clarity, connection, and confirmation* regarding **expectancy** being stirred by this **word of worth**, seek *Him* and *His Word first*. To possibly assist you in the process the list of **ION** words is available in the Appendix.

*Footnotes: Chapter 7 Day 5 C names / * See Gensis 16, Gensis 1, Revelation 22, Genesis 4, Numbers 13/14, Joshua 14, Hosea 10:11, Genesis 49:10-12, Isaiah 44/45, Ezra 1, 2 Chronicles 36:22, Proverbs 21:1-9 Revelation 1:5-6, 5, 1 Peter 2:9, Habakkuk 2, John 18:14, Luke 15:17, see em H517 Strongs Concordance, John 2:1-11, 1 and 2 Corinthians, 1 Corinthians 13, Acts 10, see chloe G5514 Strongs Concordance, Christian > Acts 11:26, Acts 26:28, and 1 Peter 4:16, Revelation 3:15-16 – the letter to Laodicean Church, I Kings 18:1, John 3:16. Plus, see in general Matthew, Mark, Luke, John, and Acts for New Testament C Names - all emphasis is mine and personal paraphrasing built on various translations and versions. * See Abarim Publications /The Name Caiaphas: Summary/ @abarim-publications.com.

✧ Day 6: The Journey of "c"… carry

Let *expectations*… through this **word of worth's** part to *form, birth, and emerge* in its **meaning & mission… our meditation & motivation… as movement & manifestation** *awake, arise and align* in agreement with divine eternal **expectation**!

To *carry*… there must first be a *container* or structure of some kind to hold and contain what is being **carried.** On a trip when you're traveling typically one takes varying kinds of *containers* we call *luggage* or maybe baggage… that have within them the things we want and or need to *carry* on the trip we are taking. Even when the journey we are making is an inward one like on a *pilgrimage*… there is still a necessity for what is *needed* and *necessary* to have something or someone to contain and *carry* it. We're seeing here a connectivity between two words – *carry* and *contain/container* that will be expanded as we move into this day with our "c" *word of worth* **carry.**

It is a good thing as we know and are learning… to **embrace** the **empowering** that arises because a good foundation has been established and can now provide what it was created for. Taking the time to define the meaning of words which connects to the mission of that word and all it is to be a part of… and regarding any part of or place in *the process* it manifests as what it is.

He created things to be connected in this way because He is *the Word* and moving in and through all words… especially *His*, to *connect, commune,* and *cultivate* who He is within us *His meaning, mission,* and *mandates* which are designed to be continuously revealing and manifesting *His expectancy* in it all.

Let's start with looking at what a *container* is since we need it to be what it is designed to be when it comes to the word *carry.* A *container* could simply be defined in the natural as: *a vessel, bottle, pitcher, flask, jar, jug, clay pot, box, envelope* … the something or someone receptive to receiving and *containing*…also *carrying*… what it *holds, contains* within it.

Spiritually… a *container* holds or *carries* within it the *spirit, essence, or life force* of that spirit or entity – godly or ungodly, that it is open to receiving it… and ideally in an agreeable acceptable way. We as *His* created ones *contain* and *carry His presence*; do you see the word *essence* in *presence*? We **carry** in *His* essence, *His* power, and the *DNA* of our *Father* and *Creator Elohim* in us as we are made in *His* expressed *image* and *likeness, fashioned* and *formed,* and *fearfully* and *wonderfully* as He is in *His* fullness – God the Father, Son, and Holy Spirit – you know, Them.

However, when we become *His born again children* – *His humanity family*, the *spirit of Him* in our spirit is *activated, awakened, alive, arising,* and *aligned* fully *with Him by His Spirit* to not just *carry*… but **carry out** *His* purposes and plans for us and all in and through these *earthen vessels* which are now *carrying containers*… and are *His*! As He is so are we to be and now we can begin *becoming* more so in this way.

Jonathan Cahn shares important spiritual information in his *"Book of Mysteries"* in the daily mystery titled, *"Infinity In A Jar".* He reveals how an *open container* can hold or contain something dry or liquid. A *closed container* can never contain anything – if its closed, and it can never contain anything larger than its own size. A container that is open… like a *vessel yielded, surrendered,* and *submitted* has *no limitations*… it can contain something bigger than it is… which is hard for us to grasp - but it is true. *Oh the science of God* we see in this.

There truly is a *spiritual* potential for linking to biblical kinds of principles and processes that this illustration reveals to us *if* we'll seek *Him* and *His Word* about it. It also provides a type of mental picture or image that is beneficial for receiving a fuller measure of understanding which help us to know if what's being shared is important to us in our life right now. If it *connects* to something *He's* been saying to us or doing within us, to something happening in your life, or in the lives of those we are *connected* with... and simply to grow or challenge us in a creative picturesque kind of way. *He* is creative and does use images.

That's something I enjoy about *Jonathan's* writing style in the *tellings* he shares in that book because I first grew to really appreciate them in their connections to the *tellings* in *God's Word* and still do! The *spiritual application* that may come in imagery where the *words* seem to come alive in what their *telling* because of what they **carry** within... what they *contain*... and *contain* within the *greater telling*. It can become a *conduit* for the *Spirit* to begin to do what *He* does to get our attention and make it relevant, hence more *life applicable* to us... even if it **carries** a *new thing* being presented.

It's amazing how the *presence, power, and glory of God* can and will move in and through *you... me... us,* as vessels of the *Lord.* As we begin to **carry** a *greater capacity* within our **expectancy** for the light of *Him,* which ultimately comes as the glorious **expectant** unfolding of *His eternal life energy* now alive in us by *His Spirit*, along with the essence *His* pure *everlasting covenant love* contains. Like *His Words* says... *For living within you is the Christ (the Eternal Expected One) who floods you with the* **expectation** *of glory - Christ in you, Christ in me... Christ is us (expectancy's essence as) the hope of glory!**

So don't miss out on the everyday in every way kind of *ebb and flow movings* of *Him* in you coupled with what *He* desires and will do through you too! And then... be ready for what happens when you're the *conduit* it all flows through. But I imagine, some of you know and have encountered this because you've **expected** and **experienced** it. Therefore, you could share your own *telling. He* is so very good to prompt us to do so... be obedient!

It all contains *encouraging* and **empowering** *connections,* bringing welcomed *confirmations,* and for the *co-laboring* we're to **embrace** with *His Worthy Word* and *Him as the Word* in us. Which, we saw too in the *relative realistic images* of us being *clusters* on branches *connected* to the *Vine* and *cogs* on the wheel and oiled by *His Spirit*... and all *containers* **carrying** *Him*!

We're at a place now where we can finally define, although on the peripheral we have been, our *word of worth* **carry** which means to: *transport, transfer, transmit, bring, take, hold, spread, cart, lug...* and all include a *moving from one place to another, support or bearing of the weight, to sustain, to pass on.* Often it can be heard as part of a type of phrase like **carry on, carry to, carry from, carry away, carry off, carry it off,** or **carry out...** along with *implying the ability to bear or produce.* Certainly all of these **carry** much **expectancy** within them, so let's press into the more of what *He's* saying and will order next.

But before going further, let's put into the mix the meaning of one last key word that often connects to both the words **container** and **carry** which is **conduit**. It simply means: *a canal, pipe, pipeline, channel, portal,* or *tube*. It is connected to *being or becoming what allows things to flow, move, or be transported to from one place to another.* In some religions or cults its meaning is: *being one who acts as a channel to transmit something to somewhere or someone else...* is known to be potentially controversial... and justly so in some *ways, situations,* and *circumstances.* Be certain, I'm NOT connecting this to other religions or cults.

However, in the practicality of clarity being rooted in *Godly* defining and **expectancy,** where we're enabled to see and understand a **conduit** to be: something *we are in a sense as a Believer,* someone we might come in contact and interact with like a *minister, pastor, teacher, spiritual* *mentor*... with it further being one who willingly is or serves/acts as a godly type of *c*onduit that *God*, by who *He* is in *His* person and by *His Spirit* and at work in and through them to *teach, impart, transfer, or **c**arry biblical/spiritual information, revelation, teachings, principles, preparation, equipping, impartation, activation, application*... to *His Church* and the *Body of Christ*, new Believers, and others. **E**specially in *discipling* and *equipping the saints for the work of ministry* as **E**phesians 4 specifies.

This is *c*onnected for the **m**ost part to both the person who is the type of *conduit* and the person who is the recipient of what the *conduit **c**arries* and releases through their *calling, gifting, even talent or skills*... as well as the *spiritual gifts of God* **m**oving in and operating through them. The purpose of it all is to *encourage, edify*, and *empower* as they **e**quip **m**aking ready *Believers, Followers, Disciples, Christians* like *you*... *me*... *us*, to serve *God* and **e**ffectively go forth with all *He* has ordained and *c*ommissioned... and for *His* glory.

As we invite and allow *this process* within us in being one or receiving from any of the above key words – *container, **c**arrier or conduit*, let's be sure we're willing to recognize and honor *Him* first as the type of **Container, Carrier, and Conduit** *He* is. Yes, *He* is and operates and functions in those ways particularly when you *c*onsider the fullness of *Him as Father, Son, and Holy Spirit*, and all *His* dimensions and **m**ultifacetedness enabling *Him* to *be, do*, and *accomplish*. Likewise, *Him* being and doing it in us!

In *His Worthy Word* there's a continualness of being *c*aptivated in a **m**arevelous way by this verse that's *c*oming to **m**ind at this time together with the above revelation and all the thoughts it is producing and stirring... *We can all (**expect**) to draw close to Him... with the veil removed from our faces... like beholding as in a **m**irror. And, with no veil we all become like **m**irrors too who brightly reflect in and through us... the glory of the Lord Jesus. What glorious (**expectant**) changing of us into His image by the Spirit of the Lord... like a transfiguration that comes from the Lord, who is the Spirit... even from glory to glory.**

Say with me out loud releasing this decree over yourself... *"I am a dwelling place... a unique and wonderfully **m**ade vessel... a container created by Him and for Him... that contains and carries within me His power, presence, purpose, plans, and perfected glory. A conduit that releases Christ in me to everyone and everywhere with the hope of His glory arising and glorifying Him."* Amen.

Containers… carriers… and conduits… *oh my!*

What an ***expectancy*** filled releasing of the *Word*, how it works, and is at work in us… and it's not just any kind of work but an ***expectant*** work. A work that will **m**anifest the radiance of *His* glory not just within *Him* in us, us in *Him*, and as **carriers** of *Him* who are *containers*... *earthen vessels* filled with *Him, Father – Jesus – Holy Spirit*. But, *reflecting Him*… and so **m**uch so, we are indeed becoming ones *He* **c**an partner with and use as *conduits* that produce more in what I **c**all, *His upon*.

For example… like in *His* anointed ***empowering*** enablement in *the process* as *grace <u>upon</u> grace <u>upon</u> grace*. Perhaps you **c**an see and hear it… the <u>up</u> and <u>on</u>…<u>upon</u> *you*… *me*… *us*, for the flowing of that same anointing in <u>*Him*</u> is now in us and *upon* us to be these *containers, **c**arriers, and conduits*. But there's something yet needed…

He's in *His Worthy Words* above that tell us this releasing **m**anifests a revealing by *His Spirit*… a glory, a *glory to glory*… likened to an *upon*… *up and on*… yes, a *glory upon glory* in the anointed ongoing **c**ontinuality of it all when **m**anufactured and **m**anifested by *Him* in us. There is a type of repeating here, but it's necessary as we **c**an't really grasp the fullness of what the above verse is saying if we don't believe and receive of this building. So let's add to it the verse that came before it and see what unfolds. Remember, context is everything!

It fervently says... *Now, the "Lord" I'm referring to (**expecting** you to know) is the **Holy Spirit**, and wherever <u>He is **Lord**</u>, there is freedom*!* Now that's a grabber and a keeper and certainly adds a serious depth we must recognize. It truly is *Father as **Lord**, Jesus as **Lord**, and Holy Spirit as Lord* because *They* are each and all *togethered* in *Yahweh*. If *He's Lord*, *They're Lord* too. And fullness of **Lordship shifts everything** especially to the 3rd **power**! And for *3rd power carriers*! I'm one... are you?

Paul even taught using this example in this set of scriptures we find in 2 Corinthians 3:17-18 pointing out that everywhere it says *Lord*... it is <u>not</u> always referring to *Jesus*. The reference this time is to the *Holy Spirit* and *Him* doing what *He* does in the way *He moves, speaks, convicts,* and *points to truth*... just to mention a few. This is something many do not realize. Learning it certainly shifted some things for me and how I viewed *Lordship and His*.

To be *His* pure *containers, carriers,* and *conduits,* this *ordering, aligning, and rendering* of *Lordship* to the fullness of *Him* must be established fully in us so a greater work and releasing can come *to us, in us,* and *from us* to others!   ~ You know where we each are at. *Lord,* meet us there and have *Your* way!

Carry who He is in you...

When *God* created *Adam and Eve* on the sixth day in *Genesis 1 and 2* we can recall they were made in *Him* becoming a *Conduit*, that was a **Carrier** and a *Conduit of His* **full** essence being *carried* into them, their *container*s – bodies, so they could become *His conduits*. Some conditions were set for them in the garden where they lived. Yet, *He* allowed them free will to always be able to choose. The enemy knew the power of choice; he had made his, and came quickly as a *corrupted carrier* to deceive and influence theirs... these created ones who were *Yahweh's* first earthly *carriers* made by *Him*, from *Him*, and for *Him* the *Creator*. We know this, have read this in *His* book, and this book before. We're reading now for context to our *word of word* **carry** for context always plays a significant role in what we *expect* as well as the *how, why, when,* and *where* of our *expectations*.

His success in influencing and affecting their choice *infected* them with **sin.** Now they and their future offspring, us – what they, their *bloodlines* and *all future generations* would **carry.**   With that change came several immediate changes starting with their communion, conversations, their identity, what... even who, would shape their character now, and how they'd now be clothed. But, none of this changed the ***covenant keeping God*** *He* is or the fullness of the plans *He* had in place... before the foundations of the world.

Their part... as is our part now, is in operating as *He* created us is in the world. However, *He* made a way that once man chooses to become *born again*... this full circle reconciling move would make man – us, **in the world, but not of it.** We'd return to being *His* and *His carriers*. There's just something about *His expectancy*... and it's good, very good. How incredible that ours can be too as *His expectant carriers.*

Restored to having access to the **fullness** of *Him* in us - *His* DNA, essence, character, nature, along with presence, power to live thriving not just surviving, walk with *Him,* commune and talk with *Him*, knowing and growing in *Him*, through *His* purposes, promises, and plans as *His* family, children/ sons and daughters – called and chosen ones, *His* Church – ekklesia, *His* kings and priests, a royal priesthood, and more... including as *His* Bride. With each playing its part and piece in the return and restoring of all, to the full <u>context</u> of *His original intent* and *Kingdom's* cause on earth as it is in heaven.

My, oh my... what *power, potential,* and *possibilities* in our earthen vessels... jars of clay who are *containers,* *carriers,* *and conduits.* For as is written... *Has not the potter power over the clay, of the same lump to make one vessel unto honor, and another unto dishonor?... Does the clay say to the Potter, 'What are you making?' Does your work say, 'The Potter has no hands'?* *

But then it's what *His Word* says and furthermore what it connects and confirms in the general context... *Arise, and go down (in **expectation**) to the Potter's house, and there I will cause you to hear My (**expectant**) words. Then I went down to the Potter's house, and, behold, (as **expected**) He was shaping, forming, creating a work on the wheels. And the vessel that He made of clay was manifested and was marred in the hand of the Potter: so He made it again... another vessel, as seemed good to the Potter (in His **expectancy**) to make it.* * Oh... *His making again... as seemed good.. in the being born again offered to His creation... that's you... me... us.* **Expect** *and see*!

Carriers who are covered... dressed.

It's time to call our *expectations* up for what *He* wants to do through *His* **carriers,** in the variety of types and categories they come in for *He* loves diversity... as long *His* standards are prioritized in the *expectations* we are *forming, creating, birthing,* and that will manifest – as *expected* or *un**expected.***

It's time to consider that in this *ongoing process* within *life's journey...* you must know that what you wear matters. As *carriers...* I hear *Him* saying, *"There is wearing of Me and I want you to... actually need you to wear Me well. Being dressed with My character, integrity, and attributes... which represents and reflects Me because these* **carry** *in them what they are made up of - My love, light, and life which infiltrates, permeates, and saturates you with the fullness of My very being... the* **purest** *essence of* **real** *love, light, and life.*

All these things are to be worn first... on the inside covering your soul and body as the needed and necessary undergarments they are and by My Spirit you are covered in. You should **expect** *people to begin to notice good changes in you and in your countenance due to the positive and fruitful affect they are produce in you. You'll even know... especially as your* **expectancy** *begins to align more in and with Mine... that you're beginning to 'wear' Me well."* says the *Lord...* be it so as *You* have spoken and for Your glory.

In the *Bible* there was a man of *God Samuel,* who was a priest and prophet - a **carrier** of *God's* purpose, who was searching for the one he was to anoint to be the next king. He went to a man of *God, Jesse* as he was led to, believing to anoint one of his sons. Each of them looked good on the outside as the world **expected**... but, how they were dressed inwardly is what mattered to the Lord as He told Samuel... *"Surely (**expectantly**) the Lord's anointed is before Him."* But the Lord said to Samuel, *"Do not look at his appearance or at the height of his stature, because I have rejected him. For the Lord sees not as man sees; for man looks (**expectingly**) at the outward appearance, but the Lord (His **expectancy**) looks at the heart."* * God designed how we're dressed inside to matter. Think about that. Honor that in yourself.

Carriers carry... *you... me... we,* **carry** who *He* is in us and in knowing how to dress themselves to maximize what *Jesus* has done for us, especially within how the *Armor of God* in each piece represents what's available to us to help us be the **carriers** He *desires, designed, and is developing* us to be.

So let's start by recalling what the context and reasons for why we need to *get dressed* first... *Finally, (***expect** *to) be strong in the Lord and in the strength of His* **might***. Put on (with triumphant* **expectation***) the whole* **armor of God** *(with* **expectancy***), so that you* **may** *be able to stand (***expectantly***) against the schemes of the devil. For we do not (***expect** *to) wrestle against flesh and blood, but (in our* **expectations** *know it is) against the rulers, against the authorities, against the cosmic powers over this present darkness, against the spiritual forces of evil in the heavenly places. Therefore (***expect** *to) take up the whole armor of God, that you* **may** *be able to withstand in the evil day, and having done all, (***expect***) to stand firm.**

These garments called *armor*... they do so **much more** than just **c**over. When worn for what it is... in its fullness, there is a **c**ompleted work of *God* embedded within it so it not only **c**overs those who **c**arry *His presence, power, and purpose*... but in the wearing, it secures what each piece represents in an already finished work. For example: *So stand firm and hold your ground, having tightened the* **wide band belt of truth** *- personal integrity,* **moral courage***, around your waist and having put on the* **breastplate of righteousness** *– an upright heart, having strapped on your feet the* **boots of the gospel of peace** *in preparation to face the enemy with firm-footed stability and the readiness produced by the good news. Above all, lift up the* **protective shield of faith** *with which you can extinguish all the flaming arrows of the evil one. And take the* **helmet of salvation***, and the* **sword of the Spirit***, which is the* **Word of God***.** Oh... the *expectancy* of dressing in what's ours in *Christ Jesus*!

As we *go* now... *undergirded* and *armored up* to *do* and *be* in our i*dentity* and in our *authority* of who we are in *Him* and *He* is in *us*... an interesting thought **c**omes to **m**ind as I've heard it said that, "**In authenticity comes our authority.**" You... me... we all have the same armor available to us... yet, we each uniquely and authentically wear it, have our own **expectancy** in the why and how of it all, and in the *process* of why and how we're wearing it. This **c**ouples with what level or kind of authority we are willing to genuinely **embrace and be empowered by**... particularly if one believes and desires to be *His* **armored carrier.** *He* does want us to *wear it all well* on the outside too like *He* does.

Carriers of words...

We know and are learning in this *growing process* that *life* and our *lives contain* and *carry*... and believe we **c**an now say become *conduits* in *the journey*. Just like *His Word* **carries** within its words that *contain* and *carry* varied types and level of potential and power within - life. Therefore, words do become indeed an important kind of *conduit* to release to and over ourselves and others in our everyday lives. Words in general have within them the power of *either life or death* – *blessing or cursing*... as these are *biblical principles* **m**ost likely we all know. So, it's **c**ritical to know this speaks also of the power of *tongue*'s role in *speaking life* and *blessing* filled *confessions, decrees, declarations*... words *expectantly* filled with the *God* kind of life: *zoe, dunamis, exousia*... quickening *Spirit to spirit* power.

In this armoring of ourselves inside and out with all *He* offers through things *He's* secured like **truth, righteousness, peace, faith, salvation**... and yes, the **Spirit in** the **Word of God**. And there... there is a *look again and look beyond* for us to **expect and see** in what we're told to *put on* as well in this dressing for it definitely has to do with being **carriers** of *words*... and not just those we produce, but particularly those produced by *Holy Spirit* too.

Ephesians 6 reveals it powerfully in the words of the scriptures that have released above in the clearly defined *outward pieces of armor*. Yet, we know there's a place and need for our *inner dressing* which are... *With all prayer and petition (**expectantly**) pray with specific requests at all times... (**expecting**) on every occasion and in every season **pray in the Spirit**.**

There it is *Spirit to spirit*, us praying in our **most holy faith***... *in the Spirit* as we received in our inner **m**ost being when *baptized, immersed* in the *Holy Spirit and Him in us* – remember, *He* is a person as a part of the *Godhead*. For it looks like here... now in the *continuing* of the *connecting* of words in *His Word* where there is an **inner spirit armor** to put on. For in this *dressing process* there **c**omes a **c**overing in the words <u>only the Spirit knows and produces</u> in the power filled *essence of expectancy* of *His love, light, and life* they **carry**... to *infiltrate* and *saturate* our *spirit man dressing it* – the **new creature** in us that we are now! Whew!!!

How incredibly good our *Abba Papa Father God* is. This goodness reminds me of how *He* knew to **c**over the *darkness, formless, and void* of the earth by *His Spirit* – *Holy Spirit* and how *He* wants us to know *He* has from our beginning and **c**ontinually is *covering* and *dressing* everything within us as *He covers* and *armors* with *love* – first and foremost *His* as *His Love* exclusively always intentionally covers. Even a **m**ultitude of sin.

All the **m**ore reason as *His* **carriers** we **m**ust **expect** of ourselves to **m**ake sure what we speak aligns with *Him, His Word, His heart*... so as we **m**ove in this *ebb and flow* of all forms of our **c**onfessions **c**onnecting and **carrying**... as we are *actively proceeding* in our **c**alling and all *He* has **c**ommissioned us to do... with a fresh *commitment* and *consecration* of our devotion to *Him*. This all works *together*... and what a *togethering*, that is in agreement with all *He* has done, is doing, and will do in *the process*... producing a *transformation* in us and by *His Spirit*.

Carriers... your **c**onfessions, decrees, and declarations... not to **m**ention how all you speak truly **m**atters. We, you... me **m**ust consistently heed always and in all ways what *He* says in the **expectation** that the word *He* speaks is to us... *Do not withhold good from those who deserve it when it's in your power to help them in word or deed.** Amen ~ Help us *Lord*. And... let us **c**onsider what *Ed Silvoso*, a **m**inister to the Ekklesia shares, **c**onnecting this all to the *everyday process* and **expectancy** out in the world, *"If your job is your ministry, then God, who appointed you as a minister, has a supernatural empowerment for you to be able to do it His way!"* What truth and *oh* how *He* blesses us *His* **m**inisters!

Carriers of God's good and the Good News

Moving in the **m**omentum is important because all this is **c**reating, and should be in our *inner* **expectancy** with its *depth, height, width, and breadth* of what's revealed in the **carryings** of all being **m**ade known and released in this picture of an *outward and inward dressing* of ourselves. **M**ay this expanded image of countless blessings and benefits indeed help us be the **carriers** of the *full Gospel* we're **c**alled to go... **carrying** it with *beautiful feet** to all.

For as we dress our outer and inner **m**an with the armor... dressing <u>our spirit</u> too by praying and praying in the *Spirit*; our **m**ost holy faith... which connects us to what rest of this set of verses **carries** and tells us to do and will do... *"praying in the (**expectancy** of the to our spirit) Spirit and with this in view, stay alert with all perseverance and petition... interceding in prayer... for all God's people. And pray (**expectantly**) for me, that words may be given to me when I open my mouth, (**expecting**) to proclaim boldly the (**expectant** filled) mystery of the good news of* *salvation… for which I am an ambassador in chains. And pray (with earnest **expectation**) that in proclaiming it I may speak boldly and courageously, as I should."* *

What a concluding to this way of receiving from the bolder fuller releasing of the *Ephesians* 6 armoring dressing that helps us by the *Spirit* to know and respond to the question we presented with, "*How, then, can they call (**expectantly**) on Him in whom they have not believed? And how can they (in certain **expectation**) believe in Him of whom they have not heard? And how can they hear (thru the Spirit who brings **expectancy**) without someone (He **expects** to be)preaching to them?"* *

Only fully when that someone is a **Good News carrier** covered and armored *inwardly* and *outwardly* with the *Spirit* actively manifesting what *His **expectancy*** in and through us… to the **3rd power**! Does it not create a place for them to receive from *His* moving in those who are *carrying*? Those dressed in and through the fullness of *Them*… into the beyond of just *salvation* for those they're sent to… into the fuller measure of what *He* desires to give to them in the *baptism of water* and the *baptism of the Holy Spirit* for them too? *Jesus,* being the *Container, Carrier and Conduit He* was did say *He* had to go so *He* could send the *Holy Spirit* we needed – just like *He* did, to be all *He* was-is as *Son of God, Son of Man*… and to *endue* them – us, with **power – 3rd power!!!** Be it so *Lord* and for *Your glory*… have *Your way Holy Spirit!* Even *You Yeshua,* had to receive as *You* began *Your* ministry in the earth.

As our time together in this day with the *word of worth* **carry** draws to an end, in obedience it's now time to share briefly two more dimensions of how *carrying Him* in us can serve effectively as catalysts for propelling us into an *upon* – that *up and on,* of *God by His Spirit* to enable as we *journey* in *this process.* Surely, it is from our willing partnering with *His Spirit* to press from *faith to faith, strength to strength, glory to glory in grace upon grace*… that produces and manifests in and through us so incredibly more than we can ever think, imagine and in *our expectations*. Yet, there awaits us in the *togethering* of ours with *His*… unlimited ***expectancy*** and a godly good un***expectancy*** as well. Which is truly something I'm ***encountering*** and ***experiencing*** in this *telling*… and hope you are too!

Carriers of Holy Spirit Fruit

Do we have an ***expectancy*** for knowing the more of the fruit of *Holy Spirit,* it being produced in us flowing from us… let alone being able to grab hold of what it can actually do to free us in *the process* of the *becoming the being He made us to be*… and yes, as ***carriers***? *Lord* help us to arise in our ***expectancy*** and in our *journey* and be!

For there is nothing like a *caged bird* being un*caged* to *fly, soar, explore*… when that which has been contained no longer is being constrained, confined… or that which has been restricted no longer being *bound, constricted, limited*… for remember… where the *Spirit of the Lord* is there is freedom . *Ah*…but the fullness of such *liberty* remember, only comes in its fullness of *Holy Spirit* having *Lordship* in us to set us free… to flow and overflow… and with all the varying *fruit of His Spirit* producing and manifesting …filled with the glorious ***expectancy*** it ***carries!***

We really need, or at least I did, the perspective uncovered in *Galatians of The Passion Translation*'s remarkable *telling* of the fruit… *But the fruit produced by the Holy Spirit within you is divine love in all its varied **expressions** (is **expected** to be): joy that overflows, peace that subdues, patience that endures, kindness in action, a life full of virtue, faith that prevails, gentleness of heart, and strength of spirit.** Footnote: The word *self* is <u>not</u> found in this verse;

however, most translations render this as "*self-control.*" The word is actually *"lordship,"* or by implication *"spirit-strength." "strength of spirit"* ... and concludes saying... *Never set the law above these qualities, for they are meant (in divine expectancy) to be limitless.**

Fruit produced by who? And whose control? And don't you love the *adjectives* – a describing word, connected to the potential *each fruit contains, carries,* and *are conduits of* when they are growing and manifesting in us by *Holy Spirit!* So read it again… because most are also verbs – an action word, as well. For example: *joy that overflows* – overflows is both an adjective and verb. *Oh* the more… not just joy, but joy that overflows! Be it so ~

Carriers of His gifts…with signs, miracles, and wonders following

Gifts of the *Father, Son, Holy Spirit* to us are to be working in and through *Them* in us enabled by *Holy Spirit* and are spelled out for us in *Romans 12 – Redemptive Motivational Gifts of Father, 1 Corinthians 12 Gifts of the Holy Spirit, and Ephesians 4 Ascension Grace Gifts of Jesus* and must be pursued if for no other reason than *His Word* tells us this… *"So you should earnestly (expectantly) desire the most helpful gifts... and this states (with all expectancy) that you can (even with all expectation will) pursue the greater gifts."**

… And now I will send the Holy Spirit, just as My Father (expected) promised. But stay here in the city (waiting expectantly) until the Holy Spirit comes and fills you with (all expectancy of His)power from Heaven…. For indeed… These miraculous signs will accompany those who believe. And as… God added His witness to theirs. He validated their ministry with (expectant containing) signs, astonishing wonders (that stir expectancy), all kinds of powerful (expectant carrying) miracles, and by the gifts (fruit filled expectations) of the Holy Spirit, which He distributed as He desired.**…* and as we are learning, *our expectancy* draws *His* attention to us; our desire and hunger for more.

Oh, what we've received in this overall revealing of *His Words…* and by Holy Spirit in His *empowering* us to be the *containers, carriers,* and *conduits* in the more of *Him* and *Him* in us… for the more of *Him* in us to others. *"It's not about getting us to heaven, but getting heaven in us, these earthen vessels, to the earth… and Jesus is the blueprint and prototype – the real Jesus, not our American Western Church version of Him. Remember… He chooses us and to move in and use us." (Ed Watts)*

e=mc3   every expectation = maximum measure moving continually constantly in committed consecrated containers carriers conduits connected fully by **His 3rd power Holy Spirit!**

<u>In light of this *words of worth ... carry* and what's been shared:</u>

- ❖ *Perhaps... you* **Encountered or Experienced a Question or Challenge**?
  Write it out…

- ❖ *Perhaps... more has been* **Established & Empowered by the Word?**
  Write what/which…

- ❖ *Perhaps... it's time for* **Engaging & Embracing your Expectations?**
  Write what's forming…

Reminder: For **c**larity, **c**onnection, and **c**onfirmation regarding *expectancy* being stirred by this ***word of worth***, seek Him and His Word first. To possibly assist you in the process the list of **ION** words is available in the Appendix.

*Footnotes: Chapter 7 Day 6 carry / * See Colossians 1:27, John 15:1-8, 2 Corinthians 3:18, 3:17 in TPT be sure to see footnotes, Jeremiah 18:2, Romans 9:21 21, Isaiah 45:9, Psalms 1:1-6, Ephe-sians 6:10-24, Jude 1:20-25, Romans 10:14, 1 Corinthians 12:31, Romans 10:15 and Isaiah 52:17, Galatians 5:19-26 TPT and footnotes, Luke 24:49, Mark 16:17a, Hebrews 2:4, 2:22, 4:29-30, 5:32 - all emphasis is mine and personal paraphrasing built on various translations and versions. * See *Jonathan Cahn* / @mysteriesbook.com or @charismamedia.com / The Book of Mysteries - "Infinity In A Jar".

✧ Day 7: The Journey of "c"... celebrate

Let *expectations*... through this **word of worth's** part to *form, birth, and emerge* in its **meaning & mission**... **our meditation & motivation**... as **movement & manifestation** *awake, arise and align* in agreement with divine eternal *expectation*!

We **celebrate** and *honor the fullness of You God – Father, Son, and Holy Spirit* in all we do reflecting our genuine love, sincere honor, passionate purpose filled hearts, and devoted intentional intimate lives in our *lifestyle of worship, humble service,* and *surrendered submission* in all that we do with it being unto *You* who alone is worthy of all *blessing and glory, honor and power, and praise.* Amen. That is the only way this part of the *journey...* and e**v**ery day on it should begin for *you... me... us,* with this *word of worth* **celebrate!**

In beginning the writing of this portion of the *telling,* right out the gate the word **celebrate** was stirring **expectation** as it is known to do. **Celebrating** often **c**onnects **e**specially in the fondness of some **c**hildhood or special **m**emories that **c**ome to **m**ind and where *music* or *singing* were involved. But in this **m**oment for me, a fun **celebratory** song has **c**ome rushing into my soul. You probably know it and **m**ight just be prompted to sing along as we head into this **c**oncluding seventh day of *our journey* with "**c**"...

♪ "**Celebrate** good times, **c**ome on... let's **celebrate**. **Celebrate** good times, come on... let's **celebrate**... Bring your good times and your laughter too. We're gonna **celebrate** and party with you... We're gonna have a good time tonight. Let's **celebrate**. It's alright! **Celebrate** good times, come on... let's **celebrate**." ♪ "I've got all my sisters and me"... but we've got all our brothers and sisters, *His* family – and it's time to **c**ome together all around the world... and **celebrate**! Yahoo... a **celebration** to last beyond the year into all of *eternity*!

What fun singing brings to traveling, now that stirs up some memories too... and to **celebrations**. What power in the releasing of songs in their lyrics **c**arrying and **c**ontaining **expectations**! I see your smiles and *He* does too:) *He* knows... and I do too, that it's a secular song. But, it's the **m**otive in our hearts and who we are now as *His* that *He* sees and hears in it all. **Celebrating** is a perfect time to enter into the **expecting** with the **m**anifesting of a song as it arises.

It's always good when *Judah...* our praise and song, goes before us and with us. Especially in times where we're recognizing all the *reasons, people,* and *things* we have to **celebrate** and the varying kinds of **celebration** they offer. The *Lord's Feasts,* a new day, a new **m**onth, a new year... birthdays, weddings, anniversaries, graduations... so **m**any reasons, *salvations, baptisms. healings, deliverances, miracles, signs, wonders,* and **m**ore!

Here's an **e**xample from *His Worthy Word* that we should see as an **expectant** filled foundational type of laying for **celebrating**... *To everything there is a season... an **expected** time appointed...even a reason for every delight, activity, and event or purpose under heaven... a time to be born... giving birth, and a time to die... an ending; a time to plant sowing and a time to uproot what is planted. A time to kill and a time to heal; a time to tear down and a time to build up. A time to weep and a time to laugh; a time to **m**ourn and a time to dance. A time to throw away scattering stones and a time to gather stones; a time to **embrace** and a time to refrain from **embracing**. A time to search and a time to give up as lost; a time to keep and a time to throw* *away. A time to tear apart and a time to sew together; a time to keep silent and a time to speak. A time to love and a time to hate; A time for war and a time for peace.** Time... *He* is time.

And in these times... something *awakens* or **m**ay sound an *alarm* in us... reminding us of who *He* is... who we are in *Him*, whose we are as *His*, and what *He's* done... is doing, desires to do, and will do. Times where *He* imparts *revelation*... brings *redemption*... and gives ideas for *resolution* in the *revolutionary turning* the *processing* is always *creating* regarding where we are and what we're **encountering... experiencing**, and what is ahead.

In all of this when we *remember, recall, reflect,* and *reach out* to *Him*... to know the value and importance in the *role it all plays* in **expectancy**... and the *place it should have or shouldn't have* in *the process* of our **expectations** being *formed, created, birthed,* and **m**anifesting we also discover or realize various elements of *celebrating* were involved.

For therein lies the greater **expectancy to celebrate**... *He has* **m**ade everything beautiful and appropriate in its time (His **expectancy** at work). He has also planted eternity... a sense of divine purpose (eternal **expectation**) in the human heart... as a **m**ysterious longing which nothing under the sun can satisfy, except God. Yet, **m**an cannot find out, comprehend, or grasp... what God has (**expectantly**) done in His overall plan from the beginning to the end. I know that there is nothing better for them than to rejoice (**expectantly celebrate**) and to (**expect to**) do good as long as they live; and also that every **m**an should eat and drink and see and enjoy **celebrating** the (**expectant**) good of all his labor—it is the gift of God.*

Indeed it is... and, it is alright to *celebrate* equally our *progress in the process* as we *celebrate* in the *good times, hard times, sad times,* and *in between times.* There's always something to *celebrate*... to be glad for and rejoice in... and *again* I say rejoice.

After all it's what *He's* doing *in and through,* and *over* us continually as we know *His Word* expresses to us and here's what it says... *"The Lord your God Adonai, is in your* **m***idst, a Mighty Warrior who saves* (**expect it**). *He will rejoice* (**celebrate**) *over you with joy and gladness; He will be quiet and calm in His love* (**let it be your expectation**)...**m***aking no* **m***ention of your past sins... as He delights* (**with great expectancy**) *in you as He sings songs, dances, and rejoices over you... releasing even* (**expectant** *filled* **celebratory**) *shouts of joy.**

All the **m**ore reason for *you...* **m***e... us,* to *celebrate* together on this *adventure* we're taking. For *together* in *Him* we are one. *Oh,* the *togethering.* For there's no distance in the spirit between us by *His Spirit* in us *His* children, as *His* family continuing onward. Let's head into laying a foundation for the *meaning* and the *mission* our *word of worth celebrate* in what it contains and carries.

There's *simplicity* that comes in the defining of *celebrate* when we see it is purely **m**eaning:
have a good time – did we not just sing that! *To have fun, rejoice, party, festivity, to observe or commemorate a special time, to be grateful for, to give honor to, to remember...* are just a few things to know about how it's defined. One of the results that originate when we *celebrate* is it creates *a place,* **m***oment, or atmosphere* that *encourages, exhorts, edifies, and empowers.* Sounds like something to *embrace, expecting* it to be a part of our *expectations*!

Be encouraged to not **m**iss out on this extraordinarily delightful fact in *this journey* and in *the process* therein. For in one dimension we're traveling together as we've established and been encountering, particularly as it helps us see the bigger picture of the collective and corporate side of who we are as *His* and what it can represent to the *Body of Christ, His Church*, and all *He* calls us.

Likewise, in another dimension it's good to acknowledge that it's a very *private* and *individual journey* as well. Which connects us with the idea presented previously… that it truly is, if in our *expectancy* we recognize it – even **celebrate** it… a form and fruit of a *spiritual pilgrimage*. We see this in how it's *designed* to be *engaged* in over time… and, is *designated* to be a kind of *holy journey* on the *highway He* is *forming* in the *natural* and *spiritual*… as the *beauty* of *His holiness*, true *holiness*, has its work calling us up into **embracing** and being **empowered** by *His* **expectancy** for the higher better things of *God*.

The voice and spirit of *Augustine's* words impart an image, even a need, into this… *"Nothing whatever pertaining to godliness and real holiness can be accomplished without grace."* Now… add to it this powerful expression *"Holiness is a constellation of graces."* by *Thomas Bostone*. We can certainly see the importance of *grace*. It is *needful* and *necessary* to release it to *ourselves*, to *others*, and into all the ways *expectancy* flows in the varying situations that contain diverse *expectations*… and their moving in *the process* that is *forming* us… all the while *His expectation* is calling us up… and into the greater portion.

Celebrate now thanking *Him* for how *He* is helping you to take and make time for what *He* is *revealing, requiring,* and *releasing* to you… and doing within you – *spirit, soul, and body*. Taking it all beyond me *telling* you and you just *reading* a book. Into what *He* is bringing forth in the present day manifesting as *the process* is ongoing in *His graciousness, goodness, faithfulness,* and the *sufficiency of His grace*… in the continual producing of something more and it creating a more like *Him* in us. May we *expect* it… for it will be good.

Don't worry or be concerned… afraid or unsure in *the process* of recognizing, entering into in faith with confidence, and in a *celebrating* (subtle or grand) through exhibiting a *joy in the journey*. *His joy* is our *strength*… and it does *come in the morning,* even when *weeping endures for a night* and joy comes in mourning. For like *Jesus*, we *count it all joy*. And, it comes filled with *expectancy* with its *daily dose* to *fill, refresh, strengthen,* and *renew* us! And that, my friends is a reason to **celebrate**!

The *Lord Himself* wants us to be *filled and overflowing with joy*.* That's the **celebratory** side of our *God*! So we shouldn't be surprised *He* built **celebration** into *His* calendar knowing it helps produce *joy, delight,* and many other pleasant *responses, emotions, and fruit* of *His Spirit*.

We see in the timeline *He* has established in *His Word* for us to live in and out of are *His moedims*… which if you recall are *His appointed* and *divinely assigned* times. Times *He* has ordered for our *honoring and celebrating* much. Particularly the *Feasts of the Lord* in which there are *seven feasts He* emphasizes in *His Word* along with a few festivals mentioned.

These are revealed in *Leviticus 23*. I know, it's not a book we read or receive from often… but we should for it contains something we need to know because it holds within it an essential component of *His ordering* and *ordaining* of times of **celebration** that are required by *Him* and *of His people*. And, *He* tells of them being honored and **celebrated perpetually** – that's *eternally*, thus containing an **eternal expectation**… just like our *salvation* does.

Because *He* speaks of them in this way… let me share these seven *holy convocations*, another name they're given. These times *He* says to *gather, assembling to honor,* and **celebrate**. Let's start with how *He* lists them beginning with the *Spring Feasts of the Lord*. However, let me clarify here they are called and identified as *"Feasts of the Lord – the Lord's Feasts"* and they've been mentioned before. They are not actually listed as or called *Jewish or Hebrew* feasts in *His Worthy Word*.

We certainly honor and even *celebrate* that the Jewish people are those ones– *God's chosen people*, who He initially gave them to, have largely and consistently acknowledged them giving a special intentional place in their live, and the more connected to them. Let's add to that a connectedness we have to them for we must recognize that in our *grafted in one new man humanity identity** we are to acknowledge and give place to them too… *Yeshua, Jesus* did… along with the *disciples, apostles,* and all the *early church* did for many, many years.

The *seven Lord's feasts* listed include: **Passover, Unleavened Bread, First Fruits, Shavuot Pentecost, Trumpets, Day of Atonement, and Tabernacles/Sukkot.** Be encouraged to not only learn about these, but to step into *honoring and celebrating* them in ways *He'll* lead you to. Not religiously or ritualistically, but in a *purely relational* and *enjoyable* way of *communing, connecting, and celebrating* with our *covenant God* who set them into place for us to be blessed and to encounter more of *Him* as we discover the layers of meaning, purpose, and *His* plan for us through them and their connectedness to our identity and inheritance.

A shift came to *His* plan for them in the early church foundations and structure which undeniably *celebrated* and honored not just the *Lord's Feasts,* but *God's* calendar, cycles, and seasons as established in *His Word…* like *Jesus,* and others did. This disruption brought forth a familiar pattern that came in the garden to *cause confusion, bring chaos,* and *create a crisis in identity*; a kind of theft of the identity *He* divinely determined *His Church* was to live from and walk in. Different *expectations* were arising, emerging, converging, and clashing creating a place for much confusion, persecution, martyrdom, and a mixture that began to develop in very concerning, and ungodly ways.

It wasn't long till *Constantine* arose as the first *"Christian" Roman Emperor.* A leader with great power in his *sovereign role.* After his *spiritual encounter* with what he believed to be *God/Christ* he moved to <u>set a whole new religious system in place</u>. He did help bring a form of an end to the persecution of some said *"Christians"*. He also brought in what some might see as other positive methodologies and practices into what became known as *"Christianity"*. Certainly he established much in what we came to know as "the church" and life within the *Christian* way – with much that was *"good"*… or appeared to be. But, is *good* always *God*? He *expects* us to know. Afterall, there was the *Tree of the Knowledge of Good and Evil*.

In a general kind of summarizing we can see overall how the *religious Greco-Roman and pagan influence, rituals and protocols, power, and control he* enabled… alongside and coupled with the resulting changes that manifested after the *Council of Nicaea,* that all but abolished what the church *He* birthed looked like. The divine part of our *true full identity and inheritance* designated to help us *celebrate, honor, and live out* of our foundations in *Him;* whom the true *Church* belongs to and was divinely designed and birthed by. For it became *broken, fragmented,* and in a distorted kind of way *unrecognizable.* The struggle exists still today to *embrace* and be *empowered* by the truth of who the *Church really, truly, and purely* is… and who we are, for we are *His* **Church.** And it, *His Church* should be arising for such a time… so perhaps this identity theft is real and should be recognized, and even rectified?

It was and is our foundation *in Jesus as a Jew*, the **Messiah** prophesied of, the *Anointed One*, the *Begotten Son* who was *Son of God, Son of Man* – the *Way, the Truth, and the Life* and so **m**any other things *He* was, **m**odeling, **e**ducating, and **e**mulating who we are and are to be that is so very **e**ssential for us to return to. Who *He* was, *His* nature and **c**haracter… and what *He* did showing love, honor, grace, **m**ercy, **c**alling people up into their image and likeness of *Him/Them*, in them, as in us, and beyond. It was all underpinning the **e**arly **c**hurch's true identity and it being started by *Jews* who worshiped, served, and loved *Yeshua* and *Him* as <u>the only Way</u>. For *He* did **c**ome to the *Jew* first, *He* was and is still a *Jew, and* then **c**ame to the *non-Jew/Gentiles*. Those Jews were referred to as **Messianic Jews** – *Jews* that believe in *Jesus/Yeshua* was/is the **Messiah c**ome, and *non-Jews/Gentiles* that were then grafted in. Lurking in the **m**idst was an **e**vil agenda for removing and replacing any *Jewish* form of *identity* in *His Church* arising, and **e**ventually this plan took over and took **c**ontrol.

The *Holy Spirit* was active and **e**videnced in the *boldness, courage,* and *demonstration* of the *love, grace,* and *power* of *Yahweh* displayed in **e**veryday people and **e**ven prominent ones too… as *His* saints were doing the work of **m**inistry. The *ministry of reconciliation* they – we are **c**alled to with discipling, gathering regularly, **e**quipping, flowing in the gifts, and all *He* had revealed they were to be doing in being about their *Father's* business like *Jesus,* and it was the norm. They were spreading the *love of God*, the *Gospel of Salvation*, and the *Gospel of the Kingdom*, which were advancing *His* kingdom on **e**arth as it is in heaven. Yes, the nations and generations were being **c**ompelled by *His Spirit* to *repent, turn,* and *give* their lives to following and living for *Him*. What a global harvest of souls began in *His Church going, doing, being…* truly bringing about **m**uch ***celebrating*** rooted in ***celebration*** of *Him*.

The Messianic Church Arising, The Apostolic Church Arising, and The Triumphant Kingdom, along with *A Time to Advance* * are all books I highly recommend to help you know **m**ore and grow in your understanding as to why this true history, functioning, fellowshipping, and training, along with the timing of *God,* true ***celebrations*** of the *Lord's Feasts*, **c**ycles, seasons, and beyond what I **c**an share, **c**arry tremendous value. They **e**stablish the divine *originating, ordering, orchestrating, and organizing* as *He* purposed, planned, and intended, hence important and **e**ssential to ground yourself in. *Dr. Chuck D. Pierce* and *Dr. Robert Heidler* are the authors of these respected books.

Giving honor is key, so I do and **celebrate** them as types of *apostolic prophetic* **m**inister/ *ministry models, teaching* **m**entors*, spiritual kinds of fathers, and* in my life as well. They are two leaders in the **c**orporate body, who've had an invaluable spiritual influence bringing blessings in vast ways for the process and the *journey* of **m**any *internationally*… and in mine. In what I've gained and gleaned in *the process* through *Him* **c**onnecting and aligning me with them over the past twenty plus years and the kingdom **m**inistry *He's called, anointed,* and *chosen* them for is priceless. We, my husband and I, are a *"House of Zion"…* which for us is a house that aligns with and supports the *mission, vision,* and *kingdom one new* **m**an **m**andate purpose **c**oming forth at *Glory of Zion Internationa*l (GZI), and are a part of their *Kingdom Harvest Alliance*. We look forward in this next year to finally **m**aking our first trip there. We are grateful for their website with its **e**xtremely beneficial, high quality, and wide array of online **m**inistry services, trainings, products, and **m**ore they offer to stay connected.

Now back to where we were… *let's remember*, it is in <u>only</u> in *Christ Jesus* – *Yeshua*, that both *Jew* and *Gentile/non-Jews* are brought together – the *togethering He* **c**reated for us to *enjoy, honor,* ***celebrate****, and partake in* and not just through the *Lord's Feasts*, but **m**ore importantly the fullness of our *identity and inheritance* in our *New Covenant* relationship with *Yahweh* in *His* fullness; as *His* and as **His Church**... the *Ekklesia.* A part of the returning and reconciling us back to *His original intent* as *He* is bringing heaven to earth so *His kingdom* can come and *His* will be done.

> ❖ *Perhaps*... there was a bit of seriousness and heaviness for you in the above part of the *telling He* required me to share. My obedience to *His* leading is key because truth must be shared always and unquestionably at this time we're in. And, because this is *His book – not mine.* In *His Book the Bible – which is absolute truth, He* lets us know that is *the truth that sets us free*. I'm believing there's some truth coming to the church about its real identity in this day and hour that will cause some to celebrate and some to wax cold and draw away from truth. And… that which is written and revealed in what men say or believe in their own created paradigms and doctrines that have grounded them in what they believe and determine is truth… it will be tested, tried, and judged by *Him*. There is an *expectation* from *Him* in scripture that tells us we are to study *His Word* for ourselves*… showing ourselves approved as ones who have integrity and are diligent in honoring what *He's* said to do… for in this *process* we are also *expectantly* learning in some more subtle but relational ways the importance of rightly discerning and dividing the *Word of Truth.**

We going to remain in this vein of needing to take a closer look at some things where **celebrating** is an essential part, but not the whole picture. For example, there is a form of *celebration* in the *Letter's to the Seven Churches* in *Revelation 2* and *3* that *He* gave by *His Spirit* to *Paul* to write. Not necessarily an *easy* writing assignment… but a needful one that holds critical messages, effective strategies, and critical alerts for the church – *His Church* and the church today that's loosing much of her true identity leaving very little to *celebrate.*

We see in them an acknowledging of what they are: correction with direction, an admonishment to not just listen but to have an ear to hear what the *Spirit* is saying, and then culminating with a stirring of *expectancy* to arise in a *obedience quickly to all directed* so there can be a *celebrating* in the kind of way that comes with eternal rewards. In all that it's so powerfully encouraging to see that *He* chose to have *Paul* write first **celebrating** by the recognizing and honoring of what they were doing that was good and right in *His* sight.

Now, let's look at a way we see *celebrating* manifesting in a corporate way today… which will include the *family of God,* the *Body of Christ,* and *congregational* structures within the main church structure which most I believe are familiar with. Although they're different names… the overall functions I'll share in the larger scope of the *mandate, mission,* and *commission* that *God* has given and set in place to be, it remains foundational to all who make up the greater *righteous cause of Him and His kingdom.* And, the primary dynamics of what unfolds in *the process* as set forth by *Him.*

First… it's valuable to go *vertical* since *He* is to be our first priority in all things… and as we seek *His kingdom first and righteousness,* so the things we have need of can be added unto us,* we're positioning ourselves to *celebrate* what *He* will do to provide for us in the *adding's* of *God* to us. In the corporate picture of *God's family/church/body* when we're doing this in a collective or corporate way our *expectations* should increase for *His adding.*

While pondering on the above I recalled a message I heard once from an anointed man of *God, Bill Yount,* was titled, *The Cluster Anointing.* Now I believe I can reasonably *expect* you each might already be thinking of a certain fruit – why? Because the word *cluster* contains within it, as some words amazingly do, an immediate association filled with image *expectations* that connect to what it is. In this case, the word describes a way that *grapes grow*... in a *cluster*.

What is a *cluster anointing* be speaking of? Let's go look first at what *Jesus* shares with us about grapes regarding the vines and branches they grow on and why that would be important for *us* to know We see this powerful imagery and poignant expression of *desired and expected* relationship in *John 15* where *He* speaks to being the *True Vine* and *His followers*– us, being the branches, with *Father God*, being the *Gardener or Vine Dresser*.

There's so much to love about *God's divine design* as we see it in an overwhelmingly good and necessary way in this illustration *Yeshua* gives. Out of *His* heart *He* shares that: *I desire to be the source in your life and allowing Me to be such you'll receive the nourishment and strength you need to (**expectantly**) grow and sustain you for You are the branches who are to be connected to and dependent on Me. All the while the Father is pruning and removing if necessary, any branches that are bearing fruit in the process that is needful and beneficial in many ways.** A *process* that when causing growth desired might just require *celebrating*!

For in such, the fruit that develops and grows can be seen in a spiritual way reflecting a relationship with *Him as Father and Son*. How our *abiding in Him*, in *His presence*, in *our connection*, and *communing* allows our genuine desire and intentionality to make an *expected* place for *sincere* and *authentic intimacy* a reality. All are essential for our *expectancy* to begin to lean on and learn from *Him* for growing in *the process* of being and becoming first... and, so the *ongoing process* of *expectations* forming, creating, birthing, and manifesting flows more spontaneously and consistently because of our connection with *Him* is. Ours and *His* *expectancy* remember... is not just for us but, toward and for the benefit and blessing of others too.

This is where we look to the natural a bit further into what a vine with branches produces... something that grows within the connecting of the grapes on the vine together. Grapes that grow in *clusters* and *clusters* that *together* yield a harvest. So let's turn now to the *Body of Christ* where we can see how *our defining* together with *the description* above will give a representation and vivid picture that is expressed in how when the *Body* works *collectively* and *corporately together*... it can accomplish so much more than one can individually.

*Two are better than one because they have a more satisfying return (of **expectancy**) for their labor; for if either of them falls, the one will lift up his companion. But be aware and tell the one who is alone for when he falls... there is no one there to lift him up. Again, if two lie down together, then they keep warm; but how can one (**expect** to) be warm alone – you'd shiver all night. And though one can overpower him who is alone, two together can (**expectantly**) resist facing the worst. A cord of three strands will not easily snap or be broken.**

Here are *words from the Word of God* that confirm what is being represented figuratively bringing it together with the *ministry of the Body* which gives us cause alone to *celebrate.* Especially as we recognize this kind of *connecting* in honoring and *celebrating* who *He* is in <u>every part or piece each person *offers, contributes, and places*</u> into the partnering with *Him* in *His* greater *mandate, mission* and *commission* to us. And... we see the anointing at work in the power of a *three-fold cord* at work as well... like in $e=mc^3$.

When the *Body of Christ* is *working together* and in authentic meaningful connecting... being about our *Father's* business, we can *expect*... like the *clusters of grapes* on the branches of the vine, to yield a good harvest. Most *expectantly* for them to be used to create *new wine* and for the *new wineskins*. **E**ven the old wineskins, submitted to being **m**ade new, that *He's* been **m**aking ready to *contain, carry,* and *pour out*!

Now… let's take a look at all of this in the beauty of these scriptures that say **e**xactly what we've said but, in *His words of worth* that would be written in red….*"I am a true sprouting vine, and the farmer who tends the vine is **M**y Father. He **c**ares for the branches **c**onnected to **M**e by lifting and propping up the fruitless branches and pruning **e**very fruitful branch to yield a greater (**expectant**) harvest. The words I have spoken over you have already cleansed you. So you **m**ust remain in (the **expectancy** of) life-union with **M**e, for I remain in life-union (and in **expectation**) with you. For as a branch severed from the vine will not (be **expected** to) bear fruit, so your life will be fruitless unless you (**expect** to) live your life intimately joined to **M**ine. I am the sprouting vine and you're **M**y branches. As you live in (**expectation** for) union with **M**e as your source, fruitfulness will stream from within you—but when you live separated from **M**e (**expectantly**) you are powerless. If a person is separated from **M**e, he is discarded; such branches are gathered up and thrown into the fire to be burned. But if you live in life-union with **M**e and if **M**y words live powerfully (in **expectation**) within you—then you can ask whatever you desire (**expect**) and it will be done. When your lives bear abundant fruit, you demonstrate(**expectingly**) that you are **M**y mature disciples who glorify **M**y Father!**

Christ in you, in me, in us… the hope of glory*… flowing together like in this *cluster* illustration. As *He* arises in us… **m**ay we be like that of a *well-oiled machine* where the *cogs on the wheel* are all **m**oving in *His timing, aligning,* and *assigning* **c**ausing us and *Him* to *celebrate* too!

In **c**ompleting this day… let's go out in *celebration* of revelation… and it in *His Word by His Spirit… His telling…* which so *practically* and *profoundly* **m**anifests giving you… me… us, reason for *celebrating* in *the process* while on *the journey together in Him* and out of our **m**utual **expectancy**.

Let us *celebrate*… like the people did leaving *Egypt* when the *Red Sea parted*!
Let us *celebrate*… like *Abraham* did as *God* stopped *his sacrifice of Isaac*!
Let us *celebrate*… like *Daniel* did when *God* shut the **m**outh of the lions!
Let us **celebrate**… like *Esther* did **e**xposing *Haman's* decree to annihilate her people.
Let us *celebrate*… like the *Lord's* lovers for I am my *Beloved's* and *He* is **m**ine.
Let us *celebrate*… like the at the wedding as *Jesus turned water into wine*!
Let us *celebrate*… like *Joseph, Mary* and all the **e**arth did at the birth of *Jesus – Yeshua*!
Let us *celebrate*… like the father did for his prodigal son who was now home!
Let us **celebrate**… like the blind who see, deaf who hear, and the dead who live!
Let us *celebrate*… like the women at the tomb told *He's not here, He's risen*!
Let us *celebrate*… like those redeemed *of the Lord who say so*!
Now for yours ~
Let us *celebrate*… like…

In light of this **_words of worth ... celebrate_** and what's been shared:

- ❖ *Perhaps... you* **Encountered or Experienced a Question or Challenge**?
  Write it out...

- ❖ *Perhaps... more has been* **Established & Empowered by the Word?**
  Write what/which...

- ❖ *Perhaps... it's time for* **Engaging & Embracing your Expectations?**
  Write what's forming...

Reminder: For *clarity, connection, and confirmation* regarding **expectancy** being stirred by this **word of worth**, seek *Him* and *His Word* first. To possibly assist you in the process the list of **ION** words is available in the Appendix

*Footnotes: Chapter 7 Day 7 celebrate / * See Ecclesiastes 3:1-13, Zephaniah 3:17, Nehemiah 8:10, Psalm 30:5, James 1:2, John 15:11, see moed H4150 Strongs Concordance, Ephesians 2, Romans 11, Ezekiel 37, 2 Timothy 2:15, Matthew 6:33, Ecclesiastes 4:9-12, John 15:1-8 , Colossians 1:27-28 - all emphasis is mine and personal paraphrasing built on various translations and versions .   * See *Celebration* lyrics by Kool and the Gang https://www.streetdirectory.com/lyricadvisor/song/wuulaj/celebration/
* See *Glory of Zion International* – Global Spheres Center in Denton, TX @gloryofzion.org / *Dr. Chuck Pierce and Dr. Robert Heidler* books. * See *Bill Yount* / @billyount.com /Prophetic Stones of Remembrance - A Legacy for the End Times. The cluster anointing word/teaching is in this book.

✧ *Expectancy's Look Again… at the end of the Journey with "c"*
~ *Connie*

Expectation's Reflection… a testimony

Dearest Brothers and Sisters,

As I've journeyed through *this journey with "c" words of worth*, my heart has leaped numerous times wondering what to *expect* next! Every paragraph could become a prayer or declaration in itself. I found myself reading and re-reading sentences desiring to soak up the essence of its truth and meaning… coveting the words as ones truly meant for *me*… words that undergirded and covered. I felt hugged and forever loved by our *Father God, our Lord Jesus Christ* and *His Gift* to us, *Holy Spirit*. It was 'deeper well' experience in which I was pulling up bucket after bucket of fresh, renewing water… my soul rejoicing and *expecting* more as I dug deeper. *Hope, joy,* and *expectation* were becoming a new thing within me and that's what this is all about!

Of these *"c" words of worth…* 2 stood out to me as I progressed through these defining words and all the depth given to them… **COVENANT** and **CARRY**. It goes without saying… that *Christ* is first and foremost. All these words do build upon one another creating such an *expectation* from their meaningful discussion *telling* much.

But… when I see the word *covenant,* I think of how I feel when I take of *Holy Communion*. My heart picks up speed and my stomach clenches as I repeat of the *Worthy Words of Christ* at the *Last Supper*. "Then He took the cup, gave thanks to His Father (even knowing what the next few hours would bring), and gave it to them saying, *'Drink from it all of you, for this is My blood in the NEW COVENANT, which is shed for many for the remission of sins"* (poured out). And… in others it says, *"Do this in remembrance of Me."* (Matthew 26:27-28)

I always wondered what *Jesus*… in *His* humanity… was thinking and feeling. And… no one asked any questions! The disciples weren't shy. Why didn't they ask about the *NEW covenant…* or *the body* or *the blood?* These were not usual or casual words… a line was being crossed! They could not at that time discern that without the *promise and provision* of the *NEW covenant* There was no hope for humankind. But GOD – *He* made it real and full of TRUTH that was grounded in… and yet upheld by *His mighty love* and desire for reconnecting with us and giving us an *ETERNAL PROMISE of LIFE*!

And… *God* wanted relationship with us so much and us with *Him* that *He* made us *carriers* of a deep desire for sharing *His Good News Gospel* and *Abba Father's love*. So much so… that we would share it and flow from it as kingdom influencers. The last time I vividly remember hearing the word *carrier*… I was very young… and as a word that *carried* negative connotations. It became very real to me… but, not in a kind way.

Remember… words, even *words of worth*… can have both a *positive and negative* side to them. You see… that word *carry*… in certain circumstances, can be very hurtful. But *GOD*… *He* can and will bring out the other side if we allow *Him* to. When I was a very young three year old, my 27 year old father contracted *Bulbar Polio*. My 24 year old mother, my father's family were devastated by this diagnosis, and it was two weeks before their fourth anniversary. Mom was seven months pregnant with my second sister born just before *Christmas,* with me the oldest child and my younger sister.

This was on *Friday October 19, 1952*. Ironically… all the doctors were in *Chicago* at a conference on *Polio*. A resident diagnosed him and he was put in an iron lung. While my mother was getting ready to go up on the elevator and as my dad's twin brother entering an elevator to come down… a doctor ran after him - my father had died… and quickly as it was two days later on *Sunday* morning. After what happened… one can only imagine the horrible shock that reverberated through our family. Especially for my young mother who would now be a widowed parent with three young children.

It was said that it was probably a *carrier* who unknowingly passed it on to him. Since my father drove a school bus… it could have even been a child. But *GOD*… once *again* – *He* gave us another form of a *carrier* in *Jonas Salk*. Within him was the gift of healing as the inventor of the polio vaccine which *carried* within it a way to irradicate this disease and millions were given life.
God is so good!

As *carriers* of the *Good News of the Gospel* we must always do our best in *the process*… to be responsible and accountable for what we are given to *carry*… especially the words that come forth from us and the power they *carry* to the positive or negative. The gifts we possess matter too… as they are actively being used in us as *His carriers* in this journey of life. Being aware and discerning of things that could occur or be happening around us in times of releasing to others matters.

We want to represent *Him* well… so we must pursue *God's perception, guidance,* and *direction… His expectation* always. I am amazed at the magnitude of who *He* is, how *He* moves, and permeating of *His* great love for us. How *He* created us with a need for *Him* and personally draw us unto *Himself* by *His* eternal love and desire for true communion and connection in our relationship with *Him* in life.

Expectation's Prayerful Considerations:

This has all caused me to ponder with great *expectancy*…
What kind of *carrier* am I? Am I living a *pure, holy, just and true* life that flows with covenant love to others? Am I partnering with *Him* to open hearts and doors to the one and only *Jehovah God*… and for *Him* by *Holy Spirit* to make the way for salvation through *His Son Jesus Christ*?

All the **"c"** words are connected to such
and help us proclaim *His mighty love* to all.

Prayer of Expectancy:

*Dear Lord, I pray decreeing and declaring that this battalion of believers that You are, will, and have raised up is **m**otivated, **m**obilized, and **c**atapulted onto the international stage exploding into and bringing forth an influx of new **e**xpectant and **r**adical believers that will be astounding in the scope and dimension of truth and revelation, innovation and **c**reativity, expressing the fruit of the Spirit, spiritual gifts, healing power, and exhibiting a love that has never before been seen on this **e**arth glorifying You. In Jesus's name – Amen.*

Expectation's Declaration:

*I decree we submit this all to You, our **M**ost Powerful God above ANY and ALL things, persons, and powers to have Your way so Your kingdom **c**an **c**ome and Your will be done on **e**arth as it is in heaven.*

✧ W**ORTHY** W**ORDS AS** W**E** E**NTER** C**HAPTER** 8…

*May the grace (**expectancy** filled) of the Lord Jesus Christ, and the love of God (in its **expectancy**), and the fellowship (as **expected**) of the Holy Spirit be with you all.**

*Worship God (**expectantly** with all you are)! For the (**expectant**) substance and essence of the truth revealed by Jesus (as divinely **expected**) who is the (**expectant**) spirit of all prophecy… which is the (**expectancy** filled) vital breath, the divine inspiration of and in all inspired preaching and interpretation of the divine (**expectations**) will and purpose, including both mine and yours.**

*I am the Aleph – the Alpha and the Tav – the Omega… the Beginning and the Ending – the First and the Last (**expect Me** to be such), says the Lord God, who is, who was, and who is to come, the Almighty.**

*Now, **m**ay the God of peace and harmony Himself sanctify you… setting you apart from profane things (as He **expectantly** does)… **m**aking you through and through pure and wholly consecrated to God (according to His **expectations**)… and **m**ay your entire being… spirit and soul and body (as in **expectancy** He created) be preserved sound, completely flawless, and blameless at the (**expectant**) coming of and appearing our Lord Jesus Christ our **M**essiah, the Anointed One. The One who (in **expectation**) calls you by name to Himself for your salvation… who is (**expected** to be) absolutely trustworthy… as He is (**expectantly**) guarding you, watching over you, protecting you as His own and will thoroughly complete His work (as **expected**) in you.**

*For the kingdom of God is not a **m**atter of rules about food and drink, but is first (**expectantly**) in the realm of the Holy Spirit, filled with righteousness, peace, and joy (what **expectancy**). For the one who is serving Christ, the Anointed One… by walking (in **expectation**) in these acceptable by God kingdom realities… pleases and is beautiful to God (as He **expects**) and **e**arns the respect of others being approved by **m**en.**

*Those who repent - because you are willing to **c**hange your inner self—your old way of thinking, regret your sin and live a **c**hanged life… I baptize with water (as **expected**), but there is **c**oming a **m**an after me who is **m**ore powerful than I. In fact, I'm not even worthy enough to pick up his sandals. He will (with **expectation**) submerge you into union with the Spirit of Holiness and with a raging fire!**

*And now until then… there (in all **expectancy**) remains: faith (**expectancy's** fruit) - abiding trust in God and His promises… hope (**expectancy's** eternal energy) - confident **expectation** of eternal salvation… love (**expectancy's** eternal essence) - unselfish love for others growing out of God's love for me. But for now, these three, the choicest graces last… but the greatest of these, which surpasses them all… is love.**

---

*Footnotes: Chapter 8 Worthy Words / * See 2 Corinthians 13:14, Revelation 19:10, Revelation 1:8, Romans 14:17, Matthew 3:11, I Corinthians 13:13 - all emphasis is mine and personal paraphrasing built on various translations and versions. *Footnotes: Chapter 8 – none

✧ CHAPTER 8 ✧

✧ ESTABLISHING & EMBRACING … A JOURNEY WITH "3"

As we **e**nter into this *new week* of our *journeying* together and allowing *His* process to have its work in *you… me… us… individually, collectively* - as readers **e**ncountering this book together, and even *corporately* - as those who **m**ost likely are a part of the *family of God, Body of Christ, His Church.* We are learning the importance of *looking* and *looking again,* to not look back, but to *look beyond* from where we are now. It's good to recall that this is **e**specially beneficial to do when it **c**omes to *forming, creating,* and *birthing* our **expectations.**

Oh the power in the purpose of a **three-fold cord word sets** that *He's* revealed to me to *tell* about and wants us to see in this **e**nding part of our *28 day journey* as we go **e**xploring **"3".** I'm sensing just to be still however, in this moment of beginning by taking in a deep breath, inhale and exhale… **m**aking ready for what lies ahead in the *letting go, leaving, and cleaving* to *Him* as *He* by *His Spirit leads, desires, and yes, requires… selah ~*

Now out of this place… I hear the *word of the Lord* arising by the utterance of the stirring of *Holy Spirit* within me… in which is the *testimony of Jesus* within it for that is the *spirit of prophecy…* along with that spiritual gift we're to *eagerly* desire to *edify, encourage,* and *empower* for the benefiting and blessing of others*. *He* is desiring to speak to *you… me… us*, in this place. **Holy Spirit**, give us **e**ars to hear, **e**yes to see, and a spirit that receives and responds to what is being released by **Father** to us ~

It's time My children, My family, My body… wait no longer… for you are the ones I love, have created, and call My expectant sons and daughters that you are… My created and born again ones who believe in fully and receive completely from the fullness of Me as your Father so you can receive all I have for you, and believe all I have said about you, to you, and for you. Then in the believing and the receiving a way will be made for the expectancy of a conceiving from Me by My Spirit and DNA in you. For in My fullness you see, is Me as **Father, Son, and Holy Spirit**. *Have you received Me truly, fully, completely? If you have received Me… You've received Me through My Son and that's how I can call you My created 'born again' ones. But if you have not NOW is the time of your salvation – repent of your sin, turn, and acknowledge* **Him – Jesus** *as your Lord, and be saved yes, but born again in your turning to now living a life that flows from and reflects the new creature you now are in Him – in Me. I love you. Welcome to My family. My family where there are so many that are new in Me, but have yet to receive the fullness of Me as* **Holy Spirit**. *Receiving completely of all My Spirit is My divine design – the intent of what I meant originally and still do. So I say come boldly and ask of Me to receive from Me now… for you have need of Him… as even My Son had need of Him so I sent My Spirit – Holy Spirit to rest upon and in Him so He could be and do what He was purposed and sent to as* **Son of God, Son of Man**. *So He did what He was sent to do completing My covenant requirement for the blood atonement for sin – your sin. And, the ministry I gave Him on earth. Yet knowing in the going He would return to Me so <u>you could receive</u> the fullness of Me, My Spirit – Holy Spirit. For I AM that I AM and I am the Son, and I am the Holy Spirit… the Three in One, a Holy Trinity. I AM that I AM as your covenant keeping redeeming loving Father. So continue in the process with Me and expect to see a greater aligning of your spirit in, to, and with Me."* says the **Spirit** from and as the voice of **Father**, to you… me… us, *His* sons and daughters wonderfully **m**ade **c**reated ones in the FULLNESS of the expressed image and likeness of *Them… Him.*

Now **Holy Spirit,** we ask *You* to fall afresh on us, fill us with a fresh *refilling or infilling and baptizing* of those who are not and desire to be so **Father** can use us and we can fulfill **expectations** of *Yours*... in the same way *Jesus the* **Son** did and is glorified in us when we are and do. Amen.

Don't waste the moment *He* moves upon you to be *His* vessel… that container, who is *His* carrier that becomes *His* conduit to receive the power of the *Three*… and release what *He* has said or is saying. For indeed *He* has an *expectancy* for us to be and do such as we partner with *Him*… and especially as our *expectations* and *His* are aligning more in *the process* of this *journey* we are on together with *Him* in a relationship that's very real, so very relative… so that others may see *Him* in us and want to relate to. Arise… shine!

As always, our desire should be *pleasing Him* so releasing that word was required of me. *Remember*, obedience is key; better than sacrifice. Receiving it is your choice. For *He* wants us entering into this place on the *journey* with *Him* and *together in Him* out of the momentum of the moments with the *words of worth* of **"c"** that we've *encountered* and *experienced* in *the process*. We know it's not just *our journey* with those… but, the *words of worth* through **"e"** and **"m"** that have gone before and remain a part of the *continual cycle* and *circle of momentum* within us that's *forming, growing, developing*… even *creating, birthing,* and *manifesting* within us from *Him* and to mov, pour out, and give freely of *Him* in us to others.

That's what **expectations**, ours, even others, and ours of others… carry within the **expectancy** that arises within them as we *believe, receive,* and *conceive*… *spiritually, relationally,* and *naturally* in *the process*… especially them with *God's*. Oh the cycling and circling of words that represents *this uniquely beautiful powerful process* in the ongoing *ebb and flow* of it all. Don't fight it… just enter into it with and in *Him*.

In doing so, at least from where I sit… is you *gotta love* when such moving with all this **expectant** processing in the **patterns of three** starts *kicking in*. For indeed, *two are better than one, but a* **three-fold cord** *is not easily broken.** We see a kind of principle that develops within it as *He* brings together in words… and through words… the *being, doing,* and *becoming* of what they mean and are, in *their process* going on… and ongoing.

- ❖ *Perhaps*… you've noticed that in this *telling* the coming and joining together of *three words* that are *italicized* throughout… like I above – being, doing, and becoming. But, never underestimate *the power* of just *two*… for they are better than one. It's always begins and ends between just you and *Him*… but it is by *His Spirit*.

Engage, embrace, and be **empowered** by the **expectancy** of these **three-fold cord word sets!**

✧ Day 1: The Journey of "3"… Father, Son, Holy Spirit

Let **expectations**… through this **word of worth's** part to *form, birth, and emerge* in its **meaning & mission… our meditation & motivation… as movement & manifestation** *awake, arise and align* in agreement with divine eternal **expectation**!

With the *Worthy Words* and introduction to this *Chapter* 8 which biblically always points *beyond time, beyond the natural, into new beginnings, and eternal covenant*… all in **m**ind… we **c**an start out and into what *He's* prepared for us in this *pilgrimage* and with what we're **expecting** stirring. There's an **expecting** and believing *He's* shown in my part as the one *writing* and *sharing* in this *telling*… a way to present some interesting, yet potentially good kind of way **c**hallenging, some key *words of worth* grouped together as **"3"**.

It doesn't surprise me that one of my favorite **three-fold cord sets** of words is what *He's* saying to lead out with in *our journey* with and in the exploring of **"3"**. It has become and is still becoming something I've determined to know *Him* in… **in all *His* fullness**… like will begin to be seen in our *"3" words of worth* revealing who *He* is as – **Father, Son, and Holy Spirit**.

In one sense, we know the **e**ssence of *Him* is not **c**ompleted without the *Three*… and yet, we know **He is each of the Three as the Three.** So we see the importance of **e**ach recognized individually and the necessity for all together as **e**chad and *One*. It's all been written and so it shall be. For as we're discovering, *His* '*in the beginning*' is key… when the **Spirit** was sent to *cover, hover, and brood* over the *formless, dark, and void* to *fill it, prepare it, and make it* ready the **e**arth for what it was to be and now is.

Therefore, how **m**uch **m**ore for *you… me… us, His* **c**reated ones to *receive* because we've *believed* and see now **m**ore **c**learly the need for the **Holy Spirit** to fill the void *He's* **m**eant to fill in us to **e**nable us to **c**onceive our *"let there be…"* **m**oments **c**onnected to our purpose *designed and designated* by God and **c**oming from *God and Jesus*, who is the *Word, to, in,* and *through* us.

Now… let's receive **expectantly** from the **Father, Son,** and **Holy Spirit** in us by looking a bit **c**loser at the who *They* exactly are. Remember, any underlying repeating of what's been *rooted, grounded, and established* already… is only to *expand* and *enlarge* in the greater **c**ontext as we explore **m**ore, so the foundations **c**an be *enhanced, enlightened, and enforced* in the **three-fold cord** power in and of *expectancy They* together offer in *Their* togethering.

Individually… yet collectively…

Father… the person and spirit of **Father God, Our Father in Heaven…** the **One** who is **Adonai, Yahweh, Elohim,** and **Lord God Almighty**… and yet He is **El Shaddai** and **El Roi** along with **Jehovah - Rapha, Jireh, Nissi, Tsidkenu, Shalom, Shammah**… and beyond. *Personally* and *affectionately* He is known to be **c**alled by some in *His family*… me, as **Abba Papa, Daddy**… because *He* has been invited and allowed to. *He* will to you too, if *He* hasn't already. And, it's ok to let *Him* be for *He's* your, our *Heavenly Father*… as well *He* **c**an be a form of your earthly one. Remember, *He* did know us before placing us in our **m**other's womb. And, so true are the words of this worship song which say, ♪ *You're a good, good, Father – that's who You are… and, we're loved by Him – it's who we are.** Yet, let no **m**an – glory, but only in **You Father God**… for indeed *You're a good, good, Father*. ♪

Son... the person and spirit of the ***Firstborn* Son *– Only Son of the Father* the *Only Begotten Son*,** the ***Second Adam*, *Yeshua*, *Jesus*, *Jesus Christ*, *Son of God*, *Son of Man*** – along with many other names defining who *He* is by what *He* has done and is. Here's a few: ***Messiah, Savior, Lamb of God, Redeemer, Restorer, Emmanuel, Wonderful Counselor, Prince of Peace, Living Water, Bread of Heaven, Most High Priest, Rose of Sharon, Bright and Morning Star, Mighty Warrior, King of Kings... the Righteous One, Eternal King*** who *sits upon throne*, and in which all His exquisite names stir this song within me... ♪ *I know that Your eyes are like flames of fire, I know that You're hair it's as white as wool, and I know that Your voice it sounds like waters... **Jesus** You're beautiful.** Along with this favorite ♪ ***Jesus, Jesus, Jesus****... there's just something about that Name. **Jesus, Jesus, Jesus***... like a fragrance after the rain. **Master, Savior, Jesus.** Let all heaven and earth proclaim. Kings and kingdoms will all pass away but there's something about that name.* ♪ *

Oh, the transcendent beauty *H*e carries in all *His majesty, splendor*, and yes, *His sovereignty* and in *His mighty* and *matchless name – **Jesus**...* we love *You oh Lover* of our souls.

Holy Spirit*...* the person and spirit of ***Ruach, Ruach Ha-Kodesh, Breath of God... Comforter, Teacher, Advocate, Helper, Revealer, Spirit of Truth,*** *and* ***Spirit of Revelation.*** Also known by the **Seven (7) Fold Spirit**: the ***Spirit of God/the Lord,*** the ***spirit of wisdom, understanding, counsel, might, knowledge,*** and ***the fear of the Lord.* My***...** what imagery and *songs* in the *spirit* arise and ones written as I find myself singing... ♪ ***Holy Spirit*** *You are welcome here... Come flood this place and fill the atmosphere. Your glory God is what our hearts long for. To be overcome by Your presence, Lord.** And... ♪ *No Spirit but the **Holy Spirit**... but the **Holy Spirit**... come, come, come... come, come, come.** For our song ascends saying, ♪ ***Holy Spirit*** *thou art welcome in this place... Omnipotent **Father** of mercy and grace, Thou art welcome in this place.**

There is such an overflow of *Father God* in *His* fullness and filled with ***expectancy*** because *H*e exists in each individually as *Three* persons which are each fully *God...* yet collectively connected, in essence are one – in echad as *Them* – the *Holy Trinity.*

Oh... the *exuberant excellency* and *extravagant exclusive expectancy* contained and carried all-in *Their* all-encompassing empowering *names* and *identities* within those names. What they *stir* and *stimulate* in our ***expectancy*** when spoken alone... and to a greater degree when **expectantly** coupled with our believing in *Them* as the *Three in One.*

Now, add the potential of the *possibilities, promises, and purposes* when receiving in and through them what *His* **expectations** have planned. And, in the prospect of what we can **expect** and how it then propels things moving them all together into *our process* in *the journey*! Not to mention this all magnified and multiplied when joined together in their fullness and completeness as they unquestionably are as ***Father, Son, and Holy Spirit*** - as one.. in the **One** and the only ***True One.***

Therefore, indisputably – in my opinion and perhaps in yours, this *fullness* and *completeness* creates an ***expectant*** capacity with the continual capability of enabling us to not only *believe* and *receive*, but to make us ready to *conceive* of all *power, potential, and purpose* now contained and caried within *us... you... me.* In our earthen yet, *spirit* filled vessels... *formed, fashioned, and made* in the expressed *image and likeness*... of *Them...* woven together with *Their* inclusive exclusive *DNA.* As ***Elohim*** *– Creator* our ***Father*** *H*e is**,** did design this *three-fold cord* of *Them* and all *They are* in us in *His* original intent within human kind as it is. *Remember*, there's proof in the *"HDNA"* where the two DNA helix strand become *three* strands... and, with *three* a better **expectancy.**

It benefits us to recognize *again*... this type of power in this form of *unity* we were created in and is made complete in the *Three in One*... which we know in actuality was first presented to us *in the beginning* in *Genesis Chapter 1* with the creation story. Most would think it came once man – humankind, *Adam and Eve*, were created in the expressed image and likeness of *Them*. But... He had a plan before and for the beginning... that birthed from the **expectancy** and **expectations** of *His heart* and *divine plan* and include *pouring, placing,* and *putting* all the fullness of who He is and with *His utmost excellency* into all. *I AM the foundation and I AM before the earth's foundations were ever laid*... and I believe I AM.

There was and is *His ordering* in all of creation as we see in the *telling* from the start of *His Worthy Word* which validates that He first sent *His Spirit* – **Holy Spirit** – to *move, hover* and *brood* over the surface of the deep... the waters... for what became the earth and the heavens were dark and void... but *His* moving over that which was without form so the essence of who He is as spirit could begin to breathe upon, in and through that which He would now *form, produce,* and *generate His* creative power as He would construct and create according to *His* divine design with *His* order of *timing, cycles, seasons,* and *purposes* - not what man would later determine and establish in the world and is continually attempting to usurp and change what He has, is, and will set into place.

He would and did speak **expectantly** as **Jesus, The Word – which was God**, "Let there be..." and there would be... and it would be very good – *His* good. Not just in the now of that moment, but in the *eternal* vastness of *everlasting to everlasting*... the voice of the *Lord* speaking, creating through it, and causing anticipation in **expectation** of *Him* – who is the *Word* and the power in *His breath* and *voice* through *His Word*, words – to create in our lives as we **embrace** and **expect** them to not return void. To fulfill what they ultimately within them contain in what He has established in all things for us... and for our good, which again, is not the same as the good of the world. *His* good is for *His* good to be revealed in all things.

For as Paul said, *I'm writing to you to further the (**expectant**) faith of God's chosen (**expectancy** filled) ones and lead them to the full knowledge of the truth that leads to (the expectation of) godliness, which rests on the (**expectant**) hope of eternal life. God, who never lies because He cannot... has promised this before time began.** Remember, the *John 1 in the beginning was the Word and the Word was with God and the Word was God*... these words are *His* words in *His Word* which He manifested to men... and in the life of the **Son**... and **expects** to in the lives of *His* sons and daughters too.

Now here's the thing... He is always speaking in *His* time and according to *His* **expectant** plans and purposes *His* "Let there be..." for us in *the process* and *the process* within the *journey* of our lives. Are we listening, hearing, believing, and receiving? *He's our Heavenly* **Father,** *good and giving every good and perfect gift withholding no good thing, to those who will receive.** He came to establish *His Kingdom* on earth through *His family* and that began with *Adam and Eve* who humanly lineage we're a part of... and ultimately then through *Jesus* of whose divine lineage we are a part of *adopted* and *grafted* into. This making a way for us then to also become *His born again* ones as previously discussed and come into being like *Jesus, a son of God*, but who we're first a son of **man.**

There is the term *"sons of God"* to note, mentioned in the *Bible* referring to the *"Nephilim"* that we will not cover here, yet are worthy of your study time to be informed about . Remember in *Romans 8* as we began, making mention of how all the earth waits with ***earnest expectation*** for the *manifestation of the sons of God* to arise... the sons *Father* has made and is making of and in *you... me... us*, who are *born again, His*, and willing to enter into *His* greater required desired things. Like letting *3rd power* types of principles by the *Holy Spirit* working is us to partner with *Him*. Will we let our *expectations* be set higher so the *forming, creating*, and *birthing* of them can enter in more with this *expectancy* not just of a creating to birth... but to manifest that which is fully of our Creator and *Father God*?

On to the *individuality* and the *interconnectivity* in the *collective connection* of *Them* ~ The **Son**... that is the *Word* that **is** the *Beginning* and the *Word* that **is in** the *Beginning*, that is the end eternally as *He* is also the *End*... and has been before the foundations. It was always *Father's* plan to have a *Son* and *sons, children, a family of His heirs*. *He's* a family man and wants *His* heirs to be about *His Kingdom business*...which is also their, our *Father's* business. Walking in it carrying and passing it on to their children and their children's children. It's a *generational relationship* and *process* for sure. And... that's exactly what *Jesus, Son of God and Son of Man* did being about *His Father's Kingdom* business drawing and calling others into *going, doing*, and *being* about it with *Him* through *Him*, for *Him*, and as unto *Him*.

We've looked at some *facets in part* and *portions* pertaining to and in a very simple way in the life of ***Jesus,*** obviously on a surface level since this <u>isn't</u> a book of study, let alone a book of instruction where teaching the *Word of God* is its primary purpose as has been established. It's a *journey* designed to cultivate relationship with *God* in the process and our ***expectancy.***

Keeping in mind... it is a *journey* where with *Him* along in *the process,* the challenges that come and the *quest* for greater *understanding* of and through ***Jesus's*** life and model will arise. Then the knowing and growing to be in the *becoming more like Him*... especially in *yours... mine... our* **expectancy** begins a time to *awaken, arise, and align* in and with *Him*. This yields great benefits and blessings to your life and the life of others. After all *He's* the ***Father's Son*** and so are we... yet beyond our *Messiah, He's* our amazing *big brother, model, mentor, friend,* and more; such relational roles are vital. For ***as He is, so are we*... and are we to be!**

Yeshua... Jesus, whom *I love, adore, worship, and serve,* in this *telling* you've been reading from a *personal life* and relationship based insight perspective, with godly principles primarily revealed, and given to me in <u>my life's walk with *Him*</u> and with other people and ministries *He's* connected me to. It all has included some life and spiritually applicable ***encounters*** and ***experiences*** I've had and still am in the *ongoingness* of *the process* of becoming and being more like ***Jesus.*** Aren't you glad it's a ***relational*** mutually intentional and genuine *personal journey He* desires... not a formulated completing of familiar routines and rituals in all their regulated impersonal ways and means? I am.

The days of *journeying* with our *words of worth* with their meanings and missions, the thoughts they stir, images they produce, feelings they evoke, questions they present, potential answers presented... and fresh perspectives shared are exciting. Along with what they bring forth in their relativity to relationships. Plus, *expectancy* comes from relationship with *Him* and being influenced by ***Jesus's*** *words* together with their connectedness to *His earthly mission, mandate, and message* while here... with it all culminating in *His betrayal, crucifixion, death, burial, resurrection, ascension*, into the eternal of now... which has become ours now, is in our beyond... and carries *His **expected end.***

We know each... the individual and collective aspects of it all are critical to our *identity, inheritance,* and the *inward /outward process* of *His purpose, plans,* and *promises* manifesting in our lives as He **expects**, we **expect**, others **expect**... and in all the realms of the *unexpected* too. The essentiality for **Holy Spirit's** moving and *His* being a part is critical – that is how <u>**Jesus** was doing what *He* did as **Son of God, Son of Man.**</u>

Romans 8 also reminds us... *In fact, the mind-set focused on the flesh (**expects** to) fights God's plan and refuses to submit to His (**expectation** of) direction... because it cannot! For no matter how (**expectantly**) hard they try, God finds no pleasure with those controlled by the (**expectations** of the) flesh. But when the Spirit of Christ comes and makes its home in you and (**expectantly**) empowers your life... you are not dominated by the flesh... but by the(**expectancy** of the) Spirit. And if you are not joined to the Spirit of the Anointed One, you (as **expected**) are not of Him.* *

He's bringing to my recollection somethings too that I read once in a book by *Mahesh Chavda* and this I believe is important ...

> "***Jesus*** *promised that His followers would receive power when the* **Holy Spirit** *came upon them, and that power would enable them to be His witnesses throughout the world. A corollary to this that is often overlooked because it is not directly stated is that with the power of the* **Spirit** *comes the unity of the* **Spirit.** *Divided or unfocused power often dissipates quickly, wasting much valuable energy... The baptism of the* **Holy Spirit** *is not only a baptism of power, but also a baptism of unity. In the work of God's Kingdom, power and unity go together. Where the* **Spirit of God** *holds sway, the people of God dwell in peace and one accord."**

Now that is truth we can stand on. And *corollary,* in case you're wondering means: *outcome, consequence, effect or result.* What a word whose meaning added a dimension needed!

Again, we can stand knowing and living from this truth expressed in the fullness of what he shares as it's back up in *His Worthy Word*. It's according to *His* divine design, resurrected *Jesus* through *dunamis* resurrection power ... that power that was according to the same power that quickened His mortal body resurrecting **Christ** *from the dead**... and <u>now lives in us</u>. **Jesus** knew this... so *He* had to go for *Holy Spirit* to come... and we could receive the *fullness* of the **Three in One**... the **Holy Trinity**.

Unity... it is a *fruit* of the **3rd power principle**, which is connected to *His* goodness, *His* love, and *His* light bringing life and godliness with fruit produced by **Holy Spirit** <u>or</u> the connection is to what is not good; not of the good of God... but filled with ungodliness, evil, and bringing the fruit of destruction, disorder... even wrongful or premature death. The *God* of the *Godhead* choose by *His* design to be *unified* in the *entire process* of creating the earth and all of creation when *He* first sent *His Spirit* and now *He* has sent a part of *Him* as the person of **Holy Spirit,** for all who will receive... not rejecting or denying the fullness thereof.

It is an *infinite* thing... an *intimate* thing... an *intentional* thing... that the **Father, Son, and Holy Spirit**... the **Godhead** fullness as *They* have and are pursuing with *you... me... us,* and all those out their hungry and pursuing more of God! Or... even those just searching and don't know it's *Him* yet, let alone to begin to know the *Them* of *Him* and that they truly do need all which *He* **expectantly** knows and offers as <u>only *He* can</u>. So glad *He* met me there.

Collectively and beyond....

Recently, this wonderful summarizing of thought by *Kent and Beverly Mattox,* came across my path, and I couldn't think of any better time to share in this place as we pursue ending this day with **"3"** regarding the ***Father, Son, and Holy Spirit…***

> *Have you ever considered the profoundness of how the* **Holy Trinity** *of God reflects all three expressions of how we relate to our world? Think about how* **Father** *God encompasses our identity, design, and destiny and how we relate, belong and experience favor with Him and our community!*
>
> *Think about how* **Jesus Christ** *encompasses our priestly and kingly expression as a* **Son** *in this world, and how we can walk in righteous authority and dominion as we abide in Him, respond to the* **Father,** *and move in God's time. Think about how* **Holy Spirit** *encompasses the outward expression and faith acts of the finished work of* **Christ** *in our world, and how we can partner with God to bring reconciliation to all of creation— as we bring heaven to earth.** (**E***mphasis mine.)*

In *Their…* the *Three,* there is an intricate connectivity and communion *oneness* that is obviously exhibited and necessary by design in and for *Their* relationship and representation of the *fullness of God* – the **Godhead,** as *Father, Son, and Holy Spirit.* And yes, there is no difference in what is required at the core of our relationship with and representing of *Them* either. For there is a *good of God* in the diverse, but intertwined ways that *They* are operating in *Their* separateness. Yet, it is truly impossible to bring forth the *better* and *best way…* without their **unified relationship** of **oneness in togetherness.**

Now, from where we are, *expectancy* stirs drawing us to look beyond, from the collective *tellings* as expressed by these others… to move us into the paralleling of the idea of *you… me… us*, in this intricately connected relationship built on *Him* as **Father, Son, and Holy Spirit** which must be *rooted, grounded, and established* in our mutual desire and eternal *expectation* for **His greatest expectancy** as revealed in **His love, covenant,** and ***our purpose*** as **expressed** in **our togethering** in ***Him… in Them.***

E=mc3   eternal energy essence of *El / Eternal God* = **made, molded, manifesting meaningfully,** as **created** in the **comprehensive complete Godhead** to the **3**rd **Power** of *Father, Son, Holy Spirit* in *you… me… us.*

In light of these ***words of worth... Father, Son, Holy Spirit,*** and what's been shared:

❖ *Perhaps... you **Encountered or Experienced a Question or Challenge**?*
   Write it out…

❖ *Perhaps... more has been **Established & Empowered by the Word**?*
   Write what/which…

❖ *Perhaps... it's time for **Engaging & Embracing your Expectations**?*
   Write what's forming…

Reminder: For *clarity, connection, and confirmation* regarding ***expectancy*** being stirred by this ***word of worth***, seek *Him and His Word* first. To possibly assist you in the process the list of **ION** words is available in the Appendix.

*Footnotes: Chapter 8 Day 1 Father, Son, & Holy Spirit / * See Revelation 19:10, I Corinthians 14:1, Ecclesiastes 4:9-12, Romans 8:14-30, Romans 8:6-9, Matthew 7:11, Rom 6:10-11 - all emphasis is mine and personal paraphrasing built on various translations and versions. * See Glory of Zion International / gloryofzion.org / Global Spheres Center - prophetic word of Lord released Pentecost Sunday June 8, 2025 /12 Sivan 5785. * See Father song / Good Good Father by Chris Tomlin.
* See Jesus songs / Jesus You're Beautiful by Jon Thurlow and There's Just Something About That Name by Bill & Gloria Gaither. * See Holy Spirit songs / Holy Spirit by Katie Torwalt and Bryan Torwalt, Jesus Culture / Fear of the Lord (Isaiah 11) by Jaelen Jones, Jasmine Weiler, Mercy Culture Worship, Ryan Smith / Holy Spirit Thou Art Welcome by Benny Hinn.
* See *Mahesh Chavda* / @chavdaministries.org / *The Hidden Power of Speaking in Tongues* p. 80-81.
* See *Kent & Beverly Mattox* / @waio.org / Word Alive International Outreach, Oxford, AL / The Word Alive Daily email news.

✧ Day 2: The Journey of "3"…
Alpha & Omega, First & Last, Author & Finisher

Let *expectations*… through this *word of worth's* part to *form, birth, and emerge* in its *meaning & mission*… *our meditation & motivation*… *as movement & manifestation* awake, arise and align in agreement with divine eternal *expectation*!

To call or know someone by their *name* implies a basic level of *acknowledgement* in a simple manner of *recognition* or *acquaintance* implying they are not a stranger due to the appearance of some degree of familiarity. It can imply a deeper sort of *relationship* too… which forms in a variety of ways and in diverse settings.

These relationships can represent knowing them from the past or present or that they may be a mere stranger. But, a *knowing of them* doesn't necessarily mean you *know them* beyond a basic identifying… because you may have never spoken to them or had any level of personal conversation or relationship with them. All things that mark a moment as a name is spoken.

What an interesting dynamic within *the process* of our *journey* together with each other… and, all the people out there we come into contact with daily. It brings up an important question as we enter this day and part of the journey with **"3"** in the *words of worth* found in these *names of worth*… **Alpha & Omega, Beginning & End, Author & Finisher***

Do you know *Him* and call *Him* by *His* name? How many of *His* precious, powerful names? And… how important is it really if you do or don't… especially these ?

In part knowing and calling someone by name in general, contains within it the potential of pointing to the possibility that there may be some degree of personal connection… or even some level of *relationship*. Therefore, a level of importance is assigned to such knowing because it is customary to some degree as a form of social etiquette or courtesy… and even can be *expected* to another degree, as a form of respect or honor.

Different types of connections and kinds of relationship play a huge role in determining the degree of importance of or in a name. They can carry within a form of context that's good, even essential to know. And yet deeper, what a name conjures up may shed light on its/their purpose, culture, profession, or more because quickly we can 'attach' much to a name. We at times will discover great *expectancy* arising quickly forming, creating, and birthing *expectations* in our common *life social scenarios and situations* where we are continually presented with names. Knowing the meaning of their name in its origins will influence too.

Combine that all with the thought of how does knowing and calling *God* by name or *Him* knowing and calling us by name carry any kind of *expectancy*, *relevance*, or *relativity* in our *relationship* with *Him* let alone our *expectancy* of *Him* or *Him* of us... and because of what it does or doesn't have attached to it?

Let's start by looking at a foundational truth about *Him* and that is… He knows *you*… *me*… *us* by name as is written in both the *Old* and *New Testaments* of the *Bible*. We see here in *Isaiah*… *But now, this is what Adonai— the Lord and One who formed and created you, O Jacob, the One who formed and shaped you, O Israel: "Do not fear for I have (with committed **expectation**) rescued and redeemed you from your captivity as Your Kinsman Redeemer that I am… and I have called you (with **expectancy**) by name, you are Mine.*** And in these words of the *Lord to Moses* from *Exodus*… *"This very thing that you have (with **expectation**) spoken I will do, for you have found favor in My sight, and I (**expectantly**) know you by name."***

We also attest to this truth of *Him* knowing a name and it being accompanied by an acknowledging, in this example from *Jesus*... *"If you (in sincere **expectation**) openly and publicly acknowledge Me... I will freely and openly (as **expected**) acknowledge you before My heavenly Father. But if you publicly deny that you know Me, I will also deny you before My heavenly Father.** *Oh* the full circle of the knowing and acknowledging of a name.

Perhaps... that is why *He* tells us *His* from the very beginning opening an effectual door right from the start with a desire to reveal *His* names... and we know, *He* is the *Door*. Also, an acknowledging of *dimensions* and *facets* within those names connected to their meanings, containing their mission, and purpose, as well as their function and it in the... *I AM that I AM* is always the core.* For I AM is the I AM that is our *God*. From *Genesis 1* thru *Revelation 22 His* names and the fullness therein, are continually being presented to us.

We remember that indeed it started in the beginning,... and **Beginning** is one of *His* names, was *the Word* and *the Word* was with *God,* and the *Word* was *God.* These words are *His* words in *His Word* which *He* manifested to men under *His* inspiration as breathed by *His Divine Spirit* breath which brings forth absolute truth. Here it is as written by *John*...

*In the beginning (with all **eternal expectancy**)... before all time (according to **expectation**) the Living Expression – the Word (Christ) was already there (as **expected**). And the Living Expression was with God, yet was fully God Himself. They were together—face-to-face... continually existing co-eternally with God... in the very beginning. And through His creative (**expectant**) inspiration this Living Expression made all things (from out of His **expectancy**), for nothing has existence – not even one thing... was made that has come into being apart from Him!**

Oh, the *Divine* revealing for *He* had a plan before and for the beginning in the **Beginning**... that birthed from the **expectancy** and **expectations** of *His* heart's master plan... and it included *pouring out, placing,* and *putting* the substance of that which *He* is in *His* utmost **expectant** holy essence and excellency...and as unveiled into and unto all as the *Creator Elohim He* is. *I AM the foundation and I AM before the earth's foundations were ever laid.*

So, let's take a look at something connected that *Paul* shared... *I'm writing to you to further the (**expectant**) faith of God's chosen (**expectant**) ones and lead them to the full knowledge of the truth that leads to (the **expectation** of) godliness, which rests on the (**expectant**) hope of eternal life. God, who never lies because He cannot... for He has promised this <u>before time began</u>.**

To think *He* really had a plan and of you before you began. That included in *His* **expectancy** you... me... us! *He* who is the **Beginning & End... the Alpha & Omega – First & Last**, for how could *He* but not be also the **Author & Finisher** *He* is. For, here we are! The living expressions of *Him* in us, who is the *Living Expression* of the fullness of *Them,* the *Godhead* who is our *God Yahweh, El, Adonai*... just a few of the names we have touched upon the surface of in *our journey* with *Him, Them*... and *as Father, Son,* and *Holy Spirit.*

For we know these names can speak directly of *Him* revealed and expressed in and through *Him* as *Jesus Christ, the Son, Messiah,* or *Yeshua Mashiach*. And, in the name there can be a *form of power* it carries. Rest assured however, that the <u>only power</u> contained in the words which are the names *of God* is <u>**the fullness of the full divine eternal power of the pure essence of the Godhead of Yahweh for all that He is within them**</u>. Indeed there is power in them – *His*, and *in the very act of speaking His name* that power is released. An *omnipotent, omnipresent,* and *omniscient* ever present power full of *His glory, life, light,* and *love*. After all, *at the Name of Jesus every knee will bow and tongue confess that He is Lord.**

The *beyond* holds so **m**uch and in profound ways. Like when the **m**ore of *God* is revealed in an extended way within *His names* and how they are above **e**very and all other names. In the *Beginning* is just that – in *Him* who is the *Beginning* in the *beginning*. *He* is that in the start of the *beginning* of us… the *Beginning* in us… *His* **c**reated ones. In our *beginning* in the *saved* and *born again life* we are living now… in the *purposeful process,* we press forward into on *our pilgrimage* towards the end in the *journey* through and with **"3"** in this *telling.* Endings are key, for *He* is the *End,* and has an *expected end* for us **e**ach and for all things.

His being **Alpha & Omega, Beginning & End, along with Author & Finisher** gives us solid ground to build **m**uch on and **c**redence to our knowing there is an *infinite expectation* that is indeed an *eternal* thing. It is also an *intimate* thing as **m**uch as an *intentional* thing in the spirit essence of all things that *He* **c**ame as, **c**ame to be… and *He* **c**ame and will be – **He who was, is,** and **is to come** in the *Three, the Trinity* **to** *us, you and me…*and **in** *you… me… us…* *Him* as the *Three… as Them.* Amen.

In our *amen* and our greater *'yes and amen'*… is a **be it so**… and a **let there be**. The *be it so* and *let there* be of *Him* in *His fullness* as we see in *His Word, will,* and *ways* **m**anifesting in *the process* of *the journey* of relationship we're in together. So what is our *let there be* and *be it so*? Does it partner with *His*? Does it refer or relate to a name of *His* revealed to you?

Where we are speaking and releasing our *amen* in *Him*… especially in the *forming, creating, and birthing* of our *expectations* in this kind of *expectancy* that does help aligns us with what is written in the writing of *His Word* for our now and beyond. For it **c**an be… and **m**ay it be, likened unto *His*… like it was when the world began in *His* speaking of *"Let there be…"*. It certainly stirs the waters of the **c**reative power of *expectancy* **c**oming from, in and through the *Word*… *Him* and it in us.

For *He* is not just these and in these… but in the *beyond* of these where we **c**an see the **m**anifesting of *Him* also being… *Jesus Christ… who is the same yesterday and today and forever.** The same *God,* who is these things will never fail *you… me… us.* For *He* is *Shammah,* the *Lord* who is there… *watching, waiting,* and *working* **m**oving in *beginning, ending*… and, in the **m**iddle and **m**idst all things while *He* is there. The **c**urrent of *His* **c**ontinual **c**onstancy of *His* activity in the world around us therefore, in our lives

If we invite and allow *Him* in as the **Beginning** and in our beginnings… there will be in *the let there be,* as well in our *endings* and with *Him* and the **End – Alpha & Omega – First & Last**. There's nothing like *finishing well* which in part **c**omes from letting *Him* be the **Finisher** that *He* is. There however remains, a greater need in that we **m**ust in our inviting and allowing… **let Him be completely** the **Author** *He* is so *He* **c**an be the **Finisher** *He* is.

An *author* is defined simply to be a *writer, creator, designer, developer… an originator.* Hmmm… I'm hearing **c**oupled with this that it **m**ust be *His original intent.* **M**ay the intentions which are *His* be ours in *all things, always,* and *in all ways* in *the process,* in our *expectations* … and not just be… but, **m**anifest fully.

For in the *free will* that *He* has given us… we are to be stewards in our ownership, due to the *Lordship* we've given *Him*… in being the little "a" and "f" *authors'* and *finishers* as well, determining the little "b" and "e" *beginnings and endings* as we walk out our daily lives… and, as we *think, feel, or determine* what is *good, needful,* and *right.* However… and preferably, if we are truly *His*… it **m**ust be *His* desired and required… good and right in *His sight* according to

His Word, will and *ways* that ultimately **m**atters. For it **m**anifests with all its *benefits, blessings*, and for our *best* success as its *essence* is His **expectancy**!

So from *His Worthy Word* there are some words that would be good to remember as we **m**ove through this part of the *course*… *Go ahead (***expectancy*** is waiting) and **m**ake all the plans you want… but it's the Lord who will ultimately (***expectantly***) direct your steps. We are all in love with our own (***expectant***) opinions, convinced they're correct (as the **expectations** they partner with). But, the Lord (in all His **expectancy**) is in the midst of us, testing and probing our every (***expectant***) motive. Before you do anything, put your trust (and* **expectations***) totally in God and not in yourself. Then every plan you* **m***ake will (as* **expected***)succeed. The Lord works everything together to accomplish His purpose. Again I say… within your heart you can (***expectantly***) make plans for your future, but the Lord chooses… ordering the steps you are to (in every* **expectation***) take to get there.* *

And, there it is indeed… *and I am (***expectantly***) sure of this as I pray in great (***expectant***) faith for you all… fully convinced that He – the One, who has begun this gracious good work in you will faithfully continue (toward His* **expectations** *in) the process of maturing bringing it to completion until the unveiling of our Jesus Christ.* *

His Lordship in our lives is what predominately overall gives place to such. For we are *His* – *He* owns us and willingly by our **c**hoice. And, we in our part through good stewardship… as we walk in partnership with *Him* the *beginning, middle, end*… and, **e**verything in-between align. Because, *He* being the *One* **who was and is and is to come**… is also within the *what* was, *what* is, and *what* is to **c**ome in the **c**ircle and **c**ycles being **c**reated building upon one another **m**erging and **c**onverging it all *together in Him*. This brings a distinct **c**onnection for our **expectations** **e**mbedded in the **e**ndless *endeavoring, encountering and experiencing* from this positioning of oneness **c**reates for the **m**anifestation of *His* in ours.

> ❖ *Perhaps… His* names then… in what they speak representing *His* eternal existence and nature, *His* **c**hoosing to actively participate with us in who *He* is – not just be, and the unchanging, trustworthy, and grace filled loving facet of *His* **c**haracter and being… well, they certainly give us **m**uch to *consider, contemplate,* and **e**ven let be **c**ultivated in us as we **e**nter into this **m**utual desire that postures us as well… to **e**ngage in *meaningful, purposeful, and intentional relationship* with *Him* as ALL that *He* is. And… it's definitely not a formula nor formulated. Yet… it is **c**onnected if we'll have **e**yes to see… to the **e=mc3**… by *His Spirit* 3rd **power**… and enabling us to **e**nvision in *His presence, power, and purposes* Him being such in name and in ALL that *He* is as… **Alpha & Omega, Beginning & End, Author & Finisher.**

Oh… to **c**onsider… to let our **expectancy** fully go there… along with our **expectations** take us there. To let the our times of **c**ontemplation take us beyond the normal and natural, into the timelessness eternal and supernatural realm of the beyond in *who He is… what He can, has and will do*. And, to let ourselves be in a place of **m**eaningful intimacy where *awe, wonder, reverence, and honor*… for *His sovereignty, majesty, beauty, perfection*… and, the yet to be revealed **m**ysteries… **c**ultivate in us a **c**ontinual *hunger, thirst, and desire*… for **m**ore of **Him** and **ALL that He is**… for *as He is so are we*!

With those thoughts in **m**ind… let me share an overall kind of glimpse of a relevant testimony to *His* leading and revealing to me out of such a place in my life… where my **expectancy** is still unfolding and in how *He* is so very good to be **c**ontinually uncovering **m**ore.

It began with *Him telling* me in the way *He* does by *His Spirit*… that it would be good to always return to *Genesis* with any principle, belief, question, doubt, topic, issue, concern… actually, in general all things… and particularly to chapters 1-3 especially. That everything I would have need of overall… it, would be found there in the foundations He established… *in the beginning*… in what *He* said… in *His* original intent – which opened a door originally to me learning about the "*law of first mention*" that I've shared about previously.

He would within it - *Genesis*, the first book where's a lot of *first mentions*… give *revelation, direction, and understanding*. And, in doing so… *He'd* also meet me there to reveal more of *Himself* and more regarding how important who *He* is in *you… me… us* essentially is. Along with how important the foundation laid there is to the eternalness of who we are, what we're here for, and within the how and why would be something I'd begin to discover, know, and live out of – out of *Him* as **Alpha & Omega, Beginning & End (First & Last), and Author & Finisher**. He is so very good!!! And to think… now I'm here *telling* you… and offering *His* same *counsel, guidance, and direction* simply to you. Yes…for *the journey* where in *the process* **expectancy** creates… for a life that is better because the blessings and benefits of *His* **expectation**s come together in and with ours for us to **embrace, engage,** and **be empowered!**

So… we end now where we *began*, only to propel us into another new *beginning*. What *John* was given to release to those who would read it, regarding the revealing of *Jesus Christ* in the unveiling of the words expressed in *Revelation 1*… here is a portion that will lead us to the *7 Letters to the Churches*. May it serve as a type of seal to the deposit made in this day "**3**" of *our journey* and *process*. Like usual, you may want to soon read it of this anointed chapter with all its powerful imagery and revealing.

*Blessed… happy, prosperous, (**expected**) to be admired… is he who reads and those who hear the words of the (**expect** filled) prophecy, and who keep the things which are written in it heeding them and taking them to heart (in all your **expectations**); for the time of (**expectant**) fulfillment is near…. I am (**expect Me to be**) the **Alpha and the Omega** - the **Beginning and the End**. Who is (in eternal **expectation**) existing forever and Who was continually (in **expectant**) existing in the past… and Who is to come, the **Almighty** - the **Omnipotent**, the **Ruler** of all." says the Lord God.**

Be it so and so be it Lord… for Your glory and Your expected end.

<u>In light of these *words of worth*... **Alpha & Omega, Beginning & End, Author & Finisher,**</u> and <u>what's been shared</u>:

- ❖ *Perhaps... you* **Encountered or Experienced a Question or Challenge**? Write it out...

- ❖ *Perhaps... more has been* **Established & Empowered by the Word?** Write what/which...

- ❖ *Perhaps... it's time for* **Engaging & Embracing your Expectations?** Write what's forming...

Reminder: For *clarity, connection, and confirmation* regarding *expectancy* being stirred by this **word of worth**, seek *Him* and *His Word* first. To possibly assist you in the process the list of **ION** words is available in the Appendix.

*Footnotes: Chapter 8 Day 2 Alpha & Omega, First & Last, Author & Finisher / * See Revelation 1:3-8 Isaiah 43:1, Exodus 33:17, Matthew 10:32-33, Exodus 3:14, John 1:3, Genesis 1, Revelation 22, Titus 1:1-2, Hebrews 13:8, Proverbs 16:1-4, 9, Philippians 1:6, Revelation 1:3-8 - all emphasis is mine and personal paraphrasing built on various translations and versions.

✧ Day 3: The Journey of "3"... body/soul/spirit

Let **expectations**... through this **word of worth's** part to *form, birth,* and *emerge* in its **meaning & mission**... *our meditation & motivation*... *as movement & manifestation* awake, arise and align in agreement with divine eternal **expectation**!

*Listen (with **expectancy**) **My** child intently and intentionally... giving attention to **My** words which will teach you; inclining your ear to **My** sayings (**expectantly**). Do not let them depart from your eyes; fill your **mind** and thoughts (and **expectations**) with **My** words, keep them in the **midst** of your heart (in **expectancy**) until they penetrate deep into your **spirit**; for they are life to those who (**expect** to) find and unwrap them... and impart true life and radiant health (**expectancy**) to all their flesh – into the **c**ore of their being. Keep your heart, your inner **m**ost being (as **expected**) with all diligence, for out of it flows the wellspring of life.**

*May these words, as established in Your Word Father, hover and brood by Your Spirit over this lengthier day in the journey with "3" and us together with You. You know where we **e**ach are, where we need to be, what we need to see, and what/how we need to receive or **e**ven let go of. Something You'll be good to reveal as we invite and allow You to have Your way and in the depth of what this day presents. In Jesus' Name, Amen.*

Like the words released above, scripture always presents us with a picture of the goodness of the heart of *Father* to all who *read, study*, and desire to *know* it and *know Him* through it... and, **e**specially for *His* **c**hildren who do so. He's always good and *His Word* is proof of *His* continual, consistent covenant love, particularly to redeem and restore us back to *His* right *order*, for *His purposes*, and according to *His plans*. Let's believe to remember this and see such as we **e**nter in.

When we **c**ome upon a topic or subject within *His Word*, we tend to want to go right to what we believe to be at the first read the nuts and bolts of it. There, desiring to have a part in the *process* is our assumption and or our perspective. We **m**ay already have somewhat of a foundation regarding what we're reading shares, and so there's a tendency to have an *"Oh... I know this verse"*, *"I remember reading this before..."* or **e**ven an *"I didn't really get this one"* **m**oment. Haven't we all been there and **c**an relate to some degree or another?

Along **c**omes possible past thoughts, perspectives, **encounters** or **experiences** related to it and yes, **e**ven **expectations** it *stirred, formed,* and *birthed in* us that have been **m**et or unmet... possibly put aside... with no **expectancy** to understand or apply to it, let alone to search it out further. It happens... and these **e**lements **m**atter affecting us in various ways.

In these times there's a discovery waiting to **e**njoy and **e**ven look forward to in *journeying* with *Him* through *His Word* full of *His tellings*. For what is being hindered or lingering out there on the peripheral *waiting, wanting*, **expecting** to **c**ome in... is a needful part which blesses us in the *process* of our searching and knowing that's awaiting.

Entering now into our next *"3"* words of worth – **body, soul, and spirit** always be prepared for how *He'll* bring a related *concept, topic,* or *subject* – a *word* **e**ven that's been waiting out there with a **c**onnection **m**oment. In a new way you've not thought or given a place of perspective as a viewpoint or example. It **m**ay be a different kind of way and from a broader form of **c**onnecting and intertwining then you're used... so willingness to **engage** is good.

The potential is great for *you... me... us,* to start to *see* how these forming's of **three** may just have a place that **m**atters and carry a piece to **c**onnect to all these *three parts* we're **m**ade up of, **e**specially individually. But, in a profound sense, is when a **c**onnection starts to arise and emanates in the collective unfolding of affects upon and in the functioning of our ***spirit, soul, and body*** and in their *togethering*. Yes, I changed the order which we'll soon discover why.

It does require inviting and allowing *Him by His Spirit* to help us *look, look again, and look beyond* into what we *know* the *three* to be primarily. The examples used will be somewhat simple and short due to time. So let's begin with how they *are ordered,* so to speak in man's defining and looking at what *His Word* suggests in another form of ordering from how *He originally divinely designed* the *three* within us. First… a few questions for you to begin to ponder and chew on.

What are your *body, soul, and spirit*? What do you say they are? Why would the change I made above from ***body, soul and spirit*** to ***spirit, soul and body*** be important… and more importantly in what *order* do you say they are… and why would that even matter?

These are for your personal answering as you move through this longer than usual and deeper kind of day. An answer to any or all doesn't need to manifest, but a receptivity to any seeds being sown into the soil of the answers is recommended. As always it up to you and to how much you include *Him* - the ***Three***.

Yes, we've touched on ***body, soul, and spirit*** somewhat before. There is now a circling in a cycle of revelation to unfold in *looking, looking again, and looking beyond* and as *He* brings this opportunity ***expectantly before us*** to come it with *Him* for the *continuing* of *His sharpening* and calling up into more of *His Divine* purpose and will… with its ***expectancy.***

For starters, a general knowledge based summary of meanings and in an intellectual *Greek* kind of mindedness will present some defining that include but not are not limited to:

BODY… *the physique, form, figure, physical frame/framework of a human being* or object.

SOUL… *a non-physical immaterial part of a human being, conscious, personality, identity, character.*

SPIRIT…*a non-physical immaterial part of a human being, it can be the **soul** too, the seat of character, emotions, a part of humans which may give life, energy, power to them.*

Now, let's add some *spiritual biblical perspective* in the meanings and defining that would be considered more *Hebraic* and aligned with *God's* original intent when *He* created man.

SPIRIT… *the vital life force/source if in God seen as His divine active presence, and principle factor creating and sustaining life in living human beings as it refers to breath and spirit of God too, it can include the mind, will and emotions, and some believe comes with the capacity to connect in relationship.*

SOUL… *the mind, will, and emotions in a human being's inner self, the ability to feel, think, and act, capable of relationship with God and other humans.*

BODY… *a part of the unified whole human being that God created from the earth/dust/dirt and breathed life into, it is the temple or dwelling place of the Holy Spirit.*

Now, let's recall what we have established… because this is just a *day journey,* so we'll keep this relatively general, yet adding some depth as we proceed. A basic extension to the defining's above presents two potential categories for them: a ***tripartite*** view*; a trichotomy* with tri being all three – ***body, soul, spirit*** each as separate, but connected together in functioning. OR a ***bipartite*** view*; a dichotomy* with *di* being two – the ***spirit and soul*** together as one unit with the ***body*** separate, yet there is a connection in functioning.

From what's been shared up to this point regarding my line of thought... is just as they are entwined and embedded in scripture, my primary belief flows from *Him* m**aking us *triune beings*** following *His* divine design and pattern of the *Trinity* expressed, and functioning in *Him* as **Father, Son, and Holy Spirit**.

Though I respect and understand a bipartite dichotomy view as I did follow this belief to some degree for a time... it's not my heart to argue but to encourage and enlighten you in a way to search all things out for yourself in *His Word* and through *His leading, revealing, and teaching*. *He's* not led me, as shared, to write in a theological exegesis format in this book, but to share a simple sampling of thought to create awareness and stir *expectancy* to know.

It's about the overall essence of *Him* and *His Word* coming alive for you in *the process and journey* of life with the fullness of *Him* actively having access to *move, flow, and work* within sincere intentional relationship because of the power of *Them*, the *Three* at work and now within divine design of our ***spirit, soul and body*** for *He* wants all of what we are, not just who we are. Life's **encounters** and **experiences** in *Him* flowing and operating through our ***spirit, soul, and body***... tends to bring forth a desiring to secure how we're aligned in it all with *His Word, will, and ways* which undoubtedly has *influenced, directed,* and *manifested* in my **expectancy** to search and know. Could it be an area where you desire a greater measure of knowing ? *He* will meet you, me... us there!

The desire to seek *Him*, know *Him* and with all my *heart, soul, strength*, and *mind*... and it wrapped in obedient, passionate, intentional, intimate, desire... with the *expectancy* to be pleasing to *Him* is always key for me. Equally as a committed lifestyle manifesting in that of continual *surrendering, submitting,* and *putting everything aside* so to come always with clean hands and a pure heart, determining to know nothing but *Him... and Him more fully, completely, wholly.* To live from being that which *He* made new and whole in *Him*; holy as *He* is holy – ***spirit, soul, and body*** aligned in *His expectancy* and love. *Perhaps...* you can appreciate and relate to this desire and commitment.

It is ESSENTIAL to point out, that as we enter more fully into this from *Genesis*, where *He* always directs me, we can look at the ordering as designed in *His original intent* that we return to once we're *saved; born again*. Sin separated man... us from *God,* and from the fullness of *His* divine design and plan which always goes back to the garden. They were flowing in divine order aligned through *communion, conversation,* and *connection* by their **spirits** with their and our *Creator God's spirit,* naked, unashamed and in fullness of *Them*.

After they disobeyed *God's* directive, buying the lie *"Did God really say...?"* and sin entered into them through eating of the *Tree of the Knowledge of Good and Evil* that revelation and recognition of the fact came they were indeed *'naked'*- uncovered. It's seems like a small detail... but it's actually vital to recognize seeing its underlying relativity and relevance and in our relationship with *Him* today.

In the *fullness* of our new man is a born again ***spirit***, *with a **soul** and living in a **body*** which is the order now. Our being returned and redeemed means <u>all</u> things have been made new with sin atoned for reconciling us back into *original ordering* being restored so we live now from *Him* in us, *Him* with us, and partaking from *Him* who is our *Tree of Life*.

Let's look now with this in mind at what we see in the *Tree of Life of His Worthy Word*... *"Now, if anyone is enfolded, grafted into and joined to Him by faith in Him as Savior... into Christ (as He **expectantly** ordered), he has become an entirely new person... a new creature reborn and renewed (in all eternal **expectancy**) by the Holy Spirit. All old things that are related to the old* *order – our previous moral and spiritual condition… have (as expected) passed away… vanished. Behold, everything (as expected) is fresh and new things have come… because spiritual awakening (in His expectancy) brings a new life. For all these things (with their expectations) are from God, who reconciled (as expected) us to Himself through Christ… making us acceptable to Him.**

When you're on a *pilgrimage*… as you might have decided this really is a form of one and **spiritually**, you determine to acknowledge the *'why'* at the foundation of your reasoning for desiring to take one. And… it seems to come as you realize you're more consistently *recognizing,* **encountering,** *and* **experiencing** the uncovering in the discovering of just how **spiritual** your life really is… and or that you desire it to be as *you… me… we* are being called *expectantly* up higher and into more of *Him*. Oh, indeed it is a *process*.

It's ok for life and things to be **spiritual** and operating in and from our **spirits** now as the primary leader in our tripartite/triune being with our **soul** and **body** having their place. But, they're not by any means any more to be in the *"driver's seat"*. Our **spirit** is being led now by *Holy Spirit* as *He* partners with *God's* plans, purposes, and *His* **expectancy**. Remember, what was just expressed above in *His Word* and rest in knowing it.

Draw now through these words from *Brian Simmons of The Passion Translation*, to add some perspective and establish an empowering; as they empowered me in receiving from them…

> *As believers, we are regenerated by the Holy Spirit. We are indwelt by the Spirit, baptized by the Spirit, and sealed by the Spirit. When the Holy Spirit regenerates us, we are made new, born again. We are indwelt—the Spirit lives inside of us, taking up residence in our hearts. We are baptized with the Holy Spirit, which means we are fully immersed in His power and presence. And we are sealed with the Spirit, confirming that we belong to God and are set apart for His purpose.*
>
> *Do you realize what that means? The Holy Spirit is in you. He is not a distant figure, not something you experience once and move on from. He is alive, active, and present in every moment of your life. The Holy Spirit is the one who teaches us, guides us, and empowers us. He is the anointing, the oil, the wind, and the cloud of glory. He is the one who makes us able to do what we cannot do on our own.*

This is certainly a *process* and discovery that has had to unfold and be presented to us by *Him* especially in certain *seasons, places, and parts* of *our journey* and *process* with *Him*. Maybe you can relate to what I'm sharing? No running from the idea either if you're truly *His*, for as *His* our life now is as the **spirit being** *He* made us to be and *spiritually prioritized*

- ❖ *Perhaps…* this is a good time to share a type of cautionary word with you because we do encounter many things that come from others **expectations** *and perspectives* of us – not to mention the *projection* of theirs onto us. For example, I've settled it and know how my life is to be lived and it's first for and unto *Him*. That means it's a relational **spiritual** thing first as I'm *His* and in the world, but not of it anymore. And yes… more and more I'm likening it to that of a *pilgrimage*. In it there have been times when ones, for whatever reason believe it would be good for them to share or even project their *opinion, viewpoint, or conclusion* of the life I live… which is often expressed in un**expected** words. I'm reminded of these… *"You're just to heavenly (or* **spiritually***) minded to be of any earthly good."* Ouch… but, I think I *see* some hands raising out there… as you may have heard these words before… possibly even said them before. That's ok – I have too. You know what to do – I did. In it all, *He* made a way for me to *see* a thread of truth could be in what had been said. But, *He* knew my heart, and the thread of *His* red blood and fiery love was, and is truly greater. For in it all *His redemptive purposes* work… and work to bring all things together for *our…my* good and did, because I…*we*, love *Him* and are called according to *His* purposes.*

Sadly, comments like this give way to a *projection* of a kind of *perception,* with a tone of *sarcasm* or criticism often, carrying an *implication* of a *lack* of practical *application* and responsibility to **engage** in realistic *interaction* as an **expectation** daily in the real world. Therefore, accompanied with it *rejection* can arise among other things. (Did you see those **ION** words?) Please seek *Him* to help you through this if you relate. Your **spirit and soul** are affected by such… and yes, your body may bear connected effects.

Hope arises in the midst of it all… as there's a side of this that says the potential is there to inspire greater earthly good, for this way of living provides a framework connected to godly *morality, meaningfulness, purpose,* and *godliness* – and reasonably by *His Word* it be unto *holiness* in *His* righteousness. Our **soul** is certainly apart of all this *process*… and all the more reason our **spirit** must arise to lead being led by *His Spirit.*

For me… this added to some things already attacking and affecting my body the first time I heard it. Already I was in a vulnerable place in life. Not too long after that time – in *His* timing, *He* helped me see how a kind of *"hope deferred"* was setting in, and now in part through that comment being made as it came from someone I *spiritually* admired and didn't want to disappoint. Unknowingly I bought into it in a way at first, giving a place of *access* to the enemy to *accuse* and *attack*. To the degree that a type of infirmity linked with it in my body providing a place for it to go and try to take up residency grieving me **spirit, soul and body**. *He* was so very good in how and what *He* revealed regarding it all making a way for me to repent, turn to *Him* receiving forgiveness for my part, extending forgiveness too, and healing came as that root was removed with *hope being restored* and as an anchor in my **soul.**

This of course, is shared from a personal testimonial perspective, for how revelation given by *Him* to a connected experience playing a part. It doesn't always happen that way for everyone but can. The value in it does need to be pointed out as there is a battle in our *self* that goes on in *the process* of growing by our **spirit** and our **soul** requiring a maturing and submitting along with our **body** having to yield to truth and the freedom it brings to be *healed, healthy*…and *free* for *He* sets free indeed.

Until you know or have been in a place where a form of vacillating between two opinions creeps in to or a lack of awareness arises to what's really going on… you can't fully appreciate how things can come attempting to determine and decide much for you or about you either way. This should help us extend grace to ourselves and others… and understand why I'm heading in this momentary direction in hopes to release some additional insight.

For, when your **expectancy** is connected to and coming, at least in part from *Him* and *His personal, intentional,* and *purposeful* drawing and calling you, you may find everything in you **spirit** *and* **soul**, has a knowing and desires to respond. And, it's so very good when your response comes through your *"hineni"…* Hebrew for *"Here am I"* or *"Here I am Lord."*… signifying the **encountering** of submission in an *agreement alignment* form, and a moment of **expectancy** manifesting in *the process* at hand and working within **spirit** and **soul**.

The opposite can happen as well, when you, me… we, go our own way instead of *His* due to varying *reasons, different or unmet expectations,* including the *unexpected*… but all representing a type of *disconnect* within our *soul,* in its old nature flesh and *carnality*... our *spirit*... and yes, our *body*, in the flesh it is... and it all in part or full with *Him.*

He is good to send help in **m**any ways. One way is seen in how *He* brings those who are **c**arrying words of life to us, **e**specially from *His Word* that will speak into *you*... *me*... *us*. These words **m**inister to our *spirit* and our *soul* as well our *body.* Words *He* will use from His Word to ground and root us in what we truly need and that really needs to be sown into our life then and **c**ontinually. It's so amazing when *He* **c**onnects us to *special sister and brother friends or leaders* who know we're together in this journey and process as *His* family first... so they freely impart **m**uch assisting in our *growing, maturing,* and an **e**stablishing in the sowing their a part of... which grows deep within the soil of us producing **m**ore of *Him.*

Let's turn to a sowing of *His Word* that **c**omes to us through *Jeremiah* who in *Chapter 6* presents to the people of *God* a strategy of underlying importance **c**arrying a type of principle it **c**ontains to be shared... *Thus says the Lord, "Stand by the roads and look (**expectantly**); ask (**expectantly**) for the ancient paths (in all **expectation** to receive), where the good way is; then (**expect to**) walk in it, and you will (**expect to**) find rest for your **souls**.**

My, the times *He's* taken me and others together with me to these words to *align* in them, *apply,* and *activate* what they hold and how *He* extends *His counsel, guidance, and direction* in them. For *He* knows all things *He* wants for our success as we *stand, look, ask,* and say our *"**We will.**"* At times however, *other words* are what we listen to and **e**nd up not walking in that good way or finding that promised rest for **soul.**

Words... they **c**an be hurtful or harsh, help or be a hand up. Within **e**ach lies potential to lead and lend their power which starts to form something... as they're **m**oving to **e**ntrap or inspire us to say, *I'm available, ready, willing...* to obey and in the wherever, whatever is required and whatever way *He* leads... or the opposite. Hence... a battle **c**an begin within us and sometimes outside too... a type of *war at the door* of these **threshold moments**. This is why our **soul m**ust work together with our **spirit** under *Holy Spirit's* direction in these times.

Times where the person of who we fully are: *physically, naturally, and spiritually* and all that is stirring within us *awakens, arises* and attempts to *align* with an **expectancy** – but whose? The anyone or anything influencing and directing our **expecting,** including what within **m**oves to work in this way of a *three dimensionality* **spirit, soul** and **body c**onnection.

We **c**an extend this now to see further in the *telling response* to what *Jeremiah* revealed in a fairly simple strategy to those who heard it. What began to stir and what they gave place to arising in it... as their response **c**ame in *three* words that *awakened, aligned, and arose* in and from them in their *soul*... "<u>**We will not! That's not the path we want.**</u>"* Oh my!

The moments where we've, if we are honest... had to *recognize, repent and turn,* to return to *Him*... *His Word, will and ways* because *you*... *me, we* have said in our own way, "**We or I will not.**" *That's not the path or the way we want."* In our "Here I am <u>not</u>... we are <u>not</u> here" so don't **expect** from us... or me, a *'hineni.* Not an **e**asy place or a place *He* desires. You know there are things *He* requires for those who are *His* including to be obedient and respectfully adherent. But trust me... we're going to see where this is all going and our **expectancy** in it all will be key. *Holy Spirit*... keep leading us on.

In *Genesis 22*, a small, but significant piece presents a powerful **e**xample seen in *Abraham's* response to *God* when *He* requires *Him* to sacrifice his treasured son *Isaac* whom he *loved.* He responds with his *"hineni"* and it drawing us back to a weaving and **c**onnecting *He's* doing. Every part of *Abraham* and *Isaac,* who biblical historians say *Isaac* was **m**ost likely in his early thirties at that time... what they were being required to *engage* in through this *life and death* defining **m**oment of decision which certainly took some working out between the *spirit, soul* and *body*... and it power to influence *expectancy*.

How our *soul,* led by our *spirit* **m**ust settle some things in a deciding and determining of some things. Interestingly, this is the first **m**ention of *hineni* in *His Word* along with the first **m**ention of the word *love* and all within the same **c**hapter. Biblically they say **22** is the number for *personal revelation manifesting.* It did for them and **c**an for us!

Can you believe how *He'll connect, confirm,* and *even convince* us how vital the involvement of the fullness of our *spirit* and *soul,* along with our *body* is... because of *His* great love for us? And because the design is *His*, the plan is *His* and we've seen in in this life altering moment... with a **c**onnection to *His before the foundations of the world* to rescue us wholly, **c**ompletely including what we are **m**ade up of. That's **c**ovenant love's *expectancy*!

God created us fearfully and wonderfully in the image and likeness of *Them* as *He* did with a *soul* and it is good in all that it is as a *mind;* our brain/intellect, *will;* **c**hoices, reasoning, rationale, and *emotions;* feelings... and it all **c**onnected to our fleshy **c**arnality, with it all working together in place within our *body.* *His* **c**reative order of *original intent.* Remember too... *He* is the *Lover of our Soul.*

He designed it so our *spirit* would lead our *soul* and *body* both and desirably in oneness once returned to a reconciled right ordering that comes from being unified together *in, with, from, and through His Spirit* and our *born again spirit*... now a *new man* with a *new nature*, *His*, and living as a *new creature* being one with *Him*, the *One*. Some *Hebraic* thought puts the *spirit* and *soul* together. But through revelation *Yeshua* unveiled... and the **c**arrying of it through the apostles teaching, in particular *Paul*, we **c**an be assured that we are *three-part* beings just as *God* represents *Himself* in the *Three*.

Therefore, let us ponder on these words from *His Word*, as kind of decree and declaration over ourselves... *I am – we are, complete in Christ and the fullness of God dwells in me and I'm full of (the **expectancy** of) spiritual wealth. All the treasures of wisdom and knowledge dwell in me... in us, through Christ Jesus who (as **expected**) was the complete fullness of deity in human form... and now our completeness is found in Him. For we are completely filled with God as Christ's fullness overflows (**expectantly**) within us. He is the Head of every kingdom and authority in the universe! Through our union with him we have experienced circumcision of heart. All of the guilt and power of sin has been cut away and is now extinct because of what Christ, the Anointed One, has accomplished for us.** Amen – be it so and so be it *Lord.** *Selah....*

It's been said that *our lives are not defined by any one action but by a sum of our choices.* Does the same hold true biblically... spiritually? Overall, we **c**an settle into the fact that there's a variety of scripture that points to this being true. However, we also know one **c**hoice **c**an **c**hange things to either direction positive or negative... as well as for good or evil.

> ❖ *Perhaps*... that's something I think we **c**an all relate to and extend grace to ourselves as the *spirit, soul, and body* we are... and to others when realizing it. And, it's something we **c**an always seek *Him* about asking, *"Is that You Lord speaking, directing, moving, drawing... ?" "Help me receive in what I perceive as I desire to hear clearly and ask You to bring clarity in connection and confirmation quickly to me - my spirit by Your Spirit."* If we haven't asked and already listened to a voice we're uncertain is *His*... we **c**an ask *Him...* "*Father was that You speaking to me?*" By *His Spirit – the Spirit of Truth*... and *Truth* in love will reveal. *Remember, Jesus* needed *Holy Spirit* to walk as *Son of Man*,

Son of God on the earth. So we have obvious need of *Holy Spirit* too or why would *Jesus* go to send *Him* to us as the *Father* ordered. *He* is to help in many ways which include but are not limited to *leading, directing, and convicting/correcting* us. And, I stand in the belief that it is how *He* was able to live by *His* spirit as *Son of Man*… with a **soul** in a **body** like we do. Thus, being able to claim *He* understood the *testing, temptations and trials* we go through living in world as we do for in *Hebrews* it tells us *He was tempted in all ways like we are as humans, but He did not sin.** Selah ~

They, Adam and Eve, chose to use their *free will* to listen to the voice of deception that spoke to them using the idea of questioning… which most often opens a door to *doubt, confusion,* and *uncertainty*. He, the serpent, knew to ask, "*Did God really say?*"… along with enticingly presenting the fruit on the tree which *he* knew would speak to that the *inner desire* of their **soul** and *flesh*. They both ultimately responded to what *he* said overriding and disregarding what *God* had said with the result of sin… which changed everything.

They could have chosen to continue to listen to the voice of their *spirit* within *Him* that knew *Him* and what *He* had said, what *He* faithfully had and still was providing to meet all their needs… waiting to seek *Him* before they responded, or even just stood trusting what *He* said… to keep aligned in communion with *Him* and what *He* required. But something… somewhere in *the process* involving their free will, their ***expectancy*** was forming a place of rift… sent by *the deceiver* to cause a shift creating a separation from *God* and *His* intent originally set into place… and, it still is.

That's the power in the fullness of what is at work in the wholeness of how *He* created us – ***spirit, soul, and body.*** With *His original intent* being we live by our ***spirit*** with our ***soul and body*** aligned in it because they each and together are aligned in *Him* and by the *Spirit*. Afterall, <u>*He knew us in His spirit by our spirit before He formed us in our mother's womb.*</u>

Now, in this part of *journeying* there's definitely some aspects of the ***body, soul and spirit*** – which mentioned is the typical way the world orders them in a predominately soulish, intellectual type of mindset. We are a ***body, which has a soul and a spirit.*** Rather than the ordering of how they lived as created ones: we are *a **spirit**, which has a **soul** and lives in a **body**.* The order we come back to in our being reconciled and reestablished into when truly ***born again*** through *Jesus* the *Son*, and to the *God* our *Father* through the *Holy Spirit*. Oh… the **"re"** of life in its ***again*** it brings with it, especially when it comes to our makeup as humans in *His* divine design.

We know and are learning there's always *the process He* is doing in *His* moving and within *His Word* at work in us and as *He's* drawing ones into an awareness… which is all for greater oneness with *Him* and *His* purpose for our lives.

For… *we have the living Word of God which is alive, active…is full of (**expectant** filled) energy… making it energized, effective in its operating (like **expected**)… like a sharpened two-mouthed sword. It will even penetrate to the very core of our being dividing (as **expected**) where **soul and spirit** – the completeness of a person and where the bone and marrow – the deepest parts of our nature… where they all (**expectantly**) meet! It interprets and reveals… exposing and judging the true thoughts, secret motives, and intentions (and all attached **expectations**) of our hearts.**

And… *not one person exists (as He **expectantly** created) that is concealed from His sight that can hide their thoughts from God. But all things are (as **expected**) open and exposed with nothing* *remaining a secret or concealed... but revealed, exposed, and defenseless to the (**expectant**) eyes of Him with whom we **m**ust render and to give an account to (as is His **expectation**)**

It's our responsibility, our accountability, something we should **expec**t and be in agreement because of our alignment in *Him*. It is a part of *His* **expectancy** for all... **e**specially if you're *His*. "*If we hope to **m**ove forward in complete victory, we **m**ust transform our **m**inds to think the way God thinks. We **m**ust adopt His thoughts (**expectantly**) for today rather than our own. One of the greatest wards will take place on the battlefield of the **m**ind... For every process of **m**oving into a new dimension, change is necessary. Mindsets (as **expected**) have to be altered. Old patterns **m**ust **m**ake way for the new ones. Ultimately, we **m**ust think differently.*"* His Word... so powerful in how it **c**onfirms and **c**onnects.

The information shared now is a vital part in foundations being laid here: "*The Bible divides the human race into three categories: Barbarian, Greek, and Jew (Hebrew). I believe these three represent three different **m**indsets anyone of us **c**an have. First is the Barbarian **m**indset. Secondly, there is the Greek **m**indset, and thirdly, there is the Hebrew or biblical **m**indset. We need to understand **e**ach of these and how they operate. Let **m**e reassure you that any god you **c**an reason out with your human **m**ind is not a god worth worshipping. We **m**ust break off our faith in human intellect, so we **c**an draw close to Him and learn to hear His voice and walk in His ways.** See this powerful book, *A Time To Advance,* for **m**ore

It's a good time right now to *thank* and *praise Him* for the ***expectant*** **e**fficiency and **e**ffectiveness of *His designing, aligning, and ordering...* along with the ***expectant*** *sufficiency of His blood,* which has spoken a better word and *His grace,* at *work in* and through us. Our ***spirit, soul and body*** as *Elohim our Creator* designed. *Hallelujah! Thank You Jesus!*
In **c**losing... *He's* highlighted the word *homeostasis* which defines the state of the ***body*** – the house, dwelling place our ***spirit*** and ***soul*** live in... <u>when the ***body*** is at rest</u> – and I would add, when all is well in your ***spirit*** and ***soul*** it **c**onnects to your ***body's*** being at rest too.

Let's **e**nter into a place and posture of rest speaking from our **spirit** to our ***soul and body*** to receive from this benefit and blessing we have in *Christ* – a life in rest... **e**ven transformation. In this day within *our journey* with **"3"** and the *words of worth* in the ***three fold cord set of body, soul, spirit – spirit, soul, body...*** it was an intentional **m**ove to present the information shared **m**ore indirectly... and I'm sure some of you know **m**uch already in this area.

He desires in this place that you **e**nd knowing... *God will keep him in (as **expected**) perfect peace, whose **m**ind – a part of our **soul**, is stayed on You, because he trusts in You.** Oh... the power of the **m**ind... yet we have the **m**ind of *Christ* – *power, love and a sound transformed **m**ind* **e**ven.*

If in anything was **e**xpressed in a way that you felt any kind of *guilt, shame, or condemnation* go to *Him* quickly as that is not from *Him*. Only **c**onviction through the *Spirit* **m**oving in truth and through love will **e**nable you to see differently and **m**ore **c**learly a **m**atter as *He* sees and wants you/us to see.

Any form of **c**ondemnation is **c**oming by the flesh of the old **m**an, the soul, and with or by a way the deceiver our **e**nemy, **m**ay be attempting to **c**reate *confusion, **m**isperception, or **m**isunderstanding*. Again, *go to Him, His Word* and by *His Spirit* you will break free from it. *For indeed you will know the truth and the truth/Truth will set you... **m**e... us, free!**

The *Truth* in *His Worthy Word.* Let's release it into this **e**nding for it to have its perfect work.

*For what the law could not do in that it was weak through the **flesh**, God did by (**expectantly**) sending His own Son in the likeness of sinful flesh, on account of sin: He condemned sin (as **expected**) in the **flesh**, that the righteous requirement (as **expected**) of the law might be fulfilled in us who do not walk according to the **flesh** but according to the Spirit (in **expectation**). For those who live according to the **flesh** set their minds (as **expected**) on the things of the **flesh**, but those who live according to the **Spirit**, (all **expectancy** is in) the things of the **Spirit**.**

*Therefore we do not lose heart (**expectancy** stirs). Even though our outward **m**an is perishing, yet the inward **m**an is being renewed day by day (just as **expected**).**

*And we know that it's... Not that I have already attained, or am already perfected (in His **expectancy**); but I (**expect** to) press on, that I **m**ay lay hold of that for which Christ Jesus has (**expectantly**) also laid hold of me.**

If you are *born again,* you are now living as a new creature / new **m**an by your *regenerated reconciled redeemed spirit* through *His Spirit* now in you through *Christ Jesus* and the completed atoning work of the cross in *His body* given, *His* blood shed. In *Him, His image,* and *His Name Jesus, Yeshua* our identity rests in. In that identity comes authority and victory and their intertwining connectivity which is all established in *God – spirit, soul, and body.*

Remember... *the eyes of your spirit (**expect** to) allow revelation-light to enter your being. When your heart is open the light (**expectantly**) floods in. But when your heart is (**un**expectedly) hard and closed... the light cannot penetrate (as **expected**) and darkness takes its place.**

Let the ***three-fold cord*** of *knowing* this, *receiving* this, and *believing* this **m**anifest as a fruit of your ***spirit*** aligned in truth. For, it brings your ***soul and body*** into a giving *Him – Them*, total *Lordship.* Let it also be another reminder that our identity in *Him* comes with an *inheritance* that states, we're *His sons and daughters*! **M**ay we receive all benefits and blessings the *Lamb* has paid and should be a reward in us to *Him* for *His* suffering. *Salvation, healing, deliverance,* and so **m**uch **m**ore...

Let *God* arise and *His* enemies scatter far from us ***spirit, soul, and body***. For if *God* is for you... me... who can be against us... which includes our ***spirit, soul and body***. Amen.

<u>In light of these **words of worth... body, soul, spirit / spirit, soul, body** and what's been shared:</u>

- ❖ *Perhaps... you **Encountered** or **Experienced** a **Question** or **Challenge**?*
  Write it out...

- ❖ *Perhaps... more has been **Established & Empowered** by the **Word**?*
  Write what/which...

- *Perhaps… it's time for **Engaging & Embracing your Expectations?***
  Write what's forming…

Reminder: For *clarity, connection, and confirmation* regarding *expectancy* being stirred by this **word of worth**, seek *Him and His Word* first. To possibly assist you in the process the list of **ION** words is available in the Appendix.

---

*Footnotes: Chapter 8 Day 3 Body, Soul, Spirit / * See Proverbs 4:20-23, Jeremiah 6:16 -17, 2 Corinthians 5:17-18, Romans 8:28, Genesis 22, Hebrews 4:15, Hebrews 4:12-13, Isaiah 26:3, I Corinthians 2:16, 2 Timothy 1:7, John 8:31-32, Romans 8:3-5, Luke 11:34 - all emphasis is mine and personal paraphrasing built on various translations and versions. * See other related scriptures: 1 Corinthians 7:34, "body and spirit"; Matthew 10:28, "soul and body"; James 2:26, "body" and "spirit"; Luke 10:27, "heart," "soul," "strength," "mind"; Matthew 22:37, "heart," "soul," "mind".
* See *Brian Simmons* / @passionandfire.com / *Passion Newsletter – The Holy Spirit In You* * See *Chuck Pierce* / @gloryofzion.org / *God's Unfolding Battle Plan : A Field Manual For Advancing the Kingdom of God* – Introduction and Chapter The Mind War (p. 43-62).
* See *Chuck Pierce with Robert and Linda Heidler* / @ gloryofzion.org / *A Time To Advance: Understanding the Significance of the Hebrew Tribes and Months* (p. 21, 30)

✧ Day 4: The Journey of "3"… *water, fire, spirit*

Let *expectations*… through this **word of worth's** part to *form, birth, and emerge* in its **meaning & mission**… **our meditation & motivation**… **as movement & manifestation** *awake, arise and align* in agreement with divine eternal *expectation*!

Elements are the what **m**ake up the *foundations, fundamentals,* and *basics* **c**onsidered to be essentials. They **c**an be seen in what we just **e**ncountered through the **m**ain parts of our *human being* which are the *spirit, soul, and body*. Within **e**ach are *elements*. Things that are essential and necessary *main parts, workings,* or *components* that **m**ake up what they are **c**omprised of. All of that has its part and place in what we *incorporate* as vital components of the *elements* that even become the building blocks of *what* we are… additionally, *who* we are – both *naturally* and *spiritually*.

Upon recognizing this **e**lementary fact and realizing why it would be important to us as we begin *our journey* with **"3"** through the *words of worth* represented in the **three-fold cord** word set of *water, fire, and spirit*… we **c**an identify a **m**utual word from our past set of *three* – **spirit.**

We acknowledged and gave a place to the truth that a *born again child of God* now is a *spirit,* that has a *soul* and lives in a *body*. Some **m**ight say, a *spirit* that is housed in a *body* and has a *soul*. What is key is the **born again spirit** is filled with the *spirit of God* by the *Holy Spirit*… is now first, with the *soul* and *body* secondary, yet **e**ssential **c**omponents.

Yes, all things are **m**ade of **e**lements, but it is vital we understand as revealed that **m**ost often their ordering **c**an be a **c**hief factor. We will see a *significance* in the ordering of **water, fire, and spirit** as well; with the relevance unfolding in these *three* being foremost spiritually. We **m**ay discover as *He* gives us those *spiritual* eyes to *see,* ears to *hear,* and a *spirit* that responds to what *He* wants *revealed, is saying,* and *in His ordering*. For these *elements* represent a way *He* is *developing, maturing,* and *manifesting* in us through our *spirits* in *this process*… affecting then our *soul* and *body*… ideally with an **expectation** to bring them into oneness with *Him* and *His*.

Meanings of words as we've **c**ome to **expect,** and their **m**ission that's revealed as they are defined, is **m**ost valuable in our starting to bring and put together what *He* wants us to *discover, uncover,* and *receive*. So, let's do just that by providing some simple definitions to **e**ach of the *three*: **water, fire, and spirit.**

Water… *a liquid that is colorless, odorless, transparent,* and is recognized as the *essential element of fluid in all living organisms*. Often we associate **water** with *rain, rivers, ponds, lakes, seas, oceans,* and **e**ven as the **m**ain element of our *breath*. It *affects the growth* of *humans, plants, and animals* therefore it is a necessity to **m**aintain life. As well, we see it connected with *new life, renewal, refreshing, baptism, God's cleansing, rituals,* and *His* provision.

Fire… *to burn or create a burning, combustion, to discharge a gun or weapon – friendly* or *foe, detonate, to be let go or dismissed from a job, to cause to start operating – fire up, ardor,* or *passion, inspiration,* **c**an bring *death or destruction, a severe ordeal or trial,* **c**reates a *luminosity – glow, radiance, light, shine, to kindle or ignite,* and to *feed* or *apply heat*. It **c**an be associated with *God's power, presence, purifying, sanctifying, cleansing,* or *judgment* and *a form of baptism*.

Spirit... *essence of, animation/animated, non-person, soul, ghost, temper/temperament or disposition, general intent or meaning, mood, tone or tendency, a quality in a person manifesting in liveliness, quickening, brisk quality, enthusiastic, a volatile solvent or solution organic in nature, alcohol,* **c**an be a form of *tenacity,* seen as *God's divine presence, and a form of baptism.*

Each **c**an be symbolic and associate directly to *God and Him as Father, Son, and Holy Spirit* and *His Word* through its power to **m**ove, **c**hange, **c**leanse, and transform as it works within the life through death *process* and in our salvation unto eternal life. Undeniably **e**ndless ***expectancy*** begins to *form creating, and birthing* **m**uch in our ***expectations*** along with *His*.

These defining's in their own right and realm and in how they *connect, work,* and *come together naturally* and *spiritually*... **m**oving us into a place where now a re-ordering **c**an begin to form. As *Believers* we should know that it is the ***Spirit*** which is at works in *you... me... us,* and our **spirits.** We are taught in *His Word* of how *He* reveals the ***Spirit*** is working symbolically through **water** and **fire** enabling, engaging, and empowering each to be what they are **c**reated to be and do what they're **c**reated to do... particularly *spiritually.* Thus... a **c**hanged order **c**an become ***spirit, water, and fire*** emphasizing first what *He* is and we are.

A **c**onfirmation is before us now as we are witnessing the role of the *Holy Spirit*; that **3**rd **power principle** *He* brings in this *dimension, personification,* and *manifestation*. And, it **c**oming forth with **c**larification that *He* is the *Source* and the *Force*... which is behind and within what is happening in *alignment, agreement,* and on *His assignment* as a *person,* the ***Spirit of God***... and as displayed as those in the *Godhead* – the **Three**, the blessed *Trinity*.

And... when He, the truth giving *Spirit* has **(expectantly)** come, He will unveil the reality of *every truth within you, guiding you* (**as expected**) *into all truth.* For He will not speak on His own authority, but only (**in expectancy of**) *whatever He hears the Father speak, He will* **(expectantly)** *speak*... and *He will* **tell** *you* (**as expected**)... *revealing prophetically even to you.. things to come.** It's the application of this **c**onfirming truth that **m**atters not just the superficial knowing. We need the *Spirit of Truth* to *receive* it, *believe* it, and *conceive* to *achieve* what it speaks to us.

Now, the person of *Holy Spirit*, the ***Spirit*** *of God,* has **c**ome... yet *He* will **c**ome and is yet to fully **c**ome **m**anifesting the fullness in some as we will see.

After all... was the ordering of it all not **e**stablished as a pattern in *His all knowing* ***expectancy*** before and then in the beginning that *He's* showed us... in the **e**vidence of when our *Creator God, Elohim,* sent the ***Spirit*** *– His,* to hover and brood preparing a place for *Him* to **m**ove, **m**anifest, *and even* **m**inister life... and it was over the ***waters***?

With all assured ***expectation*** we know *He has, is, and will* **move, manifest, and minister** by *His Spirit* in our now, in our *beyond*... and, through **water** and **fire** too!
Speaking of ***water***... let's take a **c**loser look at it and how we see it revealed, being expressed, and with all its varying uses and applications in *Bible*. Some have been shared in the simple defining above allowing us to do a quick review of a few selected examples that will help us ***embrace*** and be ***empowered*** by the importance and ***expectancy*** within the *need to know* about ***water***... and it through and to the **3**rd **power** by *His Spirit*.

Water as a symbol figuratively shows different aspects of *God's* power. For example in **c**leansing, like in the **c**eremonial washings of the *Old Testament* sacrificial system.* We see it acting as a symbol of *destruction, danger,* and *death* in *Noah's* flood, as rains, storms, waves on bodies of **water** disrupt, devasate, and display an atmosphere of peril.

Primarily we see **water** as an amazing expression of and way to represent LIFE with its *refreshing, renewal, and refueling* power. For *He is Living Water*. We also know there is the **water** of *God's Word* as we see in this verse... *"For He died for us sacrificing Himself (as was* **expected***) that He might make her – His Bride, His Church... holy and pure sanctifying, cleansing, and showering her with the washing of the pure* **water** *of the Word of God."** Yes, there is a washing of the outward body. But *oh*, the purifying power of the inwardly washing that comes from the *holy, living, pure* **water** that *He* is and as the *Word* is.

Water*...** can represent the *Holy Spirit* in several ways. In its ability to quench our spiritual thirst, cleanse us, and bring forth life wherever *It or He* flows. Such **Spirit** *filled* **water** moves and carries out *His* ministry to our *spirit, soul, and body* as we see this in these *tellings* to the woman at the well where *Jesus* was and spoke to her saying... *"Whoever drinks of the* **water** *(especially in* **expectancy) that I will give him shall never thirst; but the* **water** *that I will give him will become (***expectant***) in him... a well of* **water** *springing up (as* **expected***) to eternal life (His* **expectation***).* *

Later in *John* 7 we see another *telling* unfold... *" Now on the last day, the great day of the (Lord's* **expected***) feast, Jesus stood and cried out, saying (with all* **expectation** *backing Him), 'If anyone is thirsty, let him come (***expectingly***) to Me and drink. For, whoever believes (***expecting***) in Me, as the Scripture has said, 'Rivers of living* **water** *will flow (with great* **expectancy***) from within them."**

Not to mention how **water** is the vital substance of *Yeshua's first miracle* performed in *His* ministry at its start while at a wedding in Cana in *John 2*. Six stone ceremonial **waterpots** were filled to the rim by the servants that *His* mother Mary had just told, *"Whatever He says... just do it!"** and so they did.

Again... obedience is key and became a catalyst for **water** being miraculously *turned into wine* in which the master of the banquet said to the bridegroom... *Everyone (is* **expected** *to)brings out the choice wine first and then the cheaper wine after the guests have had too much to drink... but you have saved the best till now'*.* And this best was *His* first miracle!

Jesus washed the feet of *His* disciples with **water** displaying a powerful model to them and us of *servant leadership*.* Within days... *His* blood with **water**, as a last kind of naturally manifesting act, poured out of *His*, the *Suffering Servant's* side* as they pierced through it while *His* body was nailed to and hanging on the cross. The blood and **water** flowing out of *His* side presents a type and shadow one could say, which came first from a *believing, receiving, and conceiving* within *Him* for the fullness of *His eternal purpose to come forth*... in that appointed moment of piercing becoming and being the **spiritual birth** *of the beginning* of *His Church* to be physically birthed and arise. What fulfillment and **water** was a part.

The power and purpose of **water** is something in which you decide and determine what you receive of *Him* and by *His* **Spirit** *as* **water**. However, let's put our **expectancy** out there to honor and heed the warning in *His Word* to not *squelch or crush His Spirit* that desires and might just be that thing you have need of or require. This kind of expression in all its **expectancy** through **water** and *Him* as **Water** and **Spirit**! Remember... in *Ezekiel 47* the vivid imagery and illustrations that show how we can go into the river *ankle, knee, waist, shoulder or beyond* of *water*. Our *expectancy* will determine everything!

Fire… is a powerful symbol biblically representing *God* as shared in the earlier mentioned simplistic defining. When it comes to *fire* connecting to or with our *body* and *soul… fire* being used as an actual physical means *He* uses to bring healing or purification comes in *His Word* ONLY metaphorically in the imagery of *fire* and in the ministry power of the ***Holy Spirit*** where there is conveyed a type of *transformative* or *purifying process* for us to see, ***embrace*** and ***be empowered*** in our *expectancy* for. *Fire* can be associated with *spiritual enlightenment* by *God* and as well with some other gods, particularly in certain cultures. In the Kingdom of *God* culture any enlightenment by **fire** would come through the ***Holy Spirit***.

Fire can connect to the representations of several things presented within *His Word*: a passion related to committed ones who serve *God* with a fervor and intensity in their worship is one. An ability to produce *honor, awe, and reverence* toward *God, His Word, will and ways* is said to be created by a ***holy fire*** within. The *redemptive, restorative, and refining* work the *Spirit of Revelation and Truth* brings by the ***fire*** of *Holy Spirit* produces a work of *God's* purposes in our lives and in powerfully working toward making us more like *Him*.

In some verses the glory of the *LORD* can come or look like a ***fire…*** even a *consuming fire* on the top of a mountain. The *tongue* in a sense is said to be like ***fire*** linking it with injustice and unrighteousness in a world of evil where amidst the parts of the body it can corrupt and contaminate the whole *body*. A potential result of this being, setting the course for one's life within our cycle of *existence* on ***fire***, so to speak, and to intent of hell setting such a ***fire***.

The Word also reveals pictures that metaphorically contain and connect to ***fire*** and are a few of my favorites. That *Jesus,* in all *His* beauty and splendor is said to have hair on *His* head as white as wool, with eyes that are like ***flames*** of blazing ***fire***, and *His* voice being like many ***waters.**** Then when *His* Church was manifesting in its time of birth in the upper room… there appeared what was likened unto ***tongues of fire*** that came to rest upon them as separate ***tongues*** on each there and it rested within them… this ***Holy Spirit fire*** .*

Remember, *Jesus* spoke to needing to go back to the *Father*, so the fullness of the *Father* can come as the *Helper* and ***all He is***, and would **endue** them with power! This happened. They were filled with the *Holy Spirit* and began to speak as the ***Spirit*** enabled them, in *other **tongues** empowering* them to be witnesses to the uttermost parts of the earth! Indeed… this is that and *fire* is involved as well as available to *you… me… us*!

Oh my… the power of **fire** and especially the ***fire of God*** to show up, manifest, partnering with *His* purposes because *the **expectancy*** of *God* required *fire…*the *fire* of the *Spirit of God*. That power! You'll know when it touches you and you will be changed for you cannot remain the same. For it is a shift from just the ***power of God and Jesus*** to the ***fullness of Holy Spirit*** power. You remember… the $e=mc^2$ to **$e=mc^3$**! Holy desire does attract *3rd **power holy fire**!*

Spirit… at the core its meaning is *wind, breath, essence*. It refers to vital power and strength when it is applied to a person. It's a creative life power like in the beginning… because it is for *Believer's* the ***Spirit*** of the *Lord*, of *God*. Interestingly, it can relate to the *soul* with its *feelings, emotions,* and *free will*. However, there can be a connected to a spirit not of *God*… which attempt to produce **similar but counterfeit** manifestations that comes from an being that is a spirit but again **NOT God's.** *God* as a ***Spirit** and the **Spirit*** *of God, the Lord,* ONLY manifests through *Holy* **Spirit** as the true *Source and Force*. For *Believers, true born again Christians,* it is God in Holy **Spirit** ALONE. There is **NO MIXTURE** acceptable to *Him*.

This is extended in revelation that manifests in the *New Testament* and *spiritually* in context. For the *human,* their **spiritual** nature is seen to be an *expansion* of the *human personality* and as a dimension of their *born again relationship with God*. It is something we can encounter and experience as we are *born again* as *spirits* primarily like in the garden before sin. It is this *human spiritual nature* that enables continuing conversation with is a part of communion, with *His Divine* **Spirit** and our *spirit* and in the *spirit* realm of *God* alone where this occurs

These summaries of scripture will bring clarity so we can attest to the above in the following: *Jesus* knew immediately in *His* **spirit** what they were thinking in their hearts and asked them why. Believers were told that when they gathered together assembling, that by the *Spirit He* is present and the power of the *Lord Jesus* is there as well. For this simple certainty of truth arises in that **God is spirit.** Those who worship *Him* – *His* worshippers… they must worship in **spirit** and in *truth*. And, it's our **spirit** being led and directed by the *Holy Spirit* that brings together the *Believer* with *Christ* placing them into the *Church* which is the *Body of Christ – Believers,* and the *Family of God*. These are foundational truths we can be assured of.

Furthermore, there is the **spirit** dimension of how we must know *Him* in *His crucifixion, death, burial,* and *resurrection… afflictions* and *sufferings*. In such we are enabled then to live in triumph over sin and our old man/nature. When we have given full *Lordship to Father, the Son Jesus,* and *the Holy Spirit* whereas, *the Holy Spirit* then **help us** and as the *One* who brings and enables a maintaining of control in our life – not self, when give *Him Lordship*.

The old man is gone, the **new man is here** – live from there. Live as the *born again spirit filled son/daughter* you now are… *surrendered, submitted, and yielding* to *God's Word, will, and ways*. This is *His* most *effectively, consistently, and aligned* in *His* **expectancy** way - by the **Spirit!** I'm hearing… *not by might, nor by power, but by My Spirit says the Lord*!* And, seven times in the *New Testament* we are told through *Paul* to "walk in the Spirit"… this helps walking in our new man in the *process* of *life's journey*!

Those who are being filled continually with the **Spirit,** and living in this *process, posture, and positioning* **in Him**… the *Holy Spirit* will convict of sin, comfort, guide, give and enable spiritual gifts to and in us, helping us to obey *God,* and more. For *He* enables us to pray and to walk beyond knowledge with understanding and wisdom from *God's Word* and it being *applied, activated,* and *appropriated* in our life with **earthly expectancy** aligned **heavenly**.

As shared early on… there is some overlapping and especially when it comes to the **spirit and spiritual** for its connectivity for us as children of *God* has to be in the purity of its ONLY *Source and Force* being in *the Holy Spirit*. As *God's Spirit* is holy *rooted, grounded,* and *established*. So always remember, there are UNHOLY, unclean, evil, and demonic spirits that are in the world around us and attempting to *distract, deter, and defer* us away from *Him* to another form of *worship and spirit* that's not **Spirit** and Truth nor is its *fire* of *Yahweh* our *God – the Tree of Life*. It is like the beginning… for the enemy does nothing new.

Now to bring closure to our day with **"3"** as expressed in our *words of worth*… let's bring them together - *water, fire and spirit* … as well as *spirit, fire and water* … and, in what is known as **baptism**. It is seen as a *symbolic individually personal act* sometimes called a *ritual, rite,* or *sacrament*... but this reference deems it to be a willing act of *obedience and identification* with **Christ** and our NEW LIFE in HIM! *Thank You Jesus, Yeshua.*

Baptism of water...

Receive now from the release words from *His Word* into this place. *Corresponding to their disobedience of long ago... when in the time of Noah, rescue came from the flood to eight souls... God in His patience waited (in **expectancy**) while the ark was built and brought them to safety through the floodwaters (as **expected**).* ***Baptism of water...*** *which is an expression of a believer's new life in Christ... now saves you, not by removing dirt from the body, but by an (**expectant**) appeal to God for a good clear conscience... demonstrating what you (**expectantly**) believe to be yours through the resurrection of Jesus Christ, who has gone into heaven and is at the right hand of God... that is, the place of honor and authority, with all angels and authorities and powers (as* ***expected*** *are)* **m**ade subservient to Him.*

Oh the fullness of what *His Word says, reveals, and* **m**akes known to us and to all who read about *baptism...* and of it through ***water***.

Johanan the Immerser... John the **Baptist c**ame preparing the way preaching a **m**essage of repentance and *baptizing* and ***water*** was definitely a part of it and still is. Remember, *Yeshua* as *Son of God and Son of Man* that *He* was... freely **e**ntered into receiving from and being ***baptized*** by *John* in the *Jordan River*.

Dying to *Himself* in *Him* being the **e**arthly representation as the *Son of Man He* was... dying and being buried in the ***water*** and rising up into the full life into who *He* was with *God* in *Him* as *Son of God*. *Oh* the power of knowing that because of *His everlasting covenant love* and ***eternal expectation*...** it was all in order before the foundation. *He* knew this and validated the *process* allowing it to prepare *Him* for living and walking out *His journey... a spiritual pilgrimage* while on **e**arth. It would require of *Him* here to be in the greater fulfillment of what this all represented and was... is required of us also, yet not like salvation.

This truly **m**ade a statement to all around of *His* **c**ommitment and obedience to representing who *He* was and, to all of the **m**essage *He* was given for *His* **m**ission and **m**andate by *Father* to *reveal, represent, and present*. How **m**uch in the **m**ore of this **m**essage and witness is given for us as *His Followers* **c**ommitted to *Him* and to do the same as *He* did... adding to *His* testimony in this public act and declaration of faith – **m**ay we also if we have not.

For we come to see how *He* later releases this act as an **e**ssential part of the **m**essage and **m**ission that would be **c**arried by *His* Disciples/ Followers... us, in the *Great Commission: Jesus commanded (with adamant **expectation**) His followers to "Go and **m**ake disciples of all nations,* ***baptizing*** *them in the name of the Father and of the Son and of the Holy Spirit (filled with all* ***expectancy***)."* **M**ay we always share the full **m**essage of our **m**ission.

Equally ***baptism*** of ***water*** has a significant part in **m**anifesting the *fruit* that **c**omes from the *transformation process* within and of our *salvation...* and of *His* greater ***expectation***. It actually opened the door to the *more* of *God* and the fullness of the *process He* set into place through *Jesus* and in *His* divine design and plan for the full work of *redemption, restoration, and reconciliation* of the world - *you... me... us*, whom *He* loves... and back fully to *Him*.

THE JOURNEY OF EXPECTATION... EMBRACE IT AND BE EMPOWERED!

Baptism of Holy Ghost/ Spirit...
John the **Baptist m**ade the way also in what he said by preparing for another **m**easure of the *baptizing* of people with a **m**ore profound *spiritual* transformation... for those who are followers of *Yeshua* to encounter... *"I indeed **baptize** you (in **expectancy**) with water; but one mightier than I **c**ometh, the latchet of whose shoes I am not worthy to unloose: He shall (as **expected**) baptize you with the Holy **Spirit** and with fire:"* This verse is in Luke 3:16 which I found interesting for we know John 3:16... it's just a numbers **c**onnection to see.

Let's not forget, *John* and all who were there witnessing *Jesus* being *baptized* in the *water*... also saw this, *After Jesus was **baptized** (as **expected**), He came up immediately out of the water; and behold, the heavenly realm (of **expectancy**) opened over Him, and John (with **expectancy** stirring) saw the **Spirit** of God descending as a dove landing and remaining on Him - Yeshua (carrying and fulfilling Divine **expectation**) and behold, a voice from heaven said, "This is My Son – the Beloved, in whom I am (and **expected** to be) well-pleased and My greatest delight is in!"*

From this there was an *expectancy* that arose in their belief and *expectation* for such to happen and it did. For *Jesus* then in *His* **m**inistry and in the *Father's* appointed time, began to share with them how. Yet, back in the *Old Testament* in *Proverbs 1*, we see a witness to what would be for *King Solomon*, and what was **c**oming **m**aking a way of *expectancy* as well... *Surely I will pour out My Spirit on you; I will **m**ake My words known to you.**

In this time of preparing them that *He* was going to leave them *He* gives the *Great Commission*. Additionally, *He* also *tells* how *He* would always be with them... but, *He* **m**ust return to the *Father* so *He* **c**ould send the *promised gift* from *Him* who would be their/our *Helper* and so very **m**uch **m**ore. *He* gives a directive to remain in the *Upper Room* praying until the *Holy Spirit* would **c**ome, to receive this gift, and endue them with power to *go, do and be* witnesses and **m**ore they were **m**eant to be... as well as *you... me... us* should **expect**.

From there we know *His Word* powerfully shares in the beginning of *Acts* of this experience and what they encounter as a ***baptism of the Holy Spirit*** falls and *together* it all is a **c**onfirming **c**onnection that this *baptism* is beyond that of which happens in our salvation. Along with validating the importance of the fullness of the role of and place *Holy Spirit* has, and **m**ust **c**ontinue to have... in the *ongoing spiritual* process beyond that of *His* role in us being *born again*.

Let's take a look at it in scripture, words *He* released... *While being together and eating with them, He **c**ommanded them (in His **expectancy** of them) not to leave Jerusalem, but to wait (**expectantly**) for what the Father had promised, "Of which," He said, "you have heard Me speak. For John baptized with water, but you will be **baptized** and empowered and united with the Holy Spirit, not long from now (expect it – I said it)."** Simply and **c**learly... it's another *baptism* and with (of) the **Holy Spirit**. And, it wasn't just for them but all believing.

Amazingly it happened on the *Lord's* day of the *Feast of Shavuot or Pentecoast** ... which they also knew it was and in ***tothered expectation*** it happened... *When the day of Pentecost had come, they were all together in one place, and suddenly a sound came from heaven like a rushing violent wind, and it filled the whole house where they were sitting. There appeared to them tongues resembling being like or as of fire, which were being distributed among them, and they rested on each one engulfing them... as each person received the **Holy Spirit**. And they were all filled and equipped... that is, diffused throughout their being with the **empowerment** of Holy*

Spirit *and began to speak in other tongues… different languages, as the **Spirit** was giving them the ability to speak out… clearly and appropriately.**

Individually we **m**ust all search out *His Word* with the help of *Holy Spirit* enabling us to know for ourselves what this all **m**eans and just **e**xactly how it **m**anifests to us, through us, in us, and then from us. For me it was a ***baptism*** and with the **e**vidence of speaking in tongues – yet, I do not believe that it is a required part of salvation unto eternal life. *He* will reveal by *His Spirit of Truth* I'm certain and you'll know to what degree **the 3ʳᵈ power** of the ***Holy Spirit*** is to be for and in *you… me… us.* Have *Your* way oh *God* and reveal by *Your Spirit.*

Baptism of Fire…

Scripture does indicate as we see **e**arlier above that *Jesus* would ***baptize*** in the ***Holy Spirit*** and with ***fire*** and there is a **c**onfidence in knowing this. As in the above *Acts* verses, we discover the power of both at work – ***Spirit and fire***. *Again*, this is all beyond the ***baptism*** of ***water*** after the forgiveness of sins unto salvation. In all, it **m**ust include your personal searching so *you know that you know* regarding these *three* forms of ***baptisms.***

There is **e**vidence in *His Word* suggesting that the ***baptism of fire*** is **m**ore than what took place at *Pentecost* and **c**ontinues beyond all the above. These revealings and teachings include it being an *inner work* in us *spirit, soul, and body* in the *ongoing process* of *sanctification*, the *refining fire* of *God* in our lives through knowing *Him – Jesus,* in all *His* sufferings and afflictions and the refining *fire* unto *holiness* in us.

Others share the *fire* of *God* at work in us by ***His Spirit*** to develop the *fruits of the Spirit* and *gifts of the Spirit* in us with them **m**anifesting in the **m**aturing *process* and life we daily live for and in *Him.* Yet, to the **e**xtreme opposite… some teach the ***baptism of fire*** only **c**omes to those who refuse to repent and it happens to them through the lake of fire of hell and unto **e**ternal death. With this all in **m**ind… I'm praying *He* as only *He* **c**an will reveal to you… as it is an area I am not ashamed to say, that I'm searching out the **m**ore in the **m**anifesting and **m**aturing aspect He has me in… knowing *He* will **m**eet *you… me… us* who are. Actually, I do believe in the ***baptism of fire*** and with what I know believe I have most likely encountered it's work but am open to discovering and **e**ntering into the fullness of it.

It is a *journey*… a *process* and in our relationship with *Him,* as shared before… *He* knows right where we are and how to **m**eet us in **e**very need with truth and in love. We thank *You* now for how *You* are and will *Father God,* in all *Your* fullness of revelation and truth.

When we have ***encountered*** and ***experienced*** the benefits and blessings of all *three* – the *3ʳᵈ power principle* by *Holy Spirit* working *in* us, *through* us, and *from* us… there is a rest in knowing we **c**an **e**nter into the fullest **m**easure of *Father's* genuine *eternal expectancy* and passionate desire to do life with *you… me… us,* and now on earth. And with that **3ʳᵈ power** working too… it's so **m**uch easier to abide and thrive, not strive in life… because *you're… we're* **c**onnected to *Him* as the *Vine* with the life of the ***Spirit*** flowing *spiritually, naturally, and supernaturally* through us.

Here's some key points to apply daily regarding keeping in the *ebb and flow lifestyle* of living in *His* fullness. Be led by the ***Spirit***, pray in the ***Spirit***, live by the ***Spirit***, and keep in step with the ***Spirit*** as we're to be continually filled with the ***Spirit***. *Oh…* the fresh infilling.

Now, **m**ay the *Isaiah 11* seven-fold attributes of the **Holy Spirit** rest in and upon *you... me... us*, and all we do... the ***spirit*** of *God,* the ***spirit*** of wisdom, the ***spirit*** of understanding, the ***spirit*** of counsel, the ***spirit*** of **m**ight, the ***spirit*** of knowledge, and the ***spirit*** of the fear of the *Lord*. And may the ***spirit, water, and fire*** of *God* work *continually, effectively, and fervently* in and through you in the *ongoing process* as we *journey onward* in **Spirit led, Spirit born, Spirit filled** *expectancy*.

e=mc3   **expressed energy** of **expectation** = **message mission methods ministry** of **Christ continually** in **containers carriers conduits** to the **3rd power** of **Holy Spirit**

In light of these ***words of worth... water, fire, spirit*** and what's been shared:

- *Perhaps... you **Encountered or Experienced a Question or Challenge?***
  Write it out...

- *Perhaps... more has been **Established & Empowered by the Word?***
  Write what/which...

- *Perhaps... it's time for **Engaging & Embracing your Expectations?***
  Write what's forming...

Reminder: For *clarity, connection, and confirmation* regarding ***expectancy*** being stirred by this ***word of worth***, seek *Him* and *His Word* first. To possibly assist you in the process the list of **ION** words is available in the Appendix.

*Footnotes: Chapter 8 Day 4 Water, Fire, Spirit / * See John 16:13, water > Exodus 30:18-21, Leviticus 16:4 and 24, 17:15, Ephesians 5:26, John 4:7-14, John 7:37-39, John 2:6-10, John 13:19, Isaiah 52:13 – 53:12, Fire > James 3:6, Luke 3:16, Acts 2:3-4, Revelation 1:14, Joel 3, Spirit > Mark 2:8 ; Acts 7:59 ; Rom 1:9 ; 8:16 ; 1 Cor 5:3-5, Romans 8:9-17, Zechariah 4:6, 1 Peter 3:20-21, Matthew 3:13-15, 3:16-17, Proverbs 1:23, Acts 2:1-4, Romans 8:14, Ephesians 6:18, Galatians 5:16, 25, Ephesians 5:18, Isaiah 11:2 - all emphasis is mine and personal paraphrasing built on various translations and versions.

✧ Day 5: The Journey of "3"… Righteousness, Peace, & Joy

Let *expectations*… through this *word of worth's* part to form, birth, and emerge in its *meaning & mission*… our *meditation & motivation*… as *movement & manifestation* awake, arise and align in agreement with divine eternal *expectation!*

There's a likelihood… actually a certainty that in *life's journey* the *process* will present you with varying types and times of challenge. In those times *you… me… we,* might find ourselves becoming encumbered by a general sense of *frustration, indecision, and or a lack of vision.* All *three* may an attempt to sidetrack and derail you from remaining on the path you were on or believed you were to be on… and *He ideally* directed you to.

Arising within it all, these challenges seem to open a door to the questioning of something or things. Possibly hesitation sets in and almost everything about where you are and what you're actually experiencing… is now unsure. The questioning may even extend to *His* revealed or perceived *expectations* of you, and how you were certain of them before. Right?

Yet, now do you know what they are anymore? Which can really seem odd and start to give place to confusion and possibly guilt, because once within their *expectancy* was such a certainty. Always remember, *God* is not the author of confusion or guilt. And… before you know they can create a shift abruptly or subtly, making a way for the sky above your life to appear cloudy, possibly with storms in the distance. Accompanying such is usually doubt, *confusion,* and or potentially *fear* because you realize perhaps, that part of what you're dealing with is what comes in the *unexpected*.

Awareness of this is key, believing we can all relate in some way. Therefore, it's important to know *hope* is on the horizon. For if you've been in this place before or are now, all you are dealing with will quickly try to spill over into your *expectancy*. As expressed in your own *expectations*, the related relevant or not so relevancy of these in the *expectations* of others, and yes, those you believe *God* has of you… can add to the overall uncertainty.

From this place *you… me… we,* have a very important choice to make. Will you let this all begin to overwhelm and overcome you – the path you're on and *the process* within it you're in? OR, will you give yourself *grace* in this place… taking it to *His throne of grace* presenting it all to *Him* there and believing *He* has heard, is or will respond, and provide you with *solutions, strategies… success*?

What a good reason and yes, a great time to present our *three words of worth* as we enter into this particular day in *our journey* with **"3"**. For what they represent will point not only to the appreciation of the power of each… but the *collective power* in the **three-fold cord word set** they become *together*. Plus, when *adding* the exclusive *expectant* role of the 3rd *power* of the **Holy Spirit** with the enablement, varying types of assistance, and connection to *God's* good plans, very certain promises, and empowering purposes *He* will make known to you and beyond.

*For the kingdom of God (overflowing with expectancy) is not a matter of rules about food and drink, but is first (and expectantly) in the realm of the Holy Spirit, filled with **righteousness, peace, and joy** (what expectancy indeed). For the one who is serving Christ, the Anointed One… by walking (in His expectations) in these acceptable by God kingdom realities… pleases and is beautiful to God (as He expects) and earns the respect of others being approved by men.**

What a really good time for us to discover the **m**eaning and **m**ission of these ***three*** *words of worth* and the *vast richness, value, and potential* they possess. **E**specially to the *3rd* ***power*** which they literally are ordered as... did you see that >>> its ***righteousness, peace, and joy*** >>> in the *Holy Ghost*, the ***Holy Spirit****!!!*

Righteousness... the first of the ***three*** in the list and rightly so in defining this *word of worth* with its **m**eanings and **m**issions within. **S**tarting with: *a quality of being and exhibiting uprightness, right standing, justifiable, a* ***m****oral standard, decency,* and all **e**specially in *God's* **e**yes according to *His character, intrinsic to His nature,* and *a standard for moral conduct*. It is displayed and presented in *His commands, laws, statutes, actions, and judgments*.

In the *Hebrew* a word for **righteousness** is *tsedaqa* **m**eaning *rightness, rights, honesty, justice, vindication, righteous deeds or acts,* and ***m****oral virtue*. The *Greek* **m**ain word for ***righteousness*** is *dikaiosune* **m**eaning the *act or character of equity or Christian justification, and righteous*.

His people are ***expected*** to pursue being in this right relationship with *Him*. **B**elievers are **c**alled to live ***righteously*** through the ***righteousness*** of *God in Christ Jesus* that we've received in our salvation and **e**xhibit as a lifestyle in our *born again* lives **e**mpowered by the *Holy Spirit* to do so.

This is the acceptable **c**ondition of **m**an to *God* which *He* requires and goes back to *His original intent* design of and for **m**an before sin. It is not accomplished by any deeds or works of a person, but through the *process* of salvation: repenting, forgiveness of sins, with turning, and returning back to *God-His* way of life in and through *His* imputed ***righteousness*** and grace. Which is **m**ost **c**ertainly *established* fully in *Him* being love and loving us.

Let's allow *His Worthy Word* to reveal ***righteousness*** to us in this... "*Blessed (**expect** to be)... joyfully nourished by God's goodness enriching those who crave, hunger, and thirst actively seeking God's* ***righteousness****!* For (as ***expected***) *you will be completely satisfied.* And, "*Blessed... comforted by inner peace and God's enriching love (because of your* ***expectancy****)...are those who are persecuted for doing what is **m**orally right... for then you experience the realm of the kingdom of heaven now and forever (according to His* ***expectations****).** We say YES *Lord*!

Remember... *There is one who will go as a forerunner before Him in the spirit, anointing, and power of Elijah... being (as **expected**) instrumental to turn the hearts of the fathers back to the children, and the disobedient hearts to the attitude and wisdom of the* ***righteous*** *fathers... in order to make ready a united people perfectly prepared - spiritually and morally, for the (**expected**) appearing of Lord.** And that... *we might serve Him (**expectantly**) without fear and in holiness being set apart and (with the **expectation** of being) in* ***righteousness*** *before Him all our days.** Amen.

Peace... *harmony, tranquility, quietness, solitude, silence, calm, an absence of conflict or war, the result of order in situations, state of security, an agreement to resolve disagreements for the benefit of all, a greeting of hello or goodbye, and freedom from fear, worry, or anxiety* are a few **m**eanings.

One **m**ajor word for ***peace*** is **shalom** in *Hebrew* with layers of **m**eaning including *wholeness, completeness, soundness, welfare, prosperity, health, well-being* where *nothing is broken, missing, lacking,* and **e**ven to the point of said *peace crushing chaos*. Shalom in the *Hebrew* everyday language is expressed as a **c**ommon greeting like *hello or goodbye*. In the *Greek*, the word most commonly used is *eirene* which means *peace, rest, one, quietness, or by implication prosperity.*

Now, let us touch and agree in unity with *His Word* that tells us… *You will keep in perfect and constant **peace** the one whose **m**ind is steadfast, committed, and focused on You in character and inclination. Because He trusts and takes refuge in You with hope and confident **expectation**.** And… *the God of **Peace** will soon crush Satan under your feet (as **expected**). The wonderful grace of our Lord Jesus (**expectantly**) be with you.**

Joy… is an **e**motion **e**voked by delight, bliss, an **e**xperience that brings **e**njoyment, pleasure, happiness, deep and lasting contentment especially when in our relationship with *God*. It is something that is desired as a part of life and in our response to living a fulfilled life. *Chedvah* is a *Hebrew* word for **joy m**eaning *gladness, rejoicing,* and *joyfulness*. A word in *Greek chara* that **m**eans *joy* along with *cheerfulness, calm delight, joyously, joyfully, and rejoicing.*

His people, which is us as *Believers*, are **expected** to live from *joy* as a *fruit of the Spirit* which is an **e**xpression **m**anifesting from the work of *His* love within us. **Peace** is also a fruit. **Joy** comes ultimately from an intentional personal relationship with *God*… in the fullness of who *He* is not just from good **c**ircumstances or wonderful things happening to us. It is a deeper work within that is <u>not an emotion</u> at all as the world teaches… but truly a fruit and by product of a deeply *rooted, grounded, and established* sense of well-being the work of *Holy Spirit* in us. It is internally being formed when things are not happening to produce what **m**an thinks is **joy.** It is <u>not an external processing</u>, but **c**an be seen and **e**xpressed externally.

Turning to *His* words, let us be blessed in this*: Until now you have not been bold enough to (in **expectancy**) ask the Father in My name. Ask (**expectantly**) and keep on asking, and you will receive (as **expected**) that your joy **m**ay be full – without limits.* And let's remember… ***Rejoice in (expectant) hope, be patient in tribulation, and be constant (expecting) in prayer… counting it all joy!**** What a building in *the process* when *joy* at work arising.

Moving on to **c**omplete this part with a verse that **c**ertainly is appreciated by **m**any… *Go and enjoy choice food and sweet drinks, and send some to those who have nothing prepared. This day is (as **expected**) holy to the Lord. Do not grieve, (let **expectancy** arise) for the **joy** of the LORD is your (ever **expectant**) strength!** In *the journey* and in *the process* be it so *Lord*!

What great things to remember and draw from. Particularly when we are in that place and or *process* of **c**hallenge or **m**oving toward it… like defined at the start of our day. It seems like ***righteousness, peace*** and ***joy*** are indeed things *He'll* be glad to *add* to us – and depending on our perspective, *He* already has… determined in part by how we to respond to it all.

A simple godly type of *relational solution He* offers in *His worthy words* shares: *This is why I tell you to never (**expect** to) be worried or anxious or distracted by or about your life or things in it… for all that you need will be provided. Which one of you by worrying could (**expect** to) add anything to your life?... Doesn't your Heavenly Father (the **Expectant** One) already know the things you have need of and require?. So (**expect**) first and above all, to constantly seek, aim at, and strive for God's kingdom and His **righteousness** – His right way reflecting His character. Then all these less important things will be (with all **expectancy** be) **added** - given to you abundantly. Refuse to worry about tomorrow (He's **expecting** this), but deal with each challenge that comes your way, one day at a time – for one day's trouble is enough. Tomorrow will take care of itself."**

Indeed *He* is the same *yesterday, today, and tomorrow*... and *this is that*. Who *He* is... what *He* does... especially as we obey and partner with *Him* doing what *He* reveals is needful, necessary... in the midst of everywhere we are, with everyone we're in the company of, and in everything; challenge or otherwise that we're confronting. Just do it! *Seek Him first, His Kingdom, and His* **RIGHTEOUSNESS**. So *good*, so *simple*, so *true*... just do it – whatever *He* says! Like *His* mother told the servants right before *He* turned water into wine!

There's truly a *'gotta love'* in the footnotes on this one which shares that in ancient manuscripts it said... *So if you ask for great things, God will* **add** *to you little things.** Oh... the **addings** of God as my *precious sister friend* and spiritual mentor *Melissa* has shared that *He* revealed to her they were *His 'addings'*... which bears witness with me so I call them that too... for this is that! *Expected* to be ongoing and being added to continually.

It's almost like we could *add* in such *expectancy* to the end of this verse where it says... *Tomorrow will take care of itself*... bringing **peace** and **joy**. Amen. *Fruits* of the *Spirit*... added to us because of *His* great love *revealed, manifested, and expressed* in *His* **righteousness** being sought first as *He* **expects!** *Oh His expectations* and all *His benefits, blessings,* and *addings*! Our hearts should indeed be full.

This seems like the right place to share a prophetic word to *edify, encourage, and empower* us with a connection and confirmation from the *Spirit of the Lord* through the anointed prophetic ministry of *Shirley Weaver, A Clear Trumpet* released in this word...
> The Lord rewards your **righteousness**. He specifically recognizes those who favor a **righteous** cause. When you take up HIS cause and possess it, the cause becomes your cause as well. Even those standing with you are favored because of you. The Lord is magnified and "takes pleasure" in rewarding you and all who stand with you! **M**ediate in Psalm 18. **M**ake it your *receiving prayer. The Lord is ready to reward your righteousness!*

A *righteous* cause; what is it and how does it look and manifest today? One of my favorite examples illustrated in the *word of God* is when *David*, in the midst of the *disorder, distraction, and disturbance* being created by giants in the land putting *fear, trembling, and dread* in the hearts of *God's* people and the men who should be keeping them from rising up.

But *God*... *He* had been preparing one and even anointed him to be their future king – unbeknownst to them, by the priest and prophet *Samuel*. You know, the one it says was a *man after God's own heart*. Yes, *David* appears arising and releasing his, "*Is there not a cause?*" And I'm certain that when he was taken out by just one of five smooth stones from *David's* simple slingshot, there was a kind of *God's peace* and with *joy* by *His Spirit* that rose up displacing what the enemy meant for evil and had filled the hearts of the people which ultimately affected their *expectancy* and their land.

> ❖ Perhaps... like *David* there's a **righteous** cause *He's* been awakening in *you, me, us?* Will we be like *David* and *inquire of the Lord* for the strategy? Will we in our **righteous** state as *born again children of God* trust in what *He* reveals and directs and will make a way for? And... so that we can enter in with boldness, in courage... and with **peace** trusting *Him*? When or if the *unexpected* arises challenging us... will we be willing to count *it all joy* as *Jesus* did? These are some serious questions calling for a sincere kind of examining of one's self, commitment, and what *He* is calling us up and into potentially. However, *He* never gives us more than *His* grace is sufficient for... and *He's*

always there with us never leaving or forsaking us. Why not believe for and release your *hineni*, "*Here am I Lord…*" at least in part and begin to arise. *He's* waiting… in *expectancy*!

Now considering the above… and all that's transpired within this place of our day ending I must honestly say, I can't imagine these questions being asked, answering them, or picture on *our journey* what *forms, births and manifests* in our *expectations* associated with them *individually, collectively or corporately,* without the *three-fold cord power word set* of *His righteousness, peace* and *joy* and *exclusively* in the *Holy Spirit!!!* How about you? So, let's just **rejoice** in *the process*, and be glad! *Expectancy* in *Him* is everything and will not disappoint!

e=mc3   righteous *expectancy* =

<u>In light of these **words of worth…righteousness, peace, & joy** and what's been shared:</u>

- *Perhaps… you **Encountered or Experienced a Question or Challenge**?*
  Write it out…

- *Perhaps… more has been **Established & Empowered by the Word?***
  Write what/which…

- *Perhaps… it's time for **Engaging & Embracing your Expectations?***
  Write what's forming…

Reminder: For *clarity, connection,* and *confirmation* regarding **expectancy** being stirred by this **word of wort** seek *Him* and *His Word* first. To possibly assist you in the process the list of **ION** words is available in the Appendix.

*Footnotes: Chapter 8 Day 5 Righteousness, Peace, & Joy / * See Romans 14:17, Strongs Concordance H6666 tsedaqa, Strongs Concordance G1343 dikaiosune, Matthew 5:6, 10 and Luke 1:17, 75, Strongs Concordance H7965, Strongs Concordance G1515 eirene, Isaiah 26:3. Romans 16:20, Strongs Concordance H2304, H2305 chedvah, Strongs Concordance G5479, John 16:24, Romans 12:12, James 1:2a, Nehemiah 8:10, Matthew 6:25a, 27, 32-34 - all emphasis is mine and personal paraphrasing built on various translations and versions.
* See Shirley Weaver @acleartrumpet.org /Shirley Weaver Ministries / "Ready to Reward" – an email portion shared daily M-F.

✧ Day 6: The Journey of "3"... *individual, collective, corporate*

Let *expectations*... through this *word of worth's* part to *form, birth, and emerge* in its **meaning & mission**... **our meditation & motivation**... as **movement & manifestation** *awake, arise and align* in agreement with divine eternal *expectation*!

The phraseology in the wording of the expression of *you... me... us* as the author penning them throughout the *paragraphs, pages, and process* in this *telling* is a great example as we enter into this day in *our journey* with **"3"** and the *three-fold cord word set* revealed in the *words of worth* **individual, collective and corporate**. For one could easily say here... *this is that*. These *three* have unquestionably been expressed and they are not originally my idea. They, *you... me... us*, are a powerful picture of **individually, collectively, corporately**... and *incredibly, wonderfully,* and *powerfully* truly His idea.

For... *just as the human body is one, though it has many parts that together form one body, so too is Christ (expectancy completed). For by one Spirit we all were immersed and mingled into one single body (His expected design). And no matter our status—whether we are Jews or non-Jews, oppressed or free—we are all privileged to drink deeply of the same Holy Spirit. In fact, the human body is not one single part, but rather many parts mingled into one (full of expectancy).**

The **many parts** He **m**oves in and works through not just to the power of one, or two... but yes **three**... and **beyond** in all who desire and **c**ommit to be a part of this *body, His - the Body of Christ, His family, His Church, and as His Ekklesia – His* sent assembled ones as He togethers them, us. It is an **empowering** thing to witness... even **m**ore so to **encounter, experience**, and **embrace** should *you... me... we*, put our **expectancy** out there for it to be so for *He has, is and will* **c**ontinually.

Another interesting thing *He's* pointed out about the this verse above is in its numbering. Yep, you gotta look at the numbers of *1 Corinthians 12:12* – there it is that *doubling*. *For two are better than one** and in this a bearing of a witness through another display of **c**onnection. For *12* is symbolic and speaks first and foremost biblically to that of *God's perfect government* where He is in **c**ontrol and actively ruling in and through *His* perfect plan. *Troy Brewer* shares some relevant information in his book, *Numbers That Preach*. He tells how *God* likes to use the number **12** in *His* language. Reminding us not to forget, *Jacob* had **12** sons and *Israel* had **12** tribes. Not **m**ention there were 12 Disciples / Apostles.

What powerful illustrations of ***individuals collectively*** together to produce *His* purposes and plans ***corporately***... and in *that process* of perfection and purpose in them as He **m**oved in their **m**idst by *His Spirit* through them in essential foundational ways toward building *His Kingdom* and its *righteous* **c**ause. For as we **c**ontinue now in this day, we **c**an ***expect* to see m**ore within this spiritual kind of principle.

Principles in some ways **m**ake you think of scientific laws, like *Newton's Law of Gravity*... which simply states how an attractive force works between *two or more* objects with **m**ass – particles in the universe, and their gravitational force, drawing them *together.* Hmmm... amazing! But then, *He* did **c**reate the universe and surely knows this *law* and any application *spiritually* as well as *relationally* for *He* always desires such. *He* attracted me in **e=mc3**!

Keep in **m**ind, that any preparation *He* **c**alls us into through ***encountering*** and ***experiencing*** drawing us by *His* attractive force unto *Him* and *His perfecting process*... as it **c**omes and **m**ost often before revelation *He* wants to release to us to receive. Be ready for it. First as **individuals**, the groups **collectively**, and extending it always to *His* larger body **corporately**.

It's time to look now at the **m**eanings and **m**issions of these *three words of worth*, see where *He's* leading us, and discover perhaps, something new that we didn't know or see before… that *He* desires and has an **expectancy** for us to now.

Individual… *separate, distinct, single, solo, alone, solitary, unaccompanied.*

Collective… *shared, joint, mutual, cooperative, gathered, united, synergistic*

Corporate… *communal, associated, collaborative, combined, as a whole all together*

Now, go back and read through **e**ach word of the ***three*** with their defining words… and do it saying them out loud releasing them into the atmosphere. **C**an you feel that, the building of **e**ach on their own… *into* the next for the ***upon*** affect? So imagine *His* ***up-on*** affect and in the *echad* that **c**an **c**ome.

After writing these I'm hearing… *containers* that become *carriers* and *conduits* of *His presence, power,* and *possibilities* for *His purposes, plans,* and *promises* – all with "s" on the end, the plural form. Perhaps… it's like we see in the law of gravity? A drawing of us to *remember, recall, and reflect* on these because of and through the *lens (perspective) of* how they all work through a *greater force together*… and **e**ven *better together*… for an accomplishing of **m**ore. Oh… the **expectanc**y in *partnering… co-laboring.*

This points additionally to an underlying *rooting, grounding,* and *establishing* that *He's* been doing in these days as *we've journeyed together* and in *the processing* of it all. It's not just that *He* has been doing it either… but that *He* is and will **c**ontinue to. For by *His* nature and in *His* earnest desire there remains *His* **m**otive, **m**ethods, and **m**anners which always *encourage (exhort), empower (edify),* and *equip* us at all times and in all ***three*** of these dimensions *He's expected, created,* and *aligned* us in and for.

His growing, developing, and ***m**aturing* of us in our need and necessity to know, along with our overall **expectancy**, begins in the *little by little* way we know of… and in the above *process* needing to happen. First ***individually*** and *vertically* through relationship with *Him* for a *godly firm* foundation is required in the **e**stablishing *He* does, has done, and will do.

Realistically and **e**ven *rationally* I believe *you… me… we* **c**an agree with the *relevancy* as *relativity* of this **e**stablishing a *place, posture,* and *positioning* of *relationship* with and in *Him* and it being recognized as **e**ssential. **E**specially if there is to be an adjoining to the other dimensions of how it *happens, looks,* and *functions* **collectively** and **corporately**, in the *horizontally*, **e**ven diagonally of it all.

God's Word gives us numerous *examples, illustrations,* and ***m**anifestations* of this in *varying, multifaceted,* and *complex* ways. For starters let's look at these *worthy words* and what they unfold for us by the *Spirit,* to **see…hear… receive**: *With tender humility and quiet patience, always (He **expects** us to) demonstrate gentleness and generous unselfish love toward one another – forsaking yourself, especially (**expect** to) toward those who **m**ay try your…mine… our patience. Be faithful to guard the sweet (**expected**) harmony of the Holy Spirit among you in the bonds of (the **expectancy** of) peace, being one body and one spirit – in oneness, as you were all* called (**expectantly**) into the same glorious hope of divine destiny (**eternal expectation**). For the Lord God is one, and so are we, for we share in one faith, one baptism, and one sovereign God and Father (as **expected**) of us all. And He is the perfect Father who (with fervent **expectancy**) leads us all, works through us all, and lives in us all!* Amen. Let there be and so be it.

With what's now stirring within and before us let's check out these *words of worth* and allow them to add another layer through what *Lisa Bevere* shares in her book *Adamant*,

> *"We live in a day when we need core conversations, core relationships, and a core connection with the Word of God, which is the truth. We're a generation that has been stripped of our awe, and all too often we're left with empty pursuits, tossed and turned in a river of so called truth. But truth is not a river, it is a rock.*
>
> *In the midst of all this confusion and comparison, He is our Rock, our Adamant : the unmovable and unshakable. We are invited to fashion our lives in Him – not just on Him, but in Him – as our firm foundation. He is the only sure footing in a world infiltrated with gravel."**

What a powerful illustration providing for us vivid imagery to help us look at the idea that *He* indeed has **m**ade us as ***individuals*** first, yet there in the design... like in the beginning when *Adam* needed a helpmate and *God* knew... so had planned for an *Eve*. The need for us **collectively** and **corporately** to *come together*, *work together*, and all as we *live together* with it all being ideally *together* in *Him* who is our *Rock*. Who **c**alls us as *His Children, Believers, Followers*... to build our lives in such a way we know is essential as we stand on the *Rock* who is *Truth*... and, we **m**odel this to others around us who need to know and stand also.

It's important that we *keep* **c**oming to *Him* the *Living Ston* as *His Word* says... Though He was rejected and discarded by **m**en but chosen by God and is priceless in God's sight. **C**ome and be His "living stones" and be one in the One – in union with Him (as He **expects** us to). Those who share in His nature... and are continually being assembled into a sanctuary for God. For now you serve as holy priests, offering up spiritual sacrifices that He readily accepts through Jesus Christ – the Living Stone.*

In this layering of *His Words*, her words, and what *He* appears to be bringing together in and through them **c**arries a greater sense of our full identity and it functioning in *Him*... and how as such we partner with *Him* beyond fellowship. So, let's **e**xplore the rest of what **c**onnects to it all in a deeper way we've **m**ay not have seen before...

He who descended is the very same as He who also has ascended high above all the heavens, that He - His presence, might (**expectantly**) fill all things in the whole universe. And His gifts to the church were varied and He Himself appointed some as **apostles** – those special **m**essengers, also known as representatives... some as **prophets** - who speak a new **m**essage from God to the people... some as **evangelists** - who spread the good news of salvation... and some as **pastors** and **teachers** - to shepherd and guide and instruct. He (in all **expectation**) did this to fully equip and perfect the saints - God's people, for works of **m**inistry service, to build up the body of Christ - the church... until we all reach oneness in the faith and in the knowledge of the Son of God... growing spiritually (as **expected**) to become a **m**ature believer, reaching to the **m**easure of the fullness of Christ **m**anifesting His spiritual completeness and exercising our spiritual gifts in (the **expectancy** of) unity.*

Incredibly filled with *expectations,* we should *agree* with, *align* with, and be *advancing* in the earth with these. The unfolding of and operating in what *He* through the *five-fold individual, collective*, and *corporate* working of this **m**inistry has the potential and power to do as *they, you… me…. we,* partner *together* with and *togethered* in *Him*. Just look at the word *fold*. When it's added to a word… the place and power it gives to the layering and building on the idea seen and *expressed* in the **c**oncept and *process* of *His* *upon* and **m**ore

Within this we see another group of *three* words that are key… *foundation, function, fellowship.* When our *Pastor Damian,* shared these together as a strategy the *Lord* revealed to him as *fundamental* within all **m**inistry… I recall thinking I know these words as the Lord spoken them to me by them being connected to *established* (a foundation), *purpose* (to function in), *and relationship* (my fellowship with *Him first* and then others). But, as you **c**an imagine… I grabbed hold of them as a *three-fold cord word set*. I am glad I did as both are **e**ssential and one just builds upon and within the other. The greater **c**onnection and **c**onfirmation gave place for an enlarging of my *expectations* for myself, others, and beyond.

However, *He* did want me and does us… to see a parallel in the *worlds* **c**oncept of these *philosophical principals* attempting to influence the **e**stablishing of foundations, functioning in purpose, within relationship and fellowship which *are monism, dualism, and pluralism*.

Keeping it simple, *monism* means all is one. There is no distinction or duality, let alone plurality between. For example *God* and the world, **m**ind and **m**atter, and especially in relationship to our existence… our reality. There is only a unified focus on any inter connectedness. *Dualism* is where these examples like **m**ind and **m**atter, *God* and the world are seen as separate entities and the interaction and relationship between them, with a focus on distinction and interaction. *Pluralism* is the idea that I have recognition of varying perspectives, with an **e**mphasis on diversity, and a desire for all to **c**o-**e**xist in society… through **m**ultiple groups, values, and or beliefs.

Interesting… but good to know as other religions and **c**ults bring in these to their foundations, in how they influence within their functioning, and defining what fellowship **c**ould possibly be and why. Particularly in *political, social, religious, and philosophy* platforms.

Do you know what *Christians/Christianity* falls under? *Christianity* is fundamentally *monotheistic* – as we believe **Yahweh** being the one and only **God** and **Jesus** being the one and only way to salvation and **e**ternal life. There are however, leanings towards aspects within both dualism and pluralism within what is **c**alled and defined as *Christianity*. Which in the defining above you **m**ost likely **c**an understand why. So without going into detail… I'm just giving a peripheral kind of framework and awareness. If and however *He* leads you… search it out further.

Because what we believe *individually, collectively, and corporately* **m**atters. It affects and has **e**ffects on our *expectancy* and the *forming, creating, birthing, and manifesting* of *expectations,* others *expectations,* and them working *together* let alone **c**oming *together*. In this telling I certainly have shared where I stand – and tried to respectfully. But, also that I stand on what I do all in the *foundation, functioning, and fellowship* of *Him* being the One who *determines, establishes, and executes His expectancy and expectations* to me… you too I am inclined to believe. So, we **c**an be one with *Him* – and as *Them,* and it all in *His original intent, Word, will, and ways…* not the defining of the world, **m**an, or what any *"ism"* says.

It seems like there could be a lot stirring in this moment for some. But, *He's* all about us *knowing, growing, and choosing* where we stand… and standing. May *His Spirit of Truth and Revelation* come helping *you… me… us* to learn as we *eat* from *Him* – as the *Tree of Life*… not the *Tree of the Knowledge of Good and Evil*. That's where the door opened to such thinking. They were aligned and one with *God* as *He* expected, intended, and designed. But, as we know, the enemy knew this and came quickly to *kill, steal, and destroy* with his… "*Did God really say?*"

One thing that helps me bring it all together is reminding myself; I've settled it. It's ALL ABOUT HIM as the ONE and ONLY ONE. I've given *Him* – the **Three** in One all *lordship* of my life, along with full ownership. Remember, just like the "*Ship Story*" in our journey with **"m"** in what the *word of worth manifest* presented to us. *Lordship* is everything and undoubtably essential to the established foundation, functioning in our purpose – particularly eternal purpose, and in relationship/fellowship with *Him* and others.

The story was not just about the suffix *ship* being added to words to create a place revealing a need for action required of *you… me… us*. But, a picture as well of *His* **Kingdom** on earth as it is in heaven with *Him* as the *Master Ship* and all *His* people being *His Kingdom* Church and making up *His* "fleet of ships". There's truly an ***individual*** to ***collective*** and ***corporate.***

Originally in *His* design and still there is *His Kingdom* of and in *His* people who are first *His family… children.* It was for *Him* to flow *in, through,* and *out* of them as governing ones. Then *in, through,* and *out* of their homes…into their communities they *live* in, *work* in, and *beyond.* In which the original manifesting began in the garden as they were given dominion.

This doesn't seem to be what we primarily call churches - which are buildings that belong to a variety of owners from individuals, ministries, networks, denominations, and more. Can they be a type of church that's *His*? There seems to truly be some potential and possibility there… if given to *Him* to *define, determine,* and *develop* as *He* did in the *forming, creating, birthing,* and *manifesting* of *His* early first church model and prototype, *He formed, created, and birthed* in its phenomenally exclusive divine design.

He's the **Only Captain /Master /Owner of the Ship** and must have the helm as we've come to know. Make no mistake… *He* is in control and nothing else going on *changes, disrupts, or interrupts Him*. Yet, in the bigger picture of all this there may be in part…actually to a greater degree, why we tend to have some issues with ownership and stewardship in all ***three*** dimensions of the ***individual, collective,*** and ***corporate*** aspect and all it represents.

More often than *you… me… we*, care to admit we use the strength of our will to remain controller-lord of things that should be surrendered, submitted, and given *freely, gladly, and completely* to *Him*. We love the *Lord* and wouldn't purposefully disobey *His Word* and leading – right? However, deceptively, in a perceived kind of under the radar, there are areas of *lordship* that are still looming at large untethered to *Him* as *Lord*… are there not? Requiring us as ***individual***s first to examine by *His Spirit of Truth* and it in *love*. It's a *process*… it's a *journey*… and there's *grace upon grace upon grace*. Help us *Lord*.

The time is before us now as we lay all this as we should each and every day before *Him*… and invite and allow *Him* to have *His* Way. One way is through spiritual kinds of connections *He's* made that bring through them confirmation and extension of revelation beyond into what *He'll* bring. This one below is simply amazing in how *m*uch it does! But then that's a sign as well… that it's what *God* by *His Spirit* is speaking to ones.

This is one through *Shirley Weaver* again, whom I've never *m*et, but truly have appreciated and valued all she's sown in my life in a sharpening and deepening way regarding the things of *God* and of the *Spirit*. However, there's no distance in the spirit and how *He* connects. For by *His Spirit* through these writings in this *telling*… in part you have *m*et me. Believing it's been good… what you *expected* in some ways… and possibly beyond in other ways!

*M*ay what *Shirley* shares *connect, confirm, and extend* for you in where we are now in our day ending. It amazed me how it did ~

> *It's truly this way in Lordship and His leading as Father, Son, and Holy Spirit all being given Lordship individually yet collectively. Some have found a way in some sort or another to let God be Lord in our lives, it could be more in some aspects or less have found a way to let Jesus the Son be Lord. But… in my variety of life and ministry experiences I've heard very few share on the need and necessity for letting Holy Spirit be Lord.*
>
> *Why is this important here? In general its helpful in all aspects of our walk with Him in life – so that's individually. And… obviously we're going to need to let Him be Lord by His Spirit too, along with God and Jesus collectively. But… it's essential if we want to function and fellowship corporately the way He's designed us to go, do, and be His Church - the Ekklesia, if Holy Spirit isn't functioning and being honored as one in the tripartite role of Lordship too.*

"*I (you…me…us) press on toward the goal for the prize of the upward call of God in Christ Jesus. Let those of us who are mature think this way, and if in anything you think otherwise, God will reveal that also to you. Only let us hold true to what we have (**expectantly**) attained.*" Philippians 3:14-16 (ESV) - *e*nd of devotional. (Parenthesis mine.)

<u>In light of these **words of worth… *individual, collective, corporate*** and what's been shared:</u>

- ❖ *Perhaps… you **Encountered or Experienced a Question or Challenge**?*
  Write it out…

- ❖ *Perhaps… more has been **Established & Empowered by the Word?***
  Write what/which…

❖ *Perhaps… it's time for* **Engaging & Embracing your Expectations?**
  Write what's forming…

Reminder: For *clarity,* *connection,* and *confirmation* regarding *expectancy* being stirred by this **word of worth**, seek *Him* and *His Word* first. To possibly assist you in the process the list of **ION** words is available in the Appendix.

*Footnotes: Chapter 8 Day 6 Individual, Collective, & Corporate / * See1 Corinthians 12:12-13, Ephesians 4:2- 6, I Peters 2:4-5, Ephesians 4:10-13 - all emphasis is mine and personal paraphrasing built on various translations and versions.
* See *Troy Brewer* / @troybrewer.com / Troy Brewer Ministries / *Numbers That Preach,* page 133.
* See *Lisa Bevere* / @lisabevere.com/ Lisa Bevere Ministries / *Adamant* / Devotional You Version Bible App.
* See *Shirley Weaver,* A Clear Trumpet / @acleartrumpet.org. - Shirley Weaver Ministries, email devotional.

✧ Day 7: The Journey of "3"... faith, hope, love

*Let **expectations**... through this **word of worth's** part to form, birth, and emerge in its **meaning & mission**... our **meditation & motivation**... as **movement & manifestation** awake, arise and align in agreement with divine eternal **expectation**!*

Before the triumph comes the training. I recently read this anonymous quote and will have to say I agree. Immediately I found myself thinking... it's really ongoing in our lives. For some say *life is our training ground* – to the *good or bad*, the *positive or negative*, and either in *blessing or cursing*. We go into the *journey* and the *processes* therein, with one of these predominate and then what we come out with will correlate and connect.

However... if life is the training ground it is or can be, it is to the degree we invite and allow it to be. When it includes *Him/Them* we have access to everything and anything that can assist or help us. Let's determine now to pursue and grab hold of the perspective this rope of **hope** being offered is... and especially through *Holy Spirit* the essential part *He* is.

In an extending of *hope* in *Him*, there comes many opportunities to cling to the *rest* it offers within. Yes... attached to *hope* should be a form of *rest*. Given a place, it arises and with a knowing and trusting that we are indeed still moving forward. For the fruit of it comes in that *faithful process* we've become... or are becoming familiar with >>> from *faith to faith, strength to strength*, and *glory to glory* in *His grace upon grace*.

For *triumphs* that come in life events and battles with their victories they represent most often originate in the daily *little by littles*... if we're willing to acknowledge and accept this. There's no denial that there are some losses, but we do not remain there or defeated. *We arise and shine for the glory and the Spirit of the Lord is upon us.* Amen.

Like those listed in *Hebrews 11*, better known as the *Hall of* **Faith,** *the Action of* **Faith,** or the *Triumphs of* **Faith**... there's the role of *expectancy* as seen in the lives of *Abel, Enoch,* and *Noah* to *Gideon, Barak, Samson, Jephthah*... of *David and Samuel* and the *prophets*... this *cloud of witnesses* that have gone before and who *knew in the way they knew* from the seed of *faith* planted and manifesting within them.

Receive from these *Worthy Words* filled with **much EXPECTANCY**.... *Now **faith** is the assurance (title deed, confirmation) of things hoped for... divinely guaranteed... and the evidence of things not seen... the conviction of their reality—**faith** comprehends as fact what cannot be experienced by the physical senses. And... By **faith**... that is, with an inherent trust and enduring confidence in the power, wisdom and goodness of God... we understand that the worlds - universe, ages... were framed and created formed, put in order, and equipped for their intended purpose.. by the word of God, so that what is seen was not made out of things which are visible.**

*And all of these, though they gained divine approval through their **faith**, did not receive the fulfillment of what was promised, because God had us in mind and had something better for us, so that they - these men and women of authentic **faith** would not be made perfect... that is, completed in Him apart from us.** Amen and amen.

We, *you, me, us* – like those *faith* filled ones who've gone before us... if we actually allow our **expectancy** to increase to encounter and experience the ***empowering*** sensation and personal satisfaction that such a *paradigm embraces*... our thoughts and *expectations* for continual *triumphs* in life will increase too. And that kind of life... well, it is only found in the *goodness of God*. There's just something about the *fulness in Them* and it in us that enriches and grows our *faith* for such and for sure. After all... *faith* **creates!**

For *He* has told us the battle belong to *Him**, that *He* fights for us,* and *He* is our *Triumphant King* – thanks be to *God* in whom ultimately the victory and glory belongs.* Plus, *He* reminds us that *we are more than conquerors* as we put our *faith* in *Him* in whom *all things are possible*!* We are indeed on the winning side.*

Now you may sense what I'm going to say here. Yep... you gotta love the power of *His* **faith** *filled Worthy Word*! With its unfolding above to *encourage, edify, and empower*, even *equip* us in it working in the releasing of it and it stirring *expectancy*. Not to mention in its moving for the *forming, creating, and birthing of expectations* that we start to *claim, walk in* and *see manifest*. After all, *He is the Word* and therefore these words are not just *His* but a part of *Him* who is the *Word,* and therefore *His* *expectation* is assuredly in them!

It's alright if you didn't *expect* this day to begin in this way of *telling* after the depth and length of yesterday. Rest assured, there are many benefits and blessings we receive and are rewarded by in **the power of the "3"** in *this process* within *the journey* with our *words of worth* **faith, hope, and love**. Where would we be without them? I think we can safely say... there'd not be as much victory without their highly valued and greatly appreciated inclusion and influence in our lives. In part we know this to be true since *a* **three-fold cord**, *the strong (expectant) strand that it is*... *is not easily broken.**

Let's enter to this seventh day resting on the foundation of knowledge and understanding we presently have of them... *faith, hope, and love* yet, remaining open to what *He* wants to reveal to us now... here... where *you... me... we* are at this time, in this season of life, and from the place we're **encountering** and **experiencing** as we **engage** and **embrace expectancy.**

Entering in is a good time to ground ourselves in this *triumph filled* righteous saying from *Father* to us ~ *For I know the thoughts that I think toward you (My expectations) and your marvelous destiny, says Yahweh. The plans of a future planned out in hope-filled detail. My intention is not to harm you, but to surround you with thoughts of peace, prosperity, and to give you a beautiful future... glistening with hope.. and not of evil... for you have an expected end.* So just remember, this works best... *When you call on Me and come to Me in prayer (expectantly), I will listen to your every word. If you reach out to Me (in expectancy), you will find Me when you search for Me with all your heart (in expectation). I will not disappoint you," declares Yahweh.**

This is a true word... a for sure and certain word. For *Father God, He's* always looking for ways to express *His* love to us, *His* desires for us which include *His* plans with *His* promises, provision, and protection *He* makes available. **Faith, hope, and love** are words that have multiple meanings filled with missions and mandates, that *He* wants to manifest in our lives in *the process*. So let's get started with looking at what they are.

Faith... simply put is a *confidence, trust, reliance upon, belief in* – *a person or thing, and belief through a conviction that isn't based on needing to see an obvious proof... a driving force of* **expectancy.**

Here's an interesting set of thoughts shared by *Annette Capps* on **faith**... *Faith is an unseen energy force. It is not matter, but it creates matter and actually becomes matter. That is because faith-energized words convert energy to matter. Words are the catalyst that turn the substance of faith into physical manifestation. Faith is the raw material from which all matter is made.* Wow! Be sure to re-read and receive *His* truth aligned in these words before you move on. For *He* spoke... and there was... selah ~

Hope... is simply *optimism, anticipation, courage,* **expectation**, *confidence, to want something to be true or happen... a driving source of* **expectancy.**

It's interesting that **hope,** as the word *elpis* in the *Greek,* means *confident* **expectation** or *trust*— not as in wishing, but actually in trusting *God's* promises... with all your **expectancy.**

Love... simply is *endearment, deep affection, emotion, devotion, adoration, passion towards another person or object... a core element of the essence of Him and His true* **expectancy.**

Again... opportunity comes to look at **three-fold cord word sets** in their full circle cycle when seen as **love, hope, and faith**. *He* is **love**... it is first, it is why *He* gave because *He* so *loved* the world. This certainly created a place then for great **hope** to *awaken, arise, and align* the potential and possibilities before us forming the perfect place for **faith** with its **expectant hope** to help us advance moving into the more.

God is love... and *God* is to be first. There is a principle at work here to support **love** being first... because we're to *prefer one another in love* and we are to *owe no man nothing but to love them.** In *1 Corinthians 13 love* is revealed in a multifaceted way and here's a few of these powerful adjectives that describe **love**: it is *patient, kind, endures, bears, believes,* **hopes**, *not jealous or envious, not rude or self-seeking, not proud or arrogant, not easily provoked or angered, rejoices with truth not injustice, and never fails*. WOW... no wonder *God is love* for *He* is all those things! *Father,* help us receive *Your* **love**, be **love**, extend releasing *love*, and receive *love* from others as only *You* can.

It good to know and recall *His Worthy Words* which remind... *And now there remains:* **faith** ... *abiding trust in God and His promises...* **hope**... *confident* **expectation** *of eternal salvation... and* **love**... *unselfish love for others growing out of God's love for me. These* **three** *- the choicest graces... but the greatest of these is* **love.*** This verse is *1 Corinthians* 13:13 and if you'll recall 13 biblically can be seen as representing love in the Hebrew and it's doubled here in this verse! *Perhaps*... the doubling connects them to their continuing forever?

Do we even see an *e=mc3 / **eternal fruit of faith, hope in love the essence of expectancy** = the **message, mission, mandate, methods, ministry, manhood, marriage, motives in ministry** seen in **Christ continual constant consistent covenant love** in the **cross, communion, compassion, consecration,** and **counsel** of God* to us by the 3rd power of Holy Spirit – *His all, His fullness.*

Maybe it's likened to what *Jesus as Son* said of the *Father*... *"I told them what You are like, and I will tell them even more. Then the love you have for Me will become part of them, and I will be one with them (what* **expectancy***)."* What was between the two - *Father and Son*, now becomes **three** as it is extended *to, in* and *through you... me...us* and by *His Spirit.*

It's like a waltz between *heaven on earth* and in *earthen vessels*... the dance of *Mahanaim*... between two *camps;* heaven and earth* – in the power of the *Three*... 1 – 2 – 3... 1 – 2 – 3... 1 – 2 – 3... the sound of a heavenly symphony and the cloud of witnesses that join in... releasing a divine sound to come down stirring the dance of *providence*... in the provoking of **expectancy**... in which all the earth groans and travails... for the **m**anifestation of the *Sons of God* which has begun as awakening has come... and arising has begun its dance.

It's like **Faith = Holy Spirt**, **Hope = Jesus,** and **Love = Father** and we're dancing with *Them*. You just **c**an't separate *Them* from one another... and shouldn't if you want to receive the fuller better **c**omplete **m**easure in **the three-fold cord** of the doubling of the *Three as three*... and the *Three* in both *you and me – individually, collectively...* and *us corporately.*

For like *Jeremiah* penned ... *The LORD appeared to **m**e from ages past, saying, "I have loved you **M**y people, **M**y Israel.... with an everlasting love; Therefore (in all **M**y **expectancy**) with loving kindness I have drawn you and continued **M**y faithfulness to you.** And *His* faithfulness is **e**ternal, wrapped in *His* **m**erciful *love*, and sealed with **hope**.

*See what an incredible quality of **(expectant)** love the Father has shown to us, that we would be permitted to be named and called and counted as the children of God (His **expectations**)! And so we are! For this reason the world does not know us, because it did not know Him.**

Let's **c**ontinue to draw from the well of *His Worthy Word* for the *water* of it **m**oves us through our day and reminds us... *And this is the confidence (**expectant faith**) full of great boldness as we go before Him... that we have toward Him... that if we ask anything according to His agreeable will He hears us. And if we know (**expect**) that He hears us in whatever we ask... so we know that we have the requests that we have asked of Him.** And, what we need to remember in this is... *Just make sure you ask **empowered** by confident **faith** without doubting that you will receive. For the unsure person believes one **m**inute and doubts the next. Being undecided **m**akes you become like the rough seas driven and tossed by the wind. You're up one **m**inute and tossed down the next.** Lord,* help us arise in **hope** and **c**onfident bold *faith.*

Sometimes in life and in *His Word* we discover a kind of framework with biblical principles, that **c**ould appear to be a *formula* but they're not. It's an <u>effective fruitful life applicable pattern</u> for us in *the journey* and *process* we're in throughout our lives like we just read. When we look at **three-fold cord word sets** like the **c**ommon one of *faith, hope and love* it's good to begin to seek *Him* for what *He's* revealing, saying and **expecting** for us in them **e**ach and in them *collectively together.* And, in the beyond of what we know or have ***experienced.***

It's wise to pursue further seeking of *Him* and *His Word* actually applying and appropriating what they are, do, and particularly in the *togethering* of them– *faith, hope, and love* in our lives. *He's* determined we see and settle into recognizing frameworks *He* reveals and provides in real *relationship* and *fellowship* where they function through *Him, His* love.

An **e**xample I'm reminded of and have **c**ome to know ties into what we've read above and requires a further sharing. At our local **c**hurch *New Life Christian Ministries,* our lead *Pastor Damian Tibbs,* whom I've **m**entioned, when he in **c**onfident *faith* tied to his **expectation**, sought the *Lord* regarding the **m**inistry's purpose; what it was **c**reated and **expected** to be... these two words *L.I.F.E.* and *R.E.S.T..* came to him. The *Lord* heard his request, revealed **m**uch to him, our **c**hurch family, and **c**ontinually is. For bringing families to L.I.F.E in *Jesus Christ* and **c**reating a **c**ommunity of *Believers* living a victorious life in *Him* was the foundational connection of **m**ission and vision that produces *His* R.E.S.T.

My husband and I have come to truly honor, value, and appreciate what these words stand for in their all their meanings and the mission connected to them, the ease of applying them in life, how simple they are to meaningfully share with others through what their letters stand for, and what together they establish to open a door to relationship with *God* and with others in the family of *God*, the *Church*, and the world around us.

Simply: the **L** is for **Love** - loving *God*, loving others and righteous self-love. The **I** stands for **Identity** – our true one which is *His* image and likeness according to the way *Father* made us to be; fearfully and wonderfully. The **F** is for **Faith** – that which we arise in to believe and follow *Jesus Christ* for without it, it is impossible to please *God*. Lastly, **E** is for **Eternal Purpose** – that which *He* designed us for in *His* real love towards us, along with the plans *He* has for our life as we partner with *Him* and help bring others to LIFE and REST in *Him*.

R.E.S.T. stands for **R – Revelation**, **E – Empowerment**, **S – Strategy**, and **T – Triumph** which *He* moves in and through bringing them forth to us, in us, through us, for us, and from us to benefit and bless others as we live L.I.F.E. in *Him* and together with *Him* and each other. And, in the *ministry of reconciliation* we've been given to call ones to "*Come back to God!*"*

All because we *love, worship,* and *serve Him* knowing we are pleasing *Him* as we invest in the future of and the bringing forth of *His* kingdom on earth as it is in heaven to glorify *Him*. This truth revealed to *His Church* and the greater *Family of God* for L.I.F.E. & R.E.S.T. – where ***faith*** is essential, **hope** arises producing joy for *the journey*, and **love** is always the **key**… bringing triumphant blessings for a LIFE of and in REST and always together in *Him*.

Let us receive as we end our day with *His* wrapping us in *Him* and *His* **three-fold cord** of ***faith, hope, and love*** completely as and in ***love, hope, and faith*** encircling us with all they encompass for our ***engaging, embracing,*** and ***empowering*** in the *process* in *our journey* and with ***expectation***.

From *Father's* heart of ***love*** in me and in ***faith*** I now pray over you to receive… *Now may the God, the fountain of* **hope***, fill you to overflowing with uncontainable (***expectancy*** filled) joy and perfect peace as you trust in (***expectantly*** in) Him. And may the power of the Holy Spirit continually surround your life with His super-abundance until you radiate with (***expectant***)* **hope***.**

The *Lord's* eye is upon *you…me… us* as our *journey* continues into the *beyond* now with ***faith, hope, and love*** lingering in the air propelling us forward into the ending of this *telling*. Therefore, may our eyes remain on *Him*. *He* longs for us to let go of anything deemed not of *Him*, and hold onto the *good of God* in what we've received up to this point… letting it *root, ground, and establish* us more *in Him* and where we need to be as our *28 Day Journey* ends and in the momentum it's produced for life, in all aspects and areas of connection to *His* ***expectant*** end. Your Kingdom come, Your will be done on earth as it is in heaven. Amen.

Remember these words in *His Word*… *Blessed is the* **man***…woman… whose strength is (***expectantly***) in You Yahweh, whose heart is set (with great* ***expectation***) *on* ***pilgrimage***.*

May *His* blessings fall upon us for finishing well within this *telling's* portion… and into the foretold **End**… and so *He* will find ***faith*** in the earth when it and *He* comes!

In light of these ***words of worth... faith, hope, love,*** and what's been shared:

- ❖ *Perhaps... you **Encountered or Experienced a Question or Challenge**? Write it out...*

- ❖ *Perhaps... more has been **Established & Empowered by the Word**? Write what/which...*

- ❖ *Perhaps... it's time for **Engaging & Embracing your Expectations**? Write what's forming...*

Reminder: For *clarity, connection,* and *confirmation* regarding *expectancy* being stirred by this ***word of worth***, seek *Him* and *His Word* first. To possibly assist you in the process the list of **ION** words is available in the Appendix.

*Footnotes: Chapter 8 Day 7 Faith, Hope, & Love / * See Romans 1:17, Psalm 84:7, 2 Corinthians 3:18, John 1:16, Proverbs 13:11, Isaiah 60, 61, Hebrews 11:1, 3, 39-40, 2 Chronicles 7:15, 17, 2 Corinthians 2:14, 1 Corinthians 15:57, Matthew 19:26, Romans 8:37, I John 5:4, Ecclesiastes 4:12, Jeremiah 29:11-14, I Corinthians 13, Genesis 32:2, Jeremiah 31:3, I John 3:1, 1 John 5:14-15 James 1:6, Romans 15:13, Psalm 84:5 - all emphasis is mine and personal paraphrasing built on various translations and versions. * See *Annette Capps* / Quantum Faith @cappspublishing / 2003.
* See *New Life Christian Ministries* /@newlifelima.church Lima, OH / *Pastors Damian & Brooke Tibbs* and *Family Life Pastors Jim & Stacy Lewis*. With all respect and honor, this defining used the church structure for LIFE & REST, but for the most part was shared through my words and how we've – my husband and I, perceived and are discovering it to be.

✧ Expectancy's "Look Again" at the end of the Journey with "3"
~ Karen

"I Am the Alpha and Omega... the Beginning and the End," says the Lord God,
*He Who is... and Who was... and Who is (**expectantly** yet) to come,*
the Almighty, the Ruler of All!" Revelation 1:8

Expectation's Reflection: It delights my heart in how *Beth* has seen this in the scriptures of *God's Word*. As *God* is a *God* of intentionality and purpose of the **m**any pattern **words of 3**. The enlightenment that *she* brings out in the order and the sequence of *three's* in the scriptures has been exciting to see and **e**ngage with... in a whole new perspective and new lens to look thru!

In *this journey* as you have read with your heart that it will take you thru... I have seen... as I pray you have too... how **m**uch *Expectations* take an important role in our relationship with the power of **"3", Father, Son and Holy Spirit** especially. As well as our faith in operation in *the process* and growing in that relationship. We **m**ust have *expectations* in the joining of our imagination in forming that blue print of faith. *Expectation*... joined with imagination, empowered by the *Holy Spirit*... allows faith to be **c**onceived. It **c**annot be birthed unless it's first **c**onceived. *Expectancy* is what **c**arries it thru to be birthed... as *Beth* so well illustrates in so **m**any facets in this journey!

From the beginning of time in all **c**reations in *Genesis* to the end of the book in *Revelation*... she helps us to see that the number **"3"** is in a **m**ajor sequence of patterns in **m**any arrangements and facets, and *His* perfect alignment of who *He* is as *Father, Son and Holy Spirit*. As you have traveled thru *this journey*, being stirred with the seed of enlightenment to grow with greater *expectations,* birthing the **empowerment** of *Him* in you, *He* so desires for you and me to experience!

"I Am the Alpha and Omega... the Beginning and the End," says the Lord God,
*He Who is... and Who was... and Who is (**expectantly** yet) to come,*
the Almighty, the Ruler of All!" Revelation 1:8

Prayer of Expectancy: *Father, **m**ay our hearts be open and engaged in the knowing of you as we yield to the Helper... Holy Spirit, of who You really are to us, and for us. Open our understanding of how You so uniquely designed the pattern of "3's" in Your Word to **empower** us with greater **expectations** of our journey in relationship with you*!

Expectation Declaration: *We declare we will have eyes to see, and ears to hear as our hearts have a greater **expectation** as we explore thru the **power of "3".***

SECTION THREE

✧ EXPECTATION'S MANIFESTATIONS
…AN EMERGING & EMPOWERING

✧ SECTION THREE WORTHY WORDS ✧
✧ EXPECTATION'S MANIFESTATION…
EMERGING & EMPOWERING.

*Now it is God who establishes and confirms us… in joint fellowship] with you in Christ, and who has anointed us… **empowering** us with the gifts of the Spirit. It is He who has also put His seal on us (**expectantly**) that is, He has appropriated us, and certified us as His… and has given us the Holy Spirit in our hearts as a pledge like a security deposit to guarantee… an **earnest**, the fulfillment of His (**expectant**) promise of eternal life… everlasting **expectation**.**

*But I promise you this… the Holy Spirit will come upon you… **empowering** you to be witnesses to Me… unto the remotest places… yes, the ends of the earth."**
*Now **m**ay God, the fountain of hope, fill you to overflowing with exuberant joy, uncontainable, and perfect peace as you trust in Him. And **m**ay the power of the Holy Spirit continually surround your life emerging with His super-abundance until you radiate with (**expectant**) hope **empowered**!**

*Therefore become imitators of God (with an **expectancy** of) continually copying Him and following His example. As well-beloved children, you are to imitate your Father; and walk continually in love – that is, value, esteem, and honor one another practicing empathy and compassion, unselfishly seeking the best for others, just as Christ also loved you and (**expectedly**) gave Himself up for us, an offering and sacrifice to God.
He was slain for you, so that it became a sweet fragrance.**

*But all things (are **expected** to) become visible when they are exposed by the light of God's precepts, for it is light that **m**akes everything visible. For this reason He (**expectantly**) says, "Awake, sleeper, and arise from the dead, and Christ will shine as the dawn upon you and give you light." Therefore see that you walk carefully (yet in **expectation**)living life with honor, purpose, and courage; shunning those who tolerate and enable evil, not as the unwise, but as wise who are (**expecting** to be) sensible, intelligent, discerning people, **m**aking the very **m**ost of your time on earth, recognizing and taking advantage of each opportunity (in **expectancy**) and using it with wisdom and diligence, because the days are filled now… as **expected** due to sin… with evil.**

*"…for you are a chosen people, royal priests, a holy nation, God's very own possession.
As a result, you **c**an show others the goodness of God for he called you (with great **expectancy**) out of the darkness into His wonderful light."**

*"Let us think of ways (**expecting**) to **m**otivate one another to acts of love and good works. And let us not neglect our **m**eeting together, as some people do, but (**expect** to) encourage one another, especially now that the day of His (**expectant**) return is (**expectantly**) drawing near."**

---

*Footnotes: Section Three / * See 2 Corinthians 1:21-22, Acts 1:8, Romans 15:13, Ephesians 5:1-2, 13-16, I Peter 2:9, Hebrews 10:24-25 – all emphasis is mine and personal paraphrasing built on various translations and versions.

✧ WORTHY WORDS AS WE ENTER CHAPTER 9…

*Faith **(expectantly)** works… it's alive and active expressing itself by love.
For any religious ritualistic duty filled type of works is dead benefiting you nothing.
The more we know (with assured **expectancy**) we are loved by God… joined together
in Him – the Anointed One… the more **(expectant)** our faith is enabling us to
(expectingly) trust as we believe Him, rest in Him, and as it enables
you to love one another as I have loved you.* *

"In this is love… not that we loved God, but that He (with great **expectation**) loved us long before
we loved Him (or He **expected** us to). It was His love (its **expectant** essence) and not ours that
(expectantly) sent His Son, which proved His love to us as He became the pleasing sacrificial
offering **(expected** to be) given freely… even before the foundations
of the world… to take away our sins. So… delightfully loved ones, if He loved us
in this incredible way… with such tremendous love… then loving one another
should be our **(expected)** way of life! *

*Whoever confesses and acknowledges that Jesus, Yeshua is the Son of God, God abides in and is
united in him, and **(expectingly)** he in God . We have come to know (and to **expect**) through our
personal observation and experience… believing with deep, consistent **(expectant)** faith… the
love which God has for us. God is love… and the one who abides in love abides in God, and God
abides continually **(expectantly)** in him. In **(expectancy)** this union fellowship with Him where
love is completed and perfected in us, so that we may have **(expectant)** confident, bold, assurance
in the day of judgment to face Him; because as He is, **(expectantly)** so are we in this world.
There is no fear nor does dread exist in love… for perfect, complete, mature, pure love drives out
fear, because fear involves the **expectation** of divine punishment. So anyone who is afraid of
God's judgment is not perfected in love. They have not grown into a sufficient **(expectant)**
understanding of God's love. We love, because He first loved us (eternally **expect** Him to).* *

*Father God's love in us… it is (with enormous **expectancy**) large and incredibly enduring as it is
patient. Love is gentle and consistently **(expecting** to be) kind to all. It refuses to be envious or
jealous when blessing comes to someone else. Love does not **(expect** to) brag about one's
achievements nor is it haughty inflating its own importance. Love does not traffic selling out or
submitting ones in shame, disrespect, nor selfishly seek unbecomingly its own arrogant
(expecting) honor. Love is not **(expected** to be) touchy, resentful, easily irritated, provoked, or
quick to take offense. Love joyfully celebrates **(expecting)** truth, honesty and **(expects** to) pay no
attention to or finding any delight in what is wrong.
Love is a safe **(expectant)** place of shelter, for it never stops **(expectantly)**
believing the best for others. Love never takes failure as defeat,
for it never gives up (always **expecting**).* *

---

*Footnotes: Chapter 9 Worthy Words / *See Galatians 5:6, John 15:16, 1 John 4:10, Ephesians 1:4, 1 John 4:15-19, 1 Corinthians 13 Philippians 1:9-11 - all emphasis is mine and personal paraphrasing built on various translations and versions.

✧ CHAPTER 9 ✧
✧ EMERGING & EMBRACING... FOR NOW!

May these words from *His Worthy Word* **e**merge with revelation by *His Spirit* of impartation to **empower** us as we **embrace** them and the **expectancy** they **c**ontain and **c**arry... *Yahweh your Kinsman-Redeemer, the Holy One of Israel is saying (in all **expectation**)... I am the Lord your God, who teaches you to profit benefiting you with success... leading you by the way you should go.**

May we not just hear these words... but allow what they are saying about how *His teaching, leading, and directing* us in all things... **e**specially in this place of finishing... and **expecting to finish well.** **M**uch has been *released* and *revealed* to be *received*. For in the receiving we've learned there **m**ust be the *believing* for the *conceiving* of our **m**utual *expectancy* in the *togethering*. *His* in ours – ours in *His*... *His* in ours together in *Him* – and our *togethered* in *Him*. It is the... **as He is so must you... me... we... be** and **do... and expect**! There are those **expectations** of others. But, when knowing *His* is our focus... we'll simply know how *to approach, handle, and respond* to those of others.

Now *breathe in*... and let *His Living Waters of* **expectancy** within you stir, inviting *His* breath to blow over you, allowing *Him* to hover and brood over and within you... just as *He* did *by His Spirit – in the beginning*. Over anything attempting to remain *dark, formless, void*... for it **c**an't help but begin to **e**ventually respond to the **expectancy** that fills *His light, life, love*. For did not all of **c**reation receive life and breath from such, **e**specially once *He* spoke *His*, "*Let there be*..." And we say... "*Speak Your* **let there be** *over us now... over this final portion of this telling and have Your way.*"

Oh... *His speakings.* **M**y heart **c**annot **c**ount the number of times in *His* sayings to me and is still, in part or full and in all the varying ways or forms... that the **e**ssence of what I release as I recall it or receive it fresh and write it from *Him* to here... **e**ven *now* for this **m**oment requires an agreeing with what *He* speaks and then an aligning with it as we're discovering for us... for what we **expect.**

How **e**ssential for... *my tongue is (and* **expected** *to be) like the pen of a ready writer, inditing the heart of my King, ready (**expectantly**) to write a good thing**... to those who have an **e**ar to hear, an **e**ye so see, and a spirit to **expect** and respond. So speak... speak *oh* **Expectant Eternal King,** Your handmaiden bondservant has **m**ade ready and is listening.. to receive and release... what *You're telling* me to *tell them*... by *Your Spirit Father*... in the *finishing*.

So let's *celebrate*... for indeed it has been and is still about *fullness of and in the journey*, the **c**ourse set before *us... you, me*... in *the process* and, <u>not</u> the end product – yet now *the process* of this time of **e**nding is here. We rest and trust in that fact that *He* already knows the end in all its fullness... uniquely and wholly *for you... for me... for us.* **M**y... how that **c**hanges ones *perspective, perception, and* **expectation**... and **m**ost assuredly the outcome... **e**specially when or if **e**ndings, goodbyes, or farewells **c**an at times present a type of **c**hallenge.

We're not just reading through to get to the **e**nd for the *completion*. But, the **c**ompleting in the **c**ircles of the **c**ycles of **expectancy** *He's* begun *in, through*, and *with* you! For now and overall... in this **preparation** of our **expectation** where *He's* been **m**aking us **m**ore like *Him*. With that in mind, let's just let *Him* be the *Author and Finisher* in the beyond of what was our *in the beginning* now becoming our... *the end*.

Embrace the simplicity of it in the overall *journey*. It's one's life being lived intentionally… in one second… one **m**inute.. one hour… one day… week… **m**onth… year… and in the diverse and **e**clectic **m**erging of **m**oments into now… beyond… and the eternal unfolding in it all. Each portion and **m**easure **c**arrying an *expectancy and expectantly*. In all this… He's not **expecting** a perfect version of us as if we already have it together or will immediately once something is revealed. Just to relish the pleasure in the **m**utuality of *authentic relationship – and its relativity*.

Even *Jesus*, who was and is *Son of God Son of Man* knew this… and still had to speak and **m**ove in the timing of it all in the earth. For *He* knew *His* times were already written in *Father's* book just as they are for *you* in *His* book, about me…about *us*.

- ❖ *Perhaps*…. it is **m**ore about **becoming and being** in *the process* where *He* extends **m**uch to us… so we **c**an *expect and see*, *"It's about a **relationship**… not a formula."*

Enjoying this way of traveling in our daily life… one would **m**ost likely be **c**onsidered **w**ise to respect and appreciate timing's vital role as one **c**ontemplates *carefully, continually, and consistently* the incredible importance of *establishing expectations* in what is written in *the Word* as *He* did in *His* lifetime and short *journey* here. Trust and *expect He* has foundationally **e**stablished a place and purpose within and for us in *His* and our timelines as it is written.

Remember, **He is the Word**. Right now as we're **c**losing, **c**oming to the end of what we've… He's begun… our inviting and allowing *Him* to be **m**ore of a part of our life *encounters and experiences* filled with all their *expectations* has formed **m**uch in us. Which has **m**ade the way for a better fuller acquainting with *Him* along the way ahead and beyond. Let's press into the fullness of what is here… right now to **seize**, **"carpe diam"**… *that seizing of moments*. Those *encounters and experiences* that have **c**ome fully *from, in, and with Him*.

A seizing of the **m**oment now to *embrace* and be *empowered* by *expectation*. There is a truth lingering here to *grab*, **e**ven take hold of if we haven't or are now seeing the need to. And… I'm sensing a need to release a **c**onnection strategical to my time of **e**ntering into this season of writing as **I** *embraced* and became *empowered* by this <u>unexpected</u> connection.

Along with the deposit of godly **c**onfidence… not just for me, but for my/our book **m**inistry support team **m**entioned before. You've been blessed by them as they shared their brief, but highly valued and appreciated part in the **Forwarding Words of Worth** and in the *28 day journey* through their **Expectation's Reflections**.

Ted, a special brother friend and **m**ighty **m**an of *God* who is the only **m**ale on the team, along with his wife *Lynette* as the only **c**ouple… they had watched a live online service with *Apostle Chuck Pierce* at *Glory of Zion* in *Texas*. *Ted* texted and then later **c**alled saying I just had to watch and hear what he shared. Hearing the extreme degree of excitement and urgency in his voice, along with feeling the extent of their *expectancy* for me to do so. So, I did watch it that day. And, OH MY! It didn't take long to understand and appreciate their anticipation in this timely release.

In this portion the sharing is from notes taken while watching the replay online at the *Glory of Zion International* ministry website and notes from *Prophecy Central* replay describing an encounter *Apostle Chuck Pierce* had. It was *Sunday August 27, 2023* and he was asleep on the **c**ouch when he awoke at 3:52am feeling a hand upon his shoulder belonging to a **m**an who was standing there. This **m**an looked to be *'Albert Einstein'*. He then spoke and said, *"You need to wake up NOW!"* He awoke immediately.

Chuck shared how he then started thinking about and looking at the *Theory of Relativity*, at things about *Albert Einstein*, and how he took *Newton's Law of Gravity* and **m**oved it into a new dimension. WOW!!! As you **c**an imagine, I was blown away and **c**aptivated by this **e**ncounter the *Lord* gave to him and fascinated by its somewhat resemblance to how *He* met in a similar way with me. (And can or has with you.)

And then the *Lord* said to **Chuck**, *"I want **My** people to WAKE UP NOW. I have NEW IDEAS, NEW COMPOSITIONS FOR THEM (did he just say that) and a NEW ACCUMMULATION of DATA (really) where they will PUT TOGETHER THINGS THEY HAVE NEVER PUT TOGETHER BEFORE to ADVANCE."* WOW! WOW! WOW! – you **c**an't orchestrate these kind of divinely appointed and aligned **c**onnecting **c**onfirmations, let alone to this degree. (Parenthesis and **c**aps mine).

Chuck **e**nded by saying, *"I'm **telling** you,* (yes he said that)... **GET READY**!"

Well… if nothing **e**lse, for sure and for **c**ertain *Papa God* planted a big *love kiss* on me that day. In that **m**oment… a **m**oment where I had to **c**hoose to let my *expectancy* arise to believe a type of **m**anifesting of it had just **c**ome in this un*expected*, undeniable *confirmation*. A **this is that** **c**onnection! And not just for me, but for *you… me… us* – a *carpe diam* – a **m**oment where in the here and now **we must seize** the *opportunity* to not deny, but fully receive that *He* has been **m**aking us ready in this *journey of and with expectation*. It expressed in such a *personal relational, relative and relevant* way – yet a *collectively corporate* way, and in **the process** – like only *He* **c**an do! So just do it! **Expect**! For I'm *expecting* for and with you!

Tell Him now and out loud… **I receive with fervent expectancy from all You have been, will, and are telling me in this telling and in any kind of making ready You are doing in, through it, and beyond in this day and these times of Your 'Get Ready' we are now in. Your kingdom come, Your will be done on earth as it is in heaven and for Your glory!**

Perhaps, you've noticed, in the here and now of the world around us, that we're in, but not of… an *expediency* in today's *mindset* the seem to be need and drivenness for a *microwave, drive thru, get it now, have it now, and be it now* **m**entality with all its varying forms of *expectancy*. It is undoubtedly what seems to **m**ake up what **m**any are looking for outwardly as their *expectations* reveal too, a sign perhaps into the inwardly. How such thoughts and ways try to spill over onto us… attempting to affect our *expectancy*.

Personally, I have been there in the fluctuating degrees, within different seasons, and regarding various aspects of life – but then haven't we all? Where something so very deep within keeps driving us with such *persistency to press* through… and yes, *spiritually* in the *making ready He* is **c**ontinually doing. Yet, a need for it just to happen **c**an hover which intervenes and interferes with the potential of *fullness of the preparedness* we are pressing into and for in the **m**ore of *Him*… and **m**ore of *Him* in you… me… us.

For what arose there was an awareness of an innate inborn desire, likened unto a fire being placed there… and it within not just *me*… *but us*, from our *Creator Father God*. For *He* indeed knew us before *He* placed us in our **m**other's womb. That *longing*… and **m**ost truly for *belonging* was **emerging** and by the power of *His* **loving longing** in that we were *first loved and desired by Him to be His*. It's **c**onverging and **m**erging through the innermost part of our being…calling us up into *the being **He made you, me… us to be***. Oh… **m**ay we **c**ling to that *expectancy*. *For oh,* how *He* loves you and me.

Awakening had **c**ome… the inner posture of obedience began being key to what *He* aligned me in and had for me, as well as asked of me. **E**specially regarding the length and depth of this *telling* and its potential for pointing to how adamant the fullness of *Them* - being the fuller better way it is… it **m**ust be. Yes, it has been for me… and to a greater degree than this *telling* **c**ould **e**ver *tell* or be. The *accumulation of data*, shared from within me… for now in the fresh newness of it by *His Spirit* in this **c**omposition. <u>*Telling* it in a way never put together before</u> … isn't that what the *Lord* said to/through **C**huck? For me, I **c**an't help but believe this is indeed a form of *"**this is that**"* that I **m**ust testify to. For if you'll recall… *He* hasn't let me use notes/writings **c**ollected over the past 23 years in this *telling*… but said to write it now from out of *Him and His* deposits and downloads in me and as *Holy Spirit* leads!

Now, being real here, *I can only imagine*… let alone believe you'd pick up a book of this length without something or someone directing you…or *telling* you in some kind of way to. As well, it appears to me to **c**onnect to an interesting dimension that you **c**an now see…as I had to see. Why *journey* had to be in the title and a lengthier period of time *in the process and the journey* with *Him* was required… but **m**ore so *He* genuinely desired – remember, **His heart is for relationship** in it all, for *He* knows the **e**nd product. To truly begin to *come away, come up, and come into* a *place, posture, and positioning* to **embrace** and be **empowered** by **expectancy** *differently*… inwardly and outwardly… beyond self… to others… and to *Him* and to **His 3rd power**!

In the sharing throughout this *telling*… it has been by *Divine* invitation that there has been and is an *intentional* place for the *inspiration, impartation, interaction, illumination, imagination, information, illustration, illusion, immersion, infusion*… and the **m**ore.

Therefore, there's no denying that **e**qually as well, any underlying awareness of ungodly spirits trying to point to *imperfection, intimidation, possibility of considered indoctrination -real, religiously, or imagined*… *along with intrepidation, inconsistencies, incompatibilities, inadequacies,* and through *inclinations*… which have attempted to work and influence to keep me… and perhaps you… from **m**oving forward, through and into the beyond of<u> all</u> *His* **expectancy**. Along with the need and desire to **expect and see** things **m**anifest *in the process*. He did not fail and has been good to **m**eet me in this place of *expectancy* and I believe *He* has for you too… and will beyond what you or we **c**an sense or see now.

For within **expectancy's** general **e**very day, **e**verywhere, and in **e**very kind of way through out this, the **c**oupling within the *relativity and relevancy* of it in our lives, our *relationships*, our *circumstances*… and extended into a greater depth of the *spiritual and eternal* dynamic of our **expectations** being *uncovered… discovered…* <u>are still *unfolding*</u>. **E**ven in a form of *redemptive restoring,* for the *reconciling* and *recovering* of *His in the beginning telling*… the **expectancy** of *original intent.* Perhaps, like expressed… it truly **m**ust be this was **m**eant to be a *pilgrimage*. My love for *Him,* to do all as unto *Him* has **embraced** it fully – you **c**an too.

It seems reasonable to say in this place there has been… and is, an underlying desire that within *the process* you've… we've **encountered** *and* **experienced** in this *telling*… there's been a **reforming** and **reviving** of some things. Not through **m**ere **c**onvincing… but **c**onvicting. Not through just a reacting… but responding. Not through just a **c**onnection… but a dis**c**onnection where needed. And, not for a **c**onforming, but a transforming required and desired.

Through it all have we not *uncovered, discovered or recovered* a greater **c**ontinuum of His grace within the **e**stablished truths… that extends in an **e**nlarged way to yourself… and others in the realm and dimensions of **expectancy** with the **expectations** presented in *the process* of *life's journey?*

Did *you... me... we*, not encounter a kind of *sincerity, kindness and gracious* patient presence from *Him* in *this process*? In the *burning, churning, leading to turning* of our hearts... with vulnerability and openness being desired and understandably required? And... in *His* loving care expressed?

Especially if there was a belief to go... even enter into some types of *hidden, intentionally or unintentionally areas* of what *really* drives our *motives, methods, manners* in and on *this mission with expectancy* and all its *expectations,* not to mention because of its greater connectivity to *His* message and mandate. We may have discovered that what might feel at first as unusual... might be needful and necessary *refining* in the *processing* to help us see and know such if we *expect* to grow, and grow in the *fullness of the image and likeness* of Them... Him. Selah ~

Let the *expectancy* for the fullness in *Spirit* and in *Truth* arise. For it has been *awakened*... and there is an *activating, advancing,* and in the *aligning* at work. This isn't just a *form of optimism*... this is **God expectancy filled hope** which at its core comes in and through *God* to us... *God* in us.

Now... *Faith works by love*... not by our good works... the things we think, feel, or suppose we ought to do. We trust **(expectantly)** in the fact that God "works" – what He is leading and guiding us to... and ordering for us to do... are in large part generated by how much we **(expect to)** believe and know God loves us. Faith does not "work" by us showing God how much we love Him. It's more of a process thing in our life journey where in our ongoing relationship with Him... we grow to know and receive from Him the unending, undying, and unshakeable exceedingly abundant love He has for us.*

Again, let's remember that *we are not of this world* which seems to be, and with greater evidence manifesting... a world filled with *evil, hatred, contention,* and *disorder*... returning compared to a place like *in the beginning* where there was great darkness and now with just a disturbing kind of alarming void – **the void of God... His light, His life and... His love.**

How we feel and what we do is all out of a place within our *expectancy*. Therefore we know it will make a difference wherever we are, with whomever we're with... and however whatever happens. It is more *encouraging, edifying,* and *empowering* to do what is *good, right,* and *kind* rather than what is *selfish, offensive or even defensive*... for we are **carrier conduits** of **His light, His life and His love** to the world and to the darkness its producing.

♪ ***What's love got to do with it... everything***.   Now, and somewhere out there... there's an *expectation* of us that contains within in the question... **<u>Did you... me... we, did we learn to love?</u>**

Continually choosing the **LAW OF LOVE** – the essence of *God* in us – and that love being shed abroad in us as *He* knits together our heart with *His* and *His* perfected nature awakens within arising and aligning us back to *Him* and with *Him* – *Them*.* For *His human kingdom* on earth must be made only in and with the infinite essence and power of LOVE forming it... for HE IS LOVE.

CHOICE... is continually evolving in the *process* of the *journey*. Love vs hate... good vs evil... light vs dark... mercy vs revenge... humility vs pride... honor vs shame.. life vs death... grace vs judgement ... blessing vs cursing ... ultimately the *Tree of Life vs Tree of Knowledge of Good and Evil.*

Our choice as *Believers* reflects *His character, conduct,* and *countenance*. *His* choice of living and dying for us and thus its influence in the constructing of *expectation* – *a sacred surrender to* *a submitted life of submission to serving Him in the context of what is His good, acceptable and perfect will with His mind.** For the remaining in oneness and communion with *Him*.

Is it not because **LOVE is the law** *He* **first created for He is love** – not the laws *He* had to later write because of sin and because communion broke union… creating a need for covenant to *restore, redeem, and reconcile* back into right order and to what it was before in the beginning, for the end… and for us and us to be eternally in and a part of *His* Kingdom?

Thank God He chooses to be a real *God* to us and willingly entering through **real love**, a **real relationship** with us that's **relative,** and **relevant** as *He*, the covenant keeping *God* that *He* is… is with us continually and eternally by *His* choice… and more so **His EXPECTANCY.**

His **emc3** = in the **eternal mission of Christ in covenant** by **the 3rd power of *His* Spirit – Holy Spirit** / not the law, not religion full of its rituals and formulas… but relationship that's' everlasting and embedded in the core of *Him* **as love.**

Now… there's an explosion of **His love** ready to burst forth in my heart… filled with an **eager expectation** and *hope* that has awakened within a deeper depth, and its assuredly more of *Him*. It is my prayer you find yourself in a similar place from receiving and realizing.

It's full of greater courage and confidence now that the *again…* the **RE** of *God* has been, is, and will be forever working in it all – ***His redeeming, restoring, reviving, returning, renewing, refilling, refueling, reforming,*** *and* ***rekindling*** in the ***reconciling*** of *you… me… us*, **His children back to** *Him*. For indeed it is what ***His*** **expectations** are **rooted, grounded, and established** in alone… because the *essence* of *Them… Him* demands it.

That a foretaste as proof of our **FULL inheritance** *first fruits gift* be given to us as *His*, our *Father's* sons and daughters… the **Holy Spirit** our **earnest expectation*** given in every good intention from **Father, our Covenant Keeping God,** through **Jesus Yeshua the Son** coming, completing *His expectant earthly covenant ministry* paying the *earnest in His atoning blood*, and returning to heaven so we could receive a pledge of a deposit in *Holy Spirit* now… for the entering into becoming the *"sons"* the earth *stands on tiptoe* for as it groans for the revealing… the *manifestation* of fullness of *Them* in *them… you… me… us*.

Oh yes… *Christ* will return… but, in the meantime there's an *expectation* for us to arise bringing **His kingdom on earth as it is in heaven.**

For it's like *He* has put into our DNA *His* **expectancy**… the **expectancy** of *God* in us… just like in **His Son Yeshua, Immanual**: *God with us*… and in us and through us in **Holy Spirit**.

In it all is **power to the 3rd** and fullest degree of the **essence** *of eternal LOVE of Him who is LOVE* and it's all *true, pure, and real covenant* **LOVE** for us to **engage with, embrace, be empowered and expect!**

<blockquote>
… my soul, wait thou only upon God;
for my *expectation* is from Him…
in His *expected end*.
</blockquote>

… *For this reason I* (**expectantly**) *bow my knees before the Father, from whom every family in heaven and on earth is named, that according to the riches of His glory He* **may** *grant you to be* *strengthened with (His **expectant**) power through His Spirit in your inner being, so that Christ may dwell (**expectantly**) in your hearts through faith—that you, being rooted and grounded in love, may have strength to comprehend with all the saints what is the breadth and length and height and depth, and to know the love of Christ that surpasses (all **expected**) knowledge, that you may be filled with all the fullness of God (and His **expectations**). Now to Him who is able to do far more abundantly than all that we ask or think (**expect**), according to the (**expectant**) power at work within us, to Him be glory in the church and in Christ Jesus throughout all generations, forever and ever.* Amen.

*Footnotes: Chapter 9 / * See Isaiah 48:17, Psalms 45:1, Romans 5:5, Colossians 2:2-3, Romans 12:1-2, Psalm 62:5, Ephesians 1:13-14, Romans 8:1-19, Ephesians 3:14-21 - all emphasis is mine and personal paraphrasing built on various translations and versions. * See Chuck Pierce / Glory of Zion International @gloryofzion.org /Replay August 27, 2023 service / Prophecy Central if still there.

✧ WORTHY WORDS AS WE ENTER CHAPTER 10…

For such a time… *He* is **m**aking it **c**lear that the *personification* of the **c**oncept of ***"expectancy"*** as a *lady* is a kind of likening unto that of **Lady Wisdom** – as seen in *Proverbs 1-9* especially. Interestingly…*He's* reminding me of her in this time of **c**losure **c**onfirming her as a type of **daughter** of **Lady Wisdom**. With **Lady Expectancy's** very **e**ssence **c**oming from the *believing, receiving, and conceiving produced* in and through the benefits and blessings of **Lady Wisdom** actively at work in one's life ordered by and living for *God*. For her very being… **c**omes only through *the wisdom of the Godhead* as illustrated and portrayed in *His Worthy Wise Word…* in the *Spirit of Wisdom** of God, that **c**omes through the spiritual gift in a *Word of Wisdom.** And… overall how **e**very form of *wisdom* therein forms, **c**reates, births, and brings forth **m**anifesting as *godly wisdom* through inviting and allowing the fullness of *Me – The Three: Father, Son, and Holy Spirit* in and to the *3rd power*. Now, let's see what **Lady Wisdom** stirs for **Lady Expectancy** to arise coming to us carrying *"His voice"* as we enter into the end with another glimpse of *His expectancy.*

The Rewards of Wisdom… My child, if you truly want a long and satisfying life, never forget the things that I've taught you. Follow closely every truth that I've given you. Then you will have a full, rewarding life. Hold on to loyal love and don't let go, and be faithful to all that you've been taught. Let your life be shaped by integrity, with truth written upon your heart. That's how you will find favor and understanding with both God and men — you will gain the reputation of living life well.

This is My expectancy for you.

Wisdom's Guidance… Trust in the Lord completely, and do not rely on your own opinions. With all your heart rely on him to guide you, and he will lead you in every decision you make. Become intimate with him in whatever you do, and he will lead you wherever you go. Don't think for a moment that you know it all, for wisdom comes when you adore him with undivided devotion and avoid everything that's wrong. Then you will find the healing refreshment your body and spirit long for. Glorify God with all your wealth, honoring him with your firstfruits, with every increase that comes to you. Then every dimension of your life will overflow with blessings from an uncontainable source of inner joy!

As you expect your expectations and My expectations to align more, they will and with joy.

Wisdom's Correction… My child, when the Lord God speaks to you, never take his words lightly, and never be upset when he corrects you. For the Father's discipline comes only from his passionate love and pleasure for you. Even when it seems like his correction is harsh, it's still better than any father on earth gives to his child. Blessings pour over the ones who find wisdom, for they have obtained living-understanding. As wisdom increases, a great treasure is imparted, greater than many bars of refined gold. It is a more valuable commodity than gold and gemstones, for there is nothing you desire that could compare to her. Wisdom extends to you long life in one hand and wealth and promotion in the other. Out of her mouth flows righteousness, and her words release both law and mercy. The ways of wisdom are sweet, always drawing you into the place of wholeness. Seeking for her… brings the discovery of untold blessings, for she is the healing tree of life to those who taste her fruits.

My expectations include My loving correction..

Wisdom's Blueprints... The Lord laid the earth's foundations with wisdom's blueprints. By his living-understanding all the universe came into being. By his divine revelation he broke open the hidden fountains of the deep, bringing secret springs to the surface as the mist of the night dripped down from heaven.

There is an eternal expectation that I have had and still do for you, as I do all the earth, in My divine design.

Wisdom, Our Hiding Place... My child, never drift off course from these two goals for your life: to walk in wisdom and to discover your purpose. Don't ever forget how they empower you. For they strengthen you inside and out and inspire you to do what's right; you will be energized and refreshed by the healing they bring. They give you living hope to guide you, and not one of life's tests will cause you to stumble. You will sleep like a baby, safe and sound — your rest will be sweet and secure. You will not be subject to terror, for it will not terrify you. Nor will the disrespectful be able to push you aside, because God is your confidence in times of crisis, keeping your heart at rest in every situation.

My expectations are embedded as a part of your purpose. Let our expectations join.

Wisdom in Relationships... Why would you withhold payment on your debt when you have the ability to pay? Just do it! When your friend comes to ask you for a favor, why would you say, "Perhaps tomorrow, when you have the money right there in your pocket? Help him today! Why would you hold a grudge in your heart toward your neighbor who lives right next door? And why would you quarrel with those who have done nothing wrong to you? Is that a chip on your shoulder? Don't act like those bullies or learn their ways. Every violent thug is despised by the Lord, but every tender lover finds friendship with God and will hear his intimate secrets. The wicked walk under God's constant curse, but the righteous walk under a stream of his blessing, for they seek to do what is right. If you walk with the mockers you will learn to mock, but God's grace and favor flow to the meek. Stubborn fools fill their lives with disgrace, but glory and honor rest upon the wise.

***My** expectancy in our relationship is a model for yours with others... be wise.* *

---

*Footnotes: Chapter 10 Worthy Words / * See Proverbs 3:1-9 TPT, Philippians 1:3-11 - all emphasis is mine and personal paraphrasing built on various translations and versions

✧ CHAPTER 10 ✧
✧ EMBRACING & EMPOWERING … FOR BEYOND!

When a doctoral student at *Princeton* asked, *"What is there left in the world for original dissertation (in depth study, critique, essay) research?"* Albert Einstein replied, *"Find out about prayer. Somebody **must** find out about prayer."* Great answer *Dr. Einstein*. Perhaps however, it is not one most *expected*.

But the kind of searching, *yours… mine… ours* we've encountered while on this *spiritual pilgrimage of expectation…* we've experienced it in an assortment of ways with some researching and depth of study, at least on my part, and whatever has been yours up to this point and within… as its presented itself in a *little by little … informal line upon line and precept upon precept* kind of way in this *telling* and in the **expectancy** of *His* moving in the midst of it all – the *journey,* from its beginning and through its end… **of the process.** And yes, *prayer's* been an ongoing essential element applied and suggested directly or indirectly.

Now, an appropriate prayer is actually coming to mind in this place. One that I discovered after it was prayed over me as I recovered from a car accident near death experience. **"Blessed are you, oh Lord our God, King of the Universe, who has sustained us and brought us to this place".**

This prayer is called the *Shehecheyanu.* It is a *Jewish* blessing of thanksgiving, typically recited to commemorate special occasions or to mark the beginning of something new or infrequent or even the end as one completes and finishes a thing well, in and through *His* goodness and grace. Let's agree releasing it aloud in prayer now: . **"Blessed are you, oh Lord our God, King of the Universe, who has sustained us and brought us to this place".**

This place… this final chapter, a valuable place for *remembering* in the *returning* and *recalling* of our *"In the beginning…"* and the sharing of some powerful **encounters** and **experiences** that led to this *telling* and it being done from and through a fullness that had come and remains through the fulness of the *Godhead – The Holy Trinity / Three: Father, Son, Holy Spirit…* and to the **3rd power** of Them/Him in me to *"Tell them"…* you.

Yet… let's not forget the underlying essential foundation of *His "In the beginning…"* with the *Spirit of God* hovering and brooding for the creating about to take place in *Elohim's, "Let there be…"* or how the earth is groaning… standing on tiptoe in **earnest expectation** for the manifestation of **the sons of God**… us, to come forth, rise up, and be in their /our divinely designed original state of *let there be*!

It's an already done, paid for and purchased with all its benefits and blessings from the *Father* through *Jesus the Son*, but requiring the *One* that was yet to come sent by the *Beloved Son – Holy Spirit…* who *He* knew had to come and still desires to come fully into and continually to *you… me… us. Holy Spirit* have *Your* way ~

Remember too… that promise in its fullness of our **earnest expectation** is not just unto our salvation, but our inheritance in our adoption in its entirety of our birthright… which is sealed by *God* through the *Holy Spirit.* Paul Keith Davis shares it like this.. *The adoptions is <u>not the accepting of someone as a son, but the placing of a son</u> born into the family with full access to his inheritance.**

Amazingly, our **expectancy** from us being a *son of God, son of man new creature born again* sonship status and birthright… is to **live and walk it out now** for we have *full access* to every benefit and blessing, all promises and provision for *His* plans and purposes for us right now on earth... in the *righteousness of God in Christ Jesus*.. while we are seated through the same in heavenly places at the right hand of *Father God Almighty*... and being led by the *Spirit of God* as *sons of God*. Amen.

So... *Never doubt God's (**expected**) **m**ighty power to work in you and accomplish all this. He will achieve infinitely **m**ore than your greatest (**expected**) request... your **m**ost unbelievable (in all your **expectancy**) dream... and exceed (all your **expectations**) beyond your wildest imagination! He will outdo them all (that's His **expectation**), for His **m**iraculous (**eternally expectant**) power constantly energizes you!* *

*O**h**, what **e**ternal **e**nergy in the **c**ontinualness of the **e**ssence of Him, His lavishing constant covenant love* wrapping around us, in us, and through us to **c**ome forth in what can be seen as 3D – *3rd power dimension* of *Him* being **e**xpressed in and through us and for into the beyond of *Him*.

The **3D** of > ***Done, Doing, Do*** – an *expectation* that is grounded first in *Him* through what is already done before the foundation and in the blood/work of the **c**ross unto ascension, what *He* is doing, and to the **3rd power** of what we **expect** *He* will do within us as *His Ekklesia*.

The **3D** of > ***Grab, Glean/lean, Grow*** – an *expectation* for how in *the journey* and *the process* therein happing to us we **grab** what *He's* releasing receiving it, we **glean** from it **leaning** not on our own understanding acknowledging the fullness of *Him*, and as *He* directs our paths so we grow!

The **4D** quantum beyond > **Grab, Glean/lean, Grow, Go/Gather** – an *expectation* which takes the above to next level beyond ourselves into Kingdom to *His power* fully working in and through us to ***go, do, be***... and as we **gather** and are **gathered together** in **Him collectively and corporately**... so *His* Kingdom on earth can be as it is in heaven. And... *signs, **m**iracles and wonders* follow us in the **e**bb and flow!

David Van Kovering shares, " ... *be filled with all Truth by observing the future   God has for you. Take that quantum leap!   Our false concepts regarding time and **m**atter limit our understanding when we consider all creation and all things eternal.*" And these words from *His* back it up... *For by Him all things were created that are in heaven and that are in earth, visible and invisible... He is before all things, and in Him all things consist, exist, and are sustained.** That is *His Word* **c**onnecting it as only it truly **c**an.

Now, I'm hearing these words spoken recently and **m**ore frequently that ...   ***expectation is the breeding ground for miracles***! Be it so Lord! But then if this is true... what is the *breeding ground for expectation*?   **YOU are... I am... WE are**. As *His* children – sons and daughters, *His* family, the Body of Christ, *His* kings and priests, *His* Church, and as *His Ekklesia*. All dimensions and dynamics of who *He* is in us and has made us as individuals, to be **c**ollectively and **c**orporately such!

What *He's* been forming in us all along the way – because *He's* already formed it in us before we were placed in our **m**other's womb. It's *His **3D*** enlarged... expanded paradigm and transformed **m**indset within us as at first and in our state that **e**xisted in life as it was/is in *His* original intent. But now we're *born again* and **c**an live in and out of the ***expectancy*** it gives us access to. Which is really quite profound.

To **c**reate and **c**ultivate what's within into an atmosphere where our ***expectancy*** for good, both in our world around us – the secular which we are *in but not of*... and in the *spiritual*... **e**ven the sacred space of the life we're living. Through the active positive force, *expectant* with a determined godly **c**onscientiousness as we partner with and in *Him – His Word, will and ways*.

It was beyond *John's* "*Prepare ye the way…*" to the beyond of *Yeshua's*, "*Behold the kingdom of heaven is at hand…*" for it was the **c**ulmination of what these **m**anifestations **c**ontained in all their eternal and earth bound *expectations* the beyond would **c**ome forth. Even the "*this is that*" of what was prophesied hundreds of years ago by Joel*.. and it was unfolding in their **m**idst as *His* **C**hurch was birthed for ***His kingdom*** to **c**ome on earth as in heaven… and not that of **m**an.

It reminds me of what I recently heard *Lou Engle* so passionately release, "… everything is shifting now… this is what I'm living for right now… a **m**assive beholding of the *Lamb of God*… and a baptism like *America* and the world has never seen." Be it so *Lord*… let there be!

The *rebirth and renaissance* of *Your Church* as *You* designed who also functions as *kings, priests* and *prophets*… and as *Your Ekklesia* on earth. For indeed we in our *born again son of God son of man Jesus* nature, **embrace** not just the *Gospel of Salvation*… but the **Gospel of Your Kingdom**… with all *expectancy* for the *fullness* to **c**ome and as we *expectantly* become **His Bride.**

Preparing, **m**aking ready, and all that's being done especially in our *identity - purpose, regarding our inheritance - position,* and *authority – power*, in these **28 days** with the **words of worth** and all… there has **emerged** an **empowering** through **"The Journey's with e… m… c… 3"**. This will aid us in bringing forth what is next according to ***His timing, purposes, and plans***. We know the potential in the **words of worth**… along with *all the other words* emphasized by their highlighted "*e… m… c…*" are having a work in and through *you… me… us*. Let us believe and *expect* that they will **c**ontinue to have… just like they have in their *manifesting process* as being discovered in this *telling*… and in new ways, even wonderful un*expected* ones too!

Especially as was initially proposed, that *you… me… we*, extend our *personal invitation* and *inclusion* of *Him*… in *His fullness* – the *fullness* of **Them – God the Father, God the Son – Jesus Yeshua,** and **God the Holy Spirit**… so to **m**ake a way for *His* presence to be experienced and an intentional place of relationship, be given for *His expectations* to *move, revolve, and evolve* in the **m**idst of it all… to the **3rd power** – which enables in all things **LOVE** – the essence power of *who and what He is*.

For *together*… and *together in Him*… we have equally been on what we defined as a type of **pilgrimage**. So as we reminiscence… remember in its **m**eaning it's **c**onsidered to be… a *journey one chooses to partake in for religious or spiritual reasons… sometimes to a specific place and or for a specific reason*. But always in the **quest** for… ♪ *More love… more power… more of You in my life…* (*yours… mine… our lives*). *More love… more power… more of You in our lives*.

You're each have joined **m**e and blessed **m**e in so **m**any ways by being a part of this appointed time and that **m**akes this… an *individual, collective, and corporate* kind of *pilgrimage* within the *greater journey* and with all *the processing* of potential and possibilities of our *expectations* increasing as *you…me… we*, keep our eyes on things eternal in all the *expectancy* it **c**ontains for here on earth. A we **c**ontinue now into the beyond… into **m**ore of *Him*… and with *expectancy* in our spirit and filled with *expectations* we're *embracing to be empowered*!

The *telling* to "*Tell them*"… which has been an honor *telling to you*… and humbly through in part what I have **encountered and experienced** from the beginning through it all… and now through the **c**ompletion brings personal satisfaction. But even greater, is the delight to share what will be the final depositing of *expectancy* as we draw to our end.

A truly astounding gift from *Father,* it was and to remains to be to me as *His* daughter… and at a time when I needed deeply and desperately to know and connect with **His love**. And, it came through a profound validation and confirmation that **e=mc3** was real and really mattered beyond what *He* was speaking to me… and then in a *"re"* of *God* to **m**y husband… and now for you and all the others.

Those who will freely ***believe, receive and conceive expectingly*** of ***His limitless extravagant covenant* LOVE**… in all its connections as the *One True Source* and source… **Forc**e and force in *His* greater ***revelation, relativity, and relevancy*** of **the essence of *Them*…** ***Him*** who is our ***Expectant Eternal God of Love.*** The God who said, "***It's not about a formula… it's about a relationship***." For **He is Love**.

Let us now **m**ove forward in ***all expectancy*** and within ***every expectation embrace it to be empowered*** as we ***press into Him*** in the ***process…*** and on this ***adventurous journey*** with the ***3 fold power cord of Father, Son, and Holy Spirit working together*** in the fullness of the ***essence of love and its power filled with eternal everlasting expectancy*** as ***heaven manifests on earth*** and in all the ***Sons of God, Sons of Man* you… me…us,** and **those yet to join us!**

Expectancy's prayer as you prepare for the end's arrival to our journey and receive first from this final releasing of His Worthy Word as in Ephesians …

I pray now to our Heavenly Expectant Father in the name of Yeshua His Son over you… May the blessings of divine grace and supernatural peace that flow from God our wonderful Father, and our Messiah, the Lord Jesus, be upon your lives. My prayers for you are full of praise to God as I give him thanks for you with great joy! I'm so grateful for our union and our enduring partnership that began the first time I presented to you the gospel. I pray with great faith for you, because I'm fully convinced that the One who began this gracious work in you will faithfully continue the process of maturing you until the unveiling of our Lord Jesus Christ! It's no wonder I pray with such confidence, since you have a permanent place in my heart! You have remained partners with me in the wonderful grace of God… (even though I'm not with you in the natural)… standing up for the truth of the gospel. Only God knows how much I dearly love you with the tender affection of Jesus, the Anointed One. Continue to pray for your love to grow and increase beyond measure, bringing you into the rich revelation of spiritual insight in all things. This will enable you to choose the most excellent way of all —becoming pure and without offense until the unveiling of Christ. And you will be filled completely with the fruits of righteousness that are found in Jesus, the Anointed One—bringing great praise and glory to God! Amen and amen. Be it so and for Your glory.

✧ THE BEAUTY OF AN UNEXPECTED END...

Expectation's conclusion... receive for it's out of our Father's love to us...

Albert Einstein (14 March 18 79–18 April 1955) is perhaps best known for being a theoretical physicist and for receiving the 1921 *Noble Peace Prize* in physics "for his services to *"Theoretical Physics"*. A lesser known fact about arguably one of the **m**ost intelligent **m**en of **m**odern times is that he was also a prolific sender of personal notes and letters upon his own personalized letterhead.

In late 1980s, Einstein's daughter Lieserl donated 1400 letters written by Einstein to the Hebrew University. The text of one of them is reproduced below for you. Had it been sent by Einstein to his daughter, this letter shows a very different side to Einstein's personality and his outlook on the world.

And it begins...

"When I proposed the theory of relativity, very few understood me, and what I will reveal now to transmit to mankind will also collide with the misunderstanding and prejudice in the world. I ask you to guard the letters as long as necessary, years, decades, until society is advanced enough to accept what I will explain below.

There is an extremely powerful force that, so far, science has not found a formal explanation too. It is a force that includes and governs all others, and is even behind any phenomenon operating in the universe and has not yet been identified by us this universal force is LOVE.

When scientists looked for a unified theory of the universe they forgot the most powerful unseen force. Love is Light, that enlighten those who give and receive it. Love is gravity, because it makes some people feel attracted to others. Love is power, because it multiplies the best we have, and allows humanity not to be extinguished in their blind selfishness. Love unfolds and reveals. For love we live and die. Love is God and God is Love.

This force explains everything and gives meaning to life. This is the variable that we have ignored for too long, maybe because we are afraid of love because it is the only energy in the universe that man has not learned to drive at will.

To give visibility to love, I made a simple substitution in my most famous equation. If instead of $E=mc^2$, we accept that the energy to heal the world can be obtained through love multiplied by the speed of light squared, we arrive at the conclusion that love is the most powerful force there is, because it has no limits.

After the failure of humanity in the use and control of the other forces of the universe that have turned against us, it is urgent that we nourish ourselves with another kind of energy.

If we want our species to survive, if we are to find meaning in life, if we want to save the world and every sentient being that inhabits it, love is the one and only answer.

Perhaps we are not yet ready to make a bomb of love, a device powerful enough to entirely destroy the hate, selfishness and greed that devastate the planet. However, each individual carries within them a small but powerful generator of love, whose energy is waiting to be released.

When we learn to give and receive this universal energy, dear Lieserl, we will have affirmed that love conquers all, is able to transcend everything and anything, because love is the quintessence of life.

I deeply regret not having been able to express what is in my heart, which has quietly beaten for you all my life. Maybe it's too late to apologize, but as time is relative, I need to tell you that I love you and thanks to you I have reached the ultimate answer!".

Your father,
Albert Einstein

Here are a few quotes of *Einstein's* that I found almost profound… and believe you **m**ight too… when you hear by the ***Spirit*** and listen for *Father's* heart in them:

"The world, as we have created it, is a process of our thinking. It cannot be changed without changing our thinking".

*"Anyone who has never **m**ade a **m**istake has never tried anything new".*

*"The **m**easure of intelligence is the ability to change".*

"It is the supreme art of the teacher to awaken joy in creative expression and knowledge".

Now, as you **c**ontinue forward in your ***journey of expectation***, be **e**ncouraged to engage and ***embrace*** this **c**hallenge to seek out and encounter more of *Him* in *His Worthy Word* revealing what *He* says to brings a **c**onnection to **e**ach quote and *experience* an opportunity to be ***empowered! Holy Spirit… have Your way!***

---

*Footnotes: Chapter 10 / * See Ephesians 3:20, Genesis 1, 2, Colossians 1:16-17 - all emphasis is mine and personal paraphrasing built on various translations and versions. * See Paul Keith Davis / @whitedoveministries.com / The Voice of the Bride p 42 – 43. * See David Van Kovering / @heavensphysics.com / The Physics of Heaven by Judy Franklin and Ellyn Davis with various other authors / p 138 -139. * See Lou Engle / @LouEngleMinistries / @ Youtube "Shorts" reel
 * See Albert Einstein / google search on legitimacy of daughter Lieserl

EINSTEIN'S LETTER TO DAUGHTER

STATEMENT of VALIDITY: Regarding the controversy surrounding this letter: "'The writings were not donated by Einstein himself, nor his daughter, Lieserl. The letters were donated by Margot Einstein, the scientist's stepdaughter,' claims Diana Kormos — Buchwald, editor — in — chief at the Einstein Papers Project. Link > https://community.thriveglobal.com/a-letter-from-albert-einstein-to-his-daughter/ .

Michele Zackheim, in her book on "Lieserl", Einstein's Daughter, states that "Lieserl" had a developmental disability, and that she lived with her mother's family and probably died of scarlet fever in September 1903.

This site validates in an AE letter written at age 22 regarding when Lieserl's birth filled to questions to Mileva about her birth. https://www.theguardian.com/science/2014/dec/05/albert-einstein-archive-genius-doubts-and-loves

✧ **EXPECTATION NOW AWAKENED IS CALLING AND AWAITS…**

DO YOU HEAR HIS WISE VOICE IN HER NOW?

FOR IT IS THE VOICE OF OUR FATHER AS LOVE

FILLED WITH HIS ENDEARING ETERNAL EXPECTANCY

AND CARRYING HIS EXPECTANT END.

Let these final *Worthy Words* remind us…
We have come (in our **expectation**)… in this journey and it's process…
into an intimate experience with God's love, and
we trust in the love He has for us. He has given us His Spirit
(and **expectancy**) within us so that we can have the
assurance that He lives in us and that we live in Him.
So… delightfully loved ones, if He loved (and still loves) us
with such tremendous love, then 'loving one another'…
should be our **(expected)** way of life.
God is love! So… as those who are living in (His **expectant**) love,
you are living in God, and God lives **(expectantly)**
now in you… me… us — let us go and love **(expecting)**!*

(*Footnotes: *See I John 4 portions from TPT with added words and emphasis mine)

✧ AN EXPECTATION PROCLAMATION FOR THE JOURNEY

Yahweh God our Father, Creator, and Eternal Expectant King
… we declare and decree You are real LOVE
– the universal eternal never changing Source and Force of LOVE!
In You… Father, Son, Holy Spirit we see $e = mc3$ in its divine eternal
capacity that we contain and carry as conduits of Yours…
for as You are so are we… we're not who we used to be.
We will press in to continually turn our hearts towards You in passionate
love, reverent worship, and authentic ministry to You
who alone are worthy… receiving as well Your lavish love which
our hearts desire to receive and pour back freely to and upon You.
We choose to engage and remain in this ever evolving multifaceted
molding and making process in You…and in our life's journey.
We will minister telling others as we partner with You to reconcile them
back into right, real, and relative relationship with You.
We will keep beholding… becoming… being… for we know in You and
by Your Spirit we live, breathe, move, and have our very being. We will
embrace Your constant covenant love and be empowered by it so the fruit
and gifts of Your Spirit move and bear much to help bring forth Your
kingdom on earth as it in in heaven.
We will be intentional to let Your love overflow to others to encounter and
experience… for we know all the earth awaits earnestly expecting the
moving and manifesting of us…
as the sons of God as is reflective of Your expected end.
We will with hope filled expectancy embrace Your expectations as we
align, arise, and advance now into the more… beyond in this
eternal **m**eaningful **c**ovenant real love relationship as Yours.

✧ APPENDICES

ION Word LIST by Elizabeth Bayliff
– words highlighted by the *Holy Spirit* that affect what we expect requiring action.

ION is a suffix that when added to a word indicates *action*; *the act, state, or result described by the base word*... which implies a *process of action* is required or has taken/taking place and is connected to *expectancy* and *expectations formed and manifesting*. Many of these can come in the form of an ungodly spirit attempting to work through them. *You* are the *Word Lord*... and by *Your Spirit* may we be moved through discernment, wisdom, and in action. Let the manifestation of *Your* expectation arise in the midst of it all with *Your* expected end.

PERCEPTION... interpretation, your understanding, meaning of or assigned, perspective, view of
PERSPECTION... perspective, viewpoint, outlook, standpoint – either true or relative to subject
VISION... see, sight, perceive visualization, observation, image, imagination, future thoughts/plans
INITIATION... to start, begin, commence, inception, move forward into – the act of or lack of.
MOTIVATION... incentive, inspiration, stimulation, drive, impetus, enthusiasm-possessing or lack of
SATISFACTION... pleasure, approval, gratification, fulfillment, contentedness - experiencing it or not
VALIDATION... proof, to endorse, authenticity, genuine, justification, connection, confirmation
INHABITIION... occupancy, dwelling, residence, taking place, lodging, possessing, abiding, settling in
LIMITATION... restraint, restrict, control, constraint, hindrance, obstacles, things that are or become
CONFUSION... confuse mixed-up, misunderstand, misperception, uncertainty, indecision, doubt
INTIMIDATION... fear, coercion, bully, frightening, alarming, threatening, scare – a spirit of
DECEPTION... lie, trickery, sham, doubt, distrust, delusion, witchcraft, suspicion, superstition
PERVERSION... distortion, falsification, twisting, manipulation, control, skew, justification
ESCALATION... escalate, heighten, increase, surge, intensify, spiral, amplify, magnification
EXAGGERATION... embellishment, overemphasis, overstate, to mock, fake, simulate, imitation
SUGGESTION... idea, proposed thought, recommendation, counsel, assumption, theory, speculation
PROVISION... supply, provide needs, give, equip, assistance, benefits, blessings
REVELATION... reveal, expose, out of hiding, disclose, present, bring forth, announce, acknowledge
IMAGINATION... mind's eye, curiosity, perception, to embellish, exaggerate, overstate, fantasize
JUSTIFICATION... defense, explain, reason, to justify, rationalization, validation, corroboration
IMPARTATION... convey, transmission of information, carry into, deposit, enlighten(ment)
DIRECTION... lead, guide, show, to make, put in order, administrate, amend, correction, ordering
SUBMISSION... plan, suggest, surrender to, submit, yield, consent to, compliance, honor, respect
ACTIVATION... start, begin, initiate, apply, adhere, display, appear, show
APPLICATION... use, function, operation, utilization, practice, purpose, claim, request, submission,
MANIFESTATION... appearance, display, show, exhibit, presence, indication, proof, expression
STAGNATION... stagnate, decay, deteriorate, sluggishness, inactivity, complacency, mediocrity
RECOGNITION... cognition, awareness, identify, reason, understand, comprehend, insight, credit.
RESTORATION... repair, renew, recover, reclaim, improve, return, restore, redemption, restitution
RECONCILIATION... resolve, reunion, return back to, resolve, rectify, settle, make right
CELEBRATION... celebrate, rejoice, honor, festivity, praise, observance, remembrance, acknowledge
*PRESUMPTION... belief, conjuncture, supposition, presupposition, with higher likelihood/evidence
*ASSUMPTION... guess, speculate, assume, take up, infer, hypothesis, suspect to be true
* Note: PRESUMPTION is accepting something as true even if not for certain. ASSUMPTION is accepting as true, certain to happen, without proof, believing without evidence
SITUATION... state or condition, circumstance, state of things at hand, all things are a "situation".
DIRECTION... path, way, course, track, route, how to do, guidance, leadership, order, manage
CULTIVATION... growing, planting, sowing, reaping, raising, rearing, bettering, nurturing, working
CONVERSTATION... communicate, talk, chat, listen, share, exchange, dialog, discuss, confer
COMMUNION... union, intimacy, closeness, coming together ... relationship

*Permission to use given by Elizabeth Bayliff, without any modifications, for it is what He revealed.

The 10 M's" for Maturing & Maintaining Ministry

Dr. Bill Hamon's book "*Prophets, Pitfalls and Principles*" (Destiny Image, ©1991)

1. **Manhood (or womanhood)**
    Gen. 1:26,27 God makes the man before manifesting mighty ministry
    Rom. 8:29 Man – apart from position, message or ministry
    Heb. 2: 6,10 Personality – evaluating the person, not performance
    Tim. 2:5 Jesus – manhood thirty years; ministry – three and a half; 10:1 ratio

2. **Ministry**
    2 Cor. 6:3 No offense to ministry; 1 Cor. 2:4-5 – power and demonstration
    Mt. 7:15-21 By their fruits you shall know them – anointing, results
    Deut. 18:20-22 Prophecies or preaching productive; proven, pure, positive

3. **Message**
    Eph. 4:15 Speak the truth in love; present truth and life giving
    1 Tim. 4:2 Message balanced, scriptural, doctrinally sound and spiritually right
    Mk. 16:20 God confirms His word – not person, pride, or reputation

4. **Maturity**
    Jas. 3:17 Attitude right; mature in human relations; heavenly wisdom
    Gal. 5:22 Fruit of the Spirit, Christ-like character, dependable, steadfast
    1 Cor. 13 Not childish, Eph. 4:14, Heb. 5:14; Biblically knowledgeable and mature
    1 Tim. 3:6 Not a novice

5. **Marriage**
    1 Tim. 3:2,5 Scripturally in order, personal family versus God's family
    1 Pet. 3:1,7 Priorities straight – God first, wife and family, then ministry
    Eph. 5:22,23 Marriage to exemplify relationship of Christ and His church

6. **Methods**
    Titus 1:16 Rigidly righteous, ethical, honest, integrity – honest
    Rom. 1:18 Not manipulative or deceptive; doesn't speak 'evangelistically'
    Rom. 3:7,8 Good end results; do not justify unscriptural methods

7. **Manners**
    Titus 1:7, 3:1,2 Unselfish, polite, kind, gentlemanly or ladylike, discreet
    Eph. 4:29, 5:4 Proper speech and communication in words and mannerism

8. **Money**
    1 Tim. 3:6 Not "craving wealth and resorting to ignoble and dishonest methods of getting it", 1 Tim. 6:5,10,17/ Luke 12:15 Love of money and materialism destroys (e.g. Achan, Balaam, Judas)

9. **Morality**
    Col. 3:5 Virtuous, pure and proper relationships
    1 Cor. 6:9-10,18 / Eph. 5:3 / 1 Cor. 5:11 Biblical sexual purity in attitude and action
    Matt. 5:28 No wrong thoughts or desire to do – without opportunity to act

10. **Motive**
    Matt. 6:1 To serve or be seen? Fulfill personal drive or God's desire?
    1 Cor. 16:15-16 True motivation?
    To minister or to be a minister? To herald the truth or just be heard by man?
    1 Cor. 13:1-3 Motivated by God's love, or lust for power, fame, name, etc.?

*Permission given to use and on file.

7 Mountains by Johnny Enlow

AREA OF CULTURE	MEDIA	FAMILY	ARTS & ENTERTAINMENT	ECONOMY	RELIGION	EDUCATION	GOVERNMENT
THE SEVEN COLORS OF LOVE	RED	ORANGE	YELLOW	GREEN	BLUE	INDIGO	VIOLET
GOD AS…	COMMUNICATOR	PAPA	CREATOR	PROVIDER	REDEEMER	TEACHER	KING
REV. 5:12 LOVE DISPLAYED AS…	BLESSING	STRENGTH	GLORY	RICHES	HONOR	WISDOM	POWER
ARCHANGEL	GABRIEL	RAPHAEL	JEHUDIEL	ZERACHIEL	MICHAEL	RAZIEL	URIEL
THE BIG LIE ABOUT GOD	GOD DOESN'T HAVE A GOOD PLAN FOR US.	WE HAVE BEEN ABANDONED AND REJECTED BY GOD.	GOD DOESN'T WANT US TO HAVE FUN.	IT IS POINTLESS TO TRUST GOD FOR OUR RICHES OR PROVISION.	WE HAVE TO WORK HARD AND BE GOOD IN ORDER TO KNOW GOD.	TRUE WISDOM IS SELF-DEPENDENCE.	GOD DOESN'T CARE ABOUT US.
YOUR ASSURANCE	YOU HAVE A DESTINY.	YOU ARE ACCEPTED.	YOU ARE ENJOYED.	YOU ARE PROVIDED FOR.	YOU HAVE ETERNAL SECURITY.	YOU ARE IMPORTANT.	YOU ARE ROYALTY.

RESTORE7

Johnny Enlow / The 7 Mountain Prophecy
Restore7.org – Lead With Love

*Permission given to use and on file.

The Ship… *casting of a modern day word parable /* by Elizabeth Bayliff through the Holy Spirit

The *captain* is known for saying… *"ALL aboard"*… so come along with me on this *"word ship"* voyage! May it stir the waters and waves of *expectation* in you as it did me… and still is as *He* keeps expounding on these essential elements. Remember *SOL* – **Lordship from ownership and in stewardship**… of and in *the process* of *you… me… us* turning - particularly our *turning to, in and through Him* in *all things, all ways, and always*. You know Lord, be it so! Full steam ahead!

We know **Kingship** and **Lordship** are at the helm of the heart of *relationship* with *His* **Messiahship** in our lives as we're no longer on a *slave ship* because we're now in **sonship**, secured in *His* redemptive **kinsmanship** and reigning **rulership**, grounded in intimate **friendship** leading to covenant **courtship** flowing from loving *fellowship* as a fruit rendered through our divine **heirship**.

With **servantship**, as *Jesus* so beautifully modeled and powerfully defined, laying the foundation for ministry and leadership of any kind. And, co-laboring **partnership** prominent part of what *He* desires from out of *His* **lordship** with us, yet *in and with Him as Father, as Son, and as Holy Spirit – the three in one* making us one in the three as such unity flows from *His* **headship** down as its fire takes us higher. Oh… the expectancy for the commanded blessing that *He* says will manifests there!

Good **sportsmanship** certainly is required when you're on *His* team in ministry. It's an important trait too in being a part of *His* family. Because we're never riding alone in a *kayak* or adrift in a *sailboat* out in the sea. *Together* is best as *He's* designed in all things; *His threefold cord* in you and me.

For as we embrace that true **worship** in *Spirit and Truth* is our life, we come to know it's also our warfare **warship** helping overcome contention and strife. But remember we must, that we're living in a **citizenship** not of this world. Which offers an **ambassadorship**, along with **landownership**, and all that is our *identity, inheritance, and authority*… oh, how that makes our enemies swirl.

Discipleship, mentorship, comradeship, companionship, and **partnership** all bring about a spirit of *kingdom* **championship** in *His* sons and daughters that arise. But ultimately, every ship must be *rooted, grounded and established* in personal **ownership** with accountability for **stewardship** and **dominionship** with truth in its core and flowing from its lips.

His excellent **workmanship** evidenced in such will glorify *His* magnificent **craftsmanship** in the beauty and reflection of *Him* in the *flagship* with its fleet of *sent ships* in covenant alignment with the fullness of *Him* and under *His* heavenly hosts angelic **guardianship**.

Among the fleet *He's* gathered and is gathering, you will see **battleships, cruise ships, cargo ships,** and **transport ships. Passenger ships, hospital ships, icebreaker ships** and even **lightships** – you know the ones that are anchored like a lighthouse in the bay. Providing a steady source of light for all to see and navigate through by their **seamanship** in the midst of the calm, the waves or the storms, making the way.

Every **ship** and **shipmate** matters with their special *part, piece, and place*, so that we *don't sink the ship*, as we try to avoid **hardships**, as we desire to encourage ones not to *abandon ship* because we don't want any **ship** wrecks as we press in this race through our **heirship**.

I AM calls, surely you hear *His* voice drawing, *"Ahoy. All hands on deck* **shipmates***!"* I'm the *Captain* at the helm and it's not too late, for indeed you've not missed your calling. **I AM** the **Ship Owner, Ship Master,** and a **Shipmate** with you too, helping keep all things **shipshape** by *My compass. Drop anchor in Me* and you will see how I will carry you through."

Ship builders, **ship** buyers, and **ship** owners are in the **shipyard** about the *Captain's* business too, along with all those who are in the docks awaiting their place on our future **ship** crews.

In the skies above as the **ship** proceeds, our spirit filled prayers like **rocket ships** are continually arising, over and in all the nations and with all *He's* commissioned us to do… and, with no compromising

Then I heard the *Captain's* passionate cry arise in the midst of a manifesting moment … *"Anchors aweigh, oh* **ships** *of My glorious fleet… afloat and turning. For I love you My ekklesia, My church… My Bride of original intent for whom My heart is yearning and My Love Boat's course is set for returning.*

*Permission to use given by Elizabeth Bayliff.

THE JOURNEY OF EXPECTATION... EMBRACE IT AND BE EMPOWERED!

THE SEVEN CHURCHES OF REVELATION

CHURCHES:	STRENGTHS:	FAILURES:	INSTRUCTION:	PROMISE TO THE FAITHFUL:
EPHESUS "LOVELESS" Rev. 2:1-7	Hard work; patient endurance; rejected evil; perseverance	You have forsaken your first love	Repent and do the works you did at first	You will eat from the tree of life
SMYRNA "SUFFERING" Rev. 2:8-11	Enduring your suffering and poverty – yet you are rich	None	Remain faithful even when facing prison, persecution or death	I will give you the crown of life; you will not be hurt by the second death
PERGAMOS "WORLDLY" Rev. 2:12-17	Loyalty to Christ; refuse to deny Him	Tolerates cults, heresies, idolatry and immorality	Repent!	Hidden manna and a stone with a new name on it
THYATIRA "WRONG DOCTRINE" Rev. 2:18-29	Love, faith, works; patient endurance; constant improvement	Tolerates pagan cults, idolatry and immorality; judgment coming!	Repent!	Faithful will hold fast until I come; I will give you the morning star
SARDIS "SPIRITUALLY DEAD" Rev. 3:1-6	Only a faithful few have kept the faith; church spiritually dead	Repent and turn back to Christ	Strengthen what little faith remains	Faithful will walk with Jesus and not be blotted out of the book of life
PHILADELPHIA "SPIRITUALLY ALIVE" Rev. 3:7-13	Kept my word and have not denied my name	None	You have an open door; I will keep you from the hour of trial	I will make you a pillar in the temple of my God
LAODICEA "COMPLACENT" Rev. 3:14-22	None	Neither hot nor cold; your riches make you impoverished	Turn from indifference and repent!	I will invite those who overcome to sit with me on my throne

Jon Gary Williams / La Vergne, TN 37086 / Author gives general permission to use
https://www.thelordsway.com/site19/custompage.asp?CongregationID=1202&CustomPageID=1451

Albert Einstein's Letter to His Daughter

Albert Einstein (14 March 18 79–18 April 1955) is perhaps best known for being a theoretical physicist and for receiving the 1921 Noble Peace Prize in physics "for his services to "Theoretical Physics". A lesser known fact about arguably one of the most intelligent men of modern times is that he was also a prolific sender of personal notes and letters upon his own personalized letterhead.

In late 1980s, Einstein's daughter Lieserl donated 1400 letters written by Einstein to the Hebrew University. The text of one of them is reproduced below for you. Had you been sent by Einstein to his daughter, this letter shows a very different side to Einstein's personality and his outlook on the world.

"When I proposed the theory of relativity, very few understood me, and what I will reveal now to transmit to mankind will also collide with the misunderstanding and prejudice in the world. I ask you to guard the letters as long as necessary, years, decades, until society is advanced enough to accept what I will explain below.

There is an extremely powerful force that, so far, science has not found a formal explanation too. It is a force that includes and governs all others, and is even behind any phenomenon operating in the universe and has not yet been identified by us this universal force is love.

When scientists looked for a unified theory of the universe they forgot the most powerful unseen force. Love is Light, that enlighten those who give and receive it. Love is gravity, because it makes some people feel attracted to others. Love is power, because it multiplies the best we have, and allows humanity not to be extinguished in their blind selfishness. Love unfolds and reveals. For love we live and die. Love is God and God is Love.

This force explains everything and gives meaning to life. This is the variable that we have ignored for too long, maybe because we are afraid of love because it is the only energy in the universe that man has not learned to drive at will.

To give visibility to love, I made a simple substitution in my most famous equation. If instead of $E=mc^2$, we accept that the energy to heal the world can be obtained through love multiplied by the speed of light squared, we arrive at the conclusion that love is the most powerful force there is, because it has no limits.

After the failure of humanity in the use and control of the other forces of the universe that have turned against us, it is urgent that we nourish ourselves with another kind of energy.

If we want our species to survive, if we are to find meaning in life, if we want to save the world and every sentient being that inhabits it, love is the one and only answer.

Perhaps we are not yet ready to make a bomb of love, a device powerful enough to entirely destroy the hate, selfishness and greed that devastate the planet. However, each individual carries within them a small but powerful generator of love, whose energy is waiting to be released.

When we learn to give and receive this universal energy, dear Lieserl, we will have affirmed that love conquers all, is able to transcend everything and anything, because love is the quintessence of life.

I deeply regret not having been able to express what is in my heart, which has quietly beaten for you all my life. Maybe it's too late to apologize, but as time is relative, I need to tell you that I love you and thanks to you I have reached the ultimate answer!".

Your father,
Albert Einstein

Albert Einstein Letter To Daughter Resource / Reference Information

AUTHOR NOTE: This letter was revealed to me at a pivotal time in God's timing in my life in 2018 which was 17 years into my journey of expectation… providing immeasurable connection, confirmation, and courage to press into Him and His love and hope filled expectancy for the eventual telling of this book.

STATEMENT of VALIDITY:
Regarding the controversy surrounding this letter: "'The writings were not donated by Einstein himself, nor his daughter, Lieserl. The letters were donated by Margot Einstein, the scientist's stepdaughter,' claims Diana Kormos — Buchwald, editor — in — chief at the Einstein Papers Project. Link > https://community.thriveglobal.com/a-letter-from-albert-einstein-to-his-daughter/
.

Michele Zackheim, in her book on "Lieserl", Einstein's Daughter, states that "Lieserl" had a developmental disability, and that she lived with her mother's family and probably died of scarlet fever in September 1903.

This site validates an AE letter was written at age 22 regarding Lieserl's birth and questions to Mileva about her birth. Here is the link:
https://www.theguardian.com/science/2014/dec/05/albert-einstein-archive-genius-doubts-and-loves

*Another name this letter has become known as is "The Universal Force of Love".

✧ MINISTRY INFORMATION ✧
ELIZABETH "BETH" BAYLIFF

📖 **WATCH** for *related short books coming soon to empower you as you engage and continue your journey with Him in* **expectation***!*

✧ **PERAZIM MINISTRIES**... *connecting with you for breakthrough in Him.*

🌐 PERAZIM MINISTRIES: @ breakthroughperazim.com
✧ CONTACT: expectbreakthroughperazim@gmail.com / 419-234-4375
See the back cover for additional information about the author.

✧ **MUSICAL MANIFESTATIONS OF EXPECTATION**

🎵 Experience a creative fruit that manifested as *expectation* stirred during worship at the piano for *Him* and while this *telling* was being birthed. The links to receive from these *spirit led releases of the sound of worship to Him* are available @ breakthroughperazim.com. Sounds From The Key of "e", Key of "m"... a major/minor with *Melissa*, Key of "c", and Sounds of "3".

✧ **PUBLISHER:** *Ajoyin Publishing / Pam Eichorn* Jones, MI 49061 USA

👍 THE JOURNEY OF EXPECTATION *Ajoyin Publishing*

✧ **COVER:** *James Nesbit / @jnesbit.com*
The back cover photo is the creative expression of the author as a cover "firstfruits" offering to the Lord. (Proverbs 3:9)

👍 PROPHETIC ART OF JAMES NESBITT

What an anointed expression to bring to life the experiences and encounters... in more ways than I can share... of my personal life's journey and process of engaging, embracing, and being empowered... through my *expectations* on earth aligning with *His* heavenly eternal and loving *expectancy.* Thanks James for saying "yes". It met my *expectations* and more!

✧ **BOOK MINISTRY SUPPORT TEAM BOOKS**
✧ *Lessons from a Headache: Living Life to the Full Despite Pain by Ted Goodwin* @Tate Publishing & Enterprises. Contact: ignitetruth1@gmail.com

✧ *Vessels of Honor and Flowers of Splendor – Discovering Your Unique Creation* (Revised Edition) *by Sally Pickard & Brenda Dulmage* @ CSS Publishing, Lima, OH.

THE JOURNEY OF EXPECTATION... EMBRACE IT AND BE EMPOWERED!

JOIN YOUR EXPECTANCY IN A CORPORATE CONNECTION

THE JOURNEY OF EXPECTATION PODCAST

"TRAVEL ON TUESDAYS" IN EXPECTANCY WITH THE AUTHOR & OTHERS THROUGH
30 WEEKS OF EMBRACING & BEING EMPOWERED!

✧ CHAPTERS 1-4

✧ CHAPTER 5-8 / EACH DAY WILL BE COVERED OVER A WEEK FOR 28 WEEKS

✧ CHAPTERS 9-10

SEE @BREAKTHROUGHPERAZIM.COM

E=mC3
...it's a relationship, not a formula.

♥ Gotta love how it ended up "**333**" pages!
He is good and I felt *His* smile, as I struggled a bit with the length of this book.

www.ingramcontent.com/pod-product-compliance
Lightning Source LLC
Chambersburg PA
CBHW081427070526
44586CB00020B/2511